Undocumented Saints

Undocumented Saints

The Politics of Migrating Devotions

WILLIAM A. CALVO-QUIRÓS

Oxford University Press is a department of the University of Oxford. It furthers
the University's objective of excellence in research, scholarship, and education
by publishing worldwide. Oxford is a registered trade mark of Oxford University
Press in the UK and certain other countries.

Published in the United States of America by Oxford University Press
198 Madison Avenue, New York, NY 10016, United States of America.

© Oxford University Press 2022

Some rights reserved. No part of this publication may be reproduced, stored in a retrieval system, or
transmitted, in any form or by any means, for commercial purposes, without the prior permission in
writing of Oxford University Press, or as expressly permitted by law, by licence or under terms agreed
with the appropriate reprographics rights organization.

This is an open access publication, available online and distributed under the terms of a Creative
Commons Attribution – Non Commercial – No Derivatives 4.0 International licence (CC
BY-NC-ND 4.0), a copy of which is available at http://creativecommons.org/licenses/by-nc-nd/4.0/.

You must not circulate this work in any other form
and you must impose this same condition on any acquirer.

Library of Congress Control Number: 2022900101

ISBN 978–0–19–763023–5 (pbk.)
ISBN 978–0–19–763022–8 (hbk.)

DOI: 10.1093/oso/9780197630228.001.0001

I want to thank my mom, Cecilia (Ma, Ceci, Tita), a single immigrant woman who not only took the risk to migrate to the United States but chose to follow her heart and love me when others did not. Thank you to my grandma Guillermina, who loved (and protected) me, her nieto, unconditionally. My sisters, Alejandra and Andrea, are an example of tenacity, resiliency, and what family is all about. These women were and remain an anchor in my life and in the communities I pledge to serve. To Eva, Tally, and Camila, the light of my eyes, you remind me of why we are committed to building a better future for all . . . and to Carlos, a brother my sister gave me. To all my family, on both sides, living in Costa Rica. To nana, mi grandma Yolanda Solano, who passed away as I wrote this dedication. You were a force of change.
Thank you to all my familia!

To Brian Hanna, I miss you every day. Thank you for everything you did and keep doing for me from up there. To Horacio Roque Ramirez, my mentor and friend, you died too soon. You remind me that every day is precious. I know that you two are celebrating now. And to my loved friends, the late Tammy Zill and Richard "Dick" Meisler, it was an honor meeting you. I cannot wait for the day we will be all together in a huge celebration!

Contents

List of Figures ix
Acknowledgments xi

Introduction: The Shifting Cartographies of Religious Migration   1

1. Jesús Malverde: A Saint of the People, for the People   32

2. Santa Olguita and Juan Soldado: Unresolved Sainthood and the Unholy Rituals of Memory   86

3. Saint Toribio Romo: Racialized Border Miracles   158

4. La Santa Muerte: The Patrona of the Death-Worlds   216

Conclusion: On Earth as It Is in Heaven   270

Notes 289
Bibliography 315
Index 333

Figures

1.1.	Jesús Malverde objects from the United States	34
1.2.	The main altar at the Jesús Malverde Chapel, Culiacán, Sinaloa	40
1.3.	Main chapel to Jesús Malverde, Culiacán, Sinaloa	44
1.4.	Images of Pedro Infante and Jesús Malverde	66
1.5.	María Romero, *Quitapesares (Solace)*, 2014	75
2.1.	Images of Olga Camacho and Juan Castillo Morales	87
2.2.	Map of Tijuana's downtown and the location of the events in 1938	89
2.3.	Map detailing the locations of Juan Soldado's and Olga Camacho's graves in Tijuana	94
2.4.	Plan and photos of Olga Camacho's gravesite, Panteón Municipal no. 2	95
2.5.	Plan and photos of Juan Soldado's burial site and main chapel, Panteón Municipal no. 1	99
2.6.	Execution site and second chapel, Panteón Municipal no. 1	102
2.7.	Alma López Gaspar de Alba, *Juan Soldado*, 1997.	124
2.8.	Santa Olguita prayer card	147
3.1.	Members of the Society of Toribio Romo, Chicago	159
3.2.	Outside the shack where Romo was killed, Tequila, Jalisco	169
3.3.	Churches to Toribio Romo, Santa Ana, Jalisco	178
3.4.	Icon of Toribio Romo, Detroit	200
3.5.	Procession of Saint Toribio Romo, May 26, 2019, Tulsa, Oklahoma	207
3.6.	Mirror altars, Tulsa, Oklahoma	208
4.1.	Santa Muerte Ball poster, Queens, New York	218
4.2.	Santa Muerte objects	223
4.3.	Santa Muerte service, Puebla, Mexico	228
4.4.	Santa Muerte altar, Tepito, Mexico	231

Acknowledgments

Chiara Lubich, an influential female Catholic thinker of the twentieth century, once said that if she were to change her name, she would like to be called Thank You. It took me many years to understand her point. *Thank you* is probably the most powerful expression we have, followed by *I am sorry*. Every academic should master these two phrases. They are signals of our mutual interconnectivity. I believe a good researcher, scholar, and teacher can be measured by mastering these two expressions in their work and in their relationship with their colleagues and their students, the communities they engage, and the society they envision. We scholars are the product of our culture and our times. We always write in a context, never alone. So the phrases *thank you* and *I am sorry* keep us grounded and in contact with our joys and limitations. This project is not just a book but also a collective experience.

Thank you (gracias): This book is the product of the love and care of many people. People dead and alive have contributed to and supported this project in many ways. Some of their support is obvious. But much is not, in part because their work is invisible both by choice and because of forces out of their control. Some came before me, as they opened spaces for this type of research and for scholars like me to exist. Special thanks to George Lipsitz, Emma Pérez, Aída Hurtado, Norma E. Cantú, Alicia Gaspar de Alba, Chela Sandoval, María Herrera Sobek, Tomas Ybarra-Frausto, Rusty Barcelo, Renato Rosaldo, Mary Louise Pratt, Antonia Castañeda, Desirée Martin, Mari Soco Castañeda-Liles, Deirdre de la Cruz, Cindy Cruz, Maria Cotera, Guisella Latorre, Josie Mendez-Negrete, Deena J. Gonzalez, Ellie Hernandez, Frederick Luis Aldama, Michael R. Hames García, Ernesto Martinez, María Herrera-Sobek, Simon J. Bronner and the late David William Foster. You read, mentored, and inspired my work over the years. You remind me that I come from a long tradition of strong people committed to transforming the world of academia.

Thank you to the Andrew W. Mellon Foundation and the School for Advanced Research (specifically Michael F. Brown, Paul Ryer, and Maria Spray) for your funding. Thank you to the University of Michigan and its many support programs and grants that made this book and research possible, including but not limited to the National Center for Faculty Diversity (including Tabbye Chavous, Marie Ting, former director John C. Burkhardt, and Noe Ortega, who is now Pennsylvania's secretary of education), the Office of Diversity, Equity, and Inclusion (especially the amazing Robert Sellers), and the ADVANCE Program (specifically Jennifer Linderman and Wendy Ascione-Juska). These offices and individuals have all provided immeasurable support and resources over the years. Thank you to the TOME (Toward an Open Monograph Ecosystem) initiative, whose monetary grant allowed this book to be accessible for free online. Thank you to the Undergraduate Research Program at the University of Michigan (specifically Luciana Nemtanu) for your many years of support and dedication to my research. Thank you to Dean Anne Curzan, Angela D. Dillard, Alex Stern, and Rosario Ceballo (now at Georgetown University), an extraordinary team of scholars and administrators who have supported and cared for this project over the years.

Thank you to the many research and archive centers and institutions whose dedication to preserving and compiling history made this research possible: the Congregation for the Causes of Saints at the Vatican; the Tijuana Historical Archive and Hilario Castillo Castillo; the General Historical Archive of the State of Sinaloa and Gilberto López Alanís; the Archivo histórico de la Arquidiócesis de Guadalajara; the Border Studies Archive at the University of Texas Rio Grande Valley; the Benson Latin American Collection at the University of Texas at Austin; the California Ethnic and Multicultural Archives at the University of California Santa Barbara; the Smithsonian Latino Center and Diana Bossa Bastidas; El archivo fotográfico del Colegio de la Frontera Norte, especially Alberto Hernández Hernández and L. C. Alfonso Caraveo; the Universidad autónoma de Baja California; and La Casa Oscar Liera in Culiacán, Sinaloa, Mexico. Thank you also to historian Fernando Escobedo de la Torre, as well as to cultural archivist/activist José Saldaña for opening your personal archive of documents from Tijuana. Thank you to the Agrasánchez Film Archive in Texas, whose materials were essential to this research and especially to accessing material culture surrounding popular figures. Thank you to the Department of Anthropology at the Universidad autónoma de Puebla (especially Leticia Villalobos) for all your help during my fieldwork in Puebla. Thank you to the Sapienza Università di Roma in Rome (specifically Silvia Cataldi and Fabrizio Martire); the Università degli Studi di Salerno (specifically Gennaro Iorio); and the Sophia University Institute (specially Giuseppe Argiolas,

Bennie Callebaut and Licia Paglione). To the University of Michigan Library (especially Barbara Alvarez and Sigrid Anderson) and its copyright office, thank you for help navigating the tiring route of finding and using images for the book. Thank you to the Dicastery for Promoting Integral Human Development at the Vatican for your work at the intersection of race, migration, and religiosity.

I need to give special thanks to the Red de investigadores del fenómeno religioso en México and its many extraordinary researchers (including Renée de la Torre, Antonio Higuera-Bonfil, Carlos E. Torres Monroy, and Amílcar Carpio) for opening your academic homes to my work. Thank you to the Red nacional de religión sociedad y política, the Escuela nacional de antropología e historia, and the Instituto nacional de antropología e historia with its own set of scholars and researchers of religion (especially Elio R. Masferrer Kan and Elizabeth Díaz Brenis). You are amazing. Thank you to Adrian Yllescas, whose work and friendship accelerated my work. Also thank you to Regnar Kristensen and Wil G. Pansters, whose pioneering work on the politics and historical nature of La Santa Muerte has inspired the work of many, including me. All of you opened the door to a stranger from El Norte, and you always made me feel welcome and challenged. Thank you for all your help, patience, and compassion. You have listened, shared contacts, and guided my work in ways for which I will always be grateful. Research with you was always rigorous but fun and transformative. You all embody what it means to care for our communities with an open mind and heart. Thank you also to scholar Andrew Chesnut, who read my early chapter on La Santa Muerte and provided much-needed advice and feedback.

Thank you also to the many parishes in both Mexico and the United States that opened archives and resources for this research, particularly the wonderful people at Sts. Peter and Paul Catholic Church in Tulsa, Oklahoma (especially Fr. Mike J. Knipe, Fr. Elmer Rodriguez, and Simón Navarro), an extraordinary community wholly dedicated to serving the Latinx migrant population. Thank you also to Holy Redeemer Parish in Detroit, Michigan; St. Agnes of Bohemia Catholic Church and the Society of Saint Toribio Romo (specifically Concepción Rodríguez and Marcos Lopez) in La Villita in Chicago, Illinois; and the parishes of Tequila, Jalisco, and Our Lady of Guadalupe in Santa Ana, Jalisco. Thank you especially to Msgr. Óscar Sánchez Barba of the Arquidiócesis de Guadalajara, Jalisco, for tremendous help in providing direct access to St. Toribio Romo's canonization files. Thank you to Auxiliary Bishop Donald F. Hanchon of the Archdiocese of Detroit and to Archbishop John C. Wester of the Archdiocese of Santa Fe for the help and support during this research project. Thank you to St. Mary Student Parish in Ann Arbor, a Jesuit-centered parish that has sustained me spiritually all these years by creating an open, inclusive, caring, welcoming, and diverse Catholic community around our University of Michigan central campus. Thank you to Holy Family Parish in south Phoenix, where this project began in 2010. Thank you to all of these beautiful communities that manifest the profound demographic changes and challenges generated by migration and the extraordinary power of embracing diversity beyond fear.

These gracias also extend to many religious groups, communities, and spiritual sites, such as La capilla a Jesús Malverde in Culiacán (specifically Jesús Manuel González Sánchez); La Santa Muerte International (especially the late Enriqueta "Queta" Vargas Ortiz); La Santa Muerte Universal (specifically Carmen Sandoval and David Valencia); the Santa Muerte community in Queens, New York (specifically Arely Vázquez); the Primer santuario a La Santa Muerte in Puebla (specifically Rev. Juan Salazar Rojo); the Iglesia Arcangelista (especially Lucino Morales), and Circulo espiritual de La Santa Muerte (especially Martin George Quijano). I will always be grateful to Doña Enriqueta "Queta" Romero for opening her home to me, as well as providing me with the first interview I ever did on La Santa Muerte. All of you entrusted me with your stories of courage and resiliency that merge the drama and the hopes created by the everyday vulnerability imposed on brown bodies. Gracias for opening your homes and altares to me. I am humble and honored.

Thank you to Mexico City artist Edgar Clemente, who created the image for the cover; and to artists Alma López, María Romero, and Sr. Nancy Lee Smith, IHM, whose transformative artworks illustrate this book and manifest the beauty of the human soul and your desires for social change and justice. Thank you to Sinaloan writers Élmer Mendoza Valenzuela, Leónidas Alfaro Bedolla, and the many cultural critics I encountered during my research journey.

Thank you to the many academic organizations whose intellectual mentorship and scholarly rigor nurtured and maintained this research over the years by offering formal and informal professional feedback and by creating a network of scholars always open and willing to review the manuscript chapters at different stages of the process. To the National Association of Chicana and Chicano Studies (NACCS), you will always be my casa grande, the home I always come back to for strength and peace in el alma: thank you for the transformative work you do for our people and the causa. Thank you to the Latino Studies Association, whose interdisciplinarity nature allowed me to move out of my comfort zone and meet many other scholars in my field (particularly former president Raúl Coronado and Lee Bebout). Thank you to the Association for Joteria Arts, Activism, and Scholarship (especially Daniel Enrique E. Perez, Eddy Alvarez, Anita Tijerina Revilla, Rigoberto Gonzalez, Rita Urquijo-Ruiz, and Maya Chinchilla), where I experienced the idea that a different world was possible. Thank you to the Latinx section at the American Academy of Religion for your encouragement, patience, and rigor. Thank you to Miguel de la Torre, Felipe Hinojosa, Bobby Rivera, and Chris Tirres for creating a space for me and my work. Thank you to the American Folklore Society, where my undocumented santos were never aliens but rather everyday citizens free to walk the halls of academia; and to the Society for the Study of Gloria Anzaldúa for years nurturing and supporting el mundo zurdo.

I also thank the Department of American Culture at the University of Michigan, my intellectual and methodological home, for its leadership over all the years, especially June Howard, Alex Stern, Gregory E. Dowd, and Larry La Fountain-Stokes. Thank you to all my colleagues who read drafts, attended my presentations, and gave feedback during my manuscript workshop (especially Kristin Hass and Yeidy Rivero), the book proposal initiative (Susan [Scotti] Parrish), and my third-year review (Anthony Mora, Joshua Miller, and Jason de Leon [now at UCLA]). I also want to thank the Latina and Latino Studies Program at the University of Michigan and the other ethnic studies programs that have shaped my work. Finally, to all my dear department colleagues and friends (including Jesse Hoffnung-Garskof, Ruby C. Tapia, Anna Watkins Fisher, Silvia Pedraza, John Cheney-Lippold, Colin Gunckel, Lisa Nakamura, Magdalena Zaborowska, Julie Ellison, Melissa Borja, Umayyah Cable, Clare Croft, Ashley Lucas, and Su'ad Abdul Khabeer): thank you for guiding me and showing me the many possibilities available when we scholars work together. A special thank you to my dear friends and drinking buddies—Stephen A. Berrey, Scott Larson, Manan Desai, Retika Adhikari, and Siobhan Rigg—for many hours of mutual support and care. You have inspired me to improve as a scholar, teacher, and colleague. I am constantly learning from you. Thank you also to our amazing staff, current and previous: Judith Gray, Mary L. Freiman, JoAnne Beltran, Kathia Kitchen, Marlene Moore, and Hannah Yung. Thank you to my former colleagues Evelyn Alsultany (University of Southern California), Maria

Cotera (University of Texas at Austin), Phil Deloria (Harvard University), and Tiya Miles for everything you have done.

Thank you to the Program for Research on Black Americans postdoctoral work group, particularly Linda Chatters and Robert Taylor. You opened a community that welcomed me when I first came to Michigan. Gracias also to all my other mentors and friends in the Departments of History; Women's Studies; Digital Studies; and Film, Television, and Media at the University of Michigan, and to the Penny W. Stamps School of Art and Design (especially Petra Kuppers, Victor Mendoza, Susan Najita, Antoine Traisnel, Nadine [Dean] Hubbs, Ava Purkiss, Elizabeth Roberts, and Gayle Rubin). You have always listened with academic and human care, and sometimes you just accompanied me for a cocktail, a coffee, or a movie when the days were hard. You made my work much better by enforcing the interdisciplinary nature of our work, both in its methodology and theoretical scopes. Finally, thank you for all the support and friendship I received at the Professional Latinos at UM Alliance (especially Catalina Ormsby, Alvaro Rojas Pena, and Nardy Baeza Bickel); and thank you to the Utopian Swim Club (especially Christian Sandvig, Sophia Brueckner, John Granzow, Catie Newell, and Natalie Ngai), a space where we merge imagination and intellectual work around the digital. Thank you!

I want to thank all the many writer-travelers whom I have encountered and who have accompanied me through the years of development of this research manuscript, as fellow graduate students, postdocs, and friends: Francisco Galarte, Bernardine Hernandez, Eddy F. Alvarez, Sara V. Hinojos, Marla Ramírez, José Anguiano, Janett Barragan, Jessica Lopez Lyman, Amber Rose Gonzalez, Sebastian Ferrada, Nick Centino, Carisa Cortez, as well as Lorena Chambers, John Arroyo, Giovanni Batz, Mayanthi Fernando, Beth Semel, and Melanie Yazzie. Your dedication and love for the field have nurtured and inspired me to work hard. This book is as much yours as it is mine. To the Men of Color Writing Group at the University of Michigan (José Casas, Ebbin Dotson, Kevin Jones, Jason Young, and Myles Durkee): we did it! Thank you to Harley Etienne (now at Ohio State University) for creating that space. Thank you to sisters Jacquie and Nadine Mattis at Easton's Nook, where we had several writing retreats: a "beautiful space where scholars, artists, and activists can meet and can pursue their work individually or as a part of small, supportive, collaborative groups." To my writing buddies Aliyah Khan, Charlotte Chi Karem Albrecht, Nancy A. Khalil, and Nilo Couret: you have walked with me the long hours dedicated to writing this book, you have sustained me, and I will always be grateful for your love and care.

Going back in time, I also want to thank the Department of Chicana and Chicano Studies at the University of California Santa Barbara (especially Dolores Inés Casillas, Micaela J. Díaz-Sánchez, Mario T. Garcia, and Francisco Lomelí) and the Design School (previously the Department of Architecture and Environmental Design) at Arizona State University (especially Jacques R. Giard and Prasad Boradkar) for your dedication and care in my formation as a dual citizen of two different disciplinary worlds. Thank you for believing in me and pushing me hard.

Grazie mille to the international research group SocialOne, an international network of scholars committed to building a better society, a more just and united world. You have been my anchor, especially during those days when I felt exhausted and misunderstood and when I doubted why I should keep going in academia. Silvia Cataldi, Gennaro Iorio, Vera Araújo, the late Simonella Magari, Rolando Cristao, Paolo Contini, Lucas Galindo, Toni Braga, Rosalba Damartis, Paolo Parra, Tina Pastorelli, Angela Mongelli, Barbara Sena, Paolo De Maina, Agnès Keuho, Paula Luengo Kanacri, and Giuseppe Pellegrini: you always reminded me that love and care are the only forces capable of genuinely creating lasting social change. I felt lost until I found you. Thank you to my great friend Alberto Lo Presti, a force of social change, and responsible for the Igino Giordani Center in Rome. Thank you also to the International Network of Sociology of Sensibilities (especially Adrian Scribano). You all keep me dreaming and fixed on the goal, the promotion of a new humanity, where a new academia based on mutual care is not only possible but a reality. Thank you to the newly founded Michigan Association for Latinx in Higher Education, where I have served as an interim chair during our first years (especially to Ruben Martinez, Alejandra Rengifo, John Bender, Susan Pozo, Diana Hernández, Jim Pen, Andrew Schlewitz, and Melba Velez Ortiz). Thank you for your patience and dedication.

Thank you to the many, many people who, in one way or another, made this project possible over the years: Lucha Corpi, Roberto D. Hernandez, Rudy Busto, Ramon Rivera-Servera, Aureliano Maria De Soto, Ramon Gutierrez, P. J. DiPietro, Aureliano DeSoto, Eliza Rodriguez y Gibson, Ricky Rodriguez, Kathryn Blackmer Reyes, Maylei Blackwell, Sergio de la Mora, John A. Garcia, Sergio De La Mora, Arturo Aldama, Sara Poot-Herrera, Anita Gonzalez, Leo Cabranes-Grant, Gwyneira Isaac, the late Yolanda Lopez, Silvano Roggero, John Markey, Sandra Torijano, Iván Chaar-López, Francheska Alers, Orquídea Morales, Kristopher Hernandez, Mayela

Rodriguez, Erika Almenara, Jose Cabezon, Omar Sosa-Tzec, Cristina Montoya, Liliana Gallegos, Mario Garcia, Peter Garcia, Silvia Rodriguez, Vega Reighan Gillam, Liliana Gonzalez (Pancha), Nina Nabors, Irene Inatty, Aurelis Troncoso, Pau Nava, and Erick Santamaria. Your friendship and intellectual work has given me life.

Thank you to all the undergraduate and graduate students involved in different ways as research assistants in this book. Thank you to my research team of undergraduate students—Srujana Sinha, Ashya Smith, Eva Gonzalez, Cassidy Johnson, Andrea Perez, Elena Schmitt, Victoria Villegas, Itzel Talavera, Laura Salas, Abria Dent, Paulo Zepeda, and Caitlyn Webster—who provided assistance at the University of Michigan. Thank you as well as to the graduate students who have attended my Latinx methodology class for your trust and enthusiasm.

My deepest thanks to Anitra Grisales for her early bilingual editing work. Thank you to my developmental editor, Kim Greenwell, someone now I call my friend, whose professional eye and unstoppable work shaped each section of this book. I will always be grateful for your incisive eye for detail and for consistently reminding me about the global perspectives of the project. I also want to thank Jeanette Fast Redmond, a phenomenal editor and human being with extraordinary skills and sensibility who helped me to remain faithful to my convictions and craft a language that is accessible and kind, one that respects and recognizes people's points of reference and personal historic contexts in every single chapter. Finally, I need to mention Heath Sledge, who took on the exhausting task of line editing the final book manuscript. Each of you provided different perspectives to the overall book project. Thank you to many friends (including Eric-Christopher Garcia, Tom Hubbard, and Jay Gelnett) who at various times provided invaluable feedback on the chapters. Thank you also to Cathy Hannabach and the team at Ideas on Fire, for patience and professionalism in creating the book's index.

Finally, I need to thank my editor, Cynthia Read, former executive editor at Oxford University Press (OUP), for your faith, patience, and dedication to the project. And thank you to all the people involved in the management, production, and distribution of this book. Thank you to Theo Calderara for taking over this project. Thank you, Drew Anderla, for your early work during the process. Special thanks to Brent Matheny, editorial assistant at OUP, for walking with me throughout the arduous production process; as well as Preetham Raj, project manager, whose patience and dedication made it possible for this book to be in the hands of you, the reader. All of these people were miracle workers, especially during the health crisis created by COVID-19. Thank you!

I hope that this work honors all of these individuals, communities, faith groups, and research centers. This book is for you. I know that no book is perfect, and as I conclude this chapter of my life, I know that it will never completely capture all the gifts I have received from you. I am also sorry for the limitations imposed by this medium, for any misunderstandings, and for the impossibility of including everything and everyone I would like. I offer most profuse apologies to all persons whom by mistake I have neglected to mention here.

You all have taught me that the biggest and most beautiful project is people, and that no two individuals are ever the same. Therefore, each person is sacred. This book is finally directed to the many migrant communities worldwide, you whose faith and the hope of a better life move you into the unknown—sometimes, traveling just with a prayer in your heart. In this sense, I believe that, like you, we are all refugees, exiles, traveling people in a world that is not done yet but is always under construction until the promise of "on Earth as it is in heaven" is fulfilled. But I know it will come about, because you have shown me that a different world is not only possible but is already here among us.

Thank you.

March 14, 2022

Introduction

The Shifting Cartographies of Religious Migration

> When writing about religion you can perhaps entertain the hope to become a saint because only in this way will your words express the commitment of your soul.
>
> —Igino Giordani

For some people life begins only after death; for others, life is a shifting journey toward a better place. As a kid, I dreamed of becoming a priest, and as a young adult, I lived for a few years in a consecrated community in Florence, Italy.[1] Those years joyfully, and painfully, transformed my relationship with the Catholic Church. They helped me distinguish the institution from my own desires to both experience transcendent spirituality and to change society. More importantly, that experience allowed me to understand that the Church is not just its formal hierarchy and structure[2] but comprises its enormous and diverse body of believers. It is a Church-in-pilgrimage, if you will—one that is diverse and uneven and whose boundaries are often blurry and contradictory.

This understanding of the Church as an institution that materializes (and thus necessarily responds to) the needs and concerns and beliefs of all its adherents underpins this project. My conceptualization of the Church as historical and cultural archive is, for me, crystallized in the figures of the vernacular saints. In the late 1990s, during my time in Tuscany, I attended a class on the Church's social doctrine. Vera Araújo, a Brazilian sociologist on the faculty, told us, "Certainly, the history of the Church can be explained by the many Church councils and papal encyclical documents.... But its history can be also studied and understood by the succession of saints and charisms that have emerged over time, one after the other, as they respond to the needs of the times."[3] That encounter was one of two moments of genesis for this project.

The other moment is deeply connected to my immigration to the United States. I had my first encounter with one of the saints discussed in this book, Toribio Romo, while I was visiting my family in Phoenix, Arizona, in 2010. That year, Arizona's then-governor, Jan Brewer, signed into law the Support Our Law Enforcement and Safe Neighborhoods Act, also known as Arizona Senate Bill (SB) 1070, introduced by state senator Russell K. Pearce. This law made it a misdemeanor for individuals to be in Arizona without proper documentation and authorized local police to lawfully stop, detain, and arrest any individual suspected of fitting that description. With the support of Sheriff Joe Arpaio of Maricopa County, Arizona, SB 1070 expanded racially motivated incursions into Arizona's Latina/o/x and Chicana/o enclaves, organizations, and allied groups, particularly in Phoenix, which has the fourth-largest Latinx population in the United States.[4]

The ensuing period saw unprecedented, systematic, and explicit terror inflicted on the Latinx communities in Phoenix. Meetings were organized around the state to assess the consequences of the anti-immigrant rhetoric and legislation. One in particular took place at Holy Family Catholic Church in south Phoenix, an old working-class Latinx neighborhood where my family lived. People there expressed alarm about the multiple raids and abuses of power carried out by the local police force, led by Arpaio: assaults were targeting parents bringing their children to school, those visiting shopping centers during the holidays, and people driving to work.

Attendees at the south Phoenix event discussed a range of strategies for responding to the terror campaign, from the implementation of a text alert network using radios and cellphones to warn of incoming raids to plans for transferring custody of children to fully documented family members if parents were deported. The gathering ended with a community prayer led by a local Catholic priest. This community organizing event, held in the church, exemplified the connections between social-civil activism and faith-based services that have historically grounded civil rights movements in the United States.[5] As Jonathan E. Calvillo explains, for many immigrants living in the United States "faith infused these residents with a sense of fight that kept them pushing on, in the face of immediate financial needs, deportation, and sustained inequality."[6]

On the altar of the church, alongside the image of the Virgin of Guadalupe, was an image of a young priest, the representation almost completely covered by flower arrangements brought as offerings by parishioners and visitors. As I found out later that day, the picture was of Saint Toribio Romo, the popular—and officially canonized—patron saint of migrants, especially those lacking documentation in the United States and dealing with migration issues. In venerating this saint, the exiles meeting in the Phoenix church that day merged their religious, political, and national sentiments toward their homeland with those they felt toward their new place of settlement. As scholar Silvia Pedraza, referring to Cuban migrants in the United States, explains, "Religion [. . .] serves to express the émigrés' patriotism and heal the pain of exile."[7]

Together, the events in Italy and in Phoenix solidified my interest in popular saints—in how they serve not only as collective historical archives but also as repositories of hope as they map the processes of migration and the maneuvers of power. I see the stories of these saints as a collection of contemporary miracles, performed day after day, testifying over and over to people's resilience in the face of adversity, exploitation, violence, and greed. I present them here as manifestations of the deeply human search for meaning and connection in a world that often seems intent on destroying both. And I honor those travelers—saints and migrants alike—whose journeys, like mine, have involved struggles for spiritual survival, toward building a better world for all.

Versus Populum (Toward the People)

> [God,] at this moment I am at the border, determined to go through. I know it is against the law. But you know well that I do not do it to defy the regulations of a nation. The economic reality in which I find myself and the desperate search for a better future for my family make me cross over without the necessary documents. I feel like [I am] a citizen of the world and a member of a Church that has no borders.
>
> —Diócesis de San Juan de los Lagos, "Al cruzar sin documentos"

"Al cruzar sin documentos" (On Traveling Without Documents) is one of many prayers in *El devocionario del migrante*, a pocket-sized prayer book created in 2007 by the Diocese of San Juan de los Lagos in Jalisco, Mexico, for those leaving Mexico and migrating to El Norte (the United States and

Canada). The devotional book is structured to follow the emotional and ever-unfolding drama experienced by migrants during their journey, including racism, cultural rejection, isolation, and family separation, all in the potential contexts of labor precariousness, imprisonment, and deportation. Other prayers include "When Leaving My Family at Home," "On the Journey North," "When Crossing [the Border] Without Documents," "When Looking for Work," "For Moments of Confusion," "When Losing Your Job," and "When Imprisoned or Deported."[8] The prayers not only invoke the struggles unique to each stage of the immigration process but also engage with political, economic, and moral issues ranging from the implications of crossing the border and working without authorization to the Catholic Church's transnational status and the Mexican Church's evolving stand on migration.

As Jacqueline Maria Hagan illustrates in her book *Migration Miracle: Faith, Hope, and Meaning on the Undocumented Journey*, when it comes to matters of migration, "in the contemporary world religion is more than a vehicle for incorporation and identity reaffirmation. . . . [It] also enables us to stay closely connected to homeland and to members of shared culture, tradition, and faith throughout the world."[9] The prayers in *El devocionario* demonstrate how migrants travel: they do not carry with them only water bottles, backpacks and expectations and imaginings about life in El Norte but also rosaries, prayer stamps, holy water, amulets, and a repertoire of religious faith practices. In many ways, migration across the US-Mexico border represents not only the mobilization of people and disposable labor for profit but also a massive relocation of religious practices from the South to the North—and vice versa, as migrants bring changed practices back to Mexico, transforming their homelands' religious terrains in turn through visits to their hometowns, remittances, wire transfers of funds, and painful forced deportations back their homelands. As N. Fadeke Castor explains, "Even as people's spiritual experiences are locally grounded, they are always also globally informed."[10] Religion—particularly devotional and vernacular spiritual practices—is deeply affected on both sides by the process of migration.

The prayers in *El devocionario* include self-reflective dialogues between the migrant and God, but also between the migrant and nation-states, the International Monetary Fund, and their families and other migrants. As the book explains, the prayers are meant to help the individual "overcome all the difficulties of the journey" and to "come to positive fruition."[11] These prayers lay out the many difficulties of an agonizing journey—almost a spiritual pilgrimage—to El Norte, and the social and moral expectations that migrants' home communities and the Church hold for them. As modern versions of the Stations of the Cross, these prayers illustrate the stages of a pain inflicted on a body, in this case the social bodies of migrants. Simultaneously, these prayers, from an official diocesan prayer book, make evident that the Church is invested not only in protecting the souls of migrants but also in reinforcing fixed codes of social conduct.

A persistent element in the prayers in *El devocionario* is explanations of why the person has been forced to migrate in the first place. In a self-reflective analysis, the prayers engage the political implications of undocumented migration. But these political questions cannot be dissociated from the mobilization of faith and religiosity. Most of the immigration debates raging in the United States (and indeed in all industrialized nations) have focused on issues of citizenship, national security, labor, and so on. But what is happening in the spiritual terrain, as religious practices travel, change, and adapt, is equally important and urgent. As Manuel A. Vásquez and Marie Friedmann Marquardt argue, "Religion can provide important insights into the new cartographies produced by globalization"—that is, in the context of exploitative capitalism and/or socialism and of the mobilization of people and communities.[12]

El devocionario is, therefore, much more than a prayer book. It is a booklet of moral norms and practices, and attempt to construct an ideal immigrant and good Catholic social citizen. The moral codes are embedded in the self-reflective prayers, which ask the immigrant to identify with the implied ideal subject—one who is confronted by a dangerous, hostile world that is different from the one in Mexico. In this situation, the practice of maintaining core Mexican Catholic values becomes not only an objective but a method that helps the migrant remain both holy and whole as a Mexican in exile. As *El devocionario* illustrates, the Catholic Church in Mexico is an active player in the discursive construction of how immigrants may read their experiences of displacement. At the same time, it shows how faith and everyday religiosity merge and work to perpetuate nationalism and moral discourses about citizenship, gender performance, labor, nationhood, and even salvation.

A Tale of a Divided Flock

As the Catholic Church in the United States "is becoming more Latinx... the Latinx population is becoming less Catholic."[13] Between 34 and 40 percent of all Catholics in the United States are Latinxs,[14] yet only about 3 percent of US-based priests are Latinx.[15] For example, in Phoenix, Arizona, where my family lived and where this project began, Latinxs represent over 58 percent of all Catholics of the Phoenix diocese, but only seven out of the two hundred priests serving the communities there are US-born Latinos.[16] This disparity is crucial for contemplating issues of representation and diversity in the decision-making processes of the Church. Hosffman Ospino's work at Boston College's School of Theology and Ministry has shown that in the United States, "Latino Catholics represent 71 percent of the country's Catholic growth" and that "about 60 percent of Catholics under 18 are Hispanics."[17] Some of these Catholic Latinxs swelling the ranks of the US Catholic Church are US-born, but many are migrants: according to "Women and Men Professing Perpetual Vows in Religious Life: The Profession Class of 2019," a report by the Secretariat of Clergy, Consecrated Life, and Vocations of the United States Conference of Catholic Bishops, "among those identifying as Hispanic/Latino(a) more than six in ten (64 percent) are foreign born while almost one-third (31 percent) are U.S. born."[18] And the Latinx religious demographic is becoming increasingly important outside the Catholic Church, for about one-quarter of all Evangelicals Protestants in the United States are now Latinxs.[19] As The Pew Research Center explains, "Hispanics are transforming the nation's religious landscape . . . not only because of their growing numbers but also because they are practicing a distinctive form of Christianity."[20]

This book therefore asks two central questions of global importance. First, how does faith migrate? And second, how does migration transform devotional practices and religious meanings? These questions require investigation on both sides of the border between Mexico and the United States. In answering these questions, this book shows how Latinx communities are battling for their survival not only in the mundane world but in the worlds of faith, religiosity, and the imaginary. It illuminates how religious devotions are framed by the sociopolitical realities of exploitation, racial segregation, and religious consumption. As I show, the US-Mexico border is not only a space of economic and social conflict and struggle but also a two-thousand-mile epistemic battleground over the terrain of faith.

I call this book *Undocumented Saints* because this project documents the emergence and relocation of popular saint devotions among documented and undocumented migrants alike, many of them invisible and located at the margins of society. I see the act of documenting writ large as a political act of liberation: the processes of "legalizing" (or even canonizing) spiritual devotions to particular saints are maneuvers of sanctioning power within institutionalized religion, just as the process of legalizing the presence of "the other" takes place through the maneuvers of political power within the institutional processes of the state. The book looks at the migration of the at-large Catholic religious experience beyond institutional boundaries, taking place in marginal spaces where power is constantly navigated and inscribed and where the divine and the everyday clash. Here, the religious/political/economic thread (migration) and the religious/spiritual/imaginary thread (the saints and devotions) run in parallel throughout the whole book.

In this sense, *Undocumented Saints* reflects what feminist religious scholar María Del Socorro Castañeda-Liles calls the "intersection of the cultural and religious roots" of a "Mexican Catholic imagination," which offers many migrants the means for "understanding themselves and the world . . . that shape their lives."[21] As she explains, vernacular religious devotions to saints cannot be understood as exclusively "heavenly," for these devotions are at the same time always deeply "earthly." *Undocumented Saints* is located at the crossroads of "the sacred (vertical) and secular (horizontal) relationships," beyond the limited categories of legality or the official.[22] I approach religion very much as Hagan defines it in her work on the spiritual journey of undocumented migrants into the United States: "in its broadest sense, to include all those beliefs and practices sanctioned by the Church, as well as the rich diversity of everyday practices informed by culture and shared experience, and employed and transformed by the migrants themselves to derive meaning in the migration process."[23]

The present book therefore examines unincorporated spiritual territories that are moving and unsettled, as they participate locally in the global drama of people in movement and in faith migration. Many of these unincorporated spiritual territories are the products of pilgrimages of displacement that started more than five hundred years ago, in Christianity's first encounter in the Americas. Overall, the book spans from the end of the nineteenth century to the first two decades of the twenty-first century. Chapters 1–4 contextualize particular vernacular saints within broader discourses about the construction of masculinity and the state, the long history of violence against women in the region, discrimination against nonnormative sexualities, and US and Mexican investment in controlling religiosity within the discourses of immigration. The stories of the vernacular saints studied in this book are organized chronologically, following the ever-shifting trajectory of Mexico's encounter with modernity—from the administration of President Porfirio Díaz to the Mexican Revolution, from the post-Revolution period to the Great Depression, and through today's still-unfolding transformations wrought by neoliberal capitalism and globalization.

In this book, I catalogue more than the emergence, evolution, and migration of these spiritual characters and the cultural practices around them; I also examine the politics and struggles surrounding the migration of popular religiosity writ large and the sophisticated roles played by spirituality and faith in migrants' work to envision a future beyond oppression. As the book reveals, the appearance, popularization, and mobilization of these vernacular saints correspond to crucial periods in the relationship between Mexico and the United States, as well as to changes in how capitalism operates in relation to labor, gender, and sexuality. It is through practices of popular religiosity organized around these border saints that Latinx immigrant communities deal with, and make local sense of, the global neoliberal policies that define their everyday experiences of forced migration, labor and housing insecurity, wage dependency, and gender and sexual control.

The immigrant, non-normative faith practices that condense in the figures of the undocumented saints are deeply monitored and surveilled. They are subject to state-sanctioned organized control and violence by both the United States and Mexico because they pose a threat to the imaginary notions of each country as a cohesive normative Christian faith-nation. Far from exotic, random, or naïve cultural artifacts, popular saints are sophisticated social constructions, assembled (and adapted) across sociopolitical contexts, all carrying the transformative potential for defiance and social change.

Followers' spiritual, emotional, and public journeys and relationships with the devotions to these vernacular saints do not begin when they first enter a chapel, build an altar, or buy a prayer card. They begin much earlier, in each person's encounter with the history and the storytelling of the miracles of that saint. The chapels and spiritual practices are part of a greater journey, as each petitioner's relationship with the traveling narrative of the saint intensifies: the physical and material practices and spaces—prayers, icons, altars, chapels—serve as placeholders and amplifiers for the narration and validation of sainthood. Chapels do more than hold holy remains; they also capture people's imaginations about life and their relationships with the nation and the state.

A Border Drama in Four Chapters

Chapters 1, 3, and 4 each focus on one particular saint, and Chapter 2 focuses on two inextricably linked saints. The chapters examine the saints chronologically, according to their histories of veneration. This is because while in some cases, public veneration began immediately after death (as with Jesús Malverde and Juan Soldado), in other cases, identification and veneration of the figure as a vernacular saint happened many years later, as in the case of Olga Camacho. In still other cases, the meaning associated with the saint's veneration has changed over time. For example, Saint Toribio Romo began not as a saint for immigrants but rather as a patron saint of soccer, and his worship did not spread and catch on widely until this shift occurred, many years after his dead and long after his unofficial canonization. Similarly, we do not know with certainty when La Santa Muerte's devotion emerged in its current form and must track the progression of her hold on the popular imagination beginning from a known crucial event in her public veneration.

The stories of these saints begin in the period leading up to the Mexican Revolution (1880–1910), a period defined by deep transformations in Mexico's socioeconomic and political structures as well as in the psyche and spirituality of the nation. The book's introduction lays out the background necessary to understand these saints; how they fit into the narrative of Catholicism as it moves from Mexico to the United States; and the political and social concerns they embody. The first spiritual figure analyzed in the book is Jesús Malverde, a "generous bandit" famous for stealing from the rich and giving to the poor. As the story goes, local police forces captured and killed him just months before the official start of the Revolution, in the northwest state of Sinaloa. Over time, Malverde has become a popular saint and a caudillo-style patrón of modern drug traffickers and immigrants, with widespread veneration on both sides of the US-Mexico border.[24] This chapter examines how the people of Sinaloa, Mexico, used oral narratives about Malverde as artifacts of collective folklore to navigate encounters with late modernity and the anxieties generated by massive industrialization, land reforms, American economic intervention, and the decline of the peasant class during Díaz's tumultuous dictatorship of 1876 to 1910. Decades later, in the 1970s, Malverde's popularity surged again in response to land disputes surrounding the expansion of the local bureaucratic state and the forced relocation (and eventual reconstruction) of his main chapel. In this later period, the now-canonical image of Malverde was created by incorporating the face of Pedro Infante, the most famous movie star and singer from Mexican cinema's Golden Age, into a bust of the saint. This bust was designed to represent the saint both for commercial, market-driven reasons and for ideological reasons, for Malverde (like Infante) is as a national ideal of masculinity. Chapter 1 concludes by considering more recent iterations of Malverde within the context of narco-capitalism, the war on drugs, and the social construct of the undesirable immigrant subject.

The second chapter turns to two folk spiritual figures of the border who are intimately connected by violence: Juan Soldado and Olga Camacho. They reflect the late 1930s aftermath of the Mexican Revolution, the Cristero War, and the Great Depression. They manifest Mexico's turbulent gendered and political relationship with the United States, as well as the relationship between popular religiosity and misogyny. The chapter begins with Olga, an eight-year-old girl who was raped and murdered in Tijuana, Mexico, in 1938. It explores the strange circumstances surrounding her death and the riots that erupted after the capture of Juan Castillo Morales, a poor, low-ranking Mexican soldier who became the main suspect in the crime. The chapter traces the bizarre evolutions of the intertwined stories of these two figures. After Castillo Morales was executed, Olga—the innocent victim of a crime—somehow became the villain; she underwent a violent, gendered erasure from popular memory, due to the socio-political climate at the time of her death and the violent military responses to popular riots demanding that her killer be caught. After this reversal, Olga's burial site was repeatedly attacked, and her family was forced to relocate her remains; Castillo Morales became a popular figure of underclass resistance, eventually emerging as Juan Soldado, a local popular saint for undocumented immigrants. The chapter shows the political roots of the strange alternating canonization of the two main figures of this drama: it analyzes Olga Camacho's family history, the family's forced relocation to Tijuana, and her union organizer father's labor disputes with the local government in the months leading up to Olga's murder. As the chapter demonstrates, both Soldado's unconventional sanctification and Olga's murder are deeply tied to the longstanding and ongoing systematic killing of women along the border (e.g., women of Juárez). It argues that Olga's recent "resurrection" as a saint is a sophisticated feminist counter discourse that recreates her as a local protector against injustice, police brutality, rape, and the social erasure effected by neoliberal policies in the region, situating her current veneration within the antifemicide movement #NiUnaMas (#NotOneMore).

The saint studied in Chapter 3, Toribio Romo, is the only one to have been formally canonized by the Catholic Church. Since the 1990s, US and Mexican newspapers have reported undocumented immigrants' stories of encountering the ghost of a priest who assists people as they travel to the United States, providing water, food, money, or transportation to those in distress.[25] Known now as El Santo Pollero (the Holy Coyote) or the smuggler saint, Father Toribio Romo was a Mexican Catholic priest killed by government troops in 1928 during the anticlerical conflict known as the Cristero War.[26] The chapter begins by exploring the economic and political conditions that frame Romo's death, then shows how the saint's meaning and image have been shaped in recent decades to reflect the precarious contemporary economic and political conditions experienced by immigrants along the US-Mexico border, particularly in the wake of the terrorist attacks of September 11, 2001. The chapter explores how, since 2014, Romo's relics—in the form of bone fragments—have circulated through the United States, encoding popular resistance and religious-political mobilization and serving as part of a campaign for comprehensive immigration reform. Today, many Catholic immigration centers have incorporated "Toribio Romo" into their names, and his relics are housed in several states—including Oklahoma, Illinois, and Michigan—reflecting the new Latinx enclaves of settlement outside the Southwest. Overall, the chapter explores the evolution of the persona of El Santo Pollero within the context of the neoliberal practices of the US and Mexican governments and the shifting dynamics of the Catholic Church as they intersect with the migration of faith.

The last chapter, Chapter 4, analyzes the spread of the veneration of La Santa Muerte, a controversial female personalization of the Grim Reaper, in both Mexico and the United States. The chapter contextualizes her modern public emergence in 2001 within the extreme precariousness that characterized the implementation of the North American Free Trade Agreement (NAFTA) and the Tequila Crisis.[27] The chapter first explores how La Santa Muerte iconography has been (mis)interpreted and appropriated to promote anti-Latinx sentiments by various groups and agencies tasked with enforcing the power of both Church and state. Intimately connected to the case of Jesús Malverde, these groups range from the US Drug Enforcement Agency to for-profit, private, consulting groups within police forces in the US and Mexico to newly-emerged organized policing agents within the Catholic Church. Chapter 4 then discusses how followers of La Santa Muerte and LGBTQ Latinx communities—communities that share similar experiences of discrimination and criminalization—have converged in venerating her as a beacon of affirmation and liberation for the outcasts of society. Drawing on queer performance and religious studies, I focus on the LGBTQ network of leaders who sustain and organize La Santa Muerte worship in Mexico and the United States, in resistance to the state and state-sanctioned forces that try to turn her veneration to their own ends.

The book closes by exploring several cases that demonstrate the intersections between the Catholic Church and the politics of race around Latinxs in the American Southwest, beginning in colonial times and extending to the present. These overlaps occur around the concepts of universal citizenship, religious sovereignty, and the racial politics of religious migration. Within these case studies, I ask: How did racism frame the sexual abuse of minors by Catholic clergy in Arizona? How do assumptions around assimilation continue to permeate the discourse about Latinx faith immigration and religious visibility? And, given the difficult economic, political, and social circumstances Latinxs (and especially Latinx immigrants) face in the 21st century US, how are hope and care kept alive in the Latinx immigrant religious experience and in these immigrants' struggles toward social change?

How to Document Undocumented Saints

> Saints, far from being static icons, provide windows on events in the larger world around them, and offer ways of charting change over time.
>
> —Jodi Bilinkoff

Doing research on the Catholic experience within Latinx studies is not easy. As Anne M. Martínez points out, "There is a long-standing resistance in Latina/o and Chicano studies, in particular, to writing about religion."[28] This opposition creates what I call an epistemic religious closet, where religiosity is relegated to scholars' private life, sometimes not viewed as an appropriate, sophisticated, or emancipatory topic for research. Even putting aside the academy's views on religion, it remains a sticky topic for those invested in a decolonialized approach to religiosity, who must navigate a liminal space within a *herida*, or wound, recognizing both the oppressive and the emancipatory potentialities of spirituality. On one side, formal religiosity carries the DNA of colonial violence, especially around the processes and legacies of the forced Christianization of indigenous groups, the violence against women and queer communities, and organized religion's overall complicity in promoting subjugation and oppression. On the other hand, this unhealed wound is also a space where many religious practices emerge as sites of resistance and community organizing, where power is questioned and constantly negotiated.

Undocumented Saints is about the complications of this wound. Each of the five vernacular folk saints considered here serves as a socioepistemic entity through which to study the intersections of the divine and the mundane, within the global drama of migration, resettlement, and the translocation of meanings. In this book I chart how sainthood is culturally constructed, negotiated, and debated within the limital spaces of border realms or border zones, in art, literature, music, performance, and the politics of piety. I document the way that immigrant saints inhabit transgressive and interstitial spaces beyond the traditional Christian sites of worship. I show that these vernacular saints make manifest a religious-social body located outside the traditional pulpit of a building, a body that is transplanted and resettled from Mexico into unincorporated colonias, immigration detention centers, barrio streets, warehouses, corner malls, churches, and parking lots all over the United States. The book, like the saints it documents, exists between tensions and difficulties—both those that are created by what Frank Graziano describes as "devotion . . . rebellious [and] resistant to organization" and those created by the unstoppable flourishing of new religious practices, spaces, and forms emerging from migration across nations, the forces of faith consumption, and the always changing markets for exploitation and the creation of vulnerability.[29]

Grounded in feminist, decolonial, queer, and borderland theories, this book understands the emergence, evolution, and interconnection of border saints (and other non-sanctioned religious practices and symbols) within broader discourses about "mestiza consciousness" and the notion of "tlilli tlapalli" (writing and wisdom) proposed by Gloria Anzaldúa,[30] and within the theoretical frameworks of Américo Paredes's "sabidurías populares" (vernacular knowledges), Michel Foucault's notion of "subjugated knowledges," and Walter Mignolo's concept of "subaltern modernities."[31] All of these theories suffuse my understanding of folk or vernacular saints as archives of social knowledge that can help us unveil the hidden historical, sociopolitical, economic, and racial struggles of Latinx communities.

Undocumented Saints views border saints as sites of faith-in-making (and of social storytelling-in-the-making, in their function as traveling narratives) that manifest the "infrapolitics" that permeate the "everyday [existence in] resistance" of Latinx migrant communities.[32] As these popular saints inhabit interstitial spaces of communal memory, the book approaches them as in-situ knowledge products—byproducts of the border's knowledge-making experience—that manifest what Patricia Hill Collins and other feminists of color have called a referential epistemic standpoint. Border vernacular saints are thus far more than spiritual entities: they are also sociopolitical and historical figures who require a unique set of cultural codes to unveil their meanings and functions as they connect present oppression with the past and allow people to embrace the uncertainties of the future.[33]

Approaching the Sacred: The Poetics of the Everyday Altares

This book's methods manifest the complexity of studying religious migration, as it examines both real and suprareal people—those who venerate saints and those who are venerated—and works across a long temporal arc that encompasses significant political, economic and social changes. Given the distinct context and evolution of each saint studied here, the, each chapter required diverse research methods and forms of archival enquiry. Indeed, I hope that one of the widest-reaching outputs of this project, especially for those interested in studying vernacular religiosity, is the interdisciplinary constellation of archives and methods that it employs. This approach is partly a product of my dual training in industrial design and in Chicana/o studies, both of which attend to art theory, aesthetics, historiography, and race, class, and gender studies. Equally crucially, my approach has been informed by the context of my department, a multidisciplinary American studies department that both values and nurtures diverse disciplines, points of view, processes, and methods for research and analysis.

I have drawn here on a variety of primary and secondary sources, including legislative and juridical proceedings, historical accounts, Vatican and parish documents, oral narratives, literature, visual and audio sources (popular music, murals, and TV shows), and extensive interviews, spatial analyses, and ethnographic visits to spiritual shrines and communities over the last ten years in the United States and Mexico.

As the reader will notice, the sources of information vary among and within chapters to adjust to temporal, chronological, and geographic boundaries. For example, analyzing a late nineteenth-century case makes more relevant the use of historical archives, newspapers, and government sources. As we move into the late twentieth- and twenty-first centuries—even to look at the same figure, in some cases—sources like interviews, films, and oral histories become more viable, given the emergence of new types of archival and technology sources (e.g., TV, films, online chat rooms, social media, etc.) and the fact that some people were still alive and available to be interviewed. Because the book follows the processes of religious migration from Mexico to the United States and back as a constant, interconnected, and codependent process, my sources also shift with the geographic location of the communities and individuals studied, as people moved between the United States and Mexico—sometimes on numerous occasions and in multiple directions. For these reasons, the book's varied methodologies are defined by and chosen in response to the particularities of each saint and the communities around them.

The book studies the making of history and memory-holding among Latinx and religious groups.[34] This is a process that, as Marie-Theresa Hernández explains, has little to do with traditional history writing but more to do with how certain "events or narratives become phantasms that only surface at disparate moments," when disjunctions between the official text and the community narrative of events occur.[35] As a study of the politics and semiotics of religion and power, *UnDocumented Saints* is informed by the work of scholars such as Roland Barthes, who argues that imaginations are primarily "systems of communication"—types of social speech that are framed within specific historical, political, and cultural contexts, and with social intentionality.[36] This emphasis on the social nature of imagination and vision influences my terminology around religion: not coincidentally, I, like Latin American religious scholar Elio Masferrer Kan, prefer to use the "concept of religious system" over the simple term religion in order to accommodate the dense religious and social experience present in all of Christianity, and specifically within the Catholic Church.[37] As Masferrer Kan explains, "Religions in complex societies, in mass societies . . . are neither amorphous nor homogeneous, but instead are segmented, stratified, and split by historical, economic, cultural, social, and religious traditions." As he defines it, a "religious system" is foremost "a ritual, symbolic, mythical, and relatively consistent system developed by a set of religious specialists, which is articulated in or is part of a cultural or subcultural system."[38] Here, my approach to religiosity as a system is crucial to comprehending and embracing the multiplicity of expressions, mutations, and forms of affiliation within what may on the surface appear to be a homogenous religious group. As Vásquez and Marquardt explain, religious identities are not "fixed unitary essences but complex and shifting dynamics, always mediated by multiple forces."[39] Therefore, understanding that people, in this case migrants, circulate within a complex system of significations recognizes that their relationships with the different parts of the system of faith vary over time, affected by their positionality (access or lack) with regard to power, a plurality of beliefs and practices, and the many ambiguities in affiliation.

In this book, a religious system is never understood as rigid, stable, or fixed but rather is seen as always in movement and in transformation. Indeed, I view religious systems as systems of systems; as Masferrer Kan explains, "religious denominations have multiple distinct religious systems within themselves. Likewise, these religious systems, although different from each other, may have a set of common elements that transcends organizational, ecclesiastical, or denominational structures—a macrosystemic structure."[40] This recognition is particularly important as we discuss the issues of affiliation among many immigrants who venerate the vernacular saints examined in this book, especially the question of how almost unreconcilable points of view can coexist within the same macrosystem of beliefs and practices. The "religion in the streets" practiced by many immigrants, as Robert Orsi explained, is quite distinct from their formal Catholic worship practices: "people have their own ways, authentic and profound, of being Catholic," and their worship practices often do not "hav[e] anything to do with how often he or she went to church."[41] This understanding can help us comprehend how migrants create always-shifting devotional models within their own constellations of belief possibilities, without compromising the cohesion of their own religious beliefs as Catholics. This creation happens independent of what the "organizational, ecclesiastical, or denominational structures" may define as normative, valid, or recognizable.[42] In this way, what seem to be opposing spiritual entities can coexist simultaneously within an individual or community repertoire of saints, independent of the official ecclesiastical stand on them.[43]

As this book demonstrates, absolutist categories such as official/unofficial, saint/sinner, sacred/profane, or even vernacular/formal cannot adequately convey people's real experiences. The perpetuation of and investment in these categories is problematic, for they do not reflect the blurry gray border areas that make up the Latin American Catholic experience (and its US inflections), built on a religious system that is more porous and flexible than people might think. There is a "Catholic sensibility" that exists outside the formal structures of the Church-as-institution, and this sensibility "expresse[s] the consciousness born in centuries of oppression and colonization."[44] Latinx immigrants are not naïve victims of (or deviants from) traditional religiosity. Indeed, my research reveals precisely the opposite: these are agentic subjects trying to make sense of their experiences via the spiritual.

Undocumented Saints shows how communities under conditions of violence develop epistemic strategies for survival that merge pragmatic and profane realities with faith and spirituality. As Vásquez and Marquardt note in a discussion of religion, "globalization is not just about domination and homogenization. It also involves resistance, heterogeneity, and the active negotiation of space, time, and identity at the grassroots, even if these negotiations occur under the powerful constraints of neoliberal markets and all-pervading culture industries."[45] This book specifically examines how religious devotions can be interpreted within the terrains of resistance, self-valorization, and the creation of semiautonomous spiritualities on and across borders—political, geographic, cultural, linguistic, and religious.

Rethinking La Frontera (the Border) as an In-Between Mobile Spiritual Territory

> Like borders and borderlands, religion marks both encounter and separation, both intermixing and alternative.
> —Manuel A. Vásquez and Marie Friedmann Marquardt

As Anzaldúa has described it, the US-Mexico border is "*una herida abierta* [an open wound] where the Third World grates against the first and bleeds. And before a scab forms, it hemorrhages again."[46] We can thus read the border as a seam of long-lasting stigmata—constantly bleeding wounds generated by the legacies of colonial violence and greed as they are inflicted on the space and on those who carry the border within them—or as a site of constant social, epistemic, economic, and religious crucifixion. But (like the crucifixion itself), the border is also a place of rebirth, regeneration and resurrection. José David Saldívar argues in his 1997 book *Border Matters: Remapping American Cultural Studies*, that new typologies of cultural expressions are always emerging at the border(s).[47] This includes new religious practices and spiritual devotions. In this regard, as Emma Pérez has suggested, border communities actively engage with the imaginary (and the spiritual), using them as cognitive tools to challenge and expose oppression, retain collective memory, and navigate power[48]—a messy, painful and powerful process.

Like the people who venerate them, border saints are often citizens located between nation-states, residing not in a single zip code but in many simultaneously. I therefore look at these migrating saints not as simply Mexican vernacular saints but rather as trans-fronterizo saints, who offer a new typology of moving and translocating religiosities both because of their shifting locations of veneration and because, as spiritual patrons of those who cross the border and resettle in the United States, they respond to the needs and experiences of their worshipers. These saints' spiritual popularity is tied to their worshipers' experience of translocation, generated by globalization, forced political and social displacement, greed, violence, and (most recently) environmental disasters. Like those who venerate them, these saints have dual citizenship, Mexican but also American.

Pragmatically, "the border" refers to the political boundary between the US and Mexico. The political, geographic border is at once both real and imaginary, as it delimits discourses of sovereignty that bind the processes of migration between the nations, and it migrates as people do—carried on the shoulders of migrants, in their physical and spiritual bodies. Indeed, the border is less a place than an epistemic, racial, and legal battleground over the terrain of the spiritual and the imaginary. It demarcates social borders around and between race, class, gender, sexual orientation, and religious affiliation, emphasizing the limitations of universal religious citizenship among Christians by concretizing nationalist or xenophobic US discourses against Latinx immigrants. The border is, in fact, better thought of not as a linear border but as a mobile (not fixed) "contact zone" that manifests racialized tensions between migrant communities and national citizens.[49]

Religious borders can be found in barrios like Pilsen in Chicago, Mexicantown in Detroit, or the McKinley neighborhood north of Tulsa—all spaces located far from the literal geographic border of the southern US, but very much existing as border spaces of racial conflict. The border is everywhere: not only on school playgrounds and at bus stops, but in the parish services performed in Spanish, in the memorial altars along the migration routes, and even in the devotional candles to vernacular saints now found in mainstream US stores. These changes embody the demographic and religious shifts in the US landscape created by faith migration. Altars of all types, then—those at church, at home, and in the streets—work as flexible border points where, as scholar Castañeda-Liles explains, "the secularization of the sacred and the sacralization of the secular take place," and the line between official and unofficial sainthood is blurred and contested[50]

At borders, which are (as Vásquez and Marquardt have put it) "liminal spaces of transcultural creativity and innovation," old forms of religious expressions are repurposed and customized and new cultural productions are generated.[51] In these spaces, those forced into migration "try to make sense of their baffling world by mapping and remapping sacred landscapes through religious practices."[52] Within the context of the extreme violence of the (physical, geographic, political) border, religiosity—in this case via saints, their spiritual tales, and their milagros (miracles) and promesas (promises)—is an essential mechanism for holding together a world that seems to be falling apart.

According to Patricia A. Price's 2004 book *Dry Place: Landscapes of Belonging and Exclusion*, the apparitions of the Virgin of Guadalupe along the US-Mexico border transform a mundane everyday space into a "sacred space,"[53] exemplifying Mircea Eliade's concept of "hierophany." These apparitions—emergences of the sacred—allow border subjects to "gain a foothold in a chaotic world; it provides an axis mundi, a seam between heaven and Earth that gives life its meaning."[54] The religious and the imaginary thus allow border subjects to transform the physical border, which usually offers an experience of unlivable evil, into a latent site of holiness with intrinsic subversive power that offers them a form of liberation.

At the border, one particularly useful concept is that of "spiritual mestizaje," a term coined by Anzaldúa and developed extensively by Teresa Delgadillo in *Spiritual Mestizaje: Religion, Gender, Race and Nation in Contemporary Chicana Narrative*.[55] Within the concept of spiritual mestizaje lies a particularly important notion: "Nepantla," a Nahuatl and Aztec term recuperated by Chicana/o and Latinx scholars to refer to the space in the middle, the in-between, that characterizes the unique state of consciousness of being a citizen of the borderlands. Within this middle spiritual space lies an amalgam of spiritual innovations that cannot be identified as fully or only Mexican, but neither are they mainstream Anglo-American; rather, they are a symbiotic interweaving of both into a unique entity. This unique religiosity characteristic of the border is what Lara Medina defines as "Nepantla spirituality," or "spirituality that emerges from the middle, from the center."[56] These spiritualities may be aesthetically and institutively very Catholic, yet at the same time they are unrecognizable by the Catholic Church authorities, for nepantla spirituality is a confluence and migration of many traditions, including indigenous traditions and those of the forced African diaspora in the Americas. For Medina, the liminal space of nepantla "gives ... 'mixed race' peoples the powers to choose, critique, integrate, and balance [their] multiple cultural and biological inheritances."[57]

The inherently political nature of nepantla spirituality, where race, gender, culture, sexuality, and spirituality overlap and intertwine, is beautifully articulated by C. Alejandra Elenes in her discussion of Gloria Anzaldúa's concept of "spiritual activism": "Spirituality, then, means more than one's relationship with God or a Creator, because it is tied with struggles for social justice and gender equality. Spirituality is a way of understanding someone's (or a community's) position in the world by trying to make sense of unfair economic conditions and gender inequality, and to do something about it."[58] Norma E. Cantú makes a similar point, explaining that her "activism springs directly from [her] spiritual practice.... [S]pirituality and activist actions are related. We touch the spirit when we change the world with our actions, and it is spirit that 'inspires' right action, especially our social justice actions."[59] It is in the borderlands that these spiritual interventions are taking place, creating religious innovations that expand and nurture the religious plurality characterizing the American experience. This model can help us understand the complex mechanism at work between cultures and communities on the move and help us appreciate the shifting paradigm required to embrace social change.

Religious Intrastates and Religious Sovereignty: Beyond Transplanted Churches

Deborah E. Kanter, in her book *Chicago Católico: Making Catholic Parishes Mexican*, asks a crucial question: "How had Mexico re-created itself so faithfully every weekend at St. Francis?"[60] To answer this question, Kanter examined Catholic parishes, as St. Francis, in Chicago, which she says "served as refugio (refuge) ... had an Americanizing influence ... [and provided] a sense of mexicanidad ...The parish acted as a glue that connected immigrants parents and their US-reared children."[61] Kanter is not alone in her observations about the transformation of American Catholicism by

Mexican migrants. Something extraordinary is happening in the United States—not only in churches, but in local communities and in the United States culture at large. To address this phenomenon, I introduce the term "religious intrastates," which describes the mobile geographic, cultural, and political border zones created by spiritual and religious migration. The religious intrastates I travel in this book are cultural and religious territories that transcend official national boundaries—places (both real and imaginary) where the sacred and the spiritual bind together seemingly disparate cultural, and sovereignty territories. They are deeply cultural, religious, and political all at once, as are the devotional practices, services modalities and vernacular saints they spawn. In many ways, the saints I examine in this book can thus serve as interlocutors for a larger discussion about religious intrastates and the limitations (and ambiguities) they create for the nation-state, its assumed religious sovereignty, and "the internal partitions that gerrymandering theorists impose" on the human experience.[62] Similar to religious mappings, they also "are particularly important to transnational migrants faced with the dislocation produced by globalization, who must draw from their religious traditions 'to delineate an alternative cartography of belonging.'"[63] The cases discussed in this book demonstrate not only how spirituality migrates within and across national borders but also how new, "unauthorized" spiritual territories are created.

As the veneration of these vernacular and sometimes even criminalized saints move from Mexico into the United States and vice versa, religious intrastates reveal the limits of sovereignty (and nation-state projects), showing that its boundaries are porous and deeply insufficient to contain the flow of religious experience. Mexican migrants construct the religious intrastate within the United States when they bring their beliefs and practices with them. They do likewise within Mexico itself, both when they physically return homes from the United States and when they send money home via remittances, fulfill mandas, sponsor religious festivities, or reshape local beliefs because they experience in the United States, which I see as processes of religious retorno or return. Migrant religious events such as the annual balls to celebrate La Santa Muerte in Queens, New York, or the festivities that draw more than three thousand followers to honor Saint Toribio Romo in Tulsa, Oklahoma, do more than just venerate a vernacular saint: they actively reconstruct a Mexico-in-simulacra that is held together by prayer recitations, music, decorations, performances, food, and invocations to an almighty God to look after a community of religious exiles.

These religious intrastates create unique religious and faith constituencies that are not simply a relocation of a state religion but a new typology, one that exists between nation-states. We are witnessing faith communities evolve beyond the concept of "Iglesias Transplantadas . . . etnicas o de inmigración" (transplanted churches, ethnic or from immigration), discussed by Manuel Marzal mostly in the context of Protestant religious migrations to South America. While Iglesias Transplantadas and religious instrastates are both "formed by immigrants who take their religion to their new homeland,"[64] religious intrastates are zones of nepantla, of spiritual activism, and are necessarily deeply political.

Transplanted churches are today evolving into the more complex social and religious structures of religious intrastates, in part because of the peculiar characteristics of social interaction in recent decades that have been promoted by neoliberal practices. The new religious forms respond to three new social and cultural factors: (1) the hyper-interconnectivity created by omnipresent access to the media/internet; (2) the construction of a displaced pan-ethnicity (e.g. pan-Latinidad in the United States); and (3) a massive global mobilization of migrant regional blocs. These three factors, which contextualize the experience of the religious intrastates around migrating saints' devotions, also negotiate religious interactions in and around migrant communities. In the United States, the first factor—the Spanish-language media (e.g. Telemundo, Univision, etc.) and the internet—has allowed home, or place of origin, to be constantly virtually present for immigrants as they settle in new territories. The second factor, combined with the anti-immigrant sentiments of many host communities, has fostered new typologies of religious organizations and structures that respond to pan-ethnicity—forms of affiliation that do not fit the models of cohesion assumed by the traditional notion of transplanted churches. Indeed, for Latinx migrants, these new pan-Latinidades can be identified in many different religious denominations and groups outside of the traditional Catholic-Protestant divide, creating large blocs of migrants (whose common features move beyond the misconceptions of Spanish as their first language, and they identify only as Catholic) in many regions of the US. For example, in Ann Arbor, Michigan, the largest group of Costa Ricans, I once encountered, were part of an Adventist church whose pastor was from Argentina and whose members all came from different countries in Latin America—all bringing different religious histories, "idiosyncrasies" and focuses from their home countries. I observed the same phenomenon in parishes and communities I visited throughout the United States for this research: for the majority of poor migrants, the experience of transnational relocation represents a crucial process of religious transformation.

On Holiness: How to Become a Saint

> Every saint has a past, and every sinner has a future.
> —Oscar Wilde

Canonization—the Catholic Church's official finding that someone is a saint—is foremost an ontological statement about a person's life. It also comprises a set of faith-based assumptions about the person's afterlife—a public declaration that the individual is probably now in Heaven. But the designation of sainthood is not relevant only to the domain of the spiritual; it also relates to the mundane and to the difficulties of being human, and specifically to the social and political conditions of time and place. As Kenneth L. Woodward notes, sainthood is a universal human concept: "Saints are found in all the great world traditions, and, though sanctity means different things in each tradition, the quest for holiness (or its equivalent) is universal."[65]

In the early years of Christianity, the process of recognizing saints "was a spontaneous act of the local Christian community" that required only the approval of the bishop of the local church.[66] But since 1234 the right to proclaim canonizations has been reserved to the pope. Today the progression into sainthood entails a long process of administrative deliberations and, in many cases, political and economic input.[67] The process has responded to changes in the social and political makeup of the Catholic Church, especially vis-à-vis the standardization and centralization of the process by the Holy See. Traditional Christian saints have been individuals who either died defending or protecting the Christian faith, manifested exceptional Christian values or virtues by assisting those in need, or have a popular "reputation for producing miracles, especially . . . posthumously at their shrines or through their relics."[68] Indeed, miracle-working is an important component of canonization: both canonically and pragmatically, as Woodward explains, "saints [are] distinguished not only for their exemplary imitation of Christ but also for their thaumaturgy or wonder-working powers."[69] In other words, through the miracles associated with them, saints function as "companion" benefactors for the living.

Process Toward Official Canonization

The official entity within the Roman Catholic Church that exercises exclusive administrative control over the process of canonizing saints is the Congregation for the Causes of Saints at the Vatican (Latin name: Congregatio de Causis Sanctorum; hereafter, Congregation for the Causes). It leads the investigation into the character of a candidate, confirms all reported miracles, evaluates testimonies, and moves the case through the process. Per canon law, the canonization process cannot even begin until at least five years after the person has died, although exceptions have been made for individuals deemed unusually holy, as in the cases of Pope John Paul II and Mother Teresa.[70]

The official process has several steps, and each result in a different spiritual title or designation for the individual. The first step begins at the local level, in the diocese where the person died or is buried, according to Monsignor Óscar Sánchez Barba. Sánchez Barba, who I interviewed about Saint Toribio Romo in Guadalajara, Mexico, has been personally responsible for introducing the successful canonization cases of the first Catholic saints in Mexico. According to Sánchez Barba, the formal process "begins with the [individual's] reputation of sanctity, at the popular level. It begins with the people. It is a community that goes to their pastor and says, 'Here, we have a person who is holy.' If that does not exist, you cannot [begin the process]. That happens first!"[71] In this first stage, Church officials study the candidate's writings and collect eyewitness testimonies from those who either knew the individual personally or can offer firsthand stories about the candidate. A detailed bibliography is collected; if all goes well, the case is presented to the Congregation for the Causes for further investigation. At that moment, the individual is given the first title or designation, "Servant of God" (Latin: *servus Dei*). In some cases, an exhumation of the body is allowed, and the Congregation for the Causes investigates the practices of veneration centering on the individual to ensure that no improper veneration, superstitions, or practices against the Catholic faith have become associated with the candidate.

In the second step, the designation of "Venerable" (Latin: *venerabilis*) is conferred if sufficient evidence indicates that the candidate has heroically exemplified at least one of the theological or cardinal virtues.[72] This designation, also known as "Heroic in Virtue," must be granted by the pope. No feast day can be set at this stage, but prayer cards and other devotional materials are generated to encourage the veneration of the person and the possibility of a miracle.

The third step, beatification, designates the individual as "Blessed" (Latin: *beatus* or *beata*). Beatification requires proof of one miracle that can be irrefutably connected to the intercession of the individual under consideration. Beatification assigns a feast day on which the candidate may be venerated. Specific limitations curb the extent to which the beatified person may be venerated—for example, devotions are restricted to spaces associated with the individual or his or her diocese and to those places connected to (or owned by) a congregation or religious community founded by the individual.

Only after the Congregation for the Causes verifies that a second miracle has been granted by the exclusive intercession of the Blessed does he or she pass the fourth and last step: canonization by the pope as a saint (Latin: *sanctus* or *sancta*),[73] allowing them to be venerated anywhere and by anyone. Note, however, that not all saints with a feast day in the Catholic liturgical calendar have been formally canonized. For example, in some cases, devotions to certain saints—such as Saint Patrick or Saint Cecilia—were already immensely popular centuries before the formal process of canonization was established. So how did they come to be recognized as saints?

On the Peculiarities of "Illegal" (or Undocumented) Saints: *Vox Populi, Vox Dei*

Unsurprisingly, then, the Catholic Church does not officially recognize as saints all people who are popularly considered so, many of whom exist only in the social consciousness of communities in the form of regional, folk, or vernacular saints. As Woodward points out, "Formal canonization is part of a much 'wider,' older, and culturally more complex process of 'making saints'"—a process that includes understandings and forms of sainthood that exist outside the official definitions.[74] As a result, there are far more vernacular and folk saints than canonized saints, with only a small number of saints *vox populi* (from the people) actually receiving formal recognition.

For Woodward, *vox populi* is "not enough to sustain a reputation for holiness without support from the church's elites" to move through the official process of canonization.[75] He notes that there are political and practical elements to decisions about canonization in modern times: "the saint-making process [became] a very powerful mechanism" under John Paul II (now himself a saint), who often used "the symbolism of sanctity to transform a sticky political situation into a personal public-relations triumph."[76] Indeed, John Paul II "beatified and canonized more individuals than all of his twentieth-century predecessors combined."[77]

Although ecclesiastical elites retain the exclusive authority to confer official sainthood, everyday Catholic believers around the world are the ones who define and sustain a saint's memory and life within and beyond the church altars. All of the saints discussed in this book—with the exception of Toribio Romo, who was officially canonized in 2000—are folk and vernacular saints. All are venerated popularly but are not recognized by the Catholic Church—not today and most likely not ever. All have in common that their devotions emerged in Mexico during the twentieth century and that their venerations have journeyed with migrant communities into the United States. They were selected for this book in part because each represents a different period, as well as a different dimension for the study of the migration and religion as shaped by factors such as race, class, gender, sexuality, and US-Mexico relationships.

These saints are what Mexican American artist and activist Alma López Gaspar de Alba terms "illegal saint[s] of 'illegal' immigrants." These types of saints are intimately connected to their immigrant constituencies and to the powers in play around them,[78] responding to the extreme vulnerability imposed on their followers. Like many of their veneradores, these vernacular saints are undocumented; they lack papers, in that they are not officially recognized by the Catholic Church. These saints, and their popular devotion, inhabit a liminal space-in-between (between what is officially defined as legal and what is considered illegal)—a border zone, a nepantla spirituality—and reveal how people incorporate religiosity to deal with everyday struggles. One might say that each of these vernacular saints is no longer simply a historical figure but has been transformed into a social text. As miracle-making legends and venerations have accreted around them, they have been constructed as new entities.

Saints, real and imaginary, legal and undocumented, formal and vernacular, are a palliative resource to which one can turn and from which one can request divine intervention, especially during periods of violence and distress. They are symbolic means to transform a "topography of cruelty" such as the border into a new kind of space in which, despite the contradictions and obstacles, life, beauty, and dignity can prevail.[79]

On Manda Economics and Miracle Currencies

One does not have to believe in miracles to be Catholic, but according to canon law, a miracle is a sign from God that the individual facilitating the miracle is in close communication or union with God—is in a state of *beatific vision* (Latin: *visio beatifica*), in heaven seeing God. According to Woodward, miracles are understood as proof of an indivisible connection or "perfect friendship" with God.[80] But miracles are more than spiritual. They also work as tools to attest to institutional authority. As Woodward explains, miracles validate the "solemn papal declaration that a person is, for certain, with God" and that consequently "the faithful can, with confidence, pray to the saint to intercede with God on their behalf."[81] In the Catholic tradition, each saint makes unique types of divine interventions linked with the specific needs, professions, industries, diseases, etc. of their venerators. The Church designates patron saints for pregnant women, for electricians, for the internet, for truck drivers, and for those suffering with eye diseases—and unofficially, as demonstrated in this book, for immigrants and for those crossing borders without approved documentation.

For all saints, official and unofficial, miracles are essential to their reputation of holiness. Particularly for folk saints, like those studied in this book, a life exemplifying Christian virtue is not sufficient: Christian virtues, in these cases, come to exist not through each saint's life but through his or her qualification as a miracle-granter. As Marzal explains, many Catholics who venerate vernacular saints do so because they consider those saints "as intercessors before God, but not as models of life."[82] In other words, for some Catholics, venerating a vernacular saint is not about reproducing the saint's life in one's own life; rather, such veneration recognizes that the vernacular saint, by his or her own virtue as a saint, manifests as a potential benefactor, especially for those who must confront the limitations of their own lives.

These miracles can be taxonomized, and saints are categorized within a matrix that defines (and differentiates) each one within specific spiritual miracle boundaries, giving each a unique territory of spiritual patronage. The more generic a saint's patronage, the greater the possibility for that saint to attract larger constituencies. However, general or ambiguous designations can erode the saint's specificity, diminishing his or her potency within a niche market of believers in search of spiritual intervention. A vernacular saint's potency—his or her ability to help people resolve their own problems—is central to their veneration. As described by Frank Graziano, devotion to saints "is a practical, goal-directed, utilitarian devotion; a survival strategy; a way of interpreting reality; and a resource enhancement realized through collaboration with a sacred patron." Potent saints and intercessors are particularly necessary when their constituencies and petitioners are marginalized, for "petitions thrive in social contexts characterized by deprivation and vulnerability, poor access to basic social services . . . a loss of trust in institutions and government, and a sense that it would take a miracle to survive this inhospitable world."[83] Religious devotion (and a miracle request), then, can be an archive of the effects of social and economic distress. In this sense, as Marzal explains, for many Catholics who practice devotions to these vernacular saints, "the miracle in a popular sense is not the one that overcomes the laws of nature, but [is the one that overcomes] the real possibilities of the devotee."[84] In the veneration of a vernacular saint, the saint's holy status depends not on recognition by the Catholic Church but on people's asking for help with real problems and then believing that their requests have been (or could be) answered.

This type of veneration works quite differently than the veneration of officially canonized Catholic saints under canon law. In the Catholic tradition defined by the institution itself, for a miracle to be recognized officially, a devotee must have prayed exclusively to one holy person (in this case a deceased person, a saint), asking him or her to intercede with God for a miracle. For a saint to grant a miracle, the believer must first develop a rapport with the saint and with the narrative of the saint's heroism and holy virtues. As Woodward puts it, "Saints exist in and through their stories." Furthermore, he adds, "to make a saint, or to commune with the saints already made, one must first know their stories."[85] This communing happens only if the petitioner has access to the saint's story or reputation in the first place. It is, in short, a closed system of mutual recognition in which the "actions" of each party serve to affirm those of the other.[86]

The miracle and the saint cannot work separately—they are intimately linked,[87] illustrating Jacques Derrida's notion of the gesture, or the calling associated in the creation of meaning.[88] To this pragmatic process of interaction I have given the label "manda economics," by which I mean the miracle exchange between the petitioner and saint-as-miracle-maker (intercession). Manda is a popular term used in Mexico and among some Mexican Americans; it can be translated as "religious requests, promises or pleas."[89] As Neal Krause and Elena Batista define it, a manda is a "religious quid pro quo"[90], a pledge offered to a spiritual entity (a saint) who has enough reach to, in return, provide a favor or a miracle. Mandas vary according to the individual, the venerational characteristics associated with the entity in question, and the location and time of year. A manda may include a penitence, a sacrifice, a change in behavior, a tangible offering, a prayer, and so on.

Mandas, then, can be read as spiritual contracts or, as Graziano calls them, "votive contracts," that happen between the petitioner (believer) and the spiritual entity or grantor (e.g., God, Mary, a saint, or a spirit).[91] While the assumption is that both parties—the petitioner and the saint-as-miracle-maker—will fulfill their promises, the petitioner cannot communicate or know for sure the desires of the spiritual figure. Therefore, the contract is very much based on moral expectations and assumptions of good faith between the parties. As Graziano argues, "petitionary devotion is a way of anticipation"; although it binds the petitioner "to reciprocation . . . [in the end, the promise] is conditional, because the votary is not obligated unless the miracle is granted."[92]

Manda economics is therefore based on social norms of reciprocity, hope, good will and idealized balance within a system of asymmetrical disparities of power. Since the petitioner does not know if their request will be granted, they try to fulfill their end of the manda in order to obligate the saints to carry out the other end of the contract. The saint may "decide" not to grant the petition for any number of reasons that can never be known by the petitioner. Some petitioners interpret the non-fulfillment of their petition as a sign that the favor was not God's will and was not good for his or her overall spiritual health. On other occasions, "insufficient faith is the primary reason cited by devotes for the failure of petitions."[93] In these cases, the responsibility for the failure returns to the devotee. Devotees cannot "breach the agreements that they themselves have initiated and defined. Reciprocity . . . is an obligation but also a matter of honor, social responsibility, and correct behavior."[94] When these norms are violated—when a manda is ruptured or unfulfilled by the petitioner—there can be grave consequences.[95] According to many of the petitioners interviewed, the spiritual entity may punish the petitioner or his or her loved ones.

However, a manda should not be confused with a payment, because neither God nor any spiritual entity needs compensation from humans. This manda, as a spiritual favor or exchange between a religious entity and petitioner, is by its nature "asymmetrical. A votary's [petitioner's] ability to reciprocate is incommensurable with a miraculous image's [spiritual entity's] ability to give. The imbalance is presumed in votive contracts" and recognized socially by the community.[96] In this sense, a manda stands instead as evidence of the superlative powers of the entity, as well as of the petitioner's good heart, good intentions, and manifest gratitude.[97]

The manda economy is defined on one side by the miracle currency being produced by spiritual entities and on the other by their followers' perpetuation of their vernacular popularity. The spiritual value of one saint over another is defined by the economics of miraculous exchanges associated with each. If someone decides that the miracles attributed to a particular saint are in fact graces made possible by another, or even are unattached to any specific saint, that first saint becomes obsolete, unneeded, and forgotten. Saints rise and fall in popularity, and sufficient numbers of followers and practices around their veneration are needed to keep them alive. Therefore, as society changes, its saints also change and evolve by incorporating new meanings, new healing powers, and new areas of miraculous intervention. Similarly, other saints fall out of fashion, disappear, or are replaced by new saints. In this way, then, saints are social texts, constantly under negotiation, with significations continually changing and being added. A saint can be understood as a type of memory incarnated—in semiotic terms, as an ideal with a spiritual body as a signifier. This is illustrated by the recent popularization and beatification (in 2020) of Carlos Acutis, patron of computer programmers and the internet. In this sense, this book is about the documenting the migration of faith, but it is also about the maneuvers of transnational power that define the precarious life (and death) of people. It is about their need for the spiritual to imagine and enact a different world for them and their families, for their hope of a future on earth as it is in Heaven.

[For additional material about this book, including timelines, photos, videos, articles, news, and cocktails inspired by these saints and their followers, visit **www.UndocumentedSaints.com**]

Jesús Malverde:
A Saint of the People, for the People

1

1

Jesús Malverde

A Saint of the People, for the People

Voy a pagar una manda	I am going to pay manda, a promise
al que me hizo un gran favor	to the one who did me a big favor
al santo que a mí me ayuda	to the saint who helps me
yo le rezo con fervor	I pray to him with fervor
y lo traigo en mi cartera	and I'm carrying his picture in my wallet
con aprecio y devoción.	with appreciation and devotion.

—Los Cadetes de Linares, "Jesús Malverde"

Jesús Malverde: The Social Body of the Saint

"[Jesús] Malverde is like the devil. He's everywhere," says Father Lázaro Sánchez as he walks down the stairs of his parish house in Culiacán, Sinaloa, holding a sculpture of the vernacular saint Jesús Malverde in his hands.[1] Father Lázaro, played by Juan Luis Orendain, is a recurring character in the second season of the telenovela *El señor de los cielos* (2013–20), created by the Florida-based network Telemundo. This narco-telenovela or narco–soap opera, set in Culiacán, chronicles the adventures of drug trafficker Aurelio Casillas (played by Rafael Amaya) and his family, and the image of vernacular saint Jesús Malverde appears consistently throughout the series, both as part of the protagonists' drama and as a member of Father Lázaro's pantheon of saints. The show is purportedly based on the real-life story of 1990s Mexican drug lord Amado Carrillo Fuentes, leader of the Juárez Cartel, the largest and most powerful drug cartel in Mexico. *El señor de los cielos* (the show's title refers to Carrillo Fuentes's nickname, "Lord of the Skies," derived from the large fleet of airplanes he used to transport drugs from Colombia to Mexico and the United States) is an international hit. In January 2021, Telemundo, one of the two leading Latinx networks in the United States, released one of their "most ambitious productions," a telenovela titled *Malverde: El santo patrón*, based on the adventures of this saint.[2]

Why does Jesús Malverde—a seeming footnote in Mexican history, a man who allegedly died in 1909 in the northwestern state of Sinaloa, Mexico, in the months leading up to the Mexican Revolution—play such a large role in a US-based Spanish-language soap opera? How did Malverde's fame as a vernacular saint migrate north from turn-of-the-century Mexico and take root all over the United States? Today, Malverde is most widely known as a narco-saint, or informal patron of Mexico's transnational drug trade. Commercial busts of this handsome norteño (a term meaning anyone who lives in a state in northern Mexico) who looks like a movie star can be found in many private homes and botánicas (folk medicine stores) in Latina/o/x barrios in US cities like Los Angeles, New York, Detroit, Chicago, and Phoenix. The image of Malverde is now indelibly associated with the world of drug trafficking and all its attendant danger. Indeed, now he is part of the US Immigration and Customs Enforcement (ICE) and Drug Enforcement Administration (DEA) agent training modules on drug paraphernalia. Malverde is also mentioned in numerous Spanish- and English-language media in the context of drug trafficking, including soap operas like *El señor de los cielos*, mainstream television shows, and news outlets, including articles in the *New York Times*, the *Washington Post*, *Time* magazine, and the *Los Angeles Times*.[3]

Malverde, in his role as narco-saint, has even made appearances in US courtrooms in drug trafficking cases. According to the widely held belief in Mexico, Joaquín Guzmán Loera, otherwise known as El Chapo, one of the most notorious of all narco-traffickers, once left a note at Malverde's chapel in Culiacán that allegedly read, "Thank you, boss. Today I humbly ask you for only Juárez and Tijuana. Thanks, so much for everything else."[4] The note was signed "JGL 'el Chapo.'" This folk connection between El Chapo and Malverde was brought up during Guzmán's trial for drug trafficking, which took place in 2018–19 in Brooklyn, New York. In addition to the traditional questions asked during the selection of the prospective jurors, the prosecution also asked, "Are you familiar with Jesus Malverde?"—a question that manifests the intimate naturalized framing of Malverde as a narco-saint. The defense, too, appealed to Malverde. As reported by the *New York Post*, Ángel Eduardo Balarezo, the leading defense lawyer, said that a small statuette of Malverde "miraculously appeared" inside the defense's conference room in the federal court where El Chapo's three-month trial was taking place—coincidentally, on "the same day government cooperator and former Sinaloa

Figure 1.1 Jesús Malverde objects from the United States: Jesús Malverde memorabilia purchased in Albuquerque, New Mexico, and Phoenix, Arizona.
Photo by the author

Cartel honcho Jesus Zambada took the stand to testify against El Chapo, his former boss" (see Figure 1.1).[5]

Did Jesús Malverde Exist?

Despite the near-ubiquity of visual and cultural references to Malverde, there are no official records or photographs of Jesús Malverde, nor can we find any clear official historical traces of his existence. There was an 1888 birth certificate for a child named Jesús Malverde found by Gilberto López Alanís, director of the Archivo histórico general del estado de Sinaloa (Historical Archive of Sinaloa); the certificate describes a baby "born in the city of Paredones, on January 15, 1888 . . . at 5:00 a.m." that "was given the name of JESÚS, the natural [out-of-wedlock] son of Guadalupe Malverde, adult and single."[6] It is not clear whether this is the same Jesús Malverde. Nor is it known whether Malverde was Jesús Malverde's original surname or was instead a popular moniker assigned to him later; the name combined two Spanish words—mal (bad, ill) and verde (green), referring to the association between his figure and banana bushes and shrubs, which were added to his folk legend by his followers because they are useful camouflage for evidence of misdeeds.[7]

Thus, the figure of Jesús Malverde—whether an actual person, the convergence of several historical figures, or purely the product of popular imagination—remains shrouded in mystery.[8] Popular tradition believes Malverde to have been born on December 24, a date that (like his given name) connects him to Jesus Christ, and according to Daniel Sada, Malverde was born in the then-dangerous neighborhood of Redonda, in Culiacán; neither claim can be verified.[9] As explained by James S. Griffith in his book *Folk Saints of the Borderlands*, most theories of Malverde's origins view him not as an actual historical person but as what Sam Quinones calls an "amalgam of two bandits," a fusion of two documented historical local figures of late-nineteenth-century Sinaloan with similar characteristics: Heraclio Bernal (1855–88), a thief from southern Sinaloa, and Felipe Bachomo (1883–1916), an indigenous rebel from the northern part of the same state.[10] Both men were popular heroes who challenged the local and national authorities of their time and financed their activities by stealing from the local hacendados (landowners) and the upper classes.[11]

In the absence of a definitive historical account of Malverde, a multitude of romantic images and narratives of his miracles and epic adventures at the end of the nineteenth century have flourished. In most of these stories, he fits into the archetype of the Robin Hood–style "generous bandit."[12] The Jesús Malverde who is venerated today is a product of his followers' imaginations, expectations, and social despair. This chapter studies not only how Malverde transformed from a peasant into a saint but also—and more importantly—what his veneration says about the deep transformations experienced by northern Mexican farmers in the last century and a half and about the evolution of narco-capitalism in North America.

Everything we know about Malverde comes from people's storytelling in corridos (popular ballads), prayer cards, novels, plays, and legends. Malverde is thus purely a social body, and his followers' devotional practices, rituals, and visual representations of him reveal the politics of their own social and historical contexts. Malverde's vernacular representations are first and foremost a repository of the social histories of resiliency, adaptability, and hope that have defined the lives of peasants migrating from Mexico to the United

States for more than a hundred years. But Malverde is also an example of the trade in spiritual goods that defines the unique relationship between the South and the North, between Mexico and the United States. He is, in a sense, a capitalist byproduct of the borderlands, one through which spirituality is continually negotiated, exchanged, reconstructed, and translated.

Consequently, the emergence and evolution of different versions of Malverde—from his early framing as a generous bandito during the years leading up to the Mexican Revolution (roughly 1870 to 1910), to his reinvention during the late 1970s in the iconic form that catapulted him to wider fame and fully commercialized him as a transnational figure, and finally to his contemporary, post-1990s narco-saint representations—are intimately interconnected with changes in capitalist structures, landholding rights, and labor in the region. As a socioreligious figure, Malverde serves to record and highlight the evolving connection of capitalist development and disenfranchisement in Mexico, particularly in Sinaloa. Indeed, the early construction of Malverde as a generous bandito informs his contemporary framing as a narco-saint: the connecting thread is his status as a victim of governmental injustice—in the past as a poor peasant, and in the present as a narco-farmer.

This approach has methodological repercussions. Given the absence of firsthand historical records about Malverde (beyond oral history), tracking the changes in his narrative has required me to use multiple and diverse sources, including plays, corridos, novels, prayers, and newspaper reports. However, studying Malverde through this variety of texts, which have been produced by a broad range of authors, raises larger questions about audience and authorship. What happens when different authors and consumer constituencies use the same imagery to create cultural products with vastly different effects, levels of power, and legitimacy? How does one compare, for example, a letter written by the Catholic bishop of Sinaloa that mentions Malverde with a play written about the saint by a closeted gay man? Both reveal important insights about Malverde's connection to his followers, yet they diverge in terms of their authors' social capital. Such questions are not so much problems to be overcome as illustrations of Malverde's ever-shifting, continually negotiated meaning and his ability to aid various kinds of actors in their individual and collective journeys. In this sense Malverde frankly speaks to a history of migration—that of his followers but also his own, as he is adapted to the new realities and needs of various communities.

Don't Ask, Don't Tell: The Catholic Church and Jesús Malverde

Jesús Malverde has not been canonized, and the Catholic Church does not recognize his veneration as a saint, nor is the Church interested in starting a proper cause of investigation for his canonization. He does not fulfill the Church's official requirements for sainthood. Indeed, there is no official recognition of his existence. However, the relationships between local Catholic communities in Sinaloa, the ecclesial authorities, and Malverde are more complicated than just a simple refusal or denial.

In Culiacán, Malverde's veneration is not sanctioned or endorsed by the Catholic Church, but many Catholics consider him a local holy hero. Here, Jesús Malverde operates (and navigates) as an open secret; the Church's position on the local veneration of Jesús Malverde appears to be "don't ask, don't tell."[13] The closest the Church has come to openly discussing Malverde arose in 1979–80 during a land dispute (described later in this chapter) involving the Culiacán local government and the relocation of Malverde's chapel. It is almost as if the ecclesial authorities consider the belief in this vernacular saint to be an expression of an immature local faith.

It is unclear why the Church resists addressing the veneration of Malverde in Culiacán—whether it means they think his veneration is unimportant or they simply wish to avoid confrontation with the local community. Perhaps the Catholic Church in Sinaloa is afraid of disturbing a different type of Catholic constituency, one of the most powerful groups of financial benefactors in the region: those who perceive Malverde as the spiritual patron of their transnational drug business.

In Culiacán, Jesús Malverde and his veneration are supported exclusively by the munificence of local charities, making it difficult for the Church to justify attacking his followers and the chapel's caretakers. Those responsible for Malverde's veneration—from Don Eligio González León, the caretaker and founder of the chapel to the saint in Culiacán, to his son Jesús Manuel González Sánchez, who fills that role today—have focused on donations to help those in need: wheelchairs, caskets, and money to cover funeral costs. Yet despite Malverde's lack of official Church recognition, most beneficiaries of the chapel's assistance are Catholics, their funerals take place in Catholic churches and facilities, and the González family has consistently declared themselves devoted Catholics. Reinforcing Malverde's charitable profile has allowed followers to unofficially incorporate him into their extended canon of seemingly Catholic saints; as a Sinaloan, Malverde is framed as a personal and accessible unofficial saint who understands his community and is available to help them with everyday needs.

Jesús Malverde works within the cohesive narratives and imagination about him, representing both Culiacán and Mexico more broadly as both a local hero and a vernacular saint. In the veneration of Malverde, the Catholic Church must navigate delicate terrain, attempting to secure a consistent faith narrative while leaving space for popular folk practices to exist alongside that narrative—perhaps in hopes that the folk practices might fade over time. In other words, as the local Catholic Church works to maintain an effective presence with the community via its "don't ask, don't tell" policy, Malverde comes to exemplify the balance between celestial and terrestrial powers.

Una Capilla para el Santo (A Chapel for the Saint)

I visited Jesús Malverde's main chapel in Culiacán, Mexico, several times between 2015 and 2018. The first time, I was a postdoc fellow at the National Center for Institutional Diversity (NCID) at the University of Michigan. For that research trip, I made an online reservation for a hotel in downtown Culiacán, but the final confirmation never came. After sending several emails without reply, I called the hotel directly. The person in charge of online reservations explained that because I was coming from the United States, the hotel needed some extra documentation: a short written description of what I was planning to do in Culiacán and why, as well as my schedule and copies of my CV, my passport, and my ID. According to the hotel clerk, a city ordinance restricted the access of reporters and researchers—unusual measures that I had never encountered or even heard about in Latin America before. The town government wanted to be sure that I was not a risk to the city, to others, or to myself. While in my opinion, I was doing low-risk research into vernacular religiosity and saints, I would very soon learn that I was wrong. After I consulted my university's legal team, we submitted via secure channels all the required paperwork, including a subsequently requested "verification," and I eventually did receive the confirmation for my hotel. I cannot deny that this little interaction made me apprehensive about the visit.

It was not until my arrival in Culiacán that I understood the unique conditions that govern this city within the context of the war on drugs in

Mexico. I have been to Culiacán multiple times since, but I still remember my first visit and the novel (and unsettling) feeling of being constantly observed—in certain ways under surveillance—by some of the hotel clerks. At the time, however, I assumed this feeling was probably a combination of my own anxieties, my naiveté, and my lack of experience with fieldwork. However, my security fears were not ill-founded, given that I was in the capital of the Sinaloan cartel.

Thankfully, I was not alone during that first visit. María Romero, a local artist whose work focuses on Jesús Malverde (discussed later in this chapter), kindly accompanied me. She lives in Mexico City but is originally from Culiacán. Without her help and support, many parts of this chapter would never have been possible. She introduced me to the to the beautiful and resilient people of Culiacán and the rich history of the city, including many of its intellectuals, its cultural centers, and its historical archives; she also introduced me to the chapel of Jesús Malverde, its vendors, and its caretakers.

In Culiacán, Jesús Malverde's chapel is more than just the primary site for Malverde's veneration—more than a simple space for spiritual transactions. The rituals and spiritual practices surrounding Malverde negotiate almighty terrestrial powers, those of capital and greed—powers that define the life and death of those venerating this vernacular Mexican saint. The chapel's existence and location reflect the intersections of the main power players in Sinaloa—the Catholic Church, the local government, and the cartels in the region—at both real and imaginary levels. As journalist Ioan Gillo writes, these connections are literal as well as figurative: the chapel is located "right across the road from the grandiose state-government palace . . . [T]he twin powers of Sinaloa—political and narco—are side by side."[14] And in a typical instance of sophisticated and wicked Mexican humor, Martín Amaral, a reporter for *El Noreste*, a Culiacán newspaper, notes, "It is somewhat curious how the chapel [of Malverde] is near the other earthly power, the government palace. There, promises are always made; here [in the chapel], people say, Malverde actually fulfills them."[15] The joke exposes the complicated and interconnected power realities (and disparities) that surround Malverde's popularity in Sinaloa.

The chapel is built on land donated by the local government after it forcibly displaced the area residents to construct the government palace in the 1970s—a concession that took place only after many protests as well as a number of inexplicable, seemingly supernatural events. The government's support for the chapel was significant in part because it expressed the relationship that the local government, and to some extent the Catholic Church, has had with the cult of Jesús Malverde. In the decades that followed the building's construction, the chapel has become a driving force for the modernization of the cult.

Malverde's chapel in Culiacán is not the lavish or opulent space one might expect, particularly given his association with high-profit illicit drug trafficking. To the contrary, the chapel is a large, spartan, warehouse-style structure, made of cement, metal, and glass, with almost no ornaments other than a pair of white and yellow glass crosses, the word "Malverde" spelled out on the exterior of the building, and a statue at the top (see Figure 1.2).

The chapel is divided into different sections, each with its own function and degree of intimacy. They are like a box within a larger box, with the inner box being the extra sanctified spot, the inner sanctum, where you do most of your actual praying. The outer box, or larger gallery, is where you wait,

Figure 1.2 The exterior of the current chapel to Jesús Malverde, Culiacán, Sinaloa. Constructed by Don Eligio González Léon.
Photo by the author

purify yourself, meditate on the goodness of the saint, look at other people's experiences with the saint, and reflect on what you need.

The building's entryway is a large, covered corridor that faces the street. The entrance works as an advertisement for the chapel, with the word "Malverde" inscribed in huge letters across eight concrete benches in front of the building. The spaces between the benches hold vendor kiosks selling religious paraphernalia related to the saint, with the kiosks located in the middle receiving the most visitors. The corridor leads to a main room, the gallery, that holds the inner sanctum, located as a separate small room in the center of the larger room. The large room, or gallery, has many nichos (niches or alcoves) along the walls. A large gallery-type space with a high ceiling, this main room's walls are covered with photos and mementos that prepare the visitor for the solemnity of the central inner sanctum with the main bust of Malverde.

The gallery is organized as a series of small nichos "sponsored" by wealthy donors. All of the spaces are covered in pictures of and testimonies to Malverde's many miracles and his followers' requests. The walls around the area serve also as displays to announce future charity events, and the main gallery highlights the many wheelchairs, coffins, and toys donated over the years, made possible by the money collected at the chapel. The records of these acts of charity construct Malverde, in the community, as a benefactor, counteracting the negative publicity associating the saint with illicit practices.

Each nicho emphasizes a different aspect of Jesús Malverde's veneration. Taken together, these nichos manifest the multifaceted character and personalization of Malverde. The aisle allows visitors to move between the rooms and sections of the larger building; it also serves as a large public space that advertises the many miracles, charities, and favors attributed to Malverde, particularly those connected to powerful families in the region who can afford such displays. This aspect stratifies Malverde's believers, separating the poor from the rich, and this stratification is apparent in the different alcoves' architectural styles, qualities, and details. The alcoves, sponsored by different families or organizations, have been commissioned or rented as offerings for favors received. Each nicho's aesthetic reflects a differentiation that is simultaneously vertical and horizontal, showing divisions between classes and also among the different regional families and powerful donors. Therefore, the nichos work as a public display of power and wealth that highlights class disparities within the worship of the saint.

Each alcove is locked behind a glass or metal door. Some are curiosity boxes, displaying objects organized around specific themes—sculptures, crosses, even baby clothes to mark a successful pregnancy or a baby's recovery from an illness. Others are wallpapered with dollar bills and images of other holy entities and saints, from Jesus Christ and the Virgin Mary to Saint Jude and La Santa Muerte—another vernacular saint, whom I discuss in Chapter 4.

Visits to his chapel are part of petitioners' greater journey of intensifying their relationship with the saint. In this sense Malverde, like all social heroes and vernacular saints, is foremost a traveling narrative. Here, the chapel serves as anchor, placeholder, and amplifier for Malverde's chronicle and for the cultural—though not official—validation of his sainthood. The chapel holds both the supposed remains of Malverde and the imaginations of his followers and the myths of his history. The emphasis on believers' personal experiences, always accompanied by "proof" of the miracles granted by Malverde, is extremely moving; it makes the saint seem close to visitors' realities and struggles. The many offerings, petitions, and testimonies collected in the inner sanctum amplify the sacredness of the space, as the visitors connect their personal and local experiences to those at the global and transnational level. In this way visitors' problems are woven together to reflect the larger drama of the region: its vulnerability to the global market and government policies, and the forced mobilization and immigration that follow. The chapel also reflects a strong sense of community connection, as many visitors express spiritual gratitude and empathy for the other people who have requested favors. New requests are perceived as part of a long-lasting community spiritual experience, one that keeps unfolding over time.

The center of the gallery features a large metal cross with a banner that reads:

> The soul of Jesús Malverde
> Born: 1870
> Died: May 3, 1909

This cross was supposedly moved from the original site where Malverde was allegedly killed.

The inner sanctum is an enclosed room at the center of the building; it is the heart of Malverde's veneration in Culiacán. The inner sanctum has two small windows on the right and left sides, facing the surrounding alcoves' aisles. These windows, which open out into the main perimeter corridor of the chapel's gallery, have been covered by images, pictures, and candles, all of which limit air circulation. The location of the windows suggests that at one time the room that constitutes the inner sanctum may have been the sole structure, and perhaps the rest of the warehouse was created around it. This impression is reinforced by the fact that the inner sanctum stands by itself within the structure of the larger building, and the roof of the latter envelops it as a sort of canopy.

The inner sanctum's interior is quite hot and dark, illuminated only by the candles offered to the saint. Paradoxically, one feels part of something larger than oneself, but also captured within an almost overwhelming space. Silence prevails in this intimate space, broken only by people praying, repeating the rosary, and sometimes sobbing or singing to the saint. Recreational drugs and heavy drinking are prohibited in the chapel—though during one of my visits in 2015, several devotees and I were invited by Romero (the local artist) and the shrine custodian to drink a beer to Malverde as an act of offering to the saint inside the inner sanctum.

During brief hiatuses in their quiet prayers, people in the inner sanctum room testify to Malverde's sanctity, exchanging histories and anecdotes about the saint's miracles and their personal relationships with him. Such conversations reinforce the sense of collective devotion and create community and connection among those present. A similar effect is created by letters, pictures of individuals and their families, cigarettes, dollar bills, miracle requests, and reminders of previously granted favors that cover the walls, the windows, and even the low ceiling. These mementos all testify to Malverde's legend—but they also weave present-day petitioners into a bigger tapestry by contextualizing new requests within a long genealogy of worship. In this way Malverde unifies believers, despite wide disparities in their backgrounds and needs. In the inner sanctum, we feel connected by our own fragility, mortality, and vulnerability. We have Malverde in common.

All attention within the inner sanctum is guided to one focal point: the sculpted bust of Malverde. Petitioners regularly bring offerings of food, alcohol, and music to this bust. Indeed, a banda or a norteño group is almost always available for patrons interested in requesting a corrido or other song to Malverde. Players constantly monitor the space for new visitors and ask if they want to offer a song to Malverde. Surrounded by thousands of photos, short narratives, petitions, and tokens of gratitude, with the silence of the inner sanctum punctuated occasionally by the sounds of life—music, testimonials, praying, and crying—visitors often experience a kind of euphoria, induced by the lack of light, the close atmosphere, and the effect of seeing the sculpture of Malverde (Figure 1.3).

Regardless of whether one believes Jesús Malverde is a saint, one cannot help but be affected by the deeply personal display of memorabilia and the intimate nature of the material left behind by his followers.

The inner sanctum works as a historical archive, a holder of community memory. In addition to the Malverde relics and several holy rocks associated with Malverde, this inner room includes images of official Catholic saints; while the official Church does not welcome Malverde, he does not mind

Figure 1.3 The main altar (inner sanctum) at the Jesús Malverde Chapel, Culiacán, Sinaloa. The altar is covered with pictures and mementos from the followers. It is common to see other saint devotions in altars. To the left of Malverde one can see images of San Charbel and the beloved Niño de Atocha, two popular saints in Mexico. The two most important shrines to the Holy Infant of Atocha or El Santo Niño de Atocha are located in Plateros, Zacatecas (Mexico) and in Chimayo, New Mexico (USA).
Photo by the author

sharing sacred space with Catholic saints recognized by the Catholic Church. The room mixes a number of references to other popular and vernacular saints alongside traditional Catholic sacred objects (such as holy water) and visual references (including images of the Virgin of Guadalupe) and the traditional Catholic prayer apparatus, such as a kneeler, two benches, large sculptures of Jesus Christ and Mary, and a donation box.

Aesthetically, the inner sanctum is thus defined by a dominant, pious Catholicism despite the silence from the Catholic Church. The space is designed to tell a history—not just that of Jesús Malverde, but the history of all those touched by faith in his miracles. The inner sanctum, and the chapel as a whole, not only displays Malverde but creates Malverde as being irrefutably a saint of the community. Visitors truly encounter Malverde as a collective apparition arising from all the petitions and mementos collected in the place.

The keepers of the chapel monitor the space continually to ensure that any new valuable offerings or significant mementos are relocated to a special vault in the back, where they remain in a private collection that records the many visits to the chapel. The vault remains closed to the public; it is open only for special guests, such as researchers or chapel benefactors, whose visits are always supervised by the keepers. In this private collection, I saw an eclectic collection of offerings, many from the North, that speak to Malverde's character as a transnational miracle maker between the United States and Mexico.

In this context, the chapel can be analyzed as an example of the consumption and marketing of religiosity. As an economic enterprise based around mandas, the chapel serves as a place where diverse traders and customers meet and where various demands and offers are fulfilled. The chapel is therefore a complex venue of capitalist production. One finds in the chapel many of the traditional economic transactions typical of the commodification, consumption, and commercialization of religious sites encountered elsewhere in the world, which are often surrounded by souvenir stores selling holy objects such as rosaries, crosses, books, and other paraphernalia aimed at reproducing the religious experience of the site itself.[16]

The administrators of Malverde's chapel capitalize on the popularity of the site by renting spaces to vendors and pricing the rent for those spaces according to proximity to the main chapel. The two most central (and therefore busiest) spots next to the main entrance are reserved for the religious memorabilia sold by the family of Jesús M. González Sánchez, the self-appointed main caretaker of the chapel and the son of González León, the previous caretaker and founder of the current chapel. At the present moment there is no process for selecting future administrators; caretaking remains a family enterprise. Jesús M. González Sánchez's role at the chapel further blurs the line between the commercial and spiritual terrains, because in addition to managing the day-to-day operations of the building, González Sánchez blesses visitors' purchases and provides them with a special prayer of protection in return for voluntary donations. However, he offers these special blessings only for objects that have been purchased in his family-run shops, not for memorabilia from the other stores.

Ultimately, the chapel to Jesús Malverde is an intermediary space, revealing the struggles and expectations of poor communities and their vulnerable conditions in a world dominated by forces outside their control. The chapel embodies the stark reality of economic inequality in Mexico, and is physically located near local power (the government palace). It lies at the intersections between the local Catholic Church, with its desire to eliminate or control Malverde's veneration; the latifundium (landed estate) ruling class, which undermines his cult by treating it as folkloric superstition; and the local narco-traffickers, who drive the media narrative of Malverde as a narco-saint. Together these forces hold Malverde's community in a state of siege, always in defense mode.

The chapel to Jesús Malverde therefore performs important work on multiple levels. It generates and commemorates miracles. It inspires hope and repentance. It produces economic revenue and social relief for the community. It both marks and mediates the profound disparities that divide local residents and visitors. Exactly how much money is generated by space rentals and souvenir sales is unclear. Unknown, too, is how much of the donated money comes from narco-benefactors seeking to assuage guilt or show remorse. But in many ways, the mystery surrounding the chapel, its work, and its benefactors is precisely what keeps Malverde's mystique alive.

As a migrant saint—one venerated in both Mexico and the United States—Malverde exists within multiple and fluid sociopolitical contexts: first within Culiacán, Sinaloa, then within the country of Mexico, and now within the United States. To understand this moving semiotic faith object, one must explore how he came to exist in the first place, and also how Sinaloa's politics and economy create the conditions for his emergence and distribution. Furthermore, one must analyze how market transformations manufactured a social body for Malverde in such a way that migration and its bandito-related narco-consumption are not only possible but constantly resignified and emphasized.

A Bandito for the People

To understand Jesús Malverde as a saint of modernity, one must comprehend the Mexican Revolution (which took place roughly from 1910 to 1920) and the geopolitics of Sinaloa, for many details used to build Malverde's religious identity as a popular hero and saint reflect the years leading up to the Mexican Revolution and the subsequent fall of the Porfiriato, the government of Porfirio Díaz, the president of Mexico for seven terms (from 1876 to 1880 and again from 1884 to 1911).

One of the earliest and most prevalent narratives about Jesús Malverde, which remains very much in place today, promotes his origins as a "generous bandito" at the turn of the twentieth century in the northern state of Sinaloa. As Patricia L. Price argues, Malverde's representation as a "social or noble bandit" and as an antagonist "to the common 'blood and vengeance' criminal" came "on the heels of a larger social transformation; in this case, the modernization of Sinaloa through the coming of the railroads and large-scale agriculture."[17] In what Gerardo Gómez Michel and Jungwon Park define as a "conflict with the modernizing project," the poor classes of Sinaloa responded to this modernization by seeking "anchors in their relationship with the sacred, the magical, and the supernatural, hoping that divine intervention would save them from a world that was about to leave them behind."[18] According to Gómez Michel and Park, the emergence and worship of Malverde as a vernacular saint thus reflects "the asymmetrical power relationships in Sinaloa during the Porfiriato modernizing period."[19]

As explained previously, popular sanctification, as in the case of Malverde, should be understood first as a proactive response by those who feel disenfranchised and marginalized. The veneration of Malverde specifically must be understood in relation to the project of modernity that characterized the Sinaloan state during the Porfiriato period: for example, the introduction of electricity, extensive train transportation (for exporting goods to the United States), and the industrialization of agrarian practices, which required massive land reforms. Crucially, in Malverde's narrative of sanctification, he is not a passive victim of the institutionalized violence of the state but a subversive actor fighting back: as the story goes, he was a Robin Hood type, killed by soldiers sent by a corrupt state to capture him for the "crime" of fighting for the poor by robbing the rich. He embodies the community's desire to resist—to reject some forms of change while demanding others. The collective imagination of the working class constructs Malverde simultaneously as a victim and as a hero vis-à-vis modernity. He is a landless peasant completely dependent on the insufficient wages offered by unethical landlords and foreign corporations, yet he exemplifies the virtues of redemption that framed the subsequent Mexican Revolution: a willingness to sacrifice for the larger cause of national transformation. Malverde's legend connects the multiple events that make up the history of modern Sinaloa, told from the point of view of those disenfranchised within the writing of history.

Long after the Mexican Revolution, Jesús Malverde was retroactively envisioned as one of the many Robin Hood–style Mexican bandits who proliferated in the late nineteenth and early twentieth centuries. For the most part, legends of these generous bandits share similar structures and narrative characteristics.[20] These figures all came from modest, working-class backgrounds. They suffered through crucial events that changed their life paths—often a death in the family or the loss of land due to wrongdoing on the part of an unscrupulous government or military. Their legends represent them as being pulled reluctantly into bandito activities, and in these tales, their generosity with the proceeds of those activities atones for the brigandage itself. In these legends (which, like history, are written patriarchally), Malverde's group of bandits is made up of only men, and Malverde is shown as the only one capable of navigating between social classes: he can pass within upper-class spaces, where he always ridicules the rich. The bandits in these legends are always one step ahead of the authorities, who are portrayed as weak, foolish, and corrupt.

The narrative of Malverde's earthly life—which, you will recall, cannot be historically verified in any of its particulars—conforms to these conventions and is specifically tailored to the early twentieth-century conditions of dispossession and economic vulnerability in the Sinaloa region. A poor peasant, Malverde was forced into manual labor when his family lost their farmland to the expansion of exploitative Sinaloa hacendados, who were the main beneficiaries of the land policies of President Díaz. (As Susan R. Walsh Sanderson estimates, by the time of Malverde's reported death at the end of the Díaz regime, all of Mexico's land titles were held by only 2 percent of the population. "Nearly one-half of the rural population of Mexico were acasillado"—meaning that they were subject to some form of debt-paying arrangements with their creditors, whether by working as peons or landless laborers or by living within haciendas, in a system that created many forms of abuse.)[21]

Legend has it that both of Malverde's parents died from starvation because of regional drought and land dispossession, and the young orphan had to provide for his younger brothers.[22] Some versions of the myth say he started working as a farmhand for one of the local landlords. Others variously describe him as working as a mason, mineworker, or laborer in the construction of the Ferrocarril Occidental de México (Western Railroad of Mexico) and the Sud Pacífico de México (Southern Pacific of Mexico), railroad lines that linked Mexico City and Mexico's Pacific coast to the United States and were central players in Díaz's modernization of the northwest region of Mexico, creating the network used to extract raw materials and transport goods into the United States.[23] Regardless of the details, all of the legends show him forced into some kind of exploitative labor that served capitalist overlord interests rather than his own.

How Malverde became a fugitive is unclear. Some popular accounts argue that he escaped into the nearby Sinaloa mountains after a fight defending someone's honor; others point to him being accused of a crime he did not commit.[24] In any case, Malverde's transition into an outlaw defines the moment when he shifts from a passive victim to a hero. After several failed attempts to capture Malverde, the governor of Sinaloa, Francisco Cañedo, allegedly offered ten thousand pesos for his arrest. According to the legend, Malverde was ambushed and killed on May 3, 1909, after being betrayed by one of his compadres, Baldemar López.[25] In some versions of the story, Malverde himself told López to turn him in and to give the reward money to the poor—a narrative that recoups even Malverde's defeat as a moment of generosity toward the community and an instance of revenge against the authorities.[26]

Once captured, the legend says, Malverde was hung from a mesquite tree on a rural road on the outskirts of Culiacán, with express orders from the governor to leave the body on display.[27] His hanging body was meant to serve as a public reminder of the price paid by those who did not follow the law or submit to Cañedo's authority.[28] But over time, people brought flowers, candles, and rocks as offerings to the site in memory of the fallen hero. Rocks are easily found and inexpensive objects that can be carried inconspicuously by visitors, making them ideal sacred objects for distribution, and a pile of rocks began to accumulate, eventually becoming so large that it covered Malverde's entire body.[29] The act of leaving rocks was an act of social disobedience, defiance, and resistance to the governor's edict, honoring Malverde. The rocks became holy relics for his followers, sacred not only because of their proximity to Malverde's body and to the place where he died but also because they were understood as providing Malverde with an appropriate

50 UNDOCUMENTED SAINTS

Christian burial. I found rocks to be common offerings at other holy sites, like in the case of Juan Soldado (see Chapter 2).

The event that cemented Malverde's legendary status occurred after his death. Governor Cañedo, Malverde's archnemesis, died unexpectedly on June 2, 1909, only one month after Malverde's execution. Many saw his death as a miracle—proof of Malverde's powers. Cañedo's sudden death and the lack of an appointed successor (Heriberto Zazueta was designated the temporary governor of Sinaloa until extraordinary elections could be called) inaugurated a period of political volatility in the region, as different sectors for or against the continuation of Díaz/Cañedo-style politics battled for power.

Malverde: A Man from Culiacán

The socioeconomic transformations and ruptures within Sinaloa, and the widespread peasant resistance (both emotional and material) to capitalist development in northern Mexico these transformation produced, help to explain the timing and potency of the legend of Jesús Malverde. However, they do not account for the specific way in which he is figured today. As a bandito and popular hero, Malverde is embedded not only in the history of the community where he (purportedly) lived but also within the history and evolution of a particular type of heteronormative masculinity in Mexico, often associated with bandits. In folklore, literature, music, and mass media representations, the sex appeal of bandits has often been used to normalize gendered behavior and social desires.[30] Bandits navigate the space between what is desired and what is condemned. As ruffians and outlaws, they represent society's yearning for freedom, but also the warnings, fears, and moral condemnation associated with sexual escapades. Traditionally, the Mexican figure of the "generous bandit" has been used to normalize a version of heterosexuality that combines manliness, bravery, and benevolence. In the context of the US-Mexico relationship, banditos are usually racialized as nonwhite indigenous outlaws, embodying the racialization of criminality, which intersects with patriarchy and power in the patriarchal model of ideal bandito manliness.

Malverde's specific narrative perpetuates an idea of redemption whereby men—here, banditos—rescue the community from other men who would oppress or exploit it. The opponents of the hypermasculine bandito are attributed other, devalued forms of masculinity. In Malverde's case, this devalued form of masculinity is represented by Cañedo and Díaz. The popular lore highlights Malverde's bravery and panache and presents Governor Cañedo as a weak, feminized character who is incapable of outsmarting the hero, who with his clever misdeeds and maneuvers always escapes and wins. Malverde's "proper" heterosexuality is consolidated by the narrative's undercutting of the masculinity of Cañedo, Díaz, and their allies. The legends about Malverde use race and class to feminize and queer these upper-class male villains as it constructs them as untrustworthy, greedy, and unpatriotic.

The paired-yet-opposite social constructs of Malverde and Cañedo thus work in tandem to maintain social, gender, and sexual roles, competing in a zero-sum masculine economy. Malverde the hero cannot exist without Cañedo the villain, whose policies put in place the conditions from which Malverde's mythology springs. In the narrative, Cañedo's emasculation is proportional to Malverde's hypermasculinity, as if only one type of masculinity can prevail. Each variant of masculine expression anchors and gives meaning to its opposite, and Malverde's survival requires Cañedo's failure.

In the legend, with each day that Malverde avoids capture, he becomes more hypermasculine, and Cañedo becomes more emasculated, stripped of more and more of the respect of his peers and subordinates. Indeed, popular versions of the legend also trade in homophobic innuendo, characterizing Cañedo as feminine and sexually ambiguous. Nothing, ironically, is said about the admiration Malverde inspires among other men. Indeed, male admiration and masculine emulation are key elements of Malverde's veneration as a saint, which embodies the Revolution narratives in Mexico.[31] This same identification with hypermasculine rebellion underpins the discourses surrounding the justification of narco-trafficking activities in the region, which have become attached to the veneration of Malverde as a revolutionary of sorts: this antigovernment, antiestablishment masculine figure serves as a vernacular saint (and point of identification) for other antiestablishment figures like the narcos.

One of the anecdotes about Malverde's life condenses the themes of masculinity, race, and class that pervade the stories of his endless fight against Cañedo as an effete, upper-class agent of the state. In this story, Cañedo challenges Malverde to break into his home and capture him. Cañedo becomes the joke of the town. In some versions of the story, Malverde does indeed break into his home, but instead of capturing Cañedo (an act that would treat him as an equal, a worthy opponent), Malverde simply embarrasses him—steals a valuable sword and writes on a wall, "Jesús M. was here."[32]

In other versions of the story, Malverde is said to be in love with Cañedo's daughter and may have even kidnapped her.[33] In this version, the forbidden love between people of different classes partially motivates the animosity between the men as they fight over the affection and control of a woman.[34] Here again, the governor becomes the joke of the town, with his (paternal) masculinity erased and Malverde's (sexual, romantic) hypermasculinity in ascendance: this version of the story shows Malverde literally penetrating the privacy—the feminized intimate domestic space—of Cañedo's home.

This part of the legend only hints at the class basis of the conflict between Malverde and Cañedo. The entire legend, and the rivalry between the two, figures the drama between peasants and the ruling upper class in the years before the Mexican Revolution. During those years Sinaloa was a central player in the land conflict between indigenous, locals, and foreigners and in the idealized forms of Mexican nationalism. In the Malverde legend, this conflict is constructed as a fight between good and evil, between peasants and the rich, and between rural and urban.[35] But from a gender and sexuality studies point of view, what is striking is the deep continuity and shared investment of both sides in male domination. The fight remains one between men, who are battling one another for social visibility and control. The drama charts a shift in power among men, but it reveals no change in the paradigm used to grant and attribute power to masculine heterosexuality. Power—the power to rule the nation, to imagine its future, and to make decisions—can only be taken up by males.

The story of Malverde breaking into Cañedo's house takes on even more significance when we consider the alleged affair between Malverde and Cañedo's daughter. The governor's interest in capturing and punishing the thief becomes personal, a way to avenge and restore his family honor, because his daughter has compromised Cañedo's family reputation by sleeping with Malverde. Within the context of Mexico's patriarchal society, government—figured here by Cañedo—becomes a male patronage system, one that is constructed by caudillos (political male leader figures, like Cañedo) and by bandits (popular outlaws, like Malverde). Here, as his legend shows, women's bodies, in the form of Cañedo's daughter, are traded and negotiated as goods, independent of their own desires or agency. Thus, in addition to a struggle over money and land, the battle between Malverde and Cañedo encodes a fight for masculine power over women. Cañedo considers his daughter to be his most valuable treasure, making Malverde a thief not only of gold and goods but also of those aspects of women that are assigned capitalist value—namely, their virginity, family reputation, and reproductive power—creating an intersection between violence against women and religiosity in the veneration of Malverde.

Malverde: A Santo for the Mexicanos

As these stories show, Jesús Malverde is more than just a vernacular saint; he is also a repository of local cultural values and history. His legend has been adapted over time to incorporate the struggles and transformations of the Sinaloa region as experienced (and imagined) by his followers. The racial and class tensions generated during the modernizing period of the Díaz regime shed light on the conditions that set into motion and shaped the Malverde legend at its beginning. The modernizing policies of development in Sinaloa sparked exponential population growth and changed the demographics of the area;[36] at the turn of the century, Sinaloa hosted 65 percent of all foreign workers living in Mexico.[37] In response to this demographic change, xenophobic policies were implemented by the state and the private sector, amplifying the already existing racial tensions in the region. In Sinaloa, wage exploitation and mistreatment based on ethnicity and place of origin were already commonly used to generate profit, and there was a long history of local Mayo/Yoreme indigenous communities being exploited and used as cheap labor.[38]

These issues of race and labor are also woven into the Malverde legend. Different versions of the legend describe Malverde as a worker in the mines laboring side by side with indigenous miners or, alternatively, as an opium poppy grower working with Chinese immigrants. In the legend, these two communities are always framed as exotic outsiders who are not fully Mexican, entering Malverde's life only to help him in some way. They are presented as disengaged, not invested in the Mexican state's project of modernization. In the description of Malverde's life offered by dramaturge Óscar Liera, for example, Malverde is flogged and left to die by Cañedo, only to be miraculously rescued and hidden by a group of Mayo/Yoreme Indians from the region.[39] From there Malverde joins a clandestine community of Chinese immigrants cultivating the opium poppy (amapola). According to Manuel Esquivel's book *Jesús Malverde*, this is a group of "Shanghai immigrants, who came to Mexico originally to work in the mines and the construction of the train rail."[40] Emphasizing the Otherness of both groups, the book presents them as providing raw information and knowledge that seemingly only Malverde can understand and use. The Mayo/Yoreme Indians teach Malverde to navigate the Sinaloan mountains and sierras without getting captured and show him how to use medicinal herbs to heal—information that will be essential for his survival as a bandit. The Chinese immigrants instruct Malverde in the cultivation of opium (a process that the book details for the reader) and show him the routes by which producers smuggle goma (raw opium) to the United States.

Both of these narratives are underpinned by the concept of *terra nullius*, or unclaimed land, which has been used consistently as a legal instrument for expropriating land from indigenous communities throughout northern Mexico. Both stories implicitly apply *terra nullius*, for in both cases the stories present the two communities as incapable of fully understanding or capitalizing on what they have until Malverde arrives. He is a paternalistic savior who essentially gives value to the land, resources, and knowledge that the indigenous groups so naively possess. Malverde's seeming superiority over local communities is part of his persona. This constructs him not as antiestablishment and antigovernment but as a materialization of a state ideology used to justify colonial expansion. Malverde's legend validates the land's occupation and its development by particular forms of masculinity and Mexicanidad. His hypermasculinity and Mexican essentialism are woven together to create a persona that reproduces the national project of uniformity and homogeneity that dominated Mexican politics after the Revolution years.

This construction of him as a unifier of a post-Revolution national identity both differentiates Malverde from other vernacular saints in Mexico and defines him as a Mexican Revolutionary spiritual legend. He represents for his adherents something like what Our Lady of Guadalupe does for Mexican Catholics (though not, of course, at the same level): a unifying, sacred symbol of the nation and of Mexicanidad.[41] After the Revolution, attempts at class integration failed and social disparity persisted. Mexico therefore needed to invest in a mythology of national unification, and the government promoted the resurgence of caudillos and indigenous symbology as well as local and vernacular religious figures and pious practices. In constructing Malverde's legend, his Sinaloan followers are not only imagining the pre-Revolution period but also actively investing in the creation of a post-Revolution narrative for their present and the future.

The veneration of Jesús Malverde is less about commemorating the past and more about building a future that longs for the past. Malverde reflects the ideals of a unified community under fixed notions of heterosexuality and masculine superiority, and the past he represents is envisioned through the eyes of racial occupation, colonialism, and patriarchalism. In the decades that followed, this highly gendered, sexualized, and racialized project achieved new heights as the legend of Malverde was transformed by the effects of entrepreneurial capitalism.

The Reformation of a Saint: The Home for Malverde

Little is known of the site of Malverde's execution or what happened to his supposed remains immediately after his death. This is due at least in part to the turmoil during and after the Mexican Revolution and the years of reconstruction that followed. Sinaloa was deeply involved in the armed conflict, and its capital, Culiacán, underwent several sieges from progovernment troops. As early as 1910, Francisco Madero visited Sinaloa as part of the anti-reelection movement tour, one of the igniting forces of the Mexican Revolution.[42] During those years the existing instability in Sinaloa was amplified by the death of its governor, Cañedo; because he had no clear successor, pro- and antigovernment factions struggled for control of the state. Indeed, in Sinaloa the armed conflict of the Mexican Revolution extended beyond 1920 (the official end of the revolution): sporadic eruptions of violence persisted until 1940, in part because of land tenure reforms and disputes.[43]

During that time, veneration of Malverde increased and cemented his place as a vernacular saint in the Sinaloa region. Locally, Malverde's legend and the events surrounding his death became synonymous with the period of change surrounding the Mexican Revolution. Malverde emerged as a peasant's martyr—a victim of the state's attacks on those most dispossessed of people and an example of the revolt with which the peasants responded. Progovernment groups used the legend for their own purposes, using Malverde to represent the defeat of the rebels and the restoration of law and order, reminding people of the consequences of challenging the state.

Attention to the material elements of the narrative provides some clues to its popular dissemination and evolution. The spread of Malverde's legend during and immediately following the Mexican Revolution can likely be attributed to people's migration patterns and other groups' forced relocations to escape the violence. Malverde's eventual burial site, for example—an essential element of his story as a miracle-working saint—is located along train tracks and close to a train station. Remember that in one variant of the legend, Malverde himself was involved in constructing that same railroad; whether or not this detail was true, it buttressed Malverde's popularity among rail workers.[44] In addition, the site's accessibility was crucial for the vast numbers of peasants and soldiers mobilized within and around Sinaloa during and after the Revolution. The fact that the saint's main chapel and burial site were so close to an important migration path played an essential role in spreading his popularity.

These two elements of Malverde's legend—his location within an important network of communication and his association with a crucial moment of transformation in a community's history—contributed to the longevity of his veneration. Without the railroad as a system of distribution, Malverde's memory, like those of other saints, might have disappeared or else remained restricted to locals. The link between the location of a saint and a medium of mass communication was therefore vital in spreading his veneration beyond Sinaloa. Liera describes the localized networks with regional reaches through which Malverde's legend spread in his 1984 play *El jinete de la divina providencia*, dedicated to Jesús Malverde:

> In those days Culiacán was not the big city [that it is today]; everything where Malverde's grave is located today was once just a mountain of bainoros [bushes local to Sinaloa]. It was located in the route to the coast, to Navolato, Aguaruto, Bachigualato, and La Pipima; that route was used by farmers, milkmen, and the cheesemakers on their way back [and forth] to the market of Culiacán to sell their goods. Nearby, there was a mesquite tree that had a limb that hung over the road.[45]

According to legend, they hung him on that mesquite branch. As Liera explains, Malverde's burial at an important commercial crossroads secured the distribution of the many forms of cultural piety created around Malverde—including but not limited to corridos (examined elsewhere in this chapter), prayer cards, candles, and the chapel itself as a destination to stop, rest, and pray.

Because saints' examples live on through the memory of their miracles, virtues, and adventures, connections to influential paths of communication—such as a railway—not only extends a given saint's area of influence but also diminishes his or her risk of being forgotten or overshadowed by other religious figures. Put bluntly, saints metaphorically compete for the attention and adoration of followers. Ultimately, their longevity may sometimes rely on their veneration sites becoming not just centers of spiritual worship but also places where people gather to rest and exchange information about the market, the weather, and the tragedies and successes of the everyday. Malverde's specific positioning as a vigilante for and protector of the poor has helped his centrally located chapel become a safe space for all those who travel there.

The legend of Malverde grew and became cemented when Sinaloa's population grew dramatically during the mid-twentieth century. His ability to do miracles became fully accepted in response to Sinaloa governor Alfonso G. Calderón's decision in the late 1970s to build a complex of public buildings in Colonia Ruiz Cortines, razing the neighborhood where Malverde was supposedly buried and where his chapel is located. What followed was a series of events that would transform the aesthetics and rituals surrounding Malverde and infuse new life into his legend.

While the residents of Ruiz Cortines and other citizens resisted the governor's construction plans from the beginning, work began nonetheless. According to several accounts, the day Malverde's gravesite was supposed to be destroyed, multiple inexplicable events happened. The first bulldozer that tried to remove the rocks and candles left for the saint broke down, and several windows broke in nearby buildings and houses.[46] The rocks gathered at the site "jumped like popcorn."[47] When a heavy crane was called to remove the first bulldozer, the same misfortune befell the second and third bulldozers. Despite what locals saw as these signs, Malverde's gravesite was razed and the new construction completed. However, mysterious calamities continued to take place near the site: the death of the first bulldozer's driver, the disappearance of equipment, and the suspicious breaking of more windows in the new buildings.[48] Eventually, in 1980, following these recurrent mysterious events and persistent public pressure, the local government donated land across from the government buildings to construct a new veneration site. The current chapel now sits on the corner of Independencia and 16 de Septiembre Streets, across from the government palace of the state of Sinaloa in Culiacán—where Malverde's burial site was originally located.[49]

According to Price, the fight for the chapel made sense given the history of Sinaloa to that point—a history that included land redistribution conflicts in the Third Agricultural Revolution of the 1940s and increasing poverty among residents, as income inequality grew and the Mexican economy more broadly imploded. These conditions set the stage for the veneration of Malverde. His veneration signifies the long struggle for place and "social legitimacy" experienced by those traditionally excluded from the dominant narratives of visibility authored both by the Mexican state and the Catholic Church. As Price puts it, "Malverde's iconographic landscape at once works to provide visibility and voice to those who are denied presence in the official landscapes of Church and State."[50] This same sense of marginalization and exploitation among his adherents fuels his veneration to this day, for the fights for land and for state recognition remain constant struggles in the region.

Beyond Malverde: Land Conflict and Divine Interventions

The relocation conflicts during the 1970s over the site of Malverde's grave are particularly important in the Sinaloan imagination, and they inform the evolution of Malverde's legend. The 1970 and 1980s saw not just a resurgence in the saint's popularity but a significant reconfiguration of Malverde himself, aesthetically and imaginatively; the sudden interest in Malverde reflected his adherents' sense that the same issues that had driven the 1940s land conflicts were coming around again—if they had ever stopped at all. The events surrounding the relocation of Malverde's grave at the end of the 1970s thus did not only express anger over the government's encroachment on this particular holy site (though that is how most critics have read it). Encoded within these events were the many ongoing protests by the inhabitants of Colonia Ruiz Cortines, the barrio where the new governmental complex was being built.[51]

The Ruiz Cortines protests must be framed within the larger agrarian problems of that time. Just as they had been before the Revolution, most lands for cultivation in the 1970s were in the hands of just a few families, concentrated in hacienda plantations. Water rights, too, were primarily reserved for the rich: most poor farmers and 86 percent of ejidos (community lands) did not have water rights.[52] This existing resentment over the unfairness of land ownership informed the Ruiz Cortines protests. As journalist Sergio López Sánchez has chronicled, those residents who were forced to relocate held sit-ins, rallies, and marches during that period, with substantial support from the student body at the Universidad Autónoma de Sinaloa.[53] The resistance delayed the construction of the new complex for several years.

Those who were to be displaced perceived the proposed buildings as having no value for them. Indeed, from the perspective of the poor residents, the new palace symbolized everything that was wrong with their local government. As Cañedo had been before the Mexican Revolution, the new governor, Alfonso G. Calderón (1975–80), was perceived as an enemy of the poor. In the sarcastic humor of those affected, the new government palace was deemed perhaps the most appropriate monument to Malverde, because, in López Sánchez's words, the local "government was built, founded, erected, cemented on the grave of a thief—only this one [that is, the state building] was much bigger." Locals even adapted the tradition of leaving stones at Malverde's grave to make the association clear; according to López Sánchez, "the new thing [was] to bring rocks and offer them to the rooftop of the house of the new bandits."[54] (Perhaps these "offerings" of rocks to the thieving state may explain some of the mysterious window-breaking at the construction site.)

For those slated to be displaced because of the construction, Malverde's chapel may have represented a last chance to preserve their homes. As Price argues, the fight to save the chapel was certainly ideological and metaphorical in may ways: the chapel represents a space of defiance, resiliency, and contestation between the powers of the state and the Church, and symbolizes the long struggle over self-sovereignty and ownership. But for those fighting to preserve the chapel—poor barrio residents and students—it was not just Malverde's sacred space that was at risk (or profaned) but also their own sacred right to claim a space, raise a family, and build a home.

Unfortunately, not even Malverde's celestial powers were able to prevent the destruction of Colonia Ruiz Cortines. Today, the new chapel sits across from the government palace, and the barrio of Ruiz Cortines has been largely forgotten. However, the relocation of the chapel sparked a new phase in the evolution of the saint and a reawakening of his legend. New religious boundaries of ownership were defined, and new rituals and practices of public veneration emerged. Malverde was repositioned in a new spiritual administrative space, so to speak, one located outside the government and outside the Catholic Church in Sinaloa. Interestingly, this new space was located within the geographic and imaginative terrain of the free market, and he was eventually taken up by narcos to become part of the spiritual cosmologies of drug trafficking.

Wrestling for Control: The Emergence of New Social Authors

The supposedly miraculous inexplicable events surrounding the dismantling of the original sacred site, combined with the public protests generated by the relocation of Colonia Ruiz Cortines, brought a new wave of publicity and many new devotees to the cult of Jesús Malverde. The new explosion in adherents, in turn, generated a new level of open resistance to the veneration of Malverde from the Catholic Church in Culiacán. It was as though the land conflict and the disturbance of the holy site awakened the somewhat dormant saint, transforming Malverde's legend and the Catholic Church's relationship with him forever.

During the conflict over the sacred site, the local Culiacán Catholic diocese proposed that the problem be solved by relocating Malverde's remains to a cemetery it owns and administers. However, the local church's interest in hosting (and controlling) Malverde's remains was rejected by his followers, who saw the offer as a bid to reduce and eventually eliminate Malverde's veneration. Resistance to this proposal was led by Roberto González Mata, the self-appointed guardian of the original shrine, before the current chapel was created. Many perceived the conflict between Malverde and the official Catholic Church establishment as rooted in part in class differences, since Malverde was understood as the saint of the uneducated and poor, in clear opposition to the perceived "Catholic bourgeoisie" of Culiacán.[55]

In Mexico and specifically Culiacán, the Catholic ordained clergy were mostly perceived as an elite group who favored the rich and were too distant from the struggles of the poor. As González Mata and those seeking to protect the original chapel understood, once Malverde's remains were relocated outside the shrine, the shrine would lose its spiritual relevance as well as the social capital needed to resist the displacement of Colonia Ruiz Cortines. Furthermore, because Malverde's very existence was so tenuously established as a historical fact, exhumation could prove devastating for those who venerated the saint and all he stood for. The community's efforts to keep Malverde's remains undisturbed was a form of resistance against both state and Church.

In this context, González Mata's rejection of the local church's offer to relocate Malverde's remains onto its own property represents simultaneously a rejection of Malverde's institutionalization and a protest against making invisible the spiritual practices associated with the saint. González Mata instead created a secular organization to preserve and protect Malverde's holy site: La Orden de los Caballeros Custodios de la Tumba de Malverde

(Order of the Knights Custodians of the Tomb of Malverde), which lasted for just a few years, during the period of the displacement dispute.[56] This fraternal organization was formed by residents of Colonia Ruiz Cortines who were followers of Malverde and were directly involved in the land disputes around the construction of the new city building. Their personal commitment to the site and their close spiritual relationship to Malverde were crucial components of the organization, and these transformed its aesthetics in ways that are still visible today.

Like the debate over his legend, this debate over Malverde's meaning and location takes place among men, with no reference to the women who have followed Malverde. In the local coverage of conflicts over the shrine and Malverde's remains, there are no references to any women involved. The Knights Custodians was a male-only organization, structured as a Catholic confradía (confraternity), a voluntary association of laymen—devoted, in this case, to promoting the veneration of Malverde and particularly to preserving his shrine. The men-only, militant structure of the organization was reflected in its hierarchical non-democratic decision-making and consolidated a male-centered power structure. It emphasized, both consciously and unconsciously, Malverde's manliness as a core value of his spirituality and aesthetics.

This is a crucial point to help us understand the subsequent development of Malverde as a narco-saint whose veneration and visual codes continually reproduce and promote a particular type of masculinity. Malverde's bandito status and his direct defiance of the state and the Church merged with the imagery and ethos associated with then-contemporary notions of "real masculinity" in the northern states of Mexico. Malverde thus emerged from this period not only as a saint of the poor and disenfranchised but also as a saint of the masculinity manifested by Sinaloa's cowboys and, eventually, its narco-traffickers—two groups whose hypermasculinity is symbolized by guns and celebrated in corridos.

As Vicente T. Mendoza explains, in the last quarter of the nineteenth century there was a renaissance in "la valentía de los protagonistas" (the hypermasculine characteristics of corridos' male protagonists), which reflected popular anti-Porfirian sentiments at the dawn of the Mexican Revolution.[57] Much of Malverde's success and longevity as a vernacular saint is intimately connected to his ability (and the ability of those adapting his legend) to incarnate the region's discourses of masculinity. He has become a spiritual personification of the masculine, an omnipresent and benevolent figure who, much like a patrón (a male boss or benefactor), watches over the terrestrial and spiritual affairs of the frontier lands. Malverde's hypermasculinity must be understood within the context of Sinaloa's own cultural investment in fixed patriarchal models of masculinity.

Certainly, Malverde had been hypermasculinized before this period. However, during the late 1970s and early 1980s, a more explicit and emphasized typology of masculinity was created and used to market Malverde, especially as both the cartels and the US war on drugs were developing. By creating the Knights Custodians, who took over the existing informal worship and upkeep of the site, González Mata set in motion processes that made community involvement in the affairs of Malverde more pluralistic and decentralized—at least momentarily.

One of the lasting transformations generated by the Knights Custodians was the introduction of new social players into the Malverde veneration ecosystem. One of those was Don Eligio González León, a local stonemason who over time became a key figure in modernizing and revitalizing the legend of Jesús Malverde. González León built the new (relocated) chapel and replaced Roberto González Mata as the chapel caretaker. According to González León, a miracle in 1973 inspired him to become involved: he was shot four times during an assault near Malverde's gravesite, but he recovered—a fact he attributed to Malverde's miraculous intervention.[58] González León decided to dedicate the rest of his life and resources to preserving and spreading the memory of the saint. As a member of the Knights Custodians, he rapidly became central in the development of the new chapel, even claiming to have provided most of the funding for its construction.

Different reports dispute the exact date when the current chapel was built.[59] Some argue that it was built in 1980, while a *Washington Post* article says that the chapel was erected in 1983,[60] and Jesús M. González Sánchez (the son of González León) told me that it was built in 1979.[61] We do know for certain that the chapel was built in stages, and based on the records about the conflict, it is most likely that the first stage was not built before 1983. González León spent the next thirty years as the main caretaker of the chapel, celebrating Malverde's memory until his own death in 2004.[62] Under González León, Malverde's relationship with the Church and the state became much less openly oppositional and much more laissez-faire than it had been since the inception of his legend.

González León's gentlemanly policy toward the Catholic Church and the elite class in Sinaloa marked a new chapter in the life of Malverde. It was a period of adaptive domestication, in which Malverde was reconstituted by local Catholic leaders and elite Sinaloans as a sympathetic figure, emphasizing his benevolence toward the poor far more than his rebellion against the powerful. González León also shifted Malverde to a figure who bypassed the earthly institutions of church and state against which Malverde had previously rebelled, instead relating directly to God. González León did this by reemphasizing the role of Malverde as a vessel for God's intervention, arguing that "if it weren't for God, Malverde couldn't do anything."[63] In this way, González León positioned Malverde as a mediator who could intercede with God on behalf of his adherents. Crucially, by clarifying that God was behind anything attributed to Malverde, González León appeased Church authorities. Even when the Catholic Church recognizes a saint, it teaches that the saint intercedes with God on people's behalf. That is, miracles attributed to saints are more precisely attributed to God, with whom a saint has interceded for the believers—although this is a subtlety that many Catholics do not know, cannot explain, or do not attend to.

Under González León's influence, Malverde's legend evolved into an elaborate, transnational mythmaking machine. During his tenure as the chapel's caretaker from 1979 until his death in 2003, González León managed the building of the new chapel, the design of Malverde's bust, the promotion of corridos to narrate Malverde's history and adventures (in fact, González León, a self-styled poet, was directly involved in writing several corridos himself, with various local bands), the proliferation of commercial memorabilia and gift shops, and the launch of a very successful network of charity events.[64] After his death, one of his eighteen children, Jesús M. González Sánchez (named after Malverde), took over the administration and control of the chapel and other affairs related to Malverde.

One of the most successful campaigns González León began is the chapel's donation of thousands of wheelchairs and coffins to those in need. These donations are inspired by events in Malverde's legend: wheelchairs because he was shot in the legs before he was captured and executed, caskets because he was refused a proper Christian burial and funeral. So much money is donated in Malverde's name for people's funerals that López Sánchez describes the philanthropy as constituting "a kind of alternative Social Security."[65] According to Sada's figures, Malverde, through the "intercession" of González León, has covered the cost of more than "7,800 funerals for people from the villages of Sinaloa, including coffins, candles, floral arrangements and funeral wreaths."[66] Today pictures and testimonies regarding many of those donations adorn the entrance to the chapel. Through this charity work, the keepers of Jesús Malverde's chapel have been able to make a long-term impact in community members' lives and in the collective memory of Sinaloa.

In the last two decades, Malverde has experienced a revival that expanded his veneration into northwest Mexico and beyond, inspiring pilgrims to visit his chapel from as far away as Durango, Nayarit, Sonora, and Baja California, as well as the state of Arizona in the United States. In many ways, Malverde's repopularization has been nurtured by the resistance of the Catholic Church and the interference of the Mexican state. The Malverde of today is not the same Malverde who died at the beginning of the Mexican Revolution. He is a new transnational and deeply commercialized saint who has been resurrected from the remains of the real Malverde—if he existed at all.

Producing a Marketable Malverde

As Malverde's popularity increased in the 1980s, there was no standardized iconography of the saint—no singular visual representation of him. The multiplicity of representations emerged as a problem of self-identification for his followers and a problem of control for his promoters and marketers. Of course, there is no official picture or painting of the real Jesús Malverde, given the difficulty in verifying details of his life or even his existence. However, differentiating his persona from other holy figures requires a recognizable and consistent visual representation. In the 1980s, those seeking to synthesize the saint's narration needed a simple-to-read, mobile, and marketable symbol of him.

The images of saints on prayer cards, devotional and prayer books, and sculptures help believers learn about their lives and miracles. Such images facilitate remembrance and serve as a type of spiritual presence that allows a follower to connect intimately with the saint as a real human being, one who inspires the follower's spiritual request or perhaps even facilitates a miracle. But people need a recognizable visual image to feel this connection; their imaginations are not enough to sustain a saint as an idea. The image narrates and perpetuates the memory of the saint in ways that constantly bring them into presence, making them alive every time the image of the saint is looked at.

González León, the chapel caretaker, was very much aware of this. His son Jesús M. González Sánchez explained to me how his father went about solidifying Malverde's image:

> About the image, the true image of Jesús Malverde. My dad had to put an image to represent him as [it is done] in all churches. There was never exactly a picture of him [Jesús Malverde] or anything, and my dad talked with someone who told him, who had known him [Jesús Malverde]. He explained [to my dad] roughly what were Malverde's traits, what he looked like, and my dad made that image—made it with the face of [Mexican actor] Pedro Infante, because Pedro Infante is loved very much by the people. He [Infante] is a beloved figure.... My dad made the image, made the chapel, did the corridos and the prayer [to Malverde], all was created by my father.[67]

As González Sánchez explains here, the absence of an agreed-upon image presented a marketing dilemma. His father needed to create a recognizable image to attract people to the chapel, because all church buildings have images of their patron saints. González León's decision to design and commission from a local artist a bust of Malverde that looks like Infante was not coincidental (see Figure 1.4). Infante was one of the most famous and beloved singers and actors during the golden age of Mexican cinema (1930s–1950s), and he was therefore well known throughout Mexico. The fact that someone who had purportedly known Malverde was able to describe him to González León, and that this description produced an image that just happened to look like one of the most popular leading actors in Mexican history, was itself an event of miraculous proportions—or, more likely, an example of González León's ingenuity.

Cinema star Infante encapsulated many of the qualities of Malverde's existing legend: he was not just popular but populist—and charismatically patriarchal. As Sergio de la Mora puts it in his book *Cinemachismo: Masculinities and Sexuality in Mexican Film*, Infante was the "most revered national icon for Mexicans both inside and outside the geographic boundaries of the nation," a figure who "embodied the collective hopes and dreams of Mexico's popular sector."[68] Infante's place in the popular imagination was forged, in part, through the movie roles he played and the marketing of his persona (by himself, the media, and his manager) as "the archetypal post-revolutionary, not-quite-domesticated, working-class migrant from the provinces."[69] His

66 UNDOCUMENTED SAINTS

Figure 1.4 Images of Pedro Infante and Jesús Malverde. Notice the resemblance between Pedro Infante and the commercial busts of Malverde inspired by the one commissioned by Don Eligio González Léon. *Right:* Image of Pedro Infante, oil painting by Ángel Zamudio, property of Gilberto Javier López Alanís (director of the Archivo Historico General del Estado de Sinaloa). *Left:* Bust of Malverde purchased by the author at the chapel in Culiacán, Sinaloa.
Photos by the author

appeal was universal; he was desired as an "alter-ego for many Mexican males as well as an object of desire for both genders because of the respect, authority, and physical and sexual powers he demonstrated" in his films.[70] He was thus a perfect pictorial representation of Malverde, who similarly stood for a particular form of masculinity, Mexican nationhood, and the "commodification of Mexicanidad."[71]

While Infante was a national star, González León constructed the image of Infante as Malverde within a particular urban and regional context. Both Infante and Malverde were from Sinaloa. Infante was born on November 18, 1917, in Mazatlán, the most important Sinaloan city after its capital, Culiacán. Choosing Infante to literally provide the face for the iconic bust of Malverde thus invoked both local and national layers of familiarity. As mentioned earlier, the struggles surrounding the creation of Malverde's chapel as a recognized place of worship were part of a wider spatial conflict created by the growth of Culiacán the city and the Sinaloan government more broadly.

Infante also hooked into this conflict, for he was understood as a "prototype of the expanding working-class population, a representative of el pueblo [the people]" as it struggled "to adapt to modernity and the social problem caused by the urban explosion."[72]

Thus, Malverde and Infante both illustrate the nostalgic masculine ideals of the post-Revolutionary period as well as its class ideals. Malverde is frequently depicted as being (like Infante) light-skinned, representing the social norms and stratifications around skin color that reflected Mexico's racial politics. Ironically, though, Malverde's legend describes him as an extremely vulnerable peasant, probably with indigenous (and thus darker-skinned) ancestry. The visual racial whitening of Malverde also shows up with all the other vernacular saints analyzed in this book—Juan Soldado, Olga Camacho, and Toribio Romo—and, interestingly, also in the case of La Santa Muerte, a saint without a phenotype. This recurrent element of light skin tells us about the tacit racial norms that inform religious practices, in this case in Mexico and along the border.

Images of Malverde follow González León's reconstruction: Malverde is usually represented as a white male with a chevron mustache, black hair, a white double-pocketed charro- or mariachi-style shirt, and a short black or red tie. He looks like the light-skinned, mustached man in the Tapatío Salsa logo, only without the large hat.[73] Descriptions of Malverde as a man of "light skin complexion" can be found in Esquivel's influential book about the life of the bandit-turned-saint, as Esquivel connects Malverde's race to his "strong character."[74] Malverde's racialization has little to do with whether the "real" Malverde was dark- or light-skinned; it hooks instead into still-resonant global, national, and local narratives associating light skin with honesty, loyalty, and, in the case of saints, innate holiness.

In the legend, Malverde's light skin endows him with a seemingly magical ability to infiltrate the consciousness of Sinaloa's wealthy, who see him as one of themselves because of his light skin. Indeed, Malverde's legend often depicts him as deceiving the rich in Sinaloa, walking into their homes and events as a welcomed guest. According to his legend, for example, Malverde is able to confront Governor Cañedo, the most powerful man in the state, not just because Malverde is a smart peasant but also because his light skin allows him to cross the many social boundaries blocking his access to Cañedo in the first place. Rich Sinaloans trust Malverde because he has light skin, which carries with it assumptions regarding access to capital, education, language, and the policing of racial boundaries.

This figures the actual racial politics in Mexico: white or light skin makes social mobility possible, allowing people to overcome the disparities created by race and class. This was true also of Infante, of whom de la Mora says, "His desirability and appeal were in no small measure also based on his whiteness."[75] His light skin, like that of most stars of the golden age in Mexican cinema, was deeply connected to Mexico's preference and veneration for a criollo (white Spanish American) aesthetic, with its ties to power, class mobility, and social stability. The criollo phenotype is dominant even today in telenovelas and Mexican politics, for whiteness is still associated with beauty and power and is considered more desirable than the brown complexions associated with indigenous or slave roots.[76] In Latin American telenovelas, news shows, and television entertainment events, whiteness is directly associated with upward social mobility.

The preference for whiteness takes on even more power when combined with notions of religious sanctity. As Richard Dyer explains in his book *White*, in the Western context Christian figures tend to be represented as light-skinned; light skin becomes a semiotic tool to represent apparent enlightenment and salvation, while dark skin is associated with sin.[77] By giving Malverde the light skin of Infante, González León tacitly responded to the region's racialized norms of beauty, virtue, and social mobility. Malverde's depiction as a white Mexican, in other words, caught the popular imagination because it reflected racial stratification in Mexican society. Malverde's legend not only reflects these social disparities but also, through his veneration, perpetuates them. Malverde's holy iconography cannot escape the mundane.

Of course, we cannot determine Malverde's actual racial makeup and phenotype without historical references, photos, or human remains for DNA testing. What is interesting, however, is how little this appears to matter. The González family of caretakers has been remarkably transparent about how Malverde's image came to exist, acknowledging that it is based in a purely secondhand description of Malverde from someone who purportedly knew him and described him to González León. Indeed, if anything, the ambiguity surrounding Malverde's appearance has only reinforced the mystical status of his image and the strength of his followers' devotion. As González Sanchéz, the chapel's current caretaker, points out, "Well, no one knows really how Jesus Christ looked. There are many different images of him in the churches, but no one is questioning that he existed. It is the same with Malverde."[78] Here, González Sánchez uses the unique situation created by the politics of representation to position Malverde within the larger Christian pantheon of spiritual figures in the region, thereby claiming for Malverde the same legitimacy. The accuracy of Malverde's imagery becomes irrelevant; more importance is assigned to what the image signifies in the public imagination. In fact, González León's manufacturing of the image is often presented as an instance of divine intervention in which González León was inspired by Malverde himself.

Since its creation, the image of Malverde has been reproduced on prayer cards, escapularios (scapulars), CD covers, figurines, busts, keychains, and belt buckles. As explained by González Sánchez, his father created an entire promotional package for Malverde, manufacturing his image, building the current chapel, and writing several corridos; all of these elements worked together to foster Malverde's veneration. González León not only gave the saint a face and built him a home but also created a brand—one that united Malverde's followers, enabled recognition and reproduction, differentiated him from other saints, and made possible the global circulation he now enjoys. In short, Malverde's rebranding in the 1980s reconstituted his legend within and through global notions of modernity and neoliberalism.

This was part of a larger shift in the 1980s away from advertising and toward branding as the main promotion strategy in the global marketplace. As goods became increasingly standardized and mass-produced, companies found it imperative to differentiate their commodities. Simply having a superior product was no longer a guarantee of success. Branding emerged in the 1980s in part as a capitalist response to a dilemma of recognition and differentiation.[79] This same dilemma was expressed in practices of religious veneration in the period: in what Fredric Jameson defines as a crisis generated by late capitalism, the branding of religious icons—such as that of Jesús Malverde—emerged in response to a historical shift within neoliberalism.[80]

What we experience in Malverde's marketing is therefore the articulation of a postmodern turn. The act of branding Jesús Malverde exemplifies what Jameson identifies as characteristics of the postmodern period, creating a pastiche of historicity, a rupture. As Jameson defines it, a "pastiche is, like parody, the imitation of a peculiar or unique, idiosyncratic style, the wearing of a linguistic mask."[81] Malverde and Infante together function as a pastiche: Infante served as Malverde's "mask"—his representation—and the two men are fused in one. The two men occupy similar roles in propping up history according to cultural values of ideal norteño masculinity. Malverde existed historically before Infante, and, as a saint-symbol—a disembodied idea—he fed on the imagination of norteño ideals of Mexican-ness and masculinity. Decades later, Malverde was reinvented in the image of Infante, who materialized those ideas, distilling and recoding in the body of a male movie star. Infante came after Malverde and gave a body to the imagined saint.

With this rebranding, the temporal past (like questions of Malverde's historical existence) becomes almost irrelevant; this new Malverde is constructed solely for an everlasting present. This act of branding uses the face of Infante, a real individual, to create a false new face for Malverde, converting both figures into someone—or something—else: they are no longer just Infante and Malverde but the sanctification of a particular heteronormative masculinity in the context of an idealized post-Revolution Mexican state. As a branding tool, the new Malverde image sells a product that, like all the other vernacular saints, is designed to deliver a promise, an idea, a feeling. And as I explain later in this chapter, over time it is this repackaging that enables his resignification as a narco-saint.[82]

There is an irony here. González Mata, the Knights Custodians, and González León rebranded Malverde in order to protect him from the traditional institutions of power—the Catholic Church and the state. They sought to retain popular control over Malverde's veneration, disputing the Catholic Church's control over the narrative of Malverde and other vernacular saints and their efforts to preserve and reconstruct the chapel pushed back against the state's absolute territorial administration. In order to evade the control of those powerful institutions, Malverde's caretakers felt they needed to increase the saint's popularity and extend his spiritual domain: with a larger number of followers, they thought, Malverde's survival would be secure. So they created, standardized, and commodified his iconic image in order to enable it to circulate more widely.

But this newfound independence-by-the-numbers, intended to free Malverde's legend from outside influence, brought with it the intrusion of new narratives about the saint, ones that were outside the control of the local keepers. In other words, securing Malverde's survival by engaging with capitalist mechanisms of production and consumption opened the saint to new forms of vulnerability. Novel marketing strategies allowed Malverde's popularity to expand beyond Sinaloa, but they also exposed his mythology to new, more powerful market forces, specifically those of narco-capitalism. As a result, today the narrative of Malverde as a benevolent bandito has been reshaped into the story of a narco-saint. Now most people outside Sinaloa encounter Malverde in conjunction with images of smuggling, narco-trafficking, and violence—the same forces endangering and disempowering the populations Jesús Malverde was originally imagined to protect.

The New Malverde: More than Just a Narco-Saint

Malverde's relationship with modern narco-culture and narco-spirituality is a complex affair that can be traced to Sinaloa's relationship with the production of recreational drugs. Mexico's narco-capitalism is linked to Malverde both by geography and by the sociopolitical factors that define Sinaloa's economic history. According to R. Andrew Chesnut, the association with cartels has benefited Malverde, for his "cult skyrocketed" with the "rise of the Mexican drug cartels in the 1980s and 1990s."[83] As Patricia L. Price argues, the regional drug cartels also benefited: during the 1980s the cartels "strategically used Malverde's legend and image as a 'generous bandit' to spin their own images as Robin Hoods of sorts." The cartels saw in Malverde the opportunity to resignify their image with the masses, associating their illicit activities with the goodwill already surrounding the vernacular saint, and to cement the link, the cartels gave "some of their wealth back to their Sinaloa hometowns, in the form of schools, road improvements, [and] community celebrations."[84] This resignification of the cartels' "criminal enterprise," argues Chesnut, was further enabled by "the government's reputation as corrupt and absent."[85] In other words, the cartels presented themselves in clear contrast to, and almost as a solution for, the government's dysfunctionality, exploitation of the working class, and perceived bias in favor of the ruling class.

Ideologically, this resignification was facilitated by a shift in popular discourse that insisted that drug cartels were only "stealing from rich drug-addicted gringos," not from local communities in Sinaloa or from the Mexican nation writ large—a clear connection to the Robin Hood–like, bandito element of Malverde's legend.[86] The cartels' emphasis on rich gringos as the market for their drugs is important, for local narco-trafficking activities cannot be understood without considering the unique relations of animosity and economic disparity between the United States and Mexico, as well as the nationalist and anti-imperialist sentiments that prevail in Sinaloa. The cartels deliberately framed themselves as simply another capitalist enterprise, providing a product demanded by the United

States. Through this ideological alchemy, cartels were able to repackage drug-trafficking violence and the killing of thousands of people as merely the collateral damage generated by the development of the most profitable enterprise in the region—or on the Mexican state's attempts to stamp it out.[87]

This argument was not entirely disingenuous. Cartel members at every level of their respective organizations are intimately connected to Sinaloa, just like other forms of organized crime, such as the Mafia. For the cartels, investing in the infrastructure of their hometowns—whether motivated by guilt or by altruism—was almost expected, because their neighborhoods, extended family, and friends were all still located in Sinaloa. It is Sinaloa that first bound Malverde to them: noting that "drug trafficking is responsible for the most significant social disruption facing modern Mexico and Sinaloa," James H. Creechan and Jorge de la Herrán Garcia argue that the "narco affection for Jesús Malverde" is directly related to this common place of origin, and, they argue, "it's not surprising to find drug themes emerge in Malverdian symbolism."[88] Malverde was already a traditional folk saint in Culiacán, the capital of Sinaloa, when it became the capital of narco-trafficking in Mexico during the twentieth century. The connection between the two was cemented as Sinaloa-based narco-enterprises consolidated and expanded their influence and trading territories beyond Culiacán and into the United States: drug traffickers "didn't abandon [their] traditional roots, and in fact were instrumental in the revival and support of local customs," including the veneration of Jesús Malverde.[89]

It is crucial, however, not to overstate and oversimplify Malverde's status as a narco-saint. Narratives linking him to drug trafficking constitute but one dimension of his multilayered meaning, and a recently added one at that. Reducing him to a narco-saint ignores the many other folk elements that inform his popularity and oversimplifies the complex nature of his veneration. His chapel, like those of many other vernacular saints, is full of requests and mementos that testify to the diversity of his many attributed miracles in areas that have to do not with narco-trafficking but with the everyday concerns of his adherents, such as health, labor, security, love, harvest, and business success—requests for intercessions to counter the many calamities that define the life of his followers. Local veneration in Culiacán reflects local religious practices and needs that differ from those in Mexico City and in the United States, as different realities and struggles emerge in the sociopolitical contexts of the communities around the saint.

Assumptions about Malverde as being solely a narco-saint not only minimize the confluence of many sociopolitical significations but also manifest racist misrepresentations of the reality experienced by Mexicans and Mexican Americans. Because Malverde is associated now with drug trafficking, his imagery is used by US police as grounds for probable cause to suspect criminal activity. For example, Rico Garcia, a sergeant from the Houston police department's narcotics division, says: "We send squads out to local hotel and motel parking lots looking for cars with Malverde symbols on the windshield or hanging from the rearview mirror.... It gives us a clue that something is probably going on."[90] The US police transfer racial stereotypes onto a virtual, imaginary Mexican citizen: Jesús Malverde. In other words, as a Mexican subject reduced to a narco-saint, Malverde—as well as the semiotic symbols, meanings, and practices associated with him—is transformed into a tacit conduit of the aberrant status associated with Mexicans in the US imagination, which views them as criminals, drug smugglers, and sexual outlaws.[91] By treating Malverde as purely a narco-saint, a kind of gang sign signaling affiliation with Mexican cartels, US police and US courts alike racially reduce Mexicans (as well as Mexican Americans and other Latinxs associated with the saint) into racialized caricatures that reflect their own intolerance and criminalization. It is not only Malverde who is turned into a narco-criminal, but also all of his followers—despite the diverse reasons people venerate him.

Framing Malverde as only a narco-saint erases the sophisticated and intricate significations created by lay communities around popular religiosity, instead conflating them with those created by drug crime organizations. Certainly, these two groups are intimately connected through historical ties in regions like Sinaloa—but they are not the same, there or anywhere else. Some local drug traffickers may be followers of Malverde, but not all followers of Malverde are drug traffickers. Reducing Malverde to only a narco-saint has serious epistemic consequences: it creates a misleading sense of knowledge about a community and oversimplifies the role played by folk culture productions (such as vernacular saints) in negotiating power disparities and inequalities. As a vernacular icon, Malverde does more than just grant favors to the narco-community. He is foremost a mediator of everyday struggles, and he deals with a large constellation of demands.

Even in his role as an element of narco-aesthetics, Malverde responds to many other symbols and signifiers. His image as a male bandito reflects elements of bravado used to construct and emphasize narco-traffic as a masculine endeavor. Malverde works not in isolation but in conjunction with

74 UNDOCUMENTED SAINTS

other elements such as large cars, guns, corridos, and flags—all meant to emphasize wealth, security, loyalty, respect, and nationalism.

Malverde's Sacred Heart: María Romero, the Bride of Culiacán

Any analysis of this vernacular saint in his full complexity, beyond the narrow image of him as a hypermasculine narco-saint, would be incomplete without engaging with the work of María Romero, a contemporary artist from Culiacán who now lives in Mexico City. Her art has been deeply influenced by the figure of Jesús Malverde and by her experiences growing up in Culiacán, and it challenges many misconceptions about Malverde and about Sinaloa.

My first contact with Romero's work involved her installation titled *El sagrado corazón del beato Jesús Malverde* (The Sacred Heart of the Blessed Jesús Malverde), which I saw during my preliminary research into the saint in 2010. The installation consists of 104 black-and-white pictures of Romero's father that she has painted over, collectively forming a large red heart. Each picture has been inscribed with a common petition to the saint or the name of a male figure connected to the legend of Jesús Malverde (see Figure 1.5). The piece can be read as an interwoven homage to both Romero's father and Malverde, but it also serves as a feminist critique of the centrality given to male experience at the heart of Sinaloan life.

I first met Romero in person in Los Angeles four years later, while the exhibition titled *Sinful Saints and Saintly Sinners* was on display at the Fowler Museum of the University of California, Los Angeles (March 30–July 20, 2014).[92] Romero's was a large installation, a traveling chapel dedicated to Jesús Malverde. This work, titled *Quitapesares* (Solace), consists of multiple embroidered square quilts supported by a metal structure. The effect of the installation is exuberant and overwhelming. Three large, embroidered pieces decorate each of the chapel walls; the main piece, which serves as the installation's central altar, is a large, embroidered tree of life, and a piece on the left is a merged representation of Romero's father and González León. When visitors walk into the chapel, they are surrounded by hundreds of small quilts, each representing a different petition to or memento of Malverde. In this way the installation replicates the experience of entering Malverde's actual chapel in Culiacán, where the walls are covered by hundreds of requests,

Figure 1.5 Images of two pieces by artist María Romero.
Top: Image of *Quitapesares (Solace)*, 2014.
Photo by the artist
Bottom: Image of *Escapulario de Malverde (Scapular of Malverde)*, created and used by María Romero during her performance *La Novia de Culiacán (The Bride of Culiacán)*, 1995. Hand embroidery. Property of the author.
Photo by the author

plates, letters, pictures, and reminders of miracles. The quilts in the installation were either created by the artist or donated by followers of the saint. As part of the process, as Romero explained in one of our interviews, she held several sewing workshops in which community members created quilts, exchanged experiences of miracles and petitions, and built community around the veneration of Malverde.[93]

Many of the quilts are mementos of miracles attributed to Malverde. Some are quite witty commentaries about the precariousness of life in Mexico. The array of requests makes clear the multifaceted meanings that Malverde has for the community, well beyond the narrow representations of him as a narco-saint. Certainly, the requests collected by Romero embrace the full array of everyday calamities experienced by Sinaloans, from job scarcity to health issues, from housing to money, and of course including love. Examples include "Get me a job that pays well"; "Malverde, help me to find the companion for my life"; "Malverde, thanks for protecting me every day ... from the police"; "Thanks, Malverde, for helping me forget who broke my heart"; and "Chucho [Malverde], thanks for getting me back with my girlfriend." A notable one reads, "Thank You for helping me regain my virility."[94] Romero explained the last petition to me as follows: after suffering from impotence, a man had turned to Malverde for help, and the saint seemed to deliver the requested miracle months later, when the man was finally able to have satisfying sex again. However, Romero disclosed, this miracle happened only after the petitioner divorced his wife and got a boyfriend. Now, according to Romero, thanks to the divine intervention of Jesús Malverde, the petitioner is finally incredibly happy as an openly gay man.

In 2001, years before creating these installations, Romero had put together an exhibition and performance piece in Culiacán at the chapel of Jesús Malverde titled *La manda de María* (The Promise of Mary). In that exhibition Romero showed twelve art pieces dedicated to the figure of Malverde, including an accordion-folded ensemble of personal letters from Romero's parents, as well as another piece constructed by fusing two shirts, one from her father and another from González León.[95] Together all twelve pieces served as the canvas for an embroidered image of Jesús Malverde, presented as a symbol of the fusing and interconnectivity of three men in Romero's life: Malverde, her father, and González León.

As the performance piece in the 2001 exhibition, Romero dressed in a white wedding dress and embodied one of Culiacán's folk characters, La Lupita, as *La novia de Culiacán* (the bride of Culiacán). Guadalupe Leyva Flores, known as La Lupita, was a transient who wandered the streets of Culiacán dressed as a bride from the 1960s until her death on May 12, 1982.[96] According to local legend, she had become mentally ill after witnessing the murder of her fiancé, Jesús, at the hands of a jealous suitor during their wedding. In reality, Leyva Flores did indeed experience several calamities during her life, including the deaths of her husband and children. Although they originate several decades apart, the legends surrounding La Lupita and Malverde have been linked in the Culiacán imagination. Many people believe that Jesús Malverde was La Lupita's fiancé. In one version, Malverde never showed up to their wedding because he was killed on his way there. In another version, La Lupita suffered after the death of her fiancé but then fell in love with the bust of Malverde and began wandering Culiacán in search of him.[97] In her performance piece, Romero presented herself as a new Lupita, and part of her manda (promise) was to walk around the city in contemplation and adoration, bringing attention to the veneration of Malverde.[98]

In 2015, to celebrate her twentieth anniversary as the new Lupita, Romero put on a collective performance, *La busqueda del tesoro de la divina gracia* (The search for the treasure of divine grace), that involved the city of Culiacán. Romero had been staging this performance consistently every year from 1996 until 2002, and thereafter more sporadically, culminating in the twentieth-anniversary performance.[99] Most of the performances have followed a similar structure: after a short presentation outside the building, which includes spoken word, poetry, and music addressing the image of La Lupita, Romero then leads a contingent of more than thirty women on a walk through the neighborhoods associated with the original Lupita in what Romero calls "an act of recovering peace and justice."

For the twentieth-anniversary event in 2015, Romero summoned the women of Sinaloa to convene at the stairs leading to Culiacán's cathedral on December 22, 2015, at 10:00 a.m., all wearing white wedding dresses. As in previous iterations of the performance, the act of traveling around the city becomes a metaphor to describe Culiacán women's eternal search for happiness amid their struggle against decades of organized crime and sexual violence. Romero frames this performance piece as both a remembrance of La Lupita's perseverance and a collective act of solidarity with women afflicted by sexual and domestic violence. Metaphorically inverting imagery of the honeymoon, the brides in the performance are not losing their virginity on their wedding night; they are actively searching for the lost innocence of the city—or, as Romero put it, searching for the city's divine grace. Together the brides visit key places around the city either associated with women's oppression or recently reconstructed as spaces of inclusion, including the chapel of La Lomita (Our Lady of Guadalupe), the central municipal market, the house of the playwright Liera, the Universidad Autónoma de Sinaloa, an elementary school, the Carmen hospital, and the chapel of Jesús Malverde. As they travel around the city, the brides consistently interact with bystanders, and many of them display banners with messages such as "Tolerancia" (tolerance), "No mas violencia en contra de las mujeres" (no more violence against women), "Dialogo" (dialogue), "Confianza" (trust), "Lealtad" (loyalty), and "Paz" (peace).[100] In the 2015 performance that I witnessed, this pilgrimage section ended at 3:00 p.m. outside the cathedral of Culiacán.

In some of the previous performances over the years, local activist groups have joined the event to bring attention to other forms of violence affecting women in Sinaloa. In 2018 one of these groups was Sabuesos Guerreras A.C. (Warrior Hounds), a group of mothers and family members of missing individuals whose disappearance has been linked to police or narco violence in the region.[101] During this performance, the mother-brides wore pictures of their missing loved ones. The group describes their work, too, as a kind of pilgrimage: under the slogan "¿Donde están?" (Where are they?), the group report regularly "going out to explore the mountains, hills, valleys, rivers, and garbage dumps [of Sinaloa] where [they] try to find what the WAVE OF VIOLENCE has taken from [them]."[102]

In these various performances, the wedding dresses create a highly symbolic, visual contrast between the expectations that women be pure mothers, girlfriends, daughters, and virgins, on the one hand, and the dirty reality of their lives as women, which contain intolerance, labor discrimination, and domestic and sexual violence. Romero herself wears sunglasses, the camouflage of many a battered woman, emphasizing the invisibility of the widespread abuse experienced by women. She presents herself both as an everywoman, representing all those affected by the issue, and as deeply connected to her own racialized identity as a Mexican indigenous woman.

A few months after the December 2015 La Lupita anniversary performance, Romero performed a new work that iterated on the bridal themes: on the morning of February 13, 2016, the day before Valentine's Day, Romero performed a solo bridal show at the Zócalo—the main square in the heart of Mexico City, outside the cathedral and the national palace—during Pope Francis's public Mass in Mexico City. As he left and waved, he acknowledged her presence, completely unaware that the bride he saw dressed in white was in reality a performance artist. Romero interpreted this encounter with the pope as fulfilling a desire expressed by La Lupita to meet a pope in person. Romero explained to me, "She [La Lupita] always wanted to talk to the Holy Father... *always*."[103] It was very appropriate that the encounter between the new Lupita and the pope met at the Zócalo—the center of Mexico, in the square where the two most important Mexican powers, the Catholic Church and the state, meet.

Following the 2015 anniversary performance, Romero returned to the original long-running La Lupita, performing it in Culiacán in 2016 and in 2017.[104] Since the 2016 performance in Culiacán, which several girls attended, Romero has begun other La Lupita projects aimed at younger women. With the help of Marco Barenque Jarquín, an illustrator and graphic designer located in Mexico City, and in conjunction with design agency Grupo Horma, Romero published in 2017 a coloring book titled *La novia de Culiacán, ni loca, ni novia: Misionera*, which narrates the story of Guadalupe Leyva Flores.[105] And Romero is currently transforming the graphic story of La Lupita into an animated film.[106]

As the leading visual artist using and manipulating Malverde's iconography and history, Romero consistently and purposely avoids framing Malverde as a narco-saint, seeking instead to introduce new ways of thinking about gender into his narrative. Her work evolved from exploring the Sinaloan interconnection between her and Malverde to offering a more personal analysis of the men in her life and then to examining the precarious situation experienced by all Mexicans, but particularly Mexican women. In many ways, her work is about rupturing the mundane by manipulating what is expected and normative, as in the case of the brides. Romero's work is intimately political and deeply personal—an effect that is made possible by her use of everyday materials in the crafting of her pieces, which generate a very intimate connection with spectators without diluting her message. In this context, quilting, embroidering, toys, popular music, and everyday rituals—things associated with femininity and domesticity—become powerful tools for social change.

Romero's art, which focuses on people's intimate connection with Malverde at the everyday level, connects to people's most personal pains and triumphs. Her work reminds us that Malverde's real miracle can be found in the quotidian lives of those who follow him—the invisible, the poor, and the displaced. As Romero quilts together the many mandas or vows to the saint, Malverde's holiness emerges as a crown of thorns, constructed by his followers' many histories of despair.

Everybody Is Malverde

In January 2020, Telemundo, one of the two leading Latinx networks in the United States, announced that they would produce a telenovela titled *Malverde: El santo patrón*, to be based on the adventures of this saint. The lead role of Jesús Malverde would be played by famous Mexican actor Fernando Colunga. The project was declared "one of Telemundo's most ambitious productions" by Marcos Santana, president of Telemundo Global Studios.[107] However, early stages of the production were slowed because of the COVID-19 pandemic. A year later, in February 2021, Telemundo announced that Colunga had dropped out of the project, with no reason given for his departure. The news surprised people; he had consistently praised the project on social media, and most of the promotion and advertising materials were based on his high-profile popularity. Colunga was quickly replaced by actor/singer Pedro Fernández in the lead role, and filming wrapped in July 2021, with the Telemundo premiere taking place two months later, on September 28. During the final stages of production, news giving an "explanation" for Colunga's unexpected departure began to leak.

For quite some time, rumors and speculations that Colunga is gay have circulated in the media. According to the news headlines of the time, Colunga dropped out of the production because "narcos did not want Colunga as Malverde for believing him gay."[108] Gossip rags treated his sexual orientation almost as a contagious disease, running headlines like "They Didn't Want Him Because He Was Gay." They claimed that "the supposed THREAT to Fernando Colunga made him leave 'Malverde' ";[109] that "narcos had threatened Fernando Colunga to abandon the role of Malverde due to rumors that he is gay";[110] and that "Fernando Colunga left Malverde after being threatened by drug traffickers for being 'gay.' "[111] The stories were based on audio from an alleged inside informant that was released by the controversial Mexican show *Chisme en vivo*, from Estrella TV. The statement reads:

> In one of the meetings, they commented that they had to stop the productions. This man [Fernando Colunga] resigned since the drug

trafficking threatened him. . . . They [the drug cartels] didn't want him playing Malverde because he was gay. He was still in the project, but there were already many threats, and he decided better to leave, and the production stopped. You know, drug trafficking is the boss, he is gay, and they threatened him because they did not want him to be the one to play [Jesús] Malverde.[112]

The rumors have not been confirmed or denied by either Colunga or Telemundo. It remains unclear whether the gossip was spread to increase visibility for the TV show, to "justify" the replacement of the actor, or as an act of retaliation against Colunga for his departure. Were the narcos truly invested in preventing Colunga from playing the role of Jesús Malverde, despite his popularity? The answer to this question is almost irrelevant. Either way, a homophobic act of violence was perpetrated—one that had ramifications for Colunga (the supposed outing of his sexual orientation and the financial consequences of losing the role) but barely affected the image or popularity of the cartels.[113]

The replacement of Colunga sent a clear message of intimidation to queer people about the vulnerability of their lives and job security in Latino America. Moreover, it denied Colunga control and self-governance regarding the narratives about his sexuality. Here the cartels worked as an extension of the almighty homophobic gaze within patriarchy. The attack on him was an assault on what he represents as a potential gay man in society's imagination. Colunga continues to deny being gay, but the gossip was ultimately not just about "forcing" him to come out; it was about controlling men's behaviors, signaling the damaging consequences of public non-normative sexual behavior. Doubt becomes a metaphorical dagger used to destroy Colunga's social and professional character.

The gossip reinforced the notion that the hyper-heterosexuality and hypermasculinity associated with Malverde must be preserved and maintained; even the potential of queerness could not be associated with his legend. The story of Colunga shows the deep maneuvers of homophobia and the expected hyper-heterosexuality associated with this Mexican saint, bandito, and local caudillo. It blends the central threads that tie together the narratives of Malverde as a saint, the reconstruction of a nation-state around ideals of masculinity and heterosexuality, the maneuvers of narco-capitalism, and the transnational nature of the devotion to Malverde, which migrants have brought to communities in the United States.

If we know one thing about Jesús Malverde's legend and the practices around his veneration, it is that they are not static—they are always evolving. The construction of his legend reveals the intimate relationship between the real and the imaginary and points to the ways in which they influence each other. As explored here, Malverde's representations respond to real socioeconomic and sociopolitical events that have fundamentally transformed Sinaloa and the rest of northwest Mexico—events ranging from the pre-Revolutionary land rebellions of the late nineteenth and early twentieth centuries to the growth of twenty-first-century narco-capitalism.

Thus, although this chapter has studied the vernacular saint Jesús Malverde, in reality it has explored Mexico's encounter with modernity and the unraveling of a series of sociopolitical and religious events (e.g., the Mexican Revolution) that defined the twentieth century, examining the role played by popular religiosity as a local community experience, and giving sense to the global changes around them. We have also looked at the many transformations of Malverde's legend and of its marketing into today's transnational, hypermasculine narco-saint.

Malverde's legend constantly evolves and adapts as those who retell it struggle to make sense of new forces in their lives. The legend does not belong only to Sinaloa or Culiacán anymore; it is now exported out of Mexico and back again, traveling with the resources, drugs, and people who traverse the nation's borders—sometimes legally, sometimes illegally; sometimes by choice, sometimes by coercion. As Sinaloa continues to transform in response to market pressure, Malverde also transforms—not just in ideology but also in appearance and worship practices. The layers of interactivity—the transnational and the local elements of his veneration—are not mutually exclusive. They coexist as different constituencies relate to the saint in different forms and with different attachments.

As a set of meanings, Malverde survives through the stories and rituals performed, remembered, and created by the community that he serves. The legend of Malverde reveals not only the forces that have shaped Sinaloa over the last century but also the ways that the realm of the imaginary is permeated by issues of class, sexuality, gender performance, xenophobia, nationhood, and personal anxieties about job security and love. The complexity of Sinaloa's transformation over the twentieth and early twenty-first centuries has required the creation of an equally complex saint to accommodate a hostile world: the power of Malverde's legend reveals the tragic and precarious experiences of a community so at the mercy of external forces that divine intervention looks like the most reasonable source of relief. Indeed, this is probably Malverde's biggest miracle: keeping the hopes and faith of a community alive, despite their precarious reality.

Santa Olguita & Juan Soldado:
Unresolved Sainthood and the Unholy Rituals of Memory

2

2

Santa Olguita and Juan Soldado

Unresolved Sainthood and the Unholy Rituals of Memory

> Magnificent Holy Girl
> Daughter, protect us from injustice.
> Girl, protect us from the police.
> Protect us from being blamed
> for the crimes of the powerful. . . .
> Look after our body
> Don't let it be subject to abuse
> and don't lead us into oblivion.
> Praise to you, Olguita, pure and blessed.
> —Prayer to Olga Camacho by Efrén Rebolledo

On the evening of Sunday, February 13, 1938, Olga Camacho, an eight-year-old girl from Tijuana, Baja California, was kidnapped, raped, and killed as she was returning from a grocery store located about a block from her home. The investigation, manhunt, and arrest after her death triggered citywide protests, the burning of several city buildings, and an international incident that forced the closure of the US-Mexico border.[1] But what happened after the mayhem—and in the many decades since—makes the story of Olga Camacho not just puzzling but pivotal for this book's exploration of saints along the border.

Camacho, the victim, has been forgotten and ignored, while Juan Castillo Morales, the primary suspect in the crime, has been popularly canonized as Juan Soldado (Juan the Soldier), one of the vernacular patron saints of migrants in the Tijuana/San Diego region (Figure 2.1). What can this story tell us about the connection between religion and violence against women along the US-Mexico border?

Figure 2.1 Images of Olga Camacho and Juan Castillo Morales.
San Diego Evening Tribune, February 16, 1938

On a February day in 1938, like every Sunday, the Camacho Martínez family attended Catholic services at the cathedral in Tijuana. They had moved to this city from Mexicali, another border town, a few years earlier. Former farmers, they had lost their land to the agrarian transformations imposed by Mexican president Lázaro Cárdenas (1934–1940) in the decades following the Mexican Revolution. The family's new residence was located in Zona Centro (Central Zone) in downtown Tijuana.[2] The house was situated across from a large autonomous zona militar (military zone) that held Tijuana's old military garrison, and only a few blocks away from a historical fort.[3]

By the 1930s, Tijuana was a fast-growing melting pot. The Prohibition era in the United States (1920–33) was bringing thousands of Americans each month to the city, creating unprecedented economic growth. The population was further swelled by the many Mexicans and Mexican Americans who had been deported during from the United States during the Great Depression (1929–36). Between four hundred thousand and two million people were deported to Mexico during this period, with almost 60 percent of them being US citizens of Mexican descent.[4] As historian Marla Ramírez explains, this massive group of people was targeted for intense "promotion of colonization programs by the newly elected Mexican President, Lazaro Cárdenas, intended to populate the northern border with Mexican repatriates and their families."[5] As a consequence of this social, demographic, and cultural upheaval, there was huge social and economic unrest in Tijuana and other border towns. The influx of migrants from the United States stoked lingering fears of American expansion, which still persisted ninety years after the Mexican-American War (1846–48). Given all these conditions, the border town was in 1938 heavily militarized, with the military presence already in a tense, uneasy relationship to the population they were there to control. While the main military headquarters was on the southern edge of town, Tijuana's historical fort, located downtown, near Olga's family home, remained a symbol of the military's presence (and the state's power) in the city.

On the fateful February day, Olga returned home around 6:00 p.m. after spending the afternoon with a neighborhood family. Her father, Aurelio Camacho León, was working downtown, and her mother, Feliza Martínez de Camacho, was attending to Olga's three-month-old baby sister while she cooked dinner for the family. Olga did not want to eat the dinner her mother was making, so she was allowed to run to the nearby grocery store, La Corona, to buy meat and milk.[6] Eventually, Olga's mother realized that she had been gone a long time, and sent another daughter, Lili, to look for her. Lili returned without Olga, and Martínez de Camacho went out herself to search for Olga. The store owner, Mariano Mendívil, informed her that Olga had been there and left with groceries (see Figure 2.2 for a map of Tijuana's downtown).[7]

Olga's mother continued her search. The next person she saw was a soldier named Juan Castillo Morales, stationed in the nearby military zone. Castillo Morales was a poor private who had moved recently to Tijuana from the south of Mexico. Olga's mother approached Castillo Morales and asked him, "Did you see a little girl near here just a few moments ago?" "No, no, [señora], I've seen no one. Perhaps she went over that way," Castillo Morales responded, pointing toward the military area.[8]

Olga was never seen alive again. Her body was found the next day in a nearby empty military garage.[9] Almost immediately, protests demanding

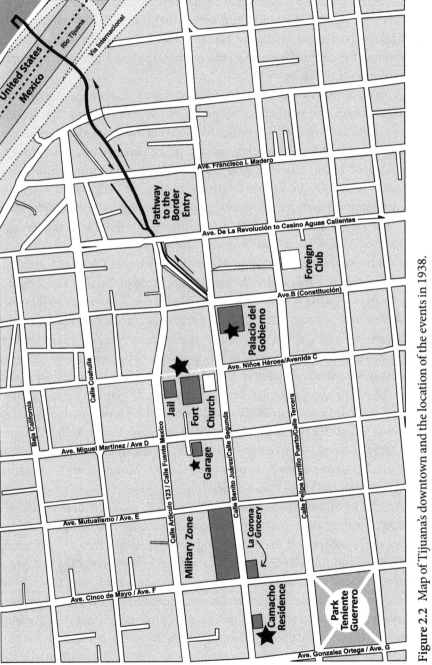

Figure 2.2 Map of Tijuana's downtown and the location of the events in 1938.
Graphic created by the author

answers broke out, as the town's simmering discontent with the government boiled over: several government buildings were burned, martial law was declared, and the US-Mexico border was closed. The authorities tried to manage the unrest quickly, and within the space of a few days, Castillo Morales was arrested, tried, and executed for Olga's murder and rape—but not before the case had become an international political affair and a spiritual and moral site of conflict.[10]

Almost immediately after Castillo Morales's execution, doubts and questions began to swirl about his guilt and the investigation. The original protests had been demanding justice for Olga, but over the following decades, public outrage shifted, centering instead on the perceived injustice done to her accused killer. A strange new narrative emerged: Castillo Morales was recast as Juan Soldado, a revered vernacular saint, and Olga faded so far into the background that she was virtually forgotten until the early 2000s, when she reemerged as Santa Olguita, a feminist saint symbolizing the struggle against men's violence against women.

Like the narratives about Jesús Malverde explored in Chapter 1, accounts of what actually happened with Olga Camacho, Juan Castillo Morales, and the town of Tijuana are far from stable. They draw on a mix of oral history and various rewritings of the past. The archive of empirical evidence about the case—the newspapers, telegrams, forensic research reports, and court evidence that I examined—provides only a fraction of the story. Over the years, the story has expanded, gaining a nimbus of both real and imaginary events that reflect changing anxieties, fears, and tensions.[11] Many of these additions to the story are rooted in legitimate doubts: as I reviewed various sources, I myself was struck by the number of inconsistencies both within and across accounts. It was these inconsistencies in the investigation that fed conspiracy theories about the alleged innocence of Castillo Morales and his eventual popular canonization as Juan Soldado.

As oral historian Alessandro Portelli has said, such "creative errors" are crucial, for they allow oral historians and researchers "to recognize the interest of the tellers, and the dreams and desires beneath them."[12] The actual events surrounding Castillo Morales and Olga become conduits to a larger narrative about the changes experienced in Tijuana during the 1930s. Most of the apparent inconsistencies and errors pertain not to the actual sequence of events but instead to "their placement in time and context," in Portelli's words.[13] The way that people assemble events to construct a narrative is crucial: when a community decides to emphasize, erase, or disqualify particular elements of a story, the decisions themselves reveal much about the anxieties, values, and distribution of power within that community.

Several questions haunt the spectacular (and, according to some, holy) histories of Olga and Castillo Morales. How and why did Castillo Morales, a convicted rapist and murderer, become revered as Juan Soldado, a saint? And what are we to make of the initial erasure of Olga Camacho, and of her recent reconstruction as Santa Olguita, a feminist saint? What do their intertwined stories tell us about the US-Mexico border in the aftermath of the Mexican Revolution, the Great Depression, and the Prohibition era in the United States? What do they tell us about the past and present culture of violence against women in Mexico?

This chapter examines Castillo Morales's and Olga's entangled yet profoundly unequal stories: the historical, social, political, and economic conditions that brought them together on that fateful day in 1938 and their divergent afterlives as Juan Soldado and (much later) Santa Olguita. Precisely because many of the details of that day and its aftermath remain unclear, the case has been fertile ground for the collective imagination. As with Malverde's divergent representations examined in Chapter 1, the goal here is not to unravel the truth of what happened but rather to explain the context that made possible the veneration of Juan Soldado and the erasure of Olga, to trace the evolution of their narratives, and to investigate what devotions to them tell us about life along the border. Together, the stories of these two vernacular saints manifest the intimate relationship between patriarchal violence and spirituality along the border. This chapter, foremost, examines how Olga's story materializes unresolved grief, pain, and violence. By tracing the spiritual journey of Santa Olguita from martyrdom through erasure and back to vernacular sainthood, we can discern the shape of many other forgotten female victims in the region, the many forms of violence in their stories, and the ways in which violence against female murder victims continues even after they have been murdered. I show the poisonous politics of (in)visibility imposed upon female victims—and the role that both formal and vernacular religiosities play as perpetrators of violence.

A note about naming in this chapter: To emphasize the temporal distinctions between the historical events and spiritual constructions in the story, and to aid their analysis, the names of Juan Castillo Morales and Juan Soldado, as well as Olga Camacho and Santa Olguita, are not used interchangeably. The name Juan Castillo Morales from this point onward refers to the historical person before his popular beatification, and Juan Soldado refers to the saint, whose name was constructed by combining the first name of Juan Castillo Morales with his position as a soldado (soldier). Similarly, henceforth, the name Olga, or Olga Camacho, refers to the eight-year-old girl who was kidnapped, raped, and murdered in 1938, whereas Santa Olguita, as she is known popularly by some, refers to the saint. This distinction manifests the transformation experienced by both Olga Camacho and Juan Castillo Morales in the consciousness of their community. In the case of Juan Castillo Morales, the distinction between the two figures seems to help Juan Soldado's followers deal with Juan Castillo Morales's conviction for Olga Camacho's rape and murder: the saint name distances the holy figure from the tainted reputation of the historical one.

Forgotten Spaces of Memory: Visiting Olga and Juan

The first of my many visits to the tombs of Olga Camacho and Juan Castillo Morales happened during the 2012 US presidential campaign. Since then, racialized narratives about the US-Mexico border have intensified and become even more central to both countries' national discourses about belonging. The stretch of wall between the United States and Mexico that existed in 2012—la linea (the line), as it known by the locals of Tijuana—is a dramatic structure in the landscape, an artificial barrier blocking the natural paths of animals and humans. It is truly a scar on the terrain, as Gloria Anzaldúa has described it.[14] As I approached the US side of the border on this first visit, highway signs instructed me to not pick up hitchhikers, because a large prison complex is in the vicinity, and a billboard alerted me that guns are illegal in Mexico.

The irony of these warnings was not lost on me. At the time of my trip, news outlets had just revealed the failure of the US federal-government-sponsored Fast and Furious program, which had intentionally delivered thousands of US guns to the drug cartels along the border and deeper into Mexico in hopes of tracking sellers and buyers. Investigations had shown that guns were transported into Mexico by US government officials, US border agents, and officers from the sheriff's departments of Arizona's Pima and Maricopa Counties, the latter under the leadership of the infamous Sheriff Joe Arpaio.[15] As I crossed into Mexico, it became evident why San Diego State University researcher Roberto D. Hernández renders it as the "US /// Mexico border"— the multiple slashes emphasize the many physical and virtual layers that separate the two countries.[16] Even though I was now an American citizen, crossing la linea gave me anxiety, for I had come of age fearing La Migra—a nickname for US Immigration and Customs Enforcement (ICE).

After many turns, I arrived at the graves of Juan Castillo Morales and Olga Camacho in Tijuana, located respectively in Tijuana's Panteón Municipal No. 1 and Panteón Municipal No. 2. Both cementerios (cemeteries) were originally situated on the outskirts of the city but now fall inside the northwestern part of Tijuana, along Avenida Venustiano Carranza. Despite being in two different cemeteries, the two graves are located within several hundred yards of each other—and both of them are less than a mile from the US-Mexico border (see Figure 2.3).[17]

In both the literal and symbolic senses, then, Juan Soldado and Santa Olguita are true border saints who, in death as in life, find themselves at the intersection of many worlds and realities. As with the evolving veneration of Jesús Malverde in Sinaloa, the cultural and spiritual practices of this border town of Tijuana arise from their transnational reality. Tijuanenses speak Spanish, but many also speak English, a combination of both, or new and complex dialects that intermingle the two. Even the city's monetary currency is mixed. On la frontera—the frontier or border—a special alchemy transforms Mexican pesos into American dollars and vice versa. The intimate interrelation between the US and Mexico, which suffuses the border zone, helps explain the emergence of border saints like Santa Olguita and Juan Soldado, whose cultural citizenship is defined not by their official zip code but by their transient (if not always voluntary) mobility—a characteristic they share with their believers. As the burial sites of Olga Camacho and Juan Castillo Morales remind us, death is omnipresent in the everyday experience of border citizens.

Death, it is often said, is the great equalizer. Yet precisely the opposite seems to be true in the cases of Olga Camacho and Juan Castillo Morales. Far from achieving closure and equality in death, both individuals' stories have been upended, raising more questions than answers. The afterlives of Olga and Juan diverge sharply, and the vast chasm between each figure's cultural and social value is exemplified by the differences between their respective burial sites. As others have noted, cemeteries are important sites of memory.[18] Mausoleums, pyramids, and chapels have long been erected as burial sites to memorialize the dead and to caution the living. It is common for graves to reflect social inequities in their layout, design, and administration, as their location and aesthetics reproduce the status differences that

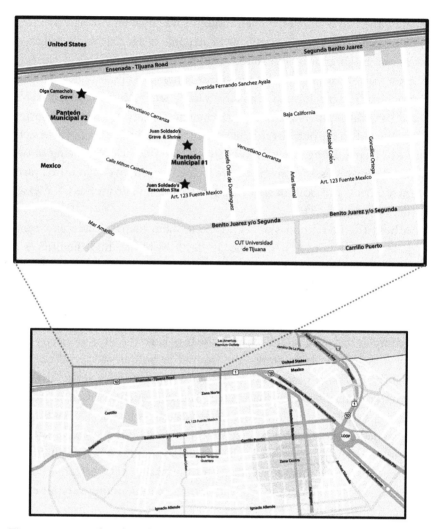

Figure 2.3 Map detailing the locations of Juan Soldado's and Olga Camacho's graves in Tijuana.
Graphic created by the author

marked their inhabitants in life. Burial sites, modern cemeteries, and spiritual chapels, like that of Jesús Malverde, are therefore rich cultural sites of historiography, because they tell us not about the dead but about the lives of those who buried them. Cemeteries are sites for the living. Chapels do more than memorize holiness and sainthood—they also recreate the sins of the believers.

Panteón Municipal No. 2: The Forgotten Olga Camacho

Olga Camacho's gravesite is located in Panteón No. 2, a few steps from the border (see Figure 2.4). Originally her remains were located at the family plot in another cemetery, the same one where Juan Castillo Morales was buried: Panteón No. 1, located just a block away along the same street.

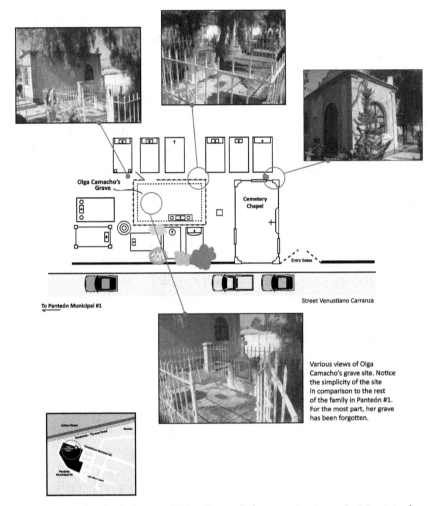

Figure 2.4 Plan and photos of Olga Camacho's gravesite, Panteón Municipal No. 2. This gravesite is just one block away from the cemetery where Juan Soldado is buried.

Graphic and photos by the author

However, the Camacho Martínez family tomb is only twenty feet from the tomb of Juan Castillo Morales, and a few years after her death, the Camacho Martínez family requested that her body be exhumed and transferred to a new plot in Panteón No. 2, which had opened in 1940 to accommodate Tijuana's growing population. Olga's grave and family (particularly her mother) was experiencing constant harassment from the growing numbers of followers of Juan Soldado.

The circumstances and timeline of how Juan Castillo Morales, the man, became Juan Soldado, the saint, are not clear. The fuzziness of the narrative probably reflect a combination of guilt and shame—in part because of the protests and cries for his blood after he was accused, and in part because of the many irregularities in the investigation and trial. The combination of these two powerful emotions led people almost immediately to venerate him as a martyr. His followers harassed Olga's family because they blamed Olga for the death of Castillo Morales. They threw rocks and other debris at her family and mourners, as well as at her burial site itself. The violence against Olga's memory and family became unbearable, and Olga was exiled to a new cemetery to minimize the conflicts.

The differences between Olga Camacho's and Juan Castillo Morales's graves are striking. Castillo Morales's gravesite is discussed at length in the next section, but suffice it to say that it presents an overwhelming display of pious popular iconography and cultural religiosity—it is a site of veneration. In contrast, Olga's grave, now to the left of Panteón No. 2's main entrance, is an inconspicuous, unmarked, white-tiled tomb surrounded by an iron fence. The only way to find out where Olga Camacho is buried is to ask the groundskeepers. Overall, the site seems truly forgotten. Her burial place looks like many of the graves around it. In stark contrast to Juan Soldado's grave, which I describe later, or the chapel of Jesús Malverde, there are on Olga's grave no flowers, candles, or pictures that refer to Olga, her mother, or the events of 1938 in any way. Nothing identifies who is buried there. People visiting loved ones at adjacent graves even use the metal fence around Olga's grave as a place to hang their coats. Those who visit the cemetery are clearly unaware of the history of the inconspicuous site.

Perhaps the Camacho Martínez family wanted this anonymity because of their experiences of harassment. Whatever their reason, Olga is now separated from her family's gravesite. So is her mother, Martínez de Camacho, who asked to be buried next to her daughter to keep Olga from being alone. These two women are now buried separately from the rest of the family. Even in the grave, Olga and her mother are subject to the compulsory invisibility and family separation imposed by the violence of patriarchy, reproducing the violence they experienced when alive. The anonymity of Olga Camacho's grave exemplifies the way that she herself has been forgotten—erased from or pushed to the margins of mainstream narratives of her death, the protests that followed it, and Castillo Morales's execution. Olga's material afterlife reflects her own disappearance from the mainstream narrative, and the comparative obscurity of her grave testifies to the difficulty of bringing visibility to the region's enduring pattern of crimes against women.

In this sense, the gravesite of Olga Camacho cannot be dissociated from the ideological, gendered narratives that define history in the region. The erasure of Olga as a person and the emergence of Juan Soldado as a vernacular saint reflect the systematic, long-standing violence committed against women at the border. Olga was eradicated not just from physical existence but also from people's memory via a series of endemic epistemic tools that favor the rapist-murderer over the victim. Patriarchal violence against Olga and her family did not end with her death in 1938 but continues in her afterlife.

During my 2012 visit, before I left Tijuana, I returned to Olga's tomb and hired some people to help me cut the grass, clean the grave, and bring flowers and candles. They asked me if I was a relative of the family, and I simply said I was a friend. After they left, I stayed to pay my respects. It was getting dark and most visitors were beginning to leave. This chapter is for Olga and the many others like her: Mexican women who are victims of femicide and who are erased from public memory.

Panteón Municipal No. 1: Juan Soldado's Chapel, a Place of Unrest

The grave of Juan Castillo Morales—now the focus of the main chapel dedicated to Juan Soldado—is located in Panteón No. 1, just twenty feet from the current crypt of the rest of the Camacho Martínez family. The Camacho Martínez family crypt is a kind of monument in its own right. Built a year after Olga was transferred to the new cemetery, the new crypt was designed to resemble a church. It is painted in robin's-egg blue with a large white sculpture of the Sacred Heart of Christ centered on the top of the façade. It has vertical iron Gothic-style windows and a wide concrete entrance that holds the main doors of the crypt. The large structure occupies space equivalent to fourteen single graves. In the context of Tijuana and this poor cemetery in particular, the family crypt is not only a fortress but a statement of wealth.

One must wonder why the Camacho Martínez family decided to build such a large, elaborate structure after Olga's body was removed. Was it a way to compensate, consciously or unconsciously, not only for the humbleness and anonymity of Olga and her mother's resting place but also for the overwhelming presence of Juan Soldado's chapel just steps away—especially considering his followers' attacks on the family site? By designing the family crypt as a church-style building, the Camacho Martínez family may have tried to intimidate Juan Soldado's followers and to prevent further attacks and vandalism. The crypt's high windows, with their decorated iron bars, along with the other aesthetic details and symbols attached to the building, are meant to secure peace for the Camacho Martínez family—as much as is possible, given the absence of their daughter/sister, Olga.

Only twenty feet away from this imposing crypt is Juan Castillo Morales's grave, where Juan Soldado's chapel is located. In contrast to Olga's faceless, nameless new gravesite, Juan Soldado's chapel is overwhelmingly full of his memory and presence. Panteón No. 1 includes not one but two separate chapels to Juan Soldado, one at the gravesite of Juan Castillo Morales and one at the spot of his actual death. As in the case of Jesús Malverde's chapel, vendors are stationed outside the entrance of Panteón No. 1, selling visitors cempazúchil (Mexican marigolds, also called flor de muertos, or flower of the dead), as well as candles, vases, rosaries, picture frames, and escapularios (scapulars)—many bearing the image of Juan Soldado.

The site has developed a vibrant economy around the image and figure of Juan Soldado: in addition to the vendors, mariachi singers perform, and young kids offer to watch visitors' cars, to clean the graves of loved ones, or to help carry flowers and water. The cemetery that houses Juan Castillo Morales's remains has become a thriving commercial site with an informal economy that feeds on and expresses the vulnerability and suffering of petitioners. The sanctified Juan Soldado constitutes a form of imagined currency that manifests the economy around mandas, the value of which rides on the hopes and fears of those who believe in him. It is easy to forget that all of this bustle rests atop a great silence: the cemetery makes no reference to Juan Castillo Morales's crime or to Olga Camacho's memory. She is erased from the explicit public narrative of Juan Soldado, the vernacular saint.

SANTA OLGUITA AND JUAN SOLDADO   99

The original veneration site—Castillo Morales's burial site, which is still the main site of veneration—is located slightly to the right of the center of the cemetery. It is easy to spot because of the unique structure of the crypt, which features a large sculpture of the santo on top (Figure 2.5). The chapel building itself is not large but a modest square concrete-and-brick shack. Like the chapel of Malverde, Juan Soldado's chapel is structured as a box

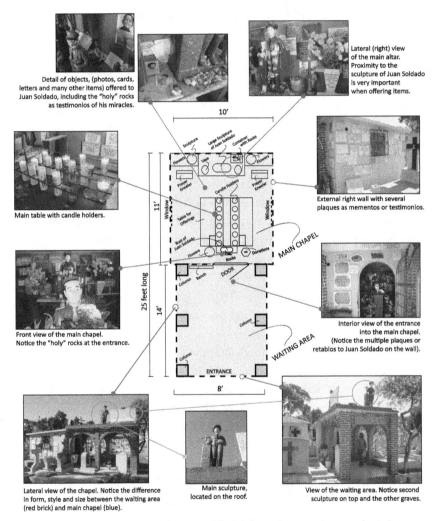

Figure 2.5 Plan and photos of Juan Soldado's burial site and main chapel, Panteón Municipal No. 1.
Graphic and photos by the author

within a box. The larger, external box (the entire building, which will I refer to as the "chapel") creates a kind of gallery (what I call the "outer chapel"), a transitional space that prepares the visitor for their journey into the inner box (which I refer to as the "inner chapel" or "inner sanctum"). It is in the inner chapel that visitors are in the heart of the saint's presence. In Juan Soldado's main chapel, these two chambers, the inner and the outer, were built at two different times with donations from his followers. Unlike that of Jesús Malverde, the chapel of Juan Soldado lacks a centralized administrative body to collect, organize, and systematize the funds received. As described in Chapter 1, the chapel of Jesús Malverde functions as a semiautonomous non-profit entity run by a family, whereas the chapel of Juan Soldado is located within a public cemetery run by the government of Tijuana.

The current chapel's inner sanctum, about ten feet wide by ten feet long by nine feet high, was built between 1974 and 1975, after the previous chapel was destroyed in a fire. The room has green walls that echo the color of the military uniform worn by the sculpture of Juan Soldado on the façade. The second chamber of the chapel, the outer room, was built between 1992 and 1993. This chamber, which is approximately ten feet wide, thirteen feet long, and nine feet high, provides a covered area for those waiting to get inside the inner sanctum and includes space for worshipers to kneel and sit on the sides as they prepare themselves for their encounter with the saint.[19] As they wait, they can read the inscriptions and permanent plaster plaques that cover the walls—messages from believers giving thanks and testimony for miracles and favors granted to individuals. An iron screen door leads from the outer chamber to the inner one, allowing people to see inside the inner sanctum even when it is closed (Figure 2.5).

The inner sanctum is a small, cluttered space decorated with plaster plaques, candles, flowers, ofrendas (offerings), prayer cards, pictures, single rocks, testimony letters, and sculptures of the saint surrounded by little piles of rocks. As they were for Jesús Malverde, that other border saint, rocks are part of the repertoire of practices venerating Juan Soldado. Lore says that after Juan Soldado was executed and buried, rocks started to appear inexplicably, piling up on his gravesite. To this day, the rocks left here serve as collective reminders, testimonies, and tokens for miracles.

The legend has it that when someone needs a favor from Juan Soldado, he or she can take one of the rocks and promise to return it once the favor has been granted. This creates a manda-economy contract, and if the person does not bring the rock back to the chapel as promised, the saint will get upset; rocks and dirt will start to appear around the person's home, work, or car. These details of the legend appeared in the testimony of people attending the grave during my visits. During my first visit, one person told me that she had been unable to bring the rock back to Juan Soldado, and she started to find dirt in her home, even after cleaning consistently. Then one day her child brought home a rock that a stranger had given him, and she realized that she needed to return the rock. The rocks become the saint's relics—not as his actual body parts, but parts from the body of the soil of Mexico. They work as extensions of his body, reproducing him everywhere. As the rocks pass from petitioner to petitioner, the legend of Juan Soldado also travels from one house to another, and devotion to him increases. In this way, the vernacular saint Juan Soldado has risen above the body of Juan Castillo Morales, replacing his memory with narratives of holiness.

Once inside the inner chapel, visitors perform rites of adoration: lighting candles, praying, touching the statuettes and busts of Juan Soldado, and exchanging rocks—actions that one sees at many similar religious sites. The aura is somber, even ritualistic, with everyone moving slowly and mostly silently. Outside the inner sanctum, in the outer chapel, those waiting talk among themselves, sharing stories of miracles granted by the saint to themselves or to others. Over and over again, people recount the story of what happened to Juan Castillo Morales back in 1938, portraying him as a victim framed for a crime, and they explain how they came in contact with the saint.

On one of my visits, a local TV station was interviewing visitors for an evening news piece. Whether speaking to each other or to the reporters, petitioners almost never dwelled at any length on Olga Camacho. The devotees find ways to differentiate between Juan, the soldier in his twenties who was the main suspect in the rape and killing of Olga Camacho, and Juan Soldado, the young man turned into a saint. The story of Juan Soldado focuses on the miracles granted by Juan Soldado as a vernacular saint, and Olga Camacho (if she is mentioned at all) is brought up only to show how Juan Soldado was martyred: framed for a crime he did not commit. In the chapel, Juan Soldado's sainthood is perpetually witnessed and affirmed, while Olga Camacho is erased. Each visitor helps to reinforce collectively the veracity and popularity of the saint through participation in both public, shared rituals and private ones.

There is also an entirely separate second chapel of Juan Soldado in Panteón No. 1, located where legend says that Juan Castillo Morales was actually executed. Under the ley de fuga (law of flight), the prisoner is given the option

102 UNDOCUMENTED SAINTS

to run free for a set number of minutes before the firing squad starts to hunt him or her.[20] If the accused escapes, he or she is set free. This second chapel marks the spot where Juan Castillo Morales was caught and actually died, and it is quite different from the previous one. It is a highly visible structure, both larger and easier to access, technically outside the boundaries of the cemetery, on private property (Figure 2.6). It can therefore hold more

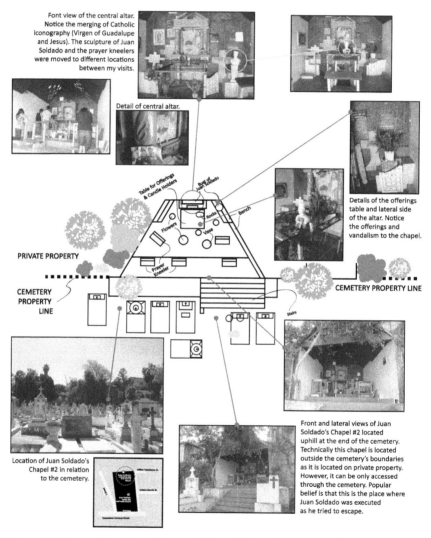

Figure 2.6 Execution site and second chapel, Panteón Municipal No. 1.
Graphic and photos by the author

venerators than the smaller chapel at the gravesite. This chapel is painted green and white and contains several kneelers, plaster plaques, candles, flowers, and holy rocks. During my visits to this chapel, the visual focal point was not a single, isolated sculpture of Juan Soldado (as it is in many sites of veneration of vernacular saints) but a painting of him that combined traditional Catholic images: the Virgin of Guadalupe and Jesus Christ looking at a childlike version of Juan Soldado. The painting was created by a believer whose request was granted by the vernacular saint.

Neither of these sites of adoration give any indication that Juan Soldado had any connection to the 1938 rape and murder of an eight-year-old girl. The chapels' design, the music, and the many flowers, letters, and plaster plaques testifying to miracles all completely erase Olga Camacho from the narratives of sainthood associated with Juan Soldado in their quest to erase a key part of his story: his conviction for rape and murder.

It is not enough for us to recognize Olga today as a martyr to misogyny. We must also understand how the current narratives about Juan Soldado perpetuate a state of violence against women. That is, despite the possibility that Juan Castillo Morales was framed, Olga Camacho, an innocent eight-year-old child, was indisputably murdered. Moreover, she was not just killed; she was raped, clear evidence of the insidious sexual character of the crime. Juan Soldado's early followers knew his history. They knew about his conviction. Whether they thought he had committed the crimes or not, they knew that someone had raped and killed Olga. While recent followers of Juan Soldado cannot be blamed for overlooking the crime, as the story has been so corrupted that they are probably unaware of the details, his early followers certainly knew—and they were fine with attacking the family of a rape and murder victim. This is one of the most inexplicable elements in this decades-old crime.

Here are the maneuvers of an epistemic apparatus of misogyny, one that reconstructs the events and creates and hides knowledge in order to normalize violence. Throwing stones at the grave and family of Olga Camacho, as early followers of Juan Soldado did, can only be understood as part of the process of diversion of responsibility and the creation of false knowledge about the crime. Olga Camacho seems to have been banished not only from the narrative but from the possibility of public redemption as a victim, for in a twisted way, she is positioned as being somehow responsible for Juan Castillo Morales's death. The narrative treats her almost as an inconvenience, collateral damage in the process of sanctifying Juan Soldado. To understand, at least in part, this spiritual crime as it may apply to similar cases, we must study the circumstances surrounding her rape and murder and the historical context leading to her disappearance.

Building (Un)Holy Chronologies: Notes on Temporality

A consistent, fixed timeline of Olga Camacho's kidnapping, rape, and murder is almost impossible to establish. The story has many versions and twists, all defined by the border experience of migration, violence against women, and women's relationships to institutionalized religion. However, to understand how border spirituality and power are working here, as well as how both figures fit into and serve the oppressive narratives of the region, we must try to figure out a cohesive sequence of events, beginning with the crimes against Olga Camacho, moving through the search for her killer and the body, and then to the trial and execution of Juan Castillo Morales. To build this chronology, I draw on primary sources, historical archives, scholarly works, newspapers, and first- and secondhand interviews conducted at the time of the crime/investigation. Because so many existing accounts are incomplete or inconsistent, I have continually cross-referenced sources. The result is by no means definitive, but it offers a relatively clear and complete picture of the context of events—the political, economic, and social conditions of 1930s Tijuana. This understanding can in turn help to explain the disparities between the historical figures of Juan Castillo Morales and Olga Camacho and the spiritual figures of Juan Soldado and Santa Olguita—the metaphorical borders that the original historical figures had to cross to be transformed into saints.

Olga's erasure from the historical narrative became very clear to me during my research, for I found very few references to Olga Camacho in the archive. Most scholars and historical records focus almost exclusively on the figure of Juan Castillo Morales, the protests that followed, and the irregularities in the investigation. This male-centered vision, which glosses over the crimes against Olga (and her family), fits within the recurrent historiography imposed on women all along the border. I work against this tendency, but the chronology leaves more questions than answers about the crime and its investigation; I point out these irregularities, but in doing so I do not mean to imply the innocence of Juan Castillo Morales. I see these irregularities as revealing the military and government's deep levels of intervention in the investigation, showing these institutions' long investment in the subjugation of women as part of a system that promotes greed and exploitation along the border. While we will probably never know if Juan Castillo Morales raped and murdered Olga, the monstrosity of the 1938 events reveals the extraordinary numbers of players taking part in the oppression experienced by this community—a region caught between, and at the mercy of, both US and Mexican powers.

The Public Timeline

On February 13, 1938, when it became clear that Olga had disappeared during her errand to the store and was missing, the Camacho Martínez family notified the police and began to scour the barrio with the help of friends and neighbors. Given the limited number of police officers in Tijuana, the military also became involved in the search.[21] Roadblocks were established around the city, radio announcements were made, and a massive group of people mobilized to search throughout the night. The search perimeter excluded the large autonomous zona militar (military zone) across from the Camacho Martínez house, because it was designated outside the administrative jurisdiction of Tijuana's civil authorities.[22] The next day, February 14, the Tijuana police department requested additional police assistance from the neighboring US city of San Diego, California. The US police became nearly as involved as the Mexican police, and many suspects in the ensuing riots eventually fled to the United States; from the beginning, the case was always a story of borders and border crossing.

On the morning of February 14, María B. de Romero, the Camacho Martínez family's neighbor, known as Meimi, found Olga's body in a deactivated garage used as a military storehouse, located two blocks from the Camacho Martínez house.[23] According to the autopsy conducted by Dr. Severano Osornio Camareña, a military doctor and Tijuana's coroner, Olga had died February 13, the same night she went missing, at around 7:00 p.m. The causes of death were strangulation and trauma to the head. Human hair and skin, as well as clothing fibers, were found under her nails, indicating that she had resisted the assault.[24] Because her body was found on military grounds, General Manuel J. Contreras—chief of military operations in Tijuana, and therefore the commander in charge of the military zone—took command of the investigation. He was assisted by the local police department; Luis Viñals Carsi, Tijuana's police chief, was also a captain in the army.[25]

Several suspects, including Juan Castillo Morales, were arrested the afternoon of the fourteenth, the day her body was found. Eventually, all but Castillo Morales were released (although details here conflict). As news of the arrests spread, the community started to congregate outside the police department, calling for a resolution to the case. The Mexican and US police were working with the military, lending their criminal investigation expertise.[26] The police departments of San Diego and Tijuana had collaborated on several previous investigations. Ed Dieckmann, a police dactylographer from San Diego, confirmed that the fingerprints of Castillo Morales matched those found on the package of meat that Olga had carried at the time of her kidnapping, which was left behind at the scene.[27] His fingerprints also matched prints in the garage where the body was found.[28] That night, Castillo Morales's girlfriend, Concha, turned over to the police a bloodstained sweater, allegedly worn by Castillo Morales the night that Olga disappeared. The fibers from the sweater matched those found under Olga's fingernails. As part of the interrogation, Concha was brought to the prison to confront Castillo Morales, and he confessed to the crime. He claimed to have been under the influence of alcohol and marijuana, and said he "slaughter[ed] her [Olga] . . . with a piece of glass."[29]

Juan Castillo Morales's confession was quickly leaked to the community, apparently by his superior officer, Contreras, who wanted to put a quick end to the protests and riots.[30] Soon after, the Tijuana police department officially and publicly declared that Juan Castillo Morales was the murderer. Almost immediately, newspaper reporters were invited to meet with Castillo Morales in prison. During the meeting, Castillo Morales confessed to the news media and was photographed.

Around 8:30 p.m. on February 14, the rioters demanded to lynch the soldier. By 2:00 am (February 15) the protesters outside the jail broke into the building but were unable to reach the suspect in custody. The fort and the city jail were burned. The protests, which began with Olga's family and friends demanding justice, eventually swelled to an insurgency, with an estimated three thousand people participating.[31] During the first clash between civilians and the military forces, "two boys and a man were killed and fourteen persons were wounded or otherwise injured as troops fired into the mob of 1500 men and women,"[32] and two more people were later reported dead.[33] At least half of the wounded victims were minors.[34] Between forty and one hundred people were arrested, although most of the detainees were freed shortly thereafter; only four people would be formally charged in connection with the arson.[35] Martial law was declared, closing cantinas as well as the US-Mexico border between San Diego and Tijuana.[36] Early on February 15, General Contreras ordered that the garage where the body was found be burned, supposedly to quiet the protests, but there were no protests happening around the garage; this is one of the suspicious moments that people now point to as indicating a cover-up.[37]

The protesters attacked city hall, the central administration building that housed the treasury, the labor arbitration board's office, the tax collector's office, and the registry of city property.[38] Protesters broke windows and set buildings on fire. Because of the rebellion, Castillo Morales was moved during the night to the new police headquarters outside town, where interrogations continued to determine whether any accomplices had participated.[39] The records of the Tijuana police include no official transcript of the interrogations. The protests affected the investigation procedures and results. Governor Sánchez Taboada explained to the Mexican department of the interior on February 28, 1938, that the protests "prevented . . . the authorities from doing the necessary inquiries, and from bringing forward the charges against the detainee."[40]

According to one of the contemporary newspaper reports, "the detainees were the leaders of CROM" (the union called Confederación Regional Obrera Mexicana, or Regional Conference of Mexican Workers) and "radical communists."[41] On February 15, several CROM members who had participated in the protests of the previous night fled to the United States, fearing retaliation from the Mexican government and military. This is another instance of the importance of borders to this story—borders that came into play with the US/Mexico collaboration in the investigation, and would later mark the soldier's development into Juan Soldado, the saint of migration.

Media reports of the events also crossed the border. On February 16, the day after they fled, *La Opinion* from Los Angeles reported on the incidents, as did the *Los Angeles Times*: "200 civilians rescued Adrián Féliz, editor of the powerful C. R. O. M. labor union newspaper, from two soldiers who had arrested him, and hurried him across the border into the United States. The soldiers opened fire."[42] That same day Olga Camacho was buried at the Panteón de la Puerta Blanca, now known as Panteón No. 1. The cemetery's original name came from the fact that Carranza Avenue, where the cemetery is located, ended on the international border, where there was an entrance to the United States known as the white door.[43]

As the protests persisted through the night of the fourteenth and into the fifteenth, Governor Sánchez Taboada kept the Mexican president, Cárdenas, abreast of the events, suspects, and plan of action.[44] On February 16, responding to Sánchez Taboada, Cárdenas ordered the local authorities not to execute the suspect but to prosecute him and any other detainees in accordance with the local law. The expectation was that the civil authorities would handle this case. However, almost immediately, the Tijuana civil court declared that "since Castillo Morales is a soldier, he should be tried in a military court."[45] General Contreras ordered the formation of an extraordinary military court, with him as the presiding judge.[46] At 5:00 p.m. on February 16, only three days after Olga's disappearance and two days after her body was discovered, the court-martial of Castillo Morales began behind closed doors. The proceedings were held in General Contreras's home, across from the fort and close to the Camacho Martínez family home; Luis G. Martínez, a civilian lawyer, was appointed as Castillo Morales's public defense attorney.[47] The trial went on until dawn, when Castillo Morales was found guilty and sentenced to death on the charges of kidnapping, first-degree murder, and rape.[48] No records of the court proceedings can be found. Unsurprisingly, it looks like Castillo Morales's punishment was decided even before the trial took place. *La Opinion*, the Latino newspaper from Los Angeles, in a piece published a day before his death, reported that Contreras was contemplating "executing him within 48 hours," in order to "satisfy the desire for revenge held by the crowd."[49]

Around 8:00 a.m. on February 17, just four days after Olga's disappearance, Juan Castillo Morales was brought to the local cemetery for execution.[50] At that time, the city had not yet engulfed the cemetery, as it has now; it was then located on the outskirts of the city, in the area known today as Colonia Castillo (no relation to Juan Castillo Morales). Several locals, military personnel, and invited members of the press attended the execution, including General Contreras (who ordered the execution) and the police inspector Jesús Medina Ríos.[51] Before the ley de fuga was carried out, Castillo Morales told the thirty soldiers tasked with his execution (members of his own military unit), "I am not afraid to die."[52] He was actually shot at the edge of the cemetery, from where, according to a newspaper at that time, "you can see very well all Tijuana and the border with the United States."[53]

Beyond the Murder: Protests of Discontent in the Context of the Great Depression

As if it were some kind of horror film, the events surrounding the deaths of Olga Camacho and Juan Castillo Morales take on a very different meaning depending on when one starts the story and how one sets the stage. Most notably, much depends on the context of the political events in Tijuana in the days leading up to Olga's attack. The protests following Olga's death were hardly the first to occur in the area. In the days before the kidnapping, another series of city protests known as the Huelga de los Sentados (literally "sitting strike," or sit-in) took place in Tijuana; these protests involved Olga's father, Camacho León, as well as other members of CROM—many of the same people who later organized and participated in the protests against Juan Castillo Morales.[54] These sit-ins were protesting the closure of casinos, which were one of the most important sources of jobs in the town.[55] The casinos were slated for closure to fulfill the moral promise of President Cárdenas's government in the aftermath of the Mexican Revolution: to "convert those centers of ill relaxation into centers for social dignity."[56]

At the center of these closure protests was the large Agua Caliente casino, an entertainment complex that included, in addition to the casino, a resort hotel (opened in 1928, when the casino opened); the large Hipódromo de Agua Caliente horse-racing track (opened in 1929); and its own airstrip, spa, hot spring baths, golf course, and bungalows. At the height of its popularity, during the first half of the 1930s, Agua Caliente drew many celebrities such as Rita Hayworth, Charlie Chaplin, and Stan Laurel and Oliver Hardy.

The Agua Caliente hippodrome was one of the main source of revenue for Tijuana. As Mario A. Carvajal notes in his book *Juan Soldado: La verdad y el mito*, at the time of the murder

> [a] climate of labor turmoil, of social unrest, was a result of the two main factions: first, the recent divisions between the various trade unions at the city, mainly CROM and CTM (Confederación de Trabajadores de México [Confederation of Mexican Workers]), which since 1936 had started a de facto war with the authorities for hierarchical supremacy. Second, the closure of the Agua Caliente Casino, which had been a source of employment for hundreds of people, occurred in July 1935.[57]

Despite the uneasy mood of the city in 1938, when Olga was killed, most narratives omit the unrest and protests preceding Olga's death, suggesting that Tijuana was a calm, peaceful city suddenly disrupted by violence. The crime's framing as exceptional justifies residents' violent reactions; the protests immediately before and after Castillo Morales's execution appear out of character for the peaceful city and its peaceful residents. Indeed, these representations suggest that the protests caused problems for Tijuana, whose economy depends heavily on tourists and their perception of the city as safe. A history of recurrent protests and political and economic tension simply does not fit the picture of security and control that the city wants to present. Therefore, most accounts of Olga Camacho's rape and murder and of Juan Castillo Morales's execution ignore the agrarian and labor disputes of the late 1930s that contextualized the events that followed. The protests are presented as an act of collective bravery against a criminal and as action in revenge for a crime against a child, not as the boiling over of existing resentments against the state and its military.

To understand the crimes against Olga Camacho and the circumstances surrounding Juan Soldado's sanctification, one must understand not only the historical context of the events within Mexico but also the context of US–Mexico relations. The years leading up to Olga Camacho's case were tumultuous ones for this cross-border relationship. As scholar Loren Lee argues, American Prohibition and Tijuana's legalization of gambling caused the explosive economic growth and demographic change that took place in Tijuana during the first quarter of the twentieth century. When Prohibition was repealed in 1933, as the Great Depression (1929–39) was creating economic chaos worldwide, it wreaked havoc on Tijuana's economy, which had become tourism-dependent.[58] In addition, during this period Tijuana was still grappling with the effects of the forced migration of over five hundred thousand people of Mexican heritage who were repatriated to Mexico from the United States between 1929 and 1936. Many of these people had settled in Tijuana, in the hope of returning to the United States when the economy improved and political hostilities subsided. The rapid population growth created in Tijuana by expatriates and landless farmers (like Olga's family) sparked many urban challenges for the city in terms of services and opportunities, creating many new colonias, or unincorporated barrios.[59]

In part to ease the social and labor unrest, the government of Mexican president Cárdenas implemented large-scale land redistribution grants in along the border, in Mexicali, Ensenada, El Rosario, Tecate, and Tijuana.[60]

In the Mexicali valley of Baja California alone, between 1937 and 1940, the Mexican government expropriated over 412,000 acres from the American-run Colorado River Land Company (CRLC)—the largest and most expensive single expropriation of that period.[61] As expected, these large expropriations of land provided Cárdenas's government and his National Revolutionary Party with a large and powerful base of progovernment farmers, the agraristas.[62] For some small Mexican rancheros, however, the results were disastrous, as they lost all rights to the lands they had been leasing from the CRLC. Olga Camacho's family was among those affected; they were forced to leave Mexicali and relocate to Tijuana when Olga's grandfather lost his land.[63]

Camacho León, Olga's father, was a union leader, the president of El Sindicato de Empleados de Cantinas, Hoteles y Restaurantes (Cantina, Hotel, and Restaurant Workers Union)—the union representing one of the groups of people who would be most affected by the casino closures. In that role, Camacho León was involved in a legal dispute opposing the government's closure of the casinos in the city.[64] This union, along with the two most powerful casino workers unions in the city (the Agua Caliente and Alba Roja unions), were all members of CROM, a powerful federation of Mexican labor unions.

Camacho León's union leadership is a crucial element of the context surrounding Olga's murder. By the time Olga was killed, Tijuana's population was deeply divided between two groups: those who opposed the government and its recent decision to close the city's casinos (this group included bar and casino workers, unified under CROM) and those who supported the government's decision (this group included the military and the agraristas, whose land rights were secured by the government). The pro-government contingent, which included the agraristas, had its own union to compete with the traditionally antigovernment CROM: CTM, a union sponsored by President Cárdenas himself. The two unions had been in direct conflict since 1936, when several progovernment members left CROM to form CTM. Before the split, CROM had been the largest federation of labor unions in Mexico, and (as we will see in Chapter 3 on Toribio Romo) an ally of the Mexican government against the Catholic Church during the Cristero War.

Throughout the 1930s, the Mexican government was in an open war against CROM, banning civil servants from membership in the organization. In a mix of politics and religiosity, as early as 1921 the Catholic Church in Mexico decreed that holding CROM membership was a mortal sin. Across the decade, CROM and CTM served as the axes of the tensions and social unrest in the city. Just a few weeks before Olga's murder, on January 25, 1938, CROM lost an important legal case: Tijuana's court of conciliation and arbitration ruled against casino workers' demand that the government force the companies that owned the casinos to pay overdue wages.[65] In the weeks following the ruling, CROM members protested in the streets of the city and outside Tijuana's city hall, clashing with progovernment groups. The protests continued all the way to the day of Olga's attack.[66]

This conflict about the casinos was a (visible, highly public) expression of the deeper anger caused by the forced migrations of the previous decade. Most of the people involved in the protests—including Camacho León—were only in Tijuana to begin with because they had been forced to migrate there after being displaced by Cárdenas's land expropriation policies.[67] The government's refusal to force casinos to pay back wages and Cárdenas's decision to close the casinos in the first place were for many protestors simply additional fuel for existing anti-government sentiments. It was no coincidence that Tijuana's city hall, briefly taken over during the Huelga de los Sentados, was destroyed in the rebellion following the murder, for this building housed all the records of the casino court case and all the information (photographs, names, addresses, etc.) gathered against those engaged in the Huelga and the street protests. With those records destroyed, many CROM members were able to avoid prosecution.

This background is crucial to understanding the events surrounding Olga's murder, for the tensions described here were playing out over those few short days. First, the agraristas, as a pronationalist group that possessed guns, were being used by the Cárdenas government as an auxiliary force to control the region, and during the Castillo Morales protests, over two hundred of them were called in to assist the city of Tijuana, further inflaming the protestors.[68] Perhaps more importantly, Juan Castillo Morales was probably one of the soldiers who, just a few days before, had helped to suppress the casino workers' demonstrations. Perhaps many of the protestors in the mob had reason to despise Castillo Morales, who (as a soldier) represented the rapacious and oppressive government they opposed.

As Carvajal explains, when the news about Olga Camacho spread and Castillo Morales was accused of her rape and murder,

> the plaintiffs [in the casino case] found in this new demonstration [against Castillo Morales] outside the Comandancia an escape from the frustration

of having seen their efforts to save the largest employer in the city fail. Probably this was the reason why those leading the demands were the same union leaders who, a few days before, were demanding labor justice, but now they were struggling to take criminal justice in their own hands.[69]

News of Olga Camacho's rape and murder, by a soldier who had helped suppress the earlier protests, only further intensified the sociopolitical fire that was already burning in Tijuana and the rest of Baja California. As one of the union leaders, Camacho León had a lot of enemies. Not surprisingly, some even wondered whether Olga's death was a warning to CROM and more specifically to her father to stop their activities. For example, Gabriel Trujillo Muñoz argues that, given the context of the labor disputes of the time, "the murder and rape of Olga Camacho was a low blow against the protest movement"—one designed to bring the unions to their knees.[70] Carvajal also notes that some of the theories circulating at that time saw Olga's murder as "revenge by members of CTM or a rival union . . . to scare the Camacho Martínez family, and to have Aurelio [Olga's father] back off from some of the syndicate's demands."[71]

The connection between the Castillo Morales protests and the sociopolitical and economic conflicts in Tijuana at the time were quite clear to many of those protesting after Castillo Morales's arrest, who demanded not only justice for Olga Camacho but the creation of jobs, increased wages, and the dismissal of various officials as well.[72] The connection was also far from lost on the Mexican government. An official press release on February 15, 1938, from the Departamento Autónomo de Prensa y Publicidad de la Secretaría de Gobernación (the Mexican Ministry of the Interior), cited Governor Sánchez Taboada in its argument that the protests were being engineered by CROM and other groups "involved in the Agua Caliente matter, [as they] burned the towers [of the Comandancia] next to the jail and the Palace of the Delegation [city hall]."[73] A similar notion was articulated by William Smale, American consul for Baja California, in a February 16, 1938, telegram to Cordell Hull, then US secretary of state:

> Agrarians have been called in to reinforce military, and military reinforcements from Ensenada and Mexicali have also been brought to Tijuana. Fracas appears to have originated as much through conflict between CROM and Federal authorities following expropriation of Agua Caliente property as through desire of vengeance for assault and murder. . . .

Not impossible, that further disorders will occur tonight although CROM leaders appear to have departed for the United States.[74]

Smale's telegram not only revealed the ongoing conflict between CROM and the Tijuana government regarding the closure of casinos but also exposed the agraristas' role in the conflict. He also noted the role of the border in the conflict, reporting that several CROM syndicate leaders had sought refuge in the United States, probably in the San Diego area—a fact that was also reported by local newspapers at the time.[75] In a follow-up telegram to the secretary of state, just two days later, Smale again insisted on the broader significance of the protests:

> I reiterate that the disturbance was more a demonstration against the government by the dissatisfied elements in Tijuana, than by persons fundamentally affected by the crime committed, and that the crime simply offered the opportunity for inciting the riot.
>
> The effect of the entire incident is likely to result in killing of the open opposition of CROM to the Government but may increase its secret activities. Because the Military was required to call upon the agrarians in support, it is not unlikely that the agrarians in the near future will be even more bold and insistent than at present respecting their demands upon the government. For these reasons, the writer is of the opinion that while the immediate incident has passed, it leads up to what may be even more serious trouble within the next few months.[76]

Smale saw the protests (and the agraristas' involvement at the state's behest) as inextricably linked to their context: social unrest against the government that was rooted in the land conflicts and labor disputes. He saw that the local Tijuana government aimed to use the rebellions as an opportunity to eliminate CROM, or at least reduce its influence, and he foresaw the problems this would cause for long-term peace in the region.

In summary, it is clear that ongoing conflicts between pro- and antigovernment forces shaped the protests that followed the Olga Camacho murder. The progovernment CTM capitalized on the unrest to gain even more leverage with the local government, organizing street vigilantes to patrol the city and "reestablish public order," and the local government decided to bring in agraristas from nearby Mexicali, Ensenada, and Rosario to reinforce the city patrols and barricades.[77] Finally, most of the people detained during the protests about Olga were CROM members.[78] These realities clearly contradict the narrative that Tijuana was a place of peace and balance before the murder—a narrative put forward by people who frame the Olga Camacho rebellion as an isolated event.

These two union groups, CROM and CTM, each with their own constituency (casino workers and agraristas, respectively), embody the socioeconomic problems of the time. While they seem to have opposite interests and opposite sources of discontent, in reality both groups were trapped by Mexican and US policies that pitted one group against the other, leaving both with few real possibilities to improve their conditions. On one side, CROM represented the precarious situation of wage workers, who were profoundly dependent on American tourism and strongly affected by the Mexican government's morality-based campaign against casinos. The marginalization and vulnerability of these workers grew out of a long series of governmental policy decisions by both Mexico and the United States. Even before the closure of Tijuana's casinos, local workers were already deeply affected by wage inequality, as Mexican workers were paid far less than Americans working at the casinos. They were therefore more affected when tourism from the United States slowed because of the Depression. In addition, gambling had been legalized in Las Vegas just a few years before, in 1931, and the rise of the Nevada casino industry was deeply connected with the demise of Tijuana's economy; California tourists, in particular, were siphoned off by the nearby Las Vegas casinos.

The CTM members and agraristas were also economically vulnerable. CTM had been created in reaction to CROM, as a way for Cárdenas to control the syndicate movement in Mexico. The Cárdenas administration prohibited government workers from joining CROM. The agraristas' tenure on and use of the land they worked were completely in the hands of the government—their land rights were secured not by the Mexican constitution but by the goodwill of the president. In essence, land rights were a political favor. This precarious position was made shakier by the fact that at that time CRLC and the US government were fighting the expropriations in court. CTM and the agraristas thus saw their future as deeply dependent on the perpetuation of President Cárdenas's administration. The actions by CROM and its allies were perceived as a direct attack on the agraristas' interests and prosperity, although the Cárdenas government was responsible for creating the entire situation for its own advantage.

The connection between social unrest and the socioeconomic situation in Tijuana that I have traced here was neatly summed up in a February 1938 news report in the *San Diego Sun*, which commented on the protests following Olga Camacho's death: "The story behind today's mob violence is seated in the stomachs of the hungry Tijuana workers, whose real interest is not in an eight-year-old child, but in getting some food in their stomachs to keep their belt buckles from rattling against their spines.... This [murder] is just what they have been waiting for."[79]

Dark Alchemy: Misogyny Along the Border Turns a Criminal into a Saint

The sociopolitical and socioeconomic reality of Tijuana during the crime can help explain how Juan Castillo Morales became the saint Juan Soldado. His transformation becomes understandable as not just a form of cultural resistance but also a profound performance of hope in the face of economic despair. His vernacular canonization was made possible by the erasure of his crime, and this erasure was in turn made possible by the existing machismo and misogyny in local Mexican culture.

In many ways the "miraculous" transformation of a rapist and murderer into a vernacular saint shows the simultaneous absurdity and extremity of misogynist violence against women along the border. The rape and murder of Olga, a child, was one event in a historical pattern of crimes against women in the region. The misogynistic character of the crime continues to be enacted today by the invisibility imposed on Olga, the exceptionality ascribed to the crime, and the recreation of Juan Soldado as an innocent—ironically, as a child himself—who was incapable of committing such a crime. He took the place of Olga as the child-victim, even though at the time of the crime she was eight and he was twenty-two—not a child by any stretch of the imagination. All of these factors manifest the constantly shifting nature of patriarchy and show how it is often interwoven with religiosity.

Why did Olga Camacho's rape and murder not resonate with the community in the same way that Juan Castillo Morales's death did? Any answer to that question must take account of the complex intersectionality of power and vulnerability in the region at the time, which left neither Juan Castillo Morales nor Olga Camacho able to tell their own story. The erasure of both voices from the narrative allowed others to tell the story in whatever way benefited themselves, and the stories that were told reveal the crucial role played by gender and race in the sequence of events.

Throughout history and around the world, rape has been part of the male-centric, patriarchal state's hegemonic project of systematic violence against women. In the California/Tijuana region, this project can be traced back to the Spanish colonial period.[80] Such violence has been enacted by state agents—recall that Juan Castillo Morales was a soldier—as part of a large array of tools to exert dominance and control over local communities, especially indigenous peoples. Olga Camacho's rape and death were enabled by larger forces. So too was the resurrection of Juan Castillo Morales as Juan Soldado: criminalization has been similarly used as a tool by the powerful to keep the lower classes (often racialized) in line, and he was adopted by protesters and rebels as a symbol of the resistance to the repressive power regimes that they fought.

The transformation of Juan Castillo Morales to Juan Soldado began in part because the case was plagued from the very beginning with questions and doubts about Castillo Morales's guilt. Some saw him as having been railroaded by the government, believing that he probably did not commit the crime at all but was a scapegoat, set up either to cover the acts of a higher-ranking figure or simply to provide the military with an easy resolution. Others saw him as being a victim of larger systems of power, whether or not he had perpetrated the atrocious crimes of which he was convicted. They perceived him as being caught in a larger network of government-sanctioned violations of people's rights. In their minds, the real criminal was not so much Castillo Morales as the military he represented, which was omnipresent in the city and operated according to its own rules. If Castillo Morales had committed the murder, some said, he was probably following orders from a superior—he was a puppet, like so many others, forced to follow the orders of those in power.

The focus of the eventual doubts about Castillo Morales's guilt (or his motivations) was General Contreras, the representative of these repressive forces. In the collective imagination of Juan Soldado's followers, Contreras, arguably more than anyone else, was responsible for the execution of Castillo Morales. In the people's consciousness Contreras represents a system that was—and still is—omnipresent and deeply involved in the lives (and deaths) of border subjects. He was not only Castillo Morales's boss but also the one in charge of the court-martial, the one who delivered the information to the masses, and the one who ordered Castillo Morales's death. He was the one who ordered that the crime scene be burned the day after Olga's body was found, ensuring that no new evidence could be collected or existing evidence confirmed. He sought to control the city in the aftermath and instituted a stringent curfew. He was allegedly the last person with whom Castillo Morales spoke before he was executed. Contreras and his actions continue to loom large in followers' representations of Castillo Morales's demise: he is presented as the ultimate patrón ruling from the shadows, the one responsible for the calamities that culminated in Castillo Morales's execution. It was these calamities that would quickly produce Castillo Morales's sainthood.

Contreras is, in many ways, a symbol of the military and governmental power that ruled Mexico during the years under President Cárdenas (who was also a military man before becoming president). Contreras's prominent role in the narrative of Juan Castillo Morales is therefore unsurprising, for it speaks to the oppression experienced by the saint's devotees, just as Castillo Morales's resurrection and redemption as Juan Soldado speak to their hopes and desperation. The characterization of Contreras held by Juan Soldado's followers—as the untouchable villain behind Olga's attack—must be interpreted as an imaginary construct meant to do more than just secure Soldado's innocence. By constructing Contreras as the antagonist in the story of Juan Soldado and Olga Camacho, the community turns a spotlight on the Machiavellian forces that govern their lives.

Whatever the truth behind the events of Olga's murder, the community appears to have seen its own precarious status reflected in Juan Castillo Morales's closed-door trial and rushed execution. Like themselves, Castillo Morales was at the mercy of the local government, the judicial system, and the military, all three of which seemed to be united against him.[81] We may never know if he was really innocent. Whatever the truth, the devotion to Juan Soldado has been deeply defined, as Paul J. Vanderwood explains, by the "conflicting feelings of injustice and justice" that define the region.[82]

As doubts about Castillo Morales's culpability mixed with the community's own sense of guilt that an innocent man may have been executed, Tijuana residents' suspicions and anxieties began to condense around a transformed version of Juan Castillo Morales—popularly sanctified and rechristened Juan Soldado, a name that emphasized not his individual personhood but his status as a representative of the military. According to Tijuana historians Gabriel Rivera and José Saldaña Rico, the sacred dimensions of the story were born the moment Castillo Morales was executed, and they were consolidated in the legend of the holy rocks that emerged soon after. According to the legend, the day after his burial, a local woman placed a wooden cross on Castillo Morales's grave with the inscription "Everyone that goes through here, place a rock and pray an Our Father."[83] Rivera and Saldaña Rico argue that as rocks began to accumulate at the site, so too did the notion that these rocks, like those that appeared at Jesús Malverde's chapel (Chapter 1), were tokens for graces, miracles, and promises granted by Juan Soldado, all expressions of a manda currency. Alejandro F. Lugo Perales links this ritual to the community's sense of guilt; he points to an ancient Moorish rite, carried to Mexico from Spain, in which, as he says, "aggressors throw stones at the grave of their victim apologizing. That's what happened with Juan Soldado; people started throwing stones at the grave and eventually there were those who said that they [the stones] performed miracles."[84]

However, according to Marco Antonio, the groundskeeper where Castillo Morales is buried, there is a much more mundane interpretation of the origin of the rocks. As he explained when I interviewed him,:

> The famous legend of the little rocks emerged because . . . some time ago, the entrance to the cemetery was located in the upper part. All that section, where we were before, used to be pastures, and grass. . . . There used to be lots of squirrels and rabbits . . . and where he [Juan Soldado] fell dead, they built a chapel, and planted a cross. . . . That area was a passage for children. . . . Those kids collected rocks for throwing at the animals. . . . The people that came to see the place where he [the soldier] died started to say that those rocks were regenerating . . . but those were the same rocks that the kids used to play with and left there to use later on [after school]. They used them to throw at the animals. They left the rock piles and the people started believing that the rocks were regenerating because of the death of Juan Soldado.[85]

Antonio has worked as a groundskeeper at the cemetery for several decades and has witnessed the growth of the chapel and the political infighting that accompanies that growth. The chapel is the most-visited grave in the cemetery, and he explained that the city and the cemetery are constantly fighting over the donations made to Juan Soldado. As the groundskeeper, he is the one who personally ensures that petitioners' requests and mandas regarding improvements to the chapel are honored, especially when tied to monetary donations, like repainting the chapel's walls, fixing the roof, or planting flowers around the veneration site. According to Antonio, faith is the force that guides people to believe in Juan Soldado, though he did not elaborate on what faith means in this context. Although he denies the mystical origins of the rocks, he does not deny the saint's miracles; he simply gave a rational explanation of this small element of the growth of Juan Soldado's legend.

The community transformed Juan Castillo Morales into the saint Juan Soldado relatively quickly. On November 11, 1938, less than nine months after the soldier's execution, the *San Ysidro Border Press* reported that during celebrations of El Día de los Muertos that year, Castillo's grave had already become a popular pilgrimage site:

> It seemed as if fully half of the people visiting the cemetery stopped to pray at the grave of Juan [Castillo Morales]. . . . Many of them believe that [he] . . . died innocent of any crime. Some even say that when they knelt at his grave they could hear the voice of the dead soldier. . . . These [people] hold that the crime was committed by another, and that [Castillo Morales] . . . as a Christian act, decided to take the blame upon himself.[86]

The belief that, despite the evidence against him, Castillo Morales was not to blame for Olga's murder (or he did it because the military told him to) is an essential and enduring element of his vernacular sainthood as Juan Soldado. As I discuss in greater depth later in this chapter, those visiting his grave today perform various acts of veneration, including leaving letters, prayers, mementos, and other objects. An example I found during one visit in 2013 emphasizes the narrative of innocence, reconstructing Juan Castillo Morales as a victim of injustice. This offering was a preprinted form written to be signed by the petitioner, who in this case was named Jorge Manuel. This popular prayer form includes a picture of Juan Castillo Morales from the *San Diego Evening Tribune* in 1938 and space for petitioners to write their names as a faith-pledge of his innocence, a gesture intended to allow petitioners to likewise identify themselves as innocent victims.[87] It reads:

> Juanito [Little Juan, referring to Juan Soldado], thank you for
> All the favors and miracles
> That you have given me.
> Sincerely,
>
> ----
>
>   For the following reasons, I believe in the innocence of (Juan Soldado) Juan Castillo Morales ✝✝✝✝

First . . . Because the news reports of the month February 1938 in Tijuana and San Diego never mentioned that Juan declared himself guilty and he always said that he was innocent, and the civil authorities and the military just assumed he was guilty.

Second . . . In February 2005 in an AM radio station from Tijuana . . . They interviewed a family member of the girl Olga Martinez Consuelo Camacho that was killed in 1938 . . . And that person assured in the interview that when the corpse was found there were the footprints of two different persons . . .

This prayer's narrative conflicts with most of the evidence from the investigation and with articles in the media at the time. My interest comes from the way this revisionist representation speaks to the realities of the border. For the people who live there, the motives, actions, and interpretations of the authorities cannot be relied upon, and for those at the mercy of these untrustworthy powers, life hangs by threads of hope, contradiction, and uncertainty. In the narrative expressed by this prayer, Juan Soldado was innocent because "he always said that he was innocent, and the civil authorities and the military just assumed he was guilty," an assertion evidenced by the claim that "when the corpse [of Olga] was found there were the footprints of two different persons." For petitioners to Juan Soldado, this is enough: these two reasons open the door for many other theories that absolve or forgive Juan Castillo Morales. Doubt is built into the narrative, and with that, Juan Soldado takes form.

Marketing Iconographies: The Remaking of a Murder

In the dark alchemy created by patriarchy, the iconographic figures of Juan Castillo Morales and Juan Soldado are two incongruent entities, separate but interconnected. They inhabit two distinct spaces in people's imagination and construction of history, but each figure haunts the other. Castillo Morales, the soldier, is unquestionably a misogynistic symbol, yet he represents the experience of Juan Soldado's followers with tight military control in Tijuana and the occupation of the border. Juan Soldado, the saint, is framed by his followers as a poor peasant from the south who represents Mexico's long legacy of land displacement and forced economic relocation—a representation of him based on Castillo Morales's experience of being compelled by these policies to migrate north. In this unbelievable twist, Juan Soldado emerged as a heroic martyr who died at the hands of the patrón system. Soldado thus becomes a dual figure who was victimized first by the state, which forced him into precarity and pushed him into the military, and the military itself, which allowed his rushed execution.

The lingering doubts about his trial and alleged guilt enable his followers to identify with him—like them, they think, he was a victim of forces beyond his control. Once Castillo Morales's recasting as a saint was set in motion, the community constructed Juan Soldado as a local hero who understood their location and unique position in Baja California. This reconstruction allows his followers to disassociate Castillo Morales's hideous crimes from Juan Soldado's saintly miracles. As time has gone by, each miracle attributed to him has fueled the myth, increasing his spiritual social capital.

But for Juan Soldado to emerge as a vernacular saint, Olga Camacho and Juan Castillo Morales had to be erased, as both are incompatible with this new narrative of holiness. As James S. Griffith points out in his book *Beliefs and Holy Places: A Spiritual Geography of the Pimería Alta*, "If you are on the bottom of the social and economic heap in a modern, impersonal society, it must be easy to identify with a figure like Juan Soldado, who was persecuted and killed but who was judged by God and found innocent."[88]

Semiotically, this transformation is evident in the image most commonly used to represent Juan Soldado as a saint: a generic photograph of a "child" soldier. This image portrays Juan Soldado as an innocent, prepubescent kid, too young to be a soldier and certainly incapable of the serious crimes of rape and murder—a deliberate marketing decision to promote and sell his holiness. The generic image is not a real photograph of him as a child, and it was chosen over the many other actual photographs of him taken during his short imprisonment the night before he was executed. This choice to use the image of an innocent child, unrelated to the real Juan Castillo Morales, differentiates Juan Soldado from Castillo Morales. Juan Soldado is not an adult, who could be capable of rape and murder, but is innocent, harmless, gentle—traditional characteristics of a saint. The image attempts to transfer Olga's actual childhood and innocence to Juan Soldado, further erasing her from the narrative. In short, the image whitewashes the main suspect of the crimes. This is an act of violence, one that is perpetuated every time the image is consumed as valid and real. The way the community thinks about the crime is directly and unavoidably linked to the representation of Juan Soldado as a child: it not only creates ignorance and perpetuates false knowledge, but it also blurs the lines between fact and myth. The male child's image replaces and erases both of the actual protagonists in the story—both the adult man (Castillo Morales) and the female child (Olga Camacho)—making it more and more difficult to differentiate the real from the fictive. The innocent male child subsumes the narrative, becoming the only available and recognizable image through which the community can parse the events it purports to represent.

This produces semantic errors—incompatible code readings that emerge from the disjunction between the innocent associations of the child-image, on the one hand, and the historical events it occludes, on the other. The imposition of the sanitized new version of Juan Soldado normalizes his innocence, erasing all possible counternarratives; most people encounter only the innocent child-saint presented to them and are thus deflected away from the actual history of violence that the image hides, probably not even knowing it exists. Even for those who know the full story of his criminal charges, the image does important work, for it allows these people to believe that he was incapable of such crimes, as a child would be incapable of them, and that he therefore must have been framed. As I discuss in the next section, this bowdlerized version of the story of Juan Castillo Morales and Olga Camacho is further amplified by the contexts through which the sanitized image circulates: how it is delivered to the community, and how its meaning is shaped by the many undocumented and working-class immigrants who help to spread Juan Soldado's legend.

Representing Juan: Dealing with Ambiguities of the Border

In his sainthood, Juan Soldado was seen as a victim of violence enacted against him by larger forces—the government, the military. He became an avatar for border crossing because migrants experience a similar kind of state-sponsored violence during (and as a result of) forced migration. The sanitized version of his myth spread rapidly in part because in the 1990s, many desperate migrants (as well as Chicanx border artists) encountered only the innocent-saint version of Juan Soldado's legend and its associated devotional practices. Most of these new followers were likely completely unaware of the crime committed against Olga Camacho, as by this point she had been successfully erased from Juan Soldado's narrative. Many of these new followers encountered and embraced Juan Soldado *only* in his role as a vernacular spiritual expression of the despair of migration.

One of the most important representations of Castillo Morales can be found in *Juan Soldado*, a piece by Alma López Gaspar de Alba, one of the best-known, most beloved, and most respected Chicanx feminist artists in recent decades (Figure 2.7).[89] By the time López encountered him, Juan Castillo Morales had been replaced by Juan Soldado, and the crime against Olga had already been erased. López's piece, which in some ways recanonizes him, illustrates the many contradictions and ambiguities at play along the border, including how patriarchy can sneak up on us all.

Named after the saint, the work *Juan Soldado* is part of López's series 1848: Chicanos in the US Landscape After the Treaty of Guadalupe Hidalgo. The piece illustrates the impact on Mexican Americans of the interlocking

Figure 2.7 Alma López Gaspar de Alba, *Juan Soldado*, 1997. Digital print on vinyl, created in Photoshop, 6 × 4 ft. From the series 1948: Chicanos and the U.S., Landscape After the Treaty of Guadalupe Hidalgo.
Photo by the artist

of police brutality, land ownership, migration, labor, and long-standing exploitation produced by the 1848 Treaty of Guadalupe Hidalgo. López created *Juan Soldado* in 1997, before she knew about Olga Camacho's case; she had encountered Juan Soldado simply as a patron saint of migrants.[90] López used *Juan Soldado* to link the Mexican-American War, the Treaty of Guadalupe Hidalgo (which concluded the conflict), and the exclusionary immigration policies experienced by Mexicans in the United States throughout history.[91]

López's image of Juan Soldado is the focal point of the piece. The figure of the saint is tinted green and is surrounded by a white halo created by the semitransparent image of the stone table of Coyolxauhqui, the Aztec moon goddess. In his hands Juan Soldado is holding a US green card (the document given to permanent residents) bearing the name Juan Castillo Morales. In this image, Coyolxauhqui works as a protector, surrounding the image of the saint. Coyolxauhqui is a familiar image, for she is often used to symbolize the simultaneous fragmentation created by violence and the process of reconstruction of the self within Chicanx and Mexican Americans. Chicanx feminist theory has long utilized the images and narratives of the Virgin of Guadalupe and of Coyolxauhqui and her mother, Coatlicue, as epistemic tools to examine the deep connections among Catholicism, colonial conquest, patriarchy, and capitalism. López's composition thus positions Juan Soldado at the intersection of the spiritual practices at the border, immigration policies, and socioeconomic development.

During a conversation at López's home and studio in Los Angeles, she explained to me, "Probably I would have not painted the piece on Juan Soldado if I had known what I know today about him."[92] She explained that since she found out the details about the case, she refuses to "display the *Santa Niña de Mochis* and *Juan Soldado* next to each other" when she is asked to show her series 1848. The *Santa Niña de Mochis* that she mentions here uses an image of an unknown girl whom López encountered during a visit to her grandmother's grave in Los Mochis, Sinaloa.[93] López explained during our April 2014 discussion that she now feels uncomfortable having the two images too close together; after she learned of the case, she says, she "would always put another piece in between them, maybe an image of the Virgen de Guadalupe."[94] By placing the Virgin of Guadalupe between the two, she shields the girl from harm. By changing how she exhibits *Juan Soldado*, López is actively reshaping and resignifying her own work.

During our conversation we did not discuss the future of her work *Juan Soldado*. But López's efforts to shape the reception of her painting of

Juan Soldado made it clear to me that access to the information about the crime could again reshape and resignify the image of Juan Soldado and his veneration—just as the erasure of information about the crime allowed Juan Castillo Morales to be transformed into Juan Soldado in the aftermath of the crime. In López's work, we see yet another new Juan Soldado emerging from the sanitized image of the innocent child-saint; this new image reinvokes the fears about patriarchy's violence against women. Now the harmless façade of this male child hides a predator, one who represents the different maneuvers used by the patriarchy to persistently prey on innocent girls.

Later in our discussion, López used the metaphor of the border to shed light on how Juan Soldado's followers may have been able to differentiate between Juan Castillo Morales and Juan Soldado and reconstruct them as two different entities. She proposed a border compartmentalization that allows both entities—the killer and the saint—to coexist in different places, even when they are the same person. López said, "[My] painting is about Juan Soldado, the saint, not Juan Castillo the murderer. They are two different persons. The Juan Soldado I encountered, the one I used from a prayer card, is a child incapable of doing harm. This one is alive in the people's prayers. The other one was executed."[95] Once again, we see how the ambiguities of the border suffuse and shape this Tijuana story.

Given the endemic violence in the region, which manifests itself in Castillo Morales's crime but is part of a larger system of oppression, with her original painting *Juan Soldado* López sought to narrate a border history that emerges from the people, from their struggles and their hopes. However, like Juan Castillo Morales/Juan Soldado, the painting itself contained and reveal the violence of the region, which is so often occluded by patriarchy and by its relations with religiosity. López focuses on the saint/child figure (which is positioned outside the Catholic Church, as I discuss in the next section) in this piece, which can be read as a type of altar, with Juan Soldado standing in for the many anonymous undocumented persons waiting to normalize their immigration status. In the painting, Juan Soldado is constructed as representing the reality of many people under an oppressive migration system, serving as an epistemic tool to inscribe a long border history. By positioning the painting within her series 1848, López utilizes the veneration of Juan Soldado to place the migration discourses he encodes within the larger history of land exploitation, forced migration, cheap labor, and social vulnerability that defines the American Southwest and Mexican Northwest. In this regard, López is correct in her assessment that Juan Soldado has now truly replaced Juan Castillo Morales in the imagination of the community.

Juan Soldado and the Microdramas of the Global Market

Today, both of Juan Soldado's chapels in Tijuana have become sites that register not his rapist/murderer past but the history of his followers' struggles. As José Manuel Valenzuela Arce explains, "Juan Soldado has turned into a collector of ex-votos and retablos [votive offerings]."[96] Blanca Garduño Pulido describes such votive offerings as "microhistories where the intimate misfortune and happiness of life are commented on."[97] The objects and letters left behind by his followers tell microstories of the survival and resiliency of the communities that live along the border. These artifacts have become an ephemeral archive that reflects the micro-level effects of macro-level socioeconomic policies, which (as the artifacts show) range from labor to health access to home ownership and the precarities of love partnerships. As Garduño Pulido explains, "It is within this complex network, of the articulation of personal biographies and social history, that Juan Soldado achieves meaning in the collective imaginary, since he helps his believers to get a job, to be healed, the return of the absent children, the cure of 'incurable' diseases, [and] the granting of emigration."[98]

As a folk saint constructed within the dark alchemy of misogyny, a chemistry that is able to dissolve Olga's murder and transform the main suspect into a saint, Juan Soldado remains relevant, despite his crimes, because he has become necessary to his followers as they deal with their misfortunes. This is part of the violence done by the patriarchy: it kills not only the body but also the memory, and it can turn a monster into a saint. Today many of Juan Soldado's followers are unaware of the crimes against Olga Camacho; others know about the crimes, but some doubt his involvement and others have become willingly complicit in his violence against Olga (a figure for patriarchy's violence against women more broadly). Nevertheless, the letters left by petitioners are important historical, cultural, and economic records. Through them, we can map over time the tangible ramifications of oppression in the social body of border communities. It is in these ex-votos that the sometimes elusive and abstract concepts of empire, class, race, gender, and diaspora become tangible, fleshed out through the figure of Juan Soldado.

This section analyzes some of the letters, requests, and prayers left behind by the followers of this saint in his two main chapels in Tijuana. To illustrate how such petitions' registers change over time, I compare the plaster plaques and retablos found by Valenzuela Arce during his research in 1990 and 1991 with those I documented as part of my own ethnographic research at Juan Soldado's chapel from 2013 to 2015. Certainly, many more letters, pictures, and mementos have been left behind since. The number is always growing, but many of them are ephemeral, disappearing into anonymity as they disintegrate or are removed by the cemetery's groundskeepers. Many petitions are written on the edge of a page, in a rush, or by hand, making it hard sometimes to read the text or the name of the petitioner. Petitioners frequently try to keep their identities hidden. Many petitions are written in code, to remain secrets between the petitioner and Juan Soldado.

The appeals I describe here can be divided into three general categories: immigration, social vulnerability, and love and family, and I examine each of them in turn. All of these categories shed light on the precarity and vulnerability of Juan Soldado's adherents. They also shed light on the relationship between the mundane and the transcendent as it is experienced at the border; my goal in examining these specific petitions in these specific category groups is to unveil the complications of popular religiosity, especially in liminal spaces where the real and imaginary—the religious, the secular, and the monstrous—cannot always be separated by a solid border but rather bleed into one another.

Immigration

For quite some time, scholars have studied Juan Soldado's veneration almost exclusively in relation to immigration.[99] He is popularly understood as the patron saint of undocumented migrants, in part because his grave (the main site of his veneration) is located within a mile of the US-Mexico border, along what used to be a traditional path for undocumented border crossers—often the last stop before reaching the border. The journey was dangerous, and immigrants visited the cemetery for many reasons: to rest, to give respect to their ancestors, and to request spiritual and divine protection in their travels north.

However, immigrants' veneration of Juan Soldado seems to have changed over the last three decades: there are differences between the petitions recorded by Valenzuela Arce and the more recent ones I examined. On the plaster plaques found in 1990 and 1991, the issues of immigration tend to focus on access to legal status, and they are overall more hopeful; more often than not, they refer to successes or emphasize a petitioner's confidence that Juan Soldado will be able to help. For example, Valenzuela Arce quotes one petition by Arturo Monarres that expresses gratitude: "Thanks, Juan Soldado, for granting me my immigration."[100] These same types of notes of gratitude do still appear; in my own research I found a similar request from another petitioner, A.M.P., from 2013, saying "Grasias [*sic*; Thank you] for helping me Juan Soldado with my visa."

However, many of the more recent petitions that I found seem to reflect the increasingly complicated and frustrating immigration process, which has been made much more difficult since the 1990s. In 1994, Operation Gatekeeper, with its "prevention through deterrence" policies, was implemented; after September 11, 2001, ICE increased the use of high-tech surveillance and biometric identity projects; and in the late 2010s and early 2020s, the threat of possible repatriation through mass deportations has grown.[101] Recent petitions often ask Soldado to aid with complex applications or to speed processing time. For most Latinx migrants, ICE is not an abstract governmental entity; instead, as La Migra, it is a real embodiment and personalization of fear and pain. Petitioner José Antonio Rojas (a pseudonym) attaches two passport pictures to his 2012 letter, which reads:

> I ask you from the bottom of my heart for the miracle to cross into the USA, open the route to arrive to my destination where I have always wanted to be, in Los Angeles, and I promise you . . . to buy you a floral wreath, once you grant me the miracle of arriving to my destination. I will send through a family member. I also ask you for my family in the USA to support me. . . . Let me cross. Open the doors for me in the USA and blind La Migra. I ask you for a sign. I ask you to protect me from danger and evil. I am also asking you that the "guera" [a light-haired or light-skinned girl] helps me to immigrate, by softening her heart so she will help me, as well as my brothers . . . and that Sonia will never leave me and never get tired of me.[102]

This petitioner asks Juan Soldado not just to allow him to enter into the United States but to "open the doors . . . in the USA and blind La Migra"—an intervention more sophisticated than simply moving from one side of a border to the other. This is a request for Juan Soldado's help in navigating the intricate processes of finding a job without being identified or captured by government entities. The idea that La Migra must be "blinded" indicates the petitioner's awareness of the breadth of its surveillance and enforcement apparatus. He must evade not only the federal agents of ICE but city police officers, who under the 287(g) Secure Communities Program are allowed to function as immigration agents; he must also avoid the US biometric program's national database and the multiple checkpoints one encounters between Tijuana and cities like San Diego or Los Angeles.[103] Petitions like this manifest the real fears and struggles created by decades of anti-immigration policies, which have rendered the process of undocumented immigration increasingly dangerous, not only in terms of crossing the border but also for surviving once within the United States.

The petitioner asks the saint for one last miracle—that his romantic partner, Sonia, will "never leave and never get tired" of him. It is unclear if "guera" refers to Sonia or if they are two different persons. What is important here is his acknowledgment that the risks of migration are not simply legal: there are also emotional and interpersonal risks associated with separation, anxiety, and unfulfilled aspirations. As he migrates to the United States and Sonia either remains in Mexico or migrates with him, Rojas hopes that his family will remain stable and unified—an outcome that, given his knowledge of other families' fates, he likely realizes requires nothing short of a miracle. He also knows that he, most likely, will be unable to fulfill the manda and deliver on his promise of bringing a floral wreath for the saint in person (because it is difficult for undocumented migrants to move back and forth across the border)—but he pledges to find a way do so nonetheless, as if trying to force Juan Soldado to grant him this miracle. Indeed, the flowers are made contingent on the granting of the miracle. A family member living in Mexico will likely deliver the flowers on Rojas's behalf only after he arrives in Los Angeles and gives instructions. In a world in which he is so disadvantaged, the petitioner knows he needs to control all the details to ensure a positive outcome.

Social Vulnerability
Another difference between Valenzuela Arce's petitions from 1990–91 and those I found in 2013–15 lies in the complexity of issues related to social and economic vulnerability. Most petitions that Valenzuela Arce found focused on issues of health access, with the next most common plea being petitions for family members deployed in the first Gulf War:

Thank you very much, Brother Juan [Soldado], for the miracle that I so desperately asked you, to bring me my son safe and sound from war (of the Gulf), where his life was in danger. —Germán J.C.M.[104]

Thanks, Brother Juan Soldado, for letting me return from the war safe and sound. —Raúl Díaz[105]

Do not let a war that will cost thousands of lives to be unleashed; that our boy returns safe and sound. We pray this in the name of Jesus Christ. When our son returns, we will bring him here as testimony of gratitude. —Alfredo y Carmen Valdés, December 1990[106]

These petitions refer to the real threat posed by the Gulf War in the 1990s to Latinx families from the United States; there were far more Latinx soldiers in the US Army than the popular demographics would predict, and these families traveled to Mexico or had family members back home petitioning Juan Soldado for the safe return of their children. In contrast, the petitions that I documented in the mid-2010s have replaced the menace of the Gulf War with another kind of war, one defined by imprisonment, the housing crisis on both sides of the border, and the lasting effects of the 2008 economic recession. In both time periods, the petitions to Juan Soldado manifest the unique vulnerability of these communities in the face of changing threats.

Compared to the petitions quoted by Valenzuela Arce, the petitions I found focused much more on appeals related to imprisonment, with this category of appeals nearly tripling. As one mother, P.P., wrote in 2013, "Thank you Juan Soldado, for granting me the miracle that my son did not go to prison." Imprisonment affects entire families and creates long-term effects on communities of color. The survival of a prisoner's family cannot be taken for granted: in societies like the United States and Mexico, where wage disparity between men and women is the norm, the disproportionate imprisonment of men represents an overwhelming economic shock to their families, with lasting repercussions.[107]

This shock is evident in the following petition that I documented in 2013, in which the wife of an accused man asks Juan Soldado for her husband's freedom: "Juan Soldado, I come to ask you with all my heart to help my husband in this difficult case. You know he is innocent of what they accuse him of. Grant me the miracle of taking him out of prison tomorrow that is his court day, help him to make them all realize that he is innocent of what they are accusing him of. His daughters and I need him, do not forsake me." In this petition the circumstances of the man's arrest and the charges are unclear, but the petition expands our understanding of how Juan Soldado's followers construct him. What is important for the petitioner is her belief in her husband's innocence and her understanding that it will take a miracle to save him. She is all too aware that her own well-being and that of her daughters are tied to him. She knows life will be extremely difficult for her as a single mother, and she likely knows what a conviction would do to the family's future prospects. In the precarious economy of miracles, it is better to get him out of prison now than try to survive alone while he serves his sentence: one miracle granted today may save her from requesting more miracles in the future.

The recent housing crisis (2007–10) on both sides of the US-Mexico border also pervades the recent petitions to Juan Soldado. In one letter I documented in 2013, an anonymous petitioner simply attaches a picture of a home to the body of the saint's sculpture, with a note written on the back: "Thanks Juan Soldado, for the miracle of keeping my house." Nothing more is needed—the message is clear and direct. Those visiting the chapel understand the struggles of foreclosure: the agony of paperwork, phone calls, and litigation; the uncertainty of whether they will be able to stay in their homes or be forced to leave forever. For people who are unable to pay inflated mortgage rates and who are helpless against discriminatory housing practices and policies, owning a home and keeping it are miracles.[108]

Sometimes the recent petitions touch on all three of these major themes, revealing the intersectionality of oppression. As M.C.T. wrote in a letter I documented in 2013:

Dear brother
Juan Soldado. I ask you please
Grant me that I receive a Mica [US green card]
Heal my leg
Rent the houses in the Canyon and
Sell the house at Rosarito help me
Dear Juan Soldado,
Grant what I ask of you, please
And I promise you that I will bring you

Flowers and candles when
I receive my mica, thanks.

In this petition, health, immigration, and housing all come together, illustrating the compounding nature of oppression for those rendered vulnerable in multiple ways.

In other cases, the requests express local economic precarity more specifically in terms of work and business success, as in a 2013 petition written by Estéban Moya, owner of a sushi lounge in Tijuana, on the back of a bank receipt:[109]

> Help me with my restaurant, increase its sales, that we achieve many sales and that the people like the food and decide to come back. That we can restore our finances, that we can avoid closing the restaurant, and that we will always find the way to pay our debts . . . and that many customers will come. Let me resolve my debts in order to help my family. I feel so exhausted . . . and the sales have not improved.

In this desperate cry for help, we can read the effects of the economic downturn in the border community of Tijuana, whose economy depends on tourism from the United States. Moya's business sense—the understanding he displays of the importance of steady sales and their connection to food quality, customer satisfaction, and the restaurant's long-term survival—means little when tourists simply are not coming to town. Under the current political and economic conditions of Tijuana and the border region, inhabitants are virtually powerless to counter such broad structural constraints, let alone to create the conditions needed to attract tourists.

The petitions from the 2010s also include more requests for steady employment, registering the increasingly unstable and unpredictable conditions faced by workers in the twenty-first century. Petitions relating to finding, getting, and keeping a job recur again and again as aspirations associated with happiness and as elements necessary for the security of a family. As one petitioner, Carlos P., requested in 2013: "If you sent me lots of work, to distribute it to my family, they will have the money to buy their things." Here the head of household's request for work is inextricably linked to the well-being of everyone in the family. In another similar petition I found in 2013, Ricardo and Susana G.T. requested: "I ask you that I never lack work, so we can be very happy." The petitioners link job security to their happiness as a couple: for a working-class family, a job represents one of the most central elements for survival, and as these petitions show, stable work is far from guaranteed.

What emerges again and again in these petitions is the precariousness of their authors: their continual condition of being held hostage to forces well beyond their control. The structures and systems that determine people's fate—the job market, health care, the criminal justice system, global tourism—are vast and inaccessible, yet their effects on petitioners' everyday lives are all too tangible and oppressive. They are trying to exert some measure of control over these huge impersonal forces, but their only way to do it is to ask a saint to intervene, to perform miracles. Under these conditions, divine intervention may be the only way to survive.

Love and Family

For many immigrants, living along the border means being trapped in another precarious economy: that of viable romantic partners. One of the most unexpected and fascinating themes to emerge among the twenty-first-century requests is the appeal for Juan Soldado to help the petitioners find or keep romantic love and affection. The surprising thing about this is not that such appeals are made at all but that they are directed at Juan Soldado—in part because it violates the institutional Church's tradition of giving each official patron saint their own specific sphere of influence, and in part because of the specific devotions that have traditionally been associated with Juan Soldado, as well as his problematic history. In Latin America, there are other saints already charged with this type of romantic patronage, including the official Saint Anthony of Padua. In the US Catholic Church, Saint Anthony is a patron saint of lost things; perhaps the demand for love has simply outstripped the supply of saints to call upon.

The "partner recession" along the border is fueled by the rates of imprisonment for men of color, misrepresentations of Latinx women in a mainstream culture that describes them only as oversexualized objects or maids, the contradictions and tensions created by cultural shifts, and the shifting of expectations as people move to El Norte. Understandably, many believe that finding love under these conditions requires a miracle.

Saints are deeply linked with the desire for—and lack of—romantic love. A Spanish expression used to describe those who never marry is "Se quedó para vestir santos" (he or she stayed to dress saints), meaning that someone has been "left on the shelf"—they are still single, with few possibilities to get married because of advanced age. This phrase is applied to both male and females, but women are more frequently the target of this expression. In the deeply heteronormative Latino American context, this expression reflects a narrow misogynistic attitude of marriage. Reading these kinds of letters left to Juan Soldado, one gets an almost painfully personal glimpse into the romantic lives of those living along the border.[110]

Love and affection are so longed for—and so scarce and difficult to come by along the border, especially for migrants—that those pursuing them can turn to unconventional methods. We have learned lessons from the many folk stories about people getting *exactly* what they request, and in matters of love, the petitions to Juan Soldado in the 2010s suggest, it is imperative to be clear about what one wants. In one request I found, the petitioner sought to remove any doubt about the identity of the man she wanted by including with her request a picture of the man, a copy of his birth certificate issued by the Mexican government, and a detailed description of her situation. Another petitioner, Adriana Ramírez, likewise included a photograph in her 2013 petition and implored Juan Soldado, "Bring me this man, my dear Juan Soldado. I want a home, Dear Father." Ramírez's petition functions as a vignette of the intimate stories that define the border. She continues:

> Dear Juan Soldado, with all my heart I ask you to bring me this man. He is playing with me. I loaned him money when I did not have it. I helped him pay off his debts. He told me that he was going to move in with me. I waited and now he stopped talking to me. I stopped eating to give him my money and now look how he has repaid me. Dearest father, I ask you to make him call me, look for me, and to pay the money he owes me. Make him desperate day and night. Do not give him a job. Make him move in with me. I want a home, dearest sweetheart.

Ramírez describes not only her devotion to a man who has taken advantage of her but also her economic vulnerability. She demands love and affection in return for everything that she has done for this man—a kind of secular manda or contract that she feels has not been fulfilled. The debt in question is not just financial but social and emotional, and it cannot be repaid with money alone; she wants attention, companionship, recognition, and domesticity. Ramírez asks Juan Soldado not to let the man rest until he fulfills his obligation to live with her and build a home together. Ultimately, as this request shows, the line between material need and affective desire is as insubstantial and mobile as the border itself, for building a family along the border is both an emotional endeavor and an economic venture with clear consequences for survival.

A Homicide in Multiple Acts: Analysis of the Case of Olga Camacho

Certainly, as the diverse types of petitions I documented show, Juan Soldado has become in the public imagination a vernacular saint with multiple spiritual talents. But we must still ask: how is it that Olga Camacho was deleted from the religious consciousness of the community? How did Juan Castillo Morales become a vernacular saint, chosen by the people over Olga Camacho, despite his conviction for rape and murder? Why was Olga not considered deserving of vernacular sainthood herself? An analysis of this crime, and of the very different responses from the church to similar crimes, is essential in order to understand the implications of Olga's story (and those of other victimized women) within the larger narrative of the US-Mexico border. Together the crime and all the events surrounding it must be evaluated in the context of the sociopolitical conditions that produced the extreme vulnerability of women like Olga in the first place.

It is Thursday, September 20, 2018, and I am in Nettuno, Italy, in the Lazio region on the Mediterranean coast, visiting a sanctuary dedicated to Saint Maria Goretti—a beautiful church with stunning views of the Tyrrhenian Sea. The weather this afternoon could not be any better. Nettuno (which means "Neptune") is a small agricultural and fishing town located thirty-five miles from Rome, with a population of under fifty thousand inhabitants.

I had traveled to Rome a few days earlier to participate in an interreligious global discussion about immigration—a conference titled "Xenophobia, Racism, and Populist Nationalism in the Context of Global Migration." The conference was organized by the Vatican's Dicastery for Promoting Integral Human Development and the World Council of Churches, in collaboration with the Pontifical Council for Promoting Christian Unity—one of many new initiatives promoted by Pope Francis to address the global drama of migration. Earlier today, on the last day of the event, the conference participants had the chance to meet with the pope in a private audience. Now, in the afternoon, as I stand inside the sanctuary in Nettuno, I cannot put the many possibilities, tensions, and ambiguities within the Church out of my mind.

I think about the story of eleven-year-old Maria Goretti. Like Olga Camacho, she was just a child when she was murdered on July 6, 1902. Two years before her death, shortly after her impoverished family had relocated to share a house with another family, her father, a farmworker, died of malaria. On July 5, 1902, Maria was taking care of her younger sister alone, as her mother and older siblings worked in the fields. Alessandro, the twenty-year-old son of the other family living in the same building, had been interested in Maria for quite some time, but she had refused all his sexual advances. When she resisted him once again that afternoon, Alessandro stabbed Maria fourteen times before he escaped and left her to die. She was found, still alive, by her family and was taken to the local hospital, where she died the following day from her wounds. Alessandro was captured soon after and confessed to the crime. He was sentenced to thirty years in prison but was released after twenty-seven. During his imprisonment, Alessandro repented and turned to religion after having a vision of Maria in a dream. Once released, he visited Maria's mother, Assunta, who forgave him. Forty years after her death, Maria Goretti was canonized by Pope Pius XII on June 24, 1950. Over half a million people—including her surviving brothers and sisters, and her murderer—attended the ceremony at Saint Peter's Basilica. Eventually Alessandro entered a Franciscan Capuchin community as a lay brother; there he died peacefully twenty years later.

Saint Maria Goretti is one of the youngest Catholic canonized saints, and she is the patron saint of teenage girls and rape victims. My question is this: Why did Maria Goretti become a saint, but not Olga Camacho? The answer is complex, but it may rest on the patriarchy's overvaluing of virginity, which María Del Socorro Castañeda-Liles describes as the Catholic Church's "obsess[ion] with sanctifying virginity."[111] As Vanderwood explains, the idea is that "the rape deprived Olga of veneration"; in contrast, Saint Maria Goretti, who was killed for resisting rape, is framed as a virgin martyr.[112] It is telling that various news reports at the time tended to present Olga as "very friendly" and "coquettish, an impish, spirited youngster who encouraged attention"; Vanderwood says that she was also presented as "a spoiled girl who was not worthy of marriage or even acceptance."[113] Women and girls like Olga are reduced to collateral casualties of a culture that defines women as either virgins or available and loose. In this case, the line between the gendered vulnerability that exists at the border and the demonization of the entire region and the people who live there are both deeply muddy and toxic.

I relate Maria's story to highlight its contrast with that of Olga Camacho, who not only has not been recognized as an official saint but also has been virtually forgotten until only recently. How did the cultural and ecclesiastical emphasis on virginity play a role in rape victim Olga's non-eligibility for sainthood and her popular erasure? And what does this tell us about sexual violence against women along the border?

One of the main reasons that Olga became invisible is precisely the sexual nature of the crime committed against her, which under patriarchy is seen as compromising women's purity, and thus their value. Both Olga and Maria serve as prototypes in the policing and control of women's sexuality, with their paired but contrasting stories reinforcing the importance of virginity and the dangers of premarital sex. Rape becomes a central element of Olga's terrestrial struggles for spiritual recognition. She was born into a society where her sexuality and gender define the quality (or precariousness) of her life, her violent death, and her memory. As Alicia Gaspar de Alba and Georgina Guzmán explain, when thinking about social violence against women in the border town of Ciudad Juárez and elsewhere along the US-Mexico border, it is crucial to "examine the traditional machismo and misogyny that pervade social attitudes toward the victims."[114] The crimes against women that have been enacted in the border region are materializations of patriarchy.

As we contemplate the thousands of female lives lost and turned invisible by sexual violence along the border and around the world, we can see clearly that this system of oppression creates its female martyrs, saints, and subjects, who are held in a kind of purgatory—suspended in time as they wait for absolution or the resolution of the crimes against them. We see in these stories the unnecessary pain and suffering meant to control and subjugate. In this context, Olga Camacho—like the petitioners of Juan Castillo Morales in his reconstructed image as Juan Soldado—is reduced to a spectral life-in-suspension that is created by the insecurity, instability, uncertainty, and vulnerability of the border. As Hector Domínguez-Ruvalcaba and Ignacio Corona explain:

> Violence against women or sexual minorities is of course not a new phenomenon nor an uncommon one. It is particularly evident when patriarchal structures are stressed by fundamental changes in the social and economic framework that challenge their very existence. Amid the cultural conditions and socioeconomic developments of the [US-Mexico] border, there are thousands of young female workers drawn by the irresistible call

of job opportunities in the foreign-owned assembly plant called maquiladora [sweatshop].[115]

In other words, the violence against women in Juárez should be understood as an expression of the intimate connection between capitalism and misogyny, for profit is tied to the exploitation and sexualization of women. Furthermore, as Domínguez-Ruvalcaba and Corona explain, the gender-specific violence at the border responds to changes in capitalism's modus operandi, and sexual violence becomes one of the tools used to control and dominate an entire community.

In this context, Olga Camacho is the victim of a multiple homicides: the murder of her and of her memory—her story and its meaning. Juan Castillo Morales may have raped and killed her body, but multiple actors and conditions colluded in her other death. My point here is not to absolve Castillo Morales or anyone else of individual responsibility but rather to contextualize their actions within the history of the city, the region, and the two nations, Mexico and the United States. The acts of violence committed against Olga reflect a long history of varying forms of violence against women along the border; the violence associated with her memory, the attacks on her tomb and family, and her forced disappearance from popular memory must be understood as the manifestation of a type of crime that has been committed many times since her physical death.

If we analyze Olga's rape and murder within a system, rather than seeing these crimes solely as the actions of Juan Castillo Morales (or, as some speculate, General Contreras), then we find it easier to recognize the other players involved in the crime, which include the judicial system and the government's land and labor reforms. All of these are part of a matrix of power that has defined Olga's vulnerability and that of other women, including Maria Goretti. The killing of Olga must be understood within larger discourses about the violence imposed by patriarchy. Furthermore, this view allows us to recognize that the consequences of these events go beyond Olga's demise; they continue to reverberate today. When we consider an entire system as a killer, Olga's murder in the 1930s is connected with the long history of violence against women in the region since the colonial period, the more recent homicides of hundreds of women in Juárez since the 1990s, and the policies of labor exploitation created by the maquiladoras along the border today.

Olga is victimized and rendered invisible in direct and indirect ways. A disproportionate amount of the material about the case—both that printed in local newspapers at the time and contemporary research articles being published today—has emphasized Juan Castillo Morales's experience and ignored Olga altogether. These narratives center the men—either the various men involved in the event or Juan Soldado and how he was popularly canonized. In a sense, what we are dealing with is the tacit and insidious masculinization of history. This masculinization erases the women and girls in Olga's story, and in other stories of violence along the border, in multiple ways. In the tellings of these events, women are either explicitly excluded or relegated to secondary roles, there to support men—or, worst of all, blamed for their own fates.

All of these tactics of erasure are present in one way or another in the ways that Olga's case is narrated. As this chapter has shown, the modern result is a distorted, male-centered narrative that colludes in the same violence it recounts. A kind of double homicide victimizes so many border women, and this is made so clearly visible in the changes in Olga's story across time. This double homicide proceeds through four acts: institutionalization, domestic marginalization, demonization, and finally romanticization.

Act I: Institutionalization
In the case of Olga and of girls and women like her, male-centered narratives are normalized by the institutions involved with the crimes, which are not only sources of the violence experienced by these women but also history-keepers that perpetuate their domination through the ways they narrate certain events.

In Olga's case, the stories told by the military, police, labor unions, government officials, and even cemetery caretakers all reproduce a particularly narrow form of masculinity that is tailored to the border. The border generates discourses of masculinity that emphasize, for example, the cowboy, the soldier, the patrón. The hypervisibility of these narrow forms of heteromasculinity exemplifies a world managed by and centered on male domination—a world where this performance of gender is necessary to dominate the border itself, as a frontier. Most of the men in Olga's story are emblems of and instruments of patriarchy. Contreras, for example, is consistently presented as being in control of the city of Tijuana and the lives of its inhabitants. The other protagonists of the story are also men: the owner of the grocery store that Olga visited before her death, the police officers, the US detectives from San Diego, the city's medical examiners, those involved in the court-martial, and the members of the judicial system—as well as the union members involved in the labor disputes and in the subsequent revolts. Men guide the actual development of events and create the narratives around them, providing the recollections and interpretations that frame how the events are passed on. The assumptions and discourses of the narratives thus emphasize men and their perspectives, and as these narratives become normalized, Olga and the other women at the center of the crime (as victims or as witnesses to the crimes) are pushed to the periphery, reconstructed as supporting characters in the main story.

Act II: Domestic Marginalization
In the most popular narratives of Olga and Juan's story, women appear briefly and disappear quickly, both in the story of the crime itself and in the protests that ensued. Women support or corroborate the facts but never figure as active protagonists. This is the role played by Feliza Martínez de Camacho, Olga's mother; Meimi de Romero, the family's neighbor who found Olga's body; and Concha, Castillo Morales's girlfriend or common-law wife. All of these women appear briefly but are never allowed to carry the story themselves, despite their centrality to it. This secondary status is extraordinary, for these women are, respectively, the first to notice Olga's disappearance, the person who found Olga's body, and the witness who provided crucial incriminating information. Yet each of these women is disenfranchised in the narrative, reframed as occupying a space of mere domesticity and passivity.

Consider how public versus private spaces are gendered and how women and men are cast as very different kinds of actors in very different kinds of spaces. The men in this story are described as acting outside the home, actively protesting, negotiating, investigating, or working, while the women and girls in the story are described as generally remaining inside the house, cooking, taking care of children, crying, or protecting the house from external threats. Women's explorations in the outside world occur only sporadically, and when they do go outside the home, the journeys often end badly: Olga is raped and murdered, and Concha is presented as unfaithful for giving the police Juan's bloodstained clothes as evidence.

Olga's mother, in particular, bears the brunt of patriarchal disapproval of women playing an active role in events: she is usually represented as vulnerable, almost defenseless, and completely dependent on her family—first her husband and then, years later, on her adult children. Yet at the same time, narratives sometimes frame Olga's death as a case of maternal failure.

For example, the detail that Olga went to the grocery store because she did not like what her mother was making for dinner seems to indict the mother for spoiling her daughter, allowing Olga to demand something else, enabling the excursion that led to her death—and at the same time to indict Olga herself for being a brat. Both domestic discord and female passivity are vilified in this second stage of the story's violence.

Act III: Demonization
The story's third stage of violence is the demonization of the city of Tijuana as a hypersexual Latinx space of sexual deviancy and danger. Here the border is seen through the lens of the Black Legend, an anti-Latinx bias that characterizes places like Tijuana as sexually perverse and degenerate.[116] According to this enduring racialized mythology, in the depraved and deviant space of the border, crimes like Olga's rape and murder are commonplace, even expected. This bias appears even in quite recent scholarly work: for example, Vanderwood, writing about the case in 2006, describes Tijuana as a town that "had never been a calm, well-run community of inhabitants living a simple life. Just the opposite... it had courted the reputation of a wide open, rip-roaring tourist mecca where anything went and the good times rolled."[117] This narrative fits neatly within the long tradition of misrepresenting the border, including Tijuana, as a dangerous, uncivilized, and permanently wild frontier. The characterization of Tijuana as "sin city" flattens and oversimplifies the complex relations that constitute the US-Mexico border and serves to normalize the abnormal violence that occurs there.

Act IV: Romanticization
Paradoxically, the demonization stage gives way to another form of epistemic violence, equally dangerous: the romanticization stage, which insists that such acts of violence against women are unique, anomalous crimes. This final stage of the narrative presents the kidnapping, rape, and murder of Olga as an event that was uncommon, out of place, even extraordinary in the history of Tijuana and Baja California. This is the narrative strategy used to justify the protests that followed Olga's death, which are recast as the panicked reaction of the community to the extraordinary nature of the isolated crime, not as evidence of longer-term discontent with political and social conditions.

The rape and killing of Olga by a soldier in Baja California is in fact not anomalous but part of a long history of violence against women that preceded Olga and continues to this day. One of the problems with the romantic dehistoricization of sexual violence is that it presents a false version of reality, one that minimizes the everyday struggle endured by women and sexual minorities along the border.

In the fairytale version of the border, Tijuana appears almost idyllic, defined by past harmony and by balance without conflict. This vision is constructed via retellings of events that weave together nostalgic notions of the past with incomplete data. Importantly, this vision is not necessarily intentional or even conscious on the part of narrators. It may truly reflect the absence of sufficient information, as well as fact that sexual crimes tend to be underreported, especially given the social price paid by female victims. Even today, unmarried women who have been raped can be perceived as unclean and unsuitable for heterosexual marriage, and certainly they were perceived as such eighty years ago. When you add to this the normalization of hypermasculinity and the gendered camaraderie among soldiers and police forces, the romanticized belief that sexual crimes are rare is somewhat easier to understand.

In a 2005 interview with the daily newspaper *Frontera*, historian Lugo Perales—the former president of the Sociedad de Historia de Tijuana (Tijuana Historical Society)—offered some context for the case of Olga Camacho, noting that in 1938 "everyone knew each other, especially in the neighborhood where the girl lived." He noted that "from 1933 to 1938 only five sexual crimes were committed between San Diego and Tijuana" combined, and that "the city was so small that it was easy for the police to arrest suspects."[118] However, in his effort to avoid stereotypes of the border (and Tijuana in particular) as being especially violent, Perales, like many others, simplifies history and elides a pattern of violence against women.

All these processes, which converge to produce the multiple murders of Olga Camacho, have deep roots and enduring resilience in the region. Chicana historian Antonia Castañeda's research, for example, has uncovered a largely unexamined history of recurrent sexual assault and rape of women (especially indigenous women) by men in California during the eighteenth-century Spanish colonial period. As Castañeda explains, violence against women was a form of "sociopolitical terrorism and control" regularly perpetrated by soldiers, which functioned "as an institutionalized mechanism for ensuring [the] subordination and compliance" of the indigenous community under the Spanish Crown.[119] This pattern of violence was not hidden; it was well known not only to the regional California government but also to the official Spanish and Mexican establishments and to the ecclesiastical authorities in the Spanish colonies. As Castañeda explains, these sexual assaults were so frequent that Junípero Serra, the Spanish Franciscan and founder of the missions in California (Serra was, controversially, canonized as a Catholic saint in 2015), asked the governor of California, Felipe de Neve, in 1771 to restrict the transit of soldiers outside quarters and their access to the indigenous villages.[120] But just as Olga is erased from the story of her own murder, so too is this part of California history. It remains largely unknown, drowned out by celebrations of male conquest and achievement—dynamics that are still in play in the present day.

In the years leading up to the disappearance of Olga Camacho, there was a series of murders targeting women and girls in California's San Diego County.[121] These cases, and many others like them, bely claims that attacks on women and girls were (and are) unusual in the region. Indeed, looking to the present day, we find that this violence has only been amplified by the changes along the border and in US-Mexico relations in the last half of the twentieth century: increasing gender exploitation, urban segregation, labor access, and wage dependency. Within this context—the historical denial of the consistent violence experienced by women throughout the region—we can begin to see that the community's eventual sanctification of Juan Castillo Morales into Juan Soldado expresses the epistemic violence that enables the erasure of physical violence against women. This same impulse has made it possible to erase and ignore the 1990s explosion in the number of women killed along the border.

Many More Olgas: Femicides and Labor Along the Border

> In recent times a street rumor has begun that the girl Olga, "Santa Olguita," has started to do miracles and apparitions. . . . The new border mythology, it is just beginning.
> —Heriberto Yépez, *Tijuanologías*

In the years following Olga Camacho's rape and murder, the US-Mexico border was deeply affected by changes wrought by World War II, the subsequent Cold War, and the emergence of neoliberal policies that restructured labor and land ownership in the region. One of the most significant transformations experienced along the border during the second half of the twentieth century—one that disproportionately affected women—was the emergence of maquiladoras as the main source of employment in the region.

Maquiladoras are a type of assembly factory along the US-Mexico border that primarily employs women. These entities enjoy unique tax exemptions and freedom from regulation by the Mexican government. They came to exist in their modern form in 1964, at the end of the twenty-two-year Bracero Program, which allowed temporary, low-wage Mexican contract laborers, mainly farmworkers, to work legally in the United States in order to address the manual labor shortage created by World War II and its aftermath. The Bracero Program was born from a series of bilateral agreements between the United States and Mexico, in particular the signing of the 1942 Mexican Farm Labor Agreement. After the Bracero Program ended in 1964, maquiladoras, most of which were owned by US corporations, were developed to generate jobs for all those returning to Mexico from the United States. Maquiladoras are a global manufacturing venture, and they work on the premise of expendable labor as corporations relocate across borders to places where labor is cheaper. Under Mexican law, maquiladoras can be fully supported by external capital investment, and they can import materials, equipment, and technology into Mexico tax- and duty-free.

To understand the violence experienced by women along the border in the last decades, one must know how heavily maquiladoras rely on female manufacturing labor and must understand how the murders of women are interconnected with larger social issues in the region and around the globe. As Elvia Arriola argues, "Gender abuse and violence, corporate power and indifference, and government acquiescence come together. . . . [along the border to] produce an environment hostile to women and hospitable to the rise of maquiladora murders."[122] Most female victims of border violence are maquiladora workers and most of their bodies are found near factories, but the connection between femicides and the proliferation of maquiladoras is even broader: maquiladoras simply exemplify the way that socioeconomic conditions along the border frame women as disposable commodities. Maquiladoras place women at the bottom of the hierarchical production line, exacerbating the traditional gendered division of labor that places men at the top of the decision-making and salary chain.[123] It is in this context that we can understand the massacre of women as a byproduct of capitalist expansion, exemplified by the maquiladora industry.

The thread that connects the rape of women during colonial times in California to the murder of Olga Camacho and to the femicides in Ciudad

Juárez is the consistent, long-lasting war against women and against peasants—a war that is linked to the constant resignification of capitalism in the region. As Silvia Federici explains in her book *Caliban and the Witch: Women, the Body, and Primitive Accumulation*, gender, race, and age are intimately connected to the creation and perpetuation of a proletarian class: the persecution of women and the perpetuation of slavery are "central aspect[s] of the accumulation and formation of the modern proletariat."[124] In many ways, the experiences of the women in Ciudad Juárez and other border towns echo the experiences of earlier generations: maquiladoras, like the factories of the Industrial Revolution, represent new forms of wage slavery that are enforced by violence. The rape and murder of women in Ciudad Juárez can be understood as part of a global project of violence meant to ensure the success of the new system of exploitation imposed by late-stage capitalism. The emergence of maquiladoras in the north of Mexico cannot be disassociated from the privatization of land in the south: one feeds the other as part of the same machinery of exploitation.

These multiple layers of violence converge in the community, creating new phantasmagoric forms of unnatural violence and forcing the social body of the border into a type of decomposition. To explain the magnitude of the violence experienced, new fantastic hero metaphors come alive. This is, as we have seen, the source of the emergence of Juan Soldado; he is a response to the multiple intensifying types of violence experienced by border subjects—economic, social, bureaucratic. As the next section shows, another fantastic hero figure has recently emerged specifically in response to the exponential rise in violence against women. This violence against women is not accounted for in the figure of Juan Soldado; indeed, as we have seen, Juan Soldado's narrative participates in this violence against women. The invisibility of Olga's kidnapping, rape, and murder is an example of the deeply patriarchal patrón politics that regulate the construction of history in the region, as well as the normalization of silence around the homicide of women.

The following section traces the popular effort that has emerged in the last decade of the twentieth century in Tijuana to recognize, resurrect, and sanctify Olga Camacho as Santa Olguita. These attempts not only seek to shift the narrative surrounding Olga's death but also to inscribe new epistemic values and meanings about the oppression, subjugation, and historical degradation experienced by women in Tijuana and along the border.

Figure 2.8 Santa Olguita prayer card.
Photo archive, El Colegio de la Frontera Norte, Tijuana, Mexico

The Making of Santa Olguita: #NiUnaMás and the Drama of Forcing Her Out of the Shadows

The ambiguities surrounding the assassination (physical and historical) of Olga Camacho persist today, even in the attempts to bring her justice. In the early 2000s, Heriberto Yépez, a controversial Tijuana artist, activist, and writer of the US-Mexico border culture, has used various means—such as producing and distributing prayer cards (see Figure 2.8)—to campaign for Olga to be recognized as a popular vernacular saint, prodding people to "remember that at one time there were miracles attributed to her."[125] Yépez recounts a particular early episode that inspired him. Around 1996 or 1997, he overheard two women talking on a bus in Tijuana:

> [One of the women said they] should look for the grave of the girl (Olga Camacho) and leave some flowers to her ... [in order to petition her] for her daughter as she was going to cross to the other side [to the United States]

and she did not want her daughter to suffer anything from the immigration agents, the Mexican police, and those assaulting mojados [undocumented immigrants] or the heartless polleros [smugglers].[126]

The encounter showed Yépez that some women, at least, were already remembering and venerating Olga privately, and it inspired him to try to rescue the memory of Olga Camacho—to more broadly challenge her invisibility within Mexico's spiritual canon, which, given the country's "clear tendency to adore virgins," he sees as a function of the contradictions and tensions raised by the case of a "raped virgin."[127]

As Yépez sees it, Olga is not currently recognized as a popular spiritual benefactor because of a series of historical and sociological factors. The first factor, according to him, was her family's immediate resistance in 1938 to creating any ties between the memory of Olga and the already emerging veneration of Juan Soldado. This emotional reaction is understandable—few parents would want their murdered child associated with their killer—and, as we have seen, artist Alma López had a similar reaction when she learned the story, refusing to hang her *Juan Soldado* piece next to her *Santa Niña de Mochis* piece without her image of Our Lady of Guadalupe interposed between them. According to Yépez, the Camacho Martínez family was rejecting this real and imagined proximity to the emerging saint when they moved Olga's remains to a new location, far from the chapel of Juan Soldado. Yépez's version makes no reference to the harassment of the Camacho Martínez family by Juan Soldado's followers, or to the real implications of asking Olga's family to affiliate themselves with the main suspect in the rape and killing of their daughter. Yépez's version frames Olga's family as responsible for her erasure from history, ignoring the effects of patriarchal systems of oppression and domination that drove the elevation of Juan Soldado and the accompanying erasure of Olga—yet another instance of male violence against the victim.

Yépez also attributes responsibility for Olga's disappearance to the people who have chosen to tell the story of Juan Soldado uncritically, without reference to Olga. He notes the "neglectfulness of journalists [and] researchers" in not seeking to "change the legend or bring into light his connection to the rape of a girl."[128] He also blames those "profiting from Juan Soldado," arguing that including Olga within the popular narration of Juan Soldado's sainthood and martyrdom would compromise the marketing of Juan Soldado and thereby damage the revenues of the many merchandise vendors and service providers who have benefited from his informal sanctification. Yépez notes that vendors around the chapel refuse to sell prayer cards dedicated to Olga Camacho, and indeed that such prayer cards have been removed from the chapel when found, because Juan Soldado's sainthood is so directly linked to belief in his innocence—a narrative that silences Olga's own innocence.

Yépez recognizes how important popular practices of piety are to the emergence and perpetuation of religiosity writ large. With this in mind, in 2002 Yépez started a "playful project of vindication" meant to kickstart popular veneration of Olga and thus restore her to visibility.[129] In what Rafa Saavedra defines as a clear example of "culture jamming of the story of Santa Olguita," Yépez decided to actively intervene in multiple events commemorating Juan Soldado in Tijuana in 2002. During the celebrations, Yépez enlisted the help of graphic artists Mónica Arreola and Melisa Arreola to create and distribute more than a thousand Santa Olguita prayer cards that included the image of Olga and a prayer. Yépez called the project "interventionist art."[130]

In the bizarre alchemy that defines the border experience, and especially the case of Olga Camacho, Yépez's intervention is particularly intriguing and somewhat troubling. He himself has been a controversial subject, criticized by both literary and feminist circles for his male-centered analyses of the border and his overemphasis on Tijuana's depiction as exotic, outcast, and non-normative.[131] These critiques of his work make his investment in Olga's sanctification even more intriguing, and serve as another reflection of the ambiguities of the border.

The prayer cards' text immediately made clear the deeply political connotations of any popular sanctification of Olga; the Arreolas' work reframes Olga Camacho as Santa Olguita, a vernacular saint capable of granting miracles as well as a "fighter for social causes, patroness against urban violence, anti-Yankee avenger, a friend of children, of women, and all those who have suffered physical or sexual abuse, and the advocate soul for the forgotten (like her)."[132] The description unapologetically contextualizes her veneration within the reality of oppression experienced by everyone along the border, and in particular by women. Here, Olga comes back not as an innocent and vulnerable eight-year-old girl but as an avenger and seeker of justice for those most vulnerable in the region. The new Santa Olguita is an active mobilizer for social change, an example of the militant nature of religiosity. This resurrected Olga understands the connections between urban violence and the physical and sexual abuse of women at the intersections of class and gender along the US-Mexico border.

In this context, the emergence of Santa Olguita is not coincidental; the narrative she incarnates, as a new border saint, is neither about victims' "passivity" and helplessness nor about their responsibility for their own victimhood (which is implied by the official sanctification of Saint Maria Goretti, who was murdered because she fought off her rapist and was thus seen as blameless—a virgin saint). This Santa Olguita is an active fighter against patriarchal violence. As a cultural object that Yépez designed in order to create social transformation, Santa Olguita resurrects the collective pain that haunts the border, resisting the effects of normalized kidnapping and rape and bringing to light the voices and stories of the victims of patriarchal violence. Santa Olguita is also an "anti-Yankee avenger" because she recognizes and symbolically resists the effects of economic exploitation by the United States in the region—and, by extension, the exploitation carried out by the various governments in Mexico, which have enabled and even invited US exploitation in the form of maquiladoras. This new Olga, created by the Arreola sisters and Yépez, has been resurrected to do miracles, very unique ones defined by the legacies of colonial oppression. This is particularly evident in the prayer on the 2001 Santa Olguita prayer card:

> Magnificent Holy Girl
> Praised be your soul
>
> Daughter, protect us from injustice.
> Girl, protect us from the police.
> Protect us from being blamed
> for the crimes of the powerful.
> Don't let us end up in jail
> for the crimes of others.
>
> Protect us from politicians,
> look after all children,
> women and the vulnerable.
> Help us find
> our lost children.
>
> Look after our body
> Don't let it be subject to abuse
> and don't lead us into oblivion.
>
> Praise be to you, Olguita, pure and blessed.[133]

The prayer obliquely yet unmistakably alludes to the unique circumstances that surround Olga Camacho's rape and murder and the sequence of events that followed, the suspects in the crime, and the possible cover-up. The reference to being "blamed / for the crimes of the powerful" and wrongly imprisoned acknowledges the potential innocence of Juan Castillo Morales, but the other parts of the prayer visualize Olga as a spiritual benefactor protecting those whose vulnerability mirrors her own. The prayer refers to politicians, the police, and the powerful—all arms of the state and existing networks of power that deliver injustice and harm. The intended audience for the veneration of Olga is precisely those who are excluded from these powerful groups, both men and women. Yet the prayer's exhortation to protect "our body" from abuse reminds petitioners specifically of Olga's suffering. In the prayer, Olga's kidnapping, rape, and murder are not forgotten; they define Santa Olguita and make her the perfect figure to fight back against crimes committed against children, women, and others who are vulnerable. She is invoked to protect the bodies of the abused and to ensure they are not forgotten.

The prayer cards were envisioned as an "art-cult [project] with enough public reach to spread the story that that Santa Olguita has returned to do miracles."[134] Yépez's intervention seeks to use grassroots practices of piety to resituate a forgotten figure in the popular imagination as an active "agent of history"—an attempt that in itself reveals the power of these vernacular saints, and their power to reflect their followers' needs, fears, and vulnerabilities.[135] In this case, Yépez and the Arreolas deliberately deployed the same mechanisms that were used to popularize Juan Soldado to (re)introduce Olga into the spiritual pantheon of border saints, thereby contesting the corrosive effects of patriarchy. The prayer cards meld art and religiosity, linking the work of mythmaking to the conditions that circumscribe people's lives along the border.

However, the intervention did not seem to catch on in the popular imagination or gain many supporters. As Vanderwood explains, "Many did not recognize her as the victim," and the project seems "not to have stimulated any devotion to Olga or around much interest in that possibility."[136] It is still unclear how people in Tijuana have responded to this project overall—although it is too early to fully assess, and it is still possible that it will catch on. Nevertheless, Yépez and the Arreola sisters' reconstruction and elevation of Olga Camacho as Santa Olguita is a provocative experiment that reveals how communities appropriate and create memories, integrating new spiritual players into their faith cosmologies. It points to the emancipatory and transformative possibilities of the spiritual entities created and used by marginalized communities to respond to their difficult realities. As Yépez explains, Olguita's veneration is deeply rooted in the changes experienced by Tijuana since the turn of the twenty-first century, which is witnessing many of the same problems and popular responses that were happening when Olga was killed. Yepez points out that now, as before, "popular movements in the city" are growing out of protests over expropriated land, as disenfranchised people squat on unowned land (participating in "the invasion of the hills in order to have a parcel") and "the sweatshops . . . replace the casinos and racetracks as the architecture and economic paradigm of the city." As he points out, the same "magical thinking, however, continues intact" from this earlier period. Like Juan Soldado in the 1930s, he says, Olga in the 2020s can become a saint who reflects the needs and desires of Tijuana: "'Santa Olguita' has started to do miracles and apparitions. The new border mythology, it is just beginning."[137] As Yépez argues, under the urban and socioeconomic crisis experienced by Tijuana—where squatting becomes the only way to obtain a plot of land, and where labor exploitation is sanctioned by the state—Santa Olguita emerges as a new saint for a new Tijuana, putting an alternative spin on the events of the 1930s and their players: a history of violence that continues to repeat itself with new forms of institutionalized greed.

Olga's family remains uninterested in her sanctification. According to Vanderwood, they see the project by Yépez as "unwarranted meddling."[138] Nevertheless, Olga Camacho is a figure for the women along the border and the many other women affected by sexual harassment and violence who are refusing to be invisible. This movement is manifested in part by the larger #NiUnaMás (#NotOneMore) movement, a Mexican precursor of the #MeToo and #TimesUp movements responding to the incredibly high rates of femicide in the country: the movement demands that "not one more" woman be murdered in Mexico.

Perhaps the so-called resurrection of Santa Olguita responds more to the remarketing of suffering and the consumption of pain than it does to any real investment in Olga's memory or a wish to prevent more killings. Certainly the forces stretching the social fabric of Tijuana today are not so different from those eighty years ago. Urban explosion, unemployment, and social precariousness remain as powerful as ever—indeed, perhaps more powerful, for they are now amplified by the war on drugs, the economy of exploitative labor by maquiladoras, the most recent economic downturn, and the xenophobic policies of the contemporary United States around immigration and labor. As the monstrous conditions of neoliberal capitalism continue to evolve, new forms of divine intervention are required.

Border Hauntings and Uncanny Revenges

As shown in this chapter, the events surrounding the deaths of Olga Camacho and Juan Castillo Morales during the turbulent year of 1938 in the border town of Tijuana were marked by sociopolitical and economic unrest, defined by the effects of Prohibition, the Great Depression, and the post-Revolution years in Mexico. Certainly, the protests after the rape and murder of Olga Camacho represent an important example of community action and social agency: residents were responding both to a grievous act of violence and to the precarious status created by the closure of casinos, the agrarian reforms of the period, and Tijuana's explosive urban growth. The burning of offices that held government records about the casino closure legal disputes was no coincidence. It was a desperate move to prevent governmental retaliation and, at least for a moment, to correct wrongdoings and do justice. In the retelling of these events, both remembering and forgetting are equally essential, as the continuity of the revolts is overlooked or made invisible.

But we must recognize that beyond these protests and demonstrations, there are other forms of agency involved in the creation and perpetuation of spiritual forms like Santa Olguita and the problematic Juan Soldado. As vernacular saints, they embody the anxieties and preoccupations of their time, and they help the community negotiate the constant transformation and contradictions of its environment. From the monstrous and incoherent conditions created by exploitation and subjugation, Juan Soldado emerges as a saint and Olga Camacho disappears.

Juan's and Olga's entangled yet disparate histories illustrate the complexities and violences in the region that are created by poverty and the precarious disparities of power. At one level, these histories describe the killing of an innocent child and the injustices of a judicial system guided by a patrón power structure. At another level, they document a larger massacre: the systematic rape, killing, and disappearance of women along the border—a pattern that started many years before the events of 1938 and continues to this day. Olga's death at the hands of a member of the military, and the local authorities' subsequent inability or unwillingness to enact justice, is but one case in a long trajectory of femicides in the region. Her double homicide, real and then spiritual, reveals the intimate connection between assaults on women's bodies and the perpetuation of structures of power that benefit men, as exemplified by the involvement of the military and the disengagement of the judicial system and the local government.

Despite their many contradictions, the rewritings of the stories of Olga Camacho and Juan Castillo Morales demonstrate the sophistication with which communities are able to summarize, decipher, and unfortunately also reproduce the dramatic and violent atrocities of the region. Certainly Olga Camacho's and Juan Castillo Morales's deaths have not been resolved. As a product of the ongoing struggles of patriarchy, the crimes against Olga remain open questions, still begging for solutions. Her memory and soul—and in some ways also Castillo Morales's—have been detained at the border and kept in the limbo of the desert.

Olga's and Juan's tragedies are kept alive and relevant by the unresolved dramas and the stories of oppression experienced by their followers. As faithful traveling specters for the border communities of Baja California, these vernacular saints reflect the vulnerability created by family separation, disparities in health and access to healthcare, job insecurity, housing dispossession, police brutality, racism, misogyny, and the patrón politics that govern the region. To what extent were the protests of 1938 about Olga's crime, and to what extent were they about the community's desperation for existence in the face of colonial policies enacted by both Mexico and the United States? We may never know. The dramas that emerged between agraristas and casino workers, and between CTM and CROM, were in part imposed and staged from the outside, as the system pitted the two sides against each other. In this sense Olga and Juan mirrored the tensions of the nation at that time.

My reading of these stories seeks to highlight the moments of remembering and forgetting that are so essential to the (re)telling of a legend and the construction of vernacular saints. The point is not what really happened, but why the stories are so unstable—and why the events they narrate are as relevant today as they were in 1938. Olga's and Juan's stories, and the story of the aftermath of their collision, shed light on the intersection between capitalist transformation and violence against women. The crimes against Olga Camacho undeniably reveal the known long-term effects of misogyny and its intersections with religiosity, as well as what is missing and unresolved. The contradictions and holes in the narrative, the nontransparency of the judicial process, the handling of evidence, and the delivery of verdicts all manifest the deep complicity of power in the patrón ruling structure at the border, where the military and the government are fused. Juan Soldado, the vernacular saint, is about border violence condensed, elevated to sainthood. It is about the atrocities experienced by women, and the conditions that continue to allow these atrocities to take place today. Both border saints inhabit a different space and time outside the traditional bureaucracies of state and Church control, thereby eluding the control of any authorities or official powers. Like many of their petitioners, both saints now navigate a liminal space of insecurity, instability, and uncertainty. But they also navigate a space in which everything is possible, where the ambiguity and absurdity of border violence are managed, and where seemingly divine intervention is essential for everyday survival.

As border subjects, Olga and Juan move across and beyond nation-state boundaries. Both of them are buried within a mile of the actual US-Mexico border. Although their bodies are trapped on the Mexican side, the story of Juan Soldado—and the story of Olga that it hides within itself—has spread throughout both Mexico and the United States. They are traveling saints. They relive, through the melodramas of their followers, their own unresolved, interwoven histories.

On one hand, the story of Olga Camacho and Juan Soldado demonstrates the sophistication of cultural border productions and how they capture and contest the atrocities and violence of the region. On the other, the story reproduces over and over the murder of Olga and the patriarchal disparity of power. How and whether either vernacular saint will survive, and how their stories will continue to change, remain to be seen. More importantly, the story of how Olga Camacho has been rendered invisible and the crimes against her have been normalized, while Juan Soldado has emerged as a vernacular saint, calls attention to the deep interconnection of religiosity and the male-centered structures of power that work along the border and at large. Olga's absence from her own story shows how religiosity can participate in and perpetuate violence against women. Today the story of Olga Camacho is about her, but it is also about the hundreds of women who, like her, have been killed and erased from history.

Saint Toribio Romo:
Racialized Border Miracles

3

3
Saint Toribio Romo

Racialized Border Miracles

In November 2016, just before Election Day in the United States, emotions and anxieties were running high among the members of the parish of Saint Agnes of Bohemia in Chicago. Their old chapel, across from the main church, was to serve as a polling place for this predominantly Latinx community. Saint Agnes is in the barrio of La Villita, the self-declared Mexican capital of the Midwest, and one of the larger Latinx enclaves in the region. In the lead-up to the election, the old chapel became a nonstop prayer site, where people constantly recited rosaries for the election.

In those months Saint Agnes also served as a meeting place for the Society of Saint Toribio Romo (SSTR), an organization dedicated to helping Latinx immigrants. The SSTR was created in 2012 after an earlier Toribio Romo Immigration Center—an initiative created by the Archdiocese of Chicago in 2009 to attend to the legal needs of the city's growing immigrant communities—closed its doors due to lack of funding.[1] SSTR is made up of eight Catholic parishes around the Chicago metropolitan area. The SSTR alternates locations for its gatherings, on the first Thursday of the month, between Saint Agnes and the parish of the Good Shepherd. Meetings involve prayer and spiritual instruction. The group also organizes community town halls, spiritual fasts, and social actions in favor of comprehensive immigration reform.[2]

Concepción Rodríguez, the president of SSTR, says that this lay organization was created to "accompany . . . the most vulnerable, the immigrant."[3] As Rodríguez explains, SSTR is inspired by the Catholic ethos of society's interconnection as "one single body," unified mystically with Christ in the Eucharist.[4] According to Rodríguez, because immigrants are the most vulnerable members of this social, communal body of Christ, the SSTR feels responsible for their well-being, for everyone in the social body is affected by what happens to one of their members.

During the 2016 US election cycle, the SSTR made outreach not to recent immigrants (its usual audience) but to US citizens whom it could register to vote. The group's slogan is "Tu voto es poder. Hazlo por mi" (Your vote is power. Do it for me), and as SSTR member Rita Aguilar explains, "We know that it's important to get out and vote . . . [and] those who cannot vote need the voices and the votes of those who can vote."[5] Since starting this initiative, they have registered hundreds of new voters.

The group's voter drive, a seemingly purely political action, was always also a religious one—as can be seen in the fact that before embarking on this mission to register voters, members of SSTR met at Saint Agnes to be blessed by the pastor (Figure 3.1). In theory, the lay, nonprofit SSTR is a nonpartisan organization, but during the 2016 election it joined other religious groups and communities who were mobilizing people to go from church pews to the polls. In an election period plagued by extreme anti-immigrant language and divisive xenophobic sentiments, fears of a wall between the US-Mexico border and the prospect of mass deportations of Latinxs led many to feel that divine intervention was necessary. They turned to Saint Toribio Romo.

Figure 3.1 Members of the Society of Toribio Romo, Chicago. The society members are receiving a blessing at St. Agnes of Bohemia in Little Village, Chicago.
Photo: Alex Ortiz/MEDILL

Unlike the vernacular saints examined in the preceding chapters, Saint Toribio Romo is an official saint of the Catholic Church, but he, like these other saints, is a patron of the border. Canonized by Pope John Paul II in 2000, he is deeply linked to the politics of immigration between Mexico and the United States. Father Toribio Romo was a Mexican Catholic priest who was killed, according to official accounts, by government troops in 1928 in the state of Jalisco, Mexico, during the anticlerical conflict known as the Cristero War.[6] As this chapter exposes, Father Romo was in fact killed by someone else, but the truth has been kept secret by the Vatican and the local church.

Since the 1970s many undocumented immigrants have reported seeing his spirit along the US-Mexico border, assisting those in distress by providing water, food, transportation, and even money. Often described as "a man dressed in black, who appears out of nowhere to offer [migrants] a ride in his pickup," the helpful stranger asks only that the travelers visit him in his home village of Santa Ana in Jalisco when they can.[7] When they do so, the hopeful migrants see his picture at the town's main church, find out his name is Father Toribio Romo, and learn that he was killed in 1928. Since his canonization, several American and Mexican newspapers—including the *New York Times* (2002), the *Arizona Republic* (2002), the *Dallas Morning News* (2006), the *Chicago Tribune* (2008), and the Mexican newspaper *Excelsior* (2012)—have reported multiple cases of undocumented immigrants surviving in the Sonoran Desert after receiving help from the spirit of Saint Toribio Romo. Today, he is known as El Santo Pollero (the Holy Coyote), the Holy Smuggler, or the smuggler saint.

At the individual level, Toribio thus serves as an important figure for migrants who must negotiate the strict, often deadly migration policies in the United States. At the institutional level, he is also a key figure in the transformation of the Catholic Church's approach to immigration in Mexico, and his increasing visibility and importance within the church reflect the deep demographic shifts experienced by the Catholic Church in the United States in the last decades. Veneration of Saint Toribio (who was canonized in 2000) rapidly increased after the terrorist events of September 11, 2001, in response to an increase in xenophobic policies and an intensification of the already vitriolic anti-immigrant rhetoric in the United States.[8] Since 2001, many Catholic immigration centers in the United States have changed their names to reflect Toribio's growing importance and popularity.[9] His fame as a pro-immigrant benefactor, as a saint of vernacular piety, and as a transnational spiritual political figure is intimately connected to the historical context surrounding his martyrdom: the Cristero War and the unique place occupied by Jalisco in the history of migration from Mexico into the United States. Migration, anthropologist Alejandra Aguilar Ros argues, is "part of what has constituted the history and regionalization of Los Altos [de Jalisco], but also the transnational circuits of religious practices."[10] Saint Toribio occupies an analogous place in the history of mobility across borders: like Jalisco itself, he exists at the intersection of US and Mexican policies of labor mobilization and religiosity in the twentieth and twenty-first centuries.

Toribio's popularity as a saint cannot be disassociated from the process of migration, which is deeply linked to his region of origin. Jalisco has long been one of the top states from which Mexican migrants originate. Migration from the west-central region of Mexico, where Jalisco is located, peaked in the late 1970s, when it accounted for 60 to 70 percent of all migrants from Mexico.[11] Certainly the origin of migrants has expanded to include other states, yet Jalisco remains a central contributor to the influx into the United States.[12]

Toribio's popularity is also intextricably linked to the events of the Cristero War; as Julia G. Young, a historian of migration and Catholicism in the Americas, puts it, his popularity is deeply rooted in "devotion to the memories, myths and martyrs of the Cristero War."[13] Young notes that these two elements—the connection of Jalisco to migration and the Cristero War—have left an enduring mark on Mexican migrants to the US since the 1920s: "The geographic and temporal connections between Mexican migration and the Cristero War meant that most Mexicans in the United States during the 1920s and 1930s had been impacted in some way by the conflict: many fled Mexico as a direct result of the Cristero War, and even those who had left beforehand had friends and family who were involved."[14] Even today, she says, "many Mexican migrants still come from the same west-central region where the war was most intensely fought."[15] Furthermore, Young says, "the children and grandchildren of Cristeros and their opponents continue to migrate.... Thus, it is likely that many of the recent emigrants from this region have encountered the images and symbols of the Cristero War—including, possibly, the image of Santo Toribio."[16] Here Young explains the intimate connection between immigration and the translocation of local venerations outside their original region, but this leaves unanswered the question of why Toribio, out of all the Cristero martyrs from the region, became so popular.

This chapter begins by explaining the historical context of the Cristero War and the events of Toribio's death, canonization, and emergence into the popular imagination as the Holy Smuggler. Toribio's canonization and the politics surrounding that decision illuminate the post-1980s US Catholic Church's struggle to deal with the major demographic and religious shifts generated by the huge influx of new Catholic Latinx immigrants, many of them undocumented. I show how Toribio's veneration has accrued a specific sociopolitical meaning, one that emerged through the circulation of Toribian relics throughout the United States in the form of bone fragments—a practice that began in 2014. As I show, these relics, and Toribio himself, have become an expression of popular resistance and religious-political mobilization in the campaign for comprehensive immigration reform. The chapter ends by exploring the evolution of El Santo Pollero within the context of the neoliberal practices of the US government and the Catholic Church as they intersect with the politics of faith migration, especially in two different sites in the United States: Detroit, Michigan, and Tulsa, Oklahoma. A postscript examines new and crucial revelations about the real killer of Saint Toribio Romo.

The Cristero War: The State Seeks to Establish an Alternative Church After a Land Revolt

On the evening of Saturday, February 21, 1925, a Spanish priest named Manuel Luis Monge and a group of armed men styling themselves the Knights of the Order of Guadalupe entered the Catholic church of La Soledad, one of the oldest parishes in Mexico City. The church lay in the working-class barrio of La Merced, in what used to be an indigenous settlement. That evening, the worshipers and the clergy were gathered in the church to celebrate eight o'clock Mass. The knights forced everyone to leave the premises and publicly installed a priest, José Joaquin Pérez Budar, as head patriarch of the newly constituted Iglesia Católica Apostólica Mexicana (ICAM, or Catholic Apostolic Church of Mexico)—an alternative to the traditional Catholic Church that had long dominated Mexico's religious life.[17] When Monge tried to return and celebrate Mass the following day, riots broke out at the church. Firefighters and police were called, and during the confrontation, many were injured and one person was allegedly killed.[18]

Among the group of interlopers who installed Budar was Ricardo Treviño, general secretary of the Confederación Regional Obrera Mexicana (CROM, the Regional Conference of Mexican Workers), the most powerful syndicate of Mexican workers at that time—a group that, you may remember, would go on to play a large role in the events surrounding Juan Castillo Morales's 1938 death in Tijuana and his transformation into Juan Soldado, as discussed in Chapter 2.[19] CROM and ICAM were intimately linked; a few years earlier, in 1921, the Catholic Church in Mexico had declared membership in CROM to be a mortal sin. However, this declaration did not prevent people from joining the organization, which by the time of the La Soledad conflict was at the peak of its power.[20] The attack on La Soledad was an expression of the state's hostility toward the Catholic Church, which came to a head under the presidency of Plutarco Elías Calles (1924–28), who considered the Church to have too much political power and to be too involved in Mexico's secular affairs. Calles was a general in the Mexican Revolution. During the conflict, the Catholic Church not only seemed to be an ally of the ruling class but was itself one of the largest landowners in the nation. At the time of these events, CROM and the Mexican government were working together. The rupture between them would happen a decade later, leading to the 1936 creation of the progovernment alternative union federation, the Confederación de Trabajadores de México, or CTM (Confederation of Mexican Workers).

ICAM was thus part of an elaborate plan by the ruling Mexican government to create a Catholic Church independent from the Holy See in Rome. Eventually, with the help of the government, the schismatic group was able to take over six other parishes in different states of Mexico. The La Soledad takeover was just one of the many church/state conflicts that eventually culminated in the period of armed conflict known as La Cristiada (Guerra Cristera, the Cristero War, or the Cristero movement) between the Mexican government and several factions of the Catholic Church in Mexico.

The Cristero War officially lasted from 1926 to 1929, with sporadic violence continuing into the late 1930s.[21] This violent conflict developed in reaction to state-sponsored anti-Catholicism under Calles, who implemented of a series of anticlerical provisions in the Mexican Constitution of 1917. Known as the Ley Calles (the Calles Law), these provisions were meant to restrict the power of the Catholic Church, particularly its involvement in politics. In addition to its new provisions, the 1917 constitution also ratified previous anticlerical articles, inspired by the Enlightenment, that had been written into the constitution of 1857 by Benito Juarez. The Ley Calles closed worship centers, deported foreign priests, seized Church properties, and imposed a mandatory national registry for clerics.

The Ley Calles created significant discontent among the populace that merged with ongoing unrest against land reforms—a series of revolts by small farmers. Many of these small farmers became the Cristeros, who favored the traditional Catholic Church against the state and served as a counterweight against the state-run ICAM and CROM. Most of the land reforms and Cristero-related uprisings were concentrated in the area known as the Bajío, or lowlands. This deeply Catholic region includes Mexico City and parts of the states of Jalisco, Guanajuato, Aguascalientes, Querétano, and San Luis Potosí, as well as the states of Nayarit, Colima, Michoacán, and Zacatecas. Los Altos de Jalisco, where Toribio Romo was born and died, is located at the center of both the Bajío region and the Cristero movement.[22]

The Cristeros were a heterogeneous group, united only by the sentiments expressed by their slogan: "¡Viva Cristo Rey! ¡Viva la Virgen de Guadalupe!" (Long live Christ the King! Long live the Virgin of Guadalupe!). The Cristeros' diversity and lack of any central command made it difficult for the government to contain them, especially at the beginning of the conflict. They had no official Church backing—they did not receive the official endorsement of the Mexican Catholic bishops' conference—but there was tacit approval of them from some Church leaders.

When the conflict exploded, Toribio Romo was a young priest in Los Altos de Jalisco. Father Toribio's direct superior and mentor, one of the most powerful ecclesiastical authorities of the time, was José Francisco Orozco y Jiménez, the archbishop of Guadalajara (1913–36); he openly supported the cause of the rebels and would become a key player in beginning Romo's later canonization process.[23]

Recall that the farmers, especially those in the Bajío region, were fighting both for religious freedom and for land rights and access. The Calles administration therefore used land dispossession and redistribution as tools to control the Cristero War: once it became clear that the government could not simply quash the rebellion, the president organized a countermovement called the agraristas, a group of small farmers and farmhands who received landholding rights from the government. (The agraristas, like the CROM members they opposed, also played an important role in the Tijuana riots that took place after Olga Camacho's murder; see Chapter 2.) The agraristas' land grants depended directly on being in the state's good graces, and the agraristas were expected to defend the state's interests, serving as informants and as a progovernment militia to fight the Cristeros at the grassroots level.

The government's strategic distribution of land grants was well organized and effective: as Jean Meyer describes, "In order to win over the rebels, to recruit new adherents and restrict popular support for the Cristeros, [land] distribution was accelerated, particularly in the zones where the rebellion was strongest."[24] In the last year of the conflict, interim president Emilio Portes Gil "alone distributed 1 million hectares in 1929 to 127,00 heads of families."[25] (Portes Gil was interim president of Mexico for fourteen months, after President-elect General Álvaro Obregón was assassinated by an opponent to Calles's anti-Catholic policies on July 17, 1928, just months before he assumed the presidency.) In addition to this massive distribution of land, Meyer says, "the [Mexican] government always utilized the Agraristas for political control, as rural police and for military action."[26]

The relationship between Cristeros and agraristas was far from simple, however. Many factors were at play, and relations between the two groups often varied from place to place. On many occasions, agraristas refused to attack, kill, or even reveal the location of priests and Church personnel. There were also instances of agraristas joining the Cristeros or simply helping to hide clerics and protect Church authorities, as in the case of Archbishop Orozco y Jiménez of Guadalajara.[27] For their part, at the beginning of the revolt, the Cristeros understood the precarious situation of the agraristas. José González Romo, a leader of the Cristero revolt in Coalcomán, wrote to Jesús Morfín, the leader of the agrarista movement in Ahuijulo, "We are not against the Agraristas, we are in favor of the redistribution of land, but we are against the Agraristas when they become soldiers."[28]

However, the Cristeros' position vis-à-vis the agraristas hardened as the conflict continued. Over time, the Cristeros began to see the agraristas as thieves who had received their land unfairly from the government—and as heretical traitors who were fighting the Church (although in fact, most of the agrarista were devoted Catholics themselves and were not interested in supporting the state's efforts to install ICAM in place of the Church). As Msgr. James T. Murphy writes in his book *Saints and Sinners in the Cristero War*, "In economic, social, and cultural terms, they [the agraristas] hardly differed from the Cristeros."[29] The division between the agraristas and the Cristeros was a fracture created and manipulated by the Mexican government, which served its own interests by distributing land—and by threatening to take it away. The Cristeros and agraristas often resided in the same towns and sometimes were members of the same family. In this light, the

Cristero War, including its religious components, should be understood as an extension of the Mexican Revolution—a peasant insurrection for land rights.

Peace talks between the Calles government and the Mexican Catholic Church began in 1928, with US ambassador Dwight Whitney Morrow serving as a mediator. On June 21, 1929, the parties reached a peace accord known as los arreglos (the agreements). No changes were made to either the Mexican Constitution or the penal code; the anticlerical Ley Calles provisions remained in place, but the government promised not to enforce them. The Roman Catholic Church regained worship rights in the nation and use (but not ownership) of its properties, and Catholic clergy could occupy those premises. The Church immediately withdrew its support from the Cristeros and threatened to excommunicate anyone who continued the attacks. On June 27, 1929, after almost three years of conflict, church bells across Mexico rang out to celebrate the end of the Church's hostilities with the state. Yet the violence between the dissident groups did not end, and many Cristeros felt that they had been betrayed by the hierarchy of the Church. All told, between government troops, Cristeros, and civilians, around one hundred thousand lives were lost during the conflicts.[30]

Who Was Toribio Romo?

Assembling a narrative of Toribio's life is challenging for a number of reasons. But by relying on a combination of official records assembled by the Catholic Church, a biography written by Toribio's brother, newspapers at the time, and other popular accounts, I have pieced together the basic trajectory that brought Toribio to Tequila. As one might expect, several disparities mark the accounts found in newspapers and souvenir novels. In general, all agree on the larger narrative of the events, but the details of dates and sites are not always consistent.

The Catholic Church's official records are the best place to start in sketching out the events of Toribio Romo's life and his murder, for several reasons. He spent most of his life in Catholic institutions as an intern, a student, or a priest. The Church holds the authoritative records of his baptism, confirmation, and ordination as well as those of his family members. In addition, both his life and his death were deeply defined by his affiliation with the Church. Documents held by the Church include a detailed and systematic review of the individual records—including primary sources, archives, and oral history accounts from parishioners and subordinates—that are required for the process of canonization. In addition to these official Church records, I use Toribio's brother's account of his life in describing his family and community, for these elements do not appear in the Church documents.

I am very much aware of the Catholic Church's investment in concocting a particular narrative of sainthood and martyrdom around Toribio Romo. Indeed, as I show, the official narrative hides who really murdered Toribio Romo in order to promote a binary state-versus-Church narrative. Therefore, I am careful to confront and complement the official narrative of his history with the narratives generated at the grassroots level, especially by his followers, which serve as an alternative and parallel system of history-telling. In this chapter, as in the rest of the book, we navigate through multiple worlds inhabited (and negotiated) by holiness.

The son of Patricio Romo Pérez and Juana González, Toribio was born on April 16, 1900, in a poor village that was then called Santa Ana de Abajo, Jalostotitlán, in the area known as Los Altos of Jalisco—one of the regions most affected by the Cristero War. In 1920 the town's name was changed from Santa Ana de Abajo to Santa Ana de Guadalupe after the Virgin of Guadalupe was declared its patron. On February 11 of the same year, Father Pedro Rodriguez, the local parish priest, "placed the first stone and blessed the site" of a church dedicated to their new patron, the Virgin of Guadalupe.[31] This church is known as La Mesita, given its location at the top of a small mesa, and over time it has become the main center of Saint Toribio's veneration.[32] The Romo family was one of the four founding families of the town, having been there since the mid-1600s.[33] According to Toribio's brother Román, their life at home was shaped by the rhythms of farming and Catholicism: "Father Toribio's home was like everyone else's in the community. Everyone would get up at sunrise and say their prayers. The men would milk the cows and go about their chores on the farm while the boys would take care of the cattle. At night, families would gather to pray the rosary[,] eat[,] and go to sleep."[34] Religiosity, like division of labor by gender, was woven into the everyday life of the farming family.

At the age of thirteen, Toribio entered the auxiliary seminary of San Juan de los Lagos, a minor seminary for boys who were interested in becoming priests. In 1920, at the age of twenty, he transferred to the Seminario Conciliar de Guadalajara to continue his studies for the priesthood. There he was influenced by the local reality of San Juan de los Lagos, with its high rates of urban poverty, as well as the social teaching of Pope Leo XIII's 1831 encyclical *Rerum Novarum* on the rights and duties of capital and labor—an official papal communication that is widely considered the foundation of Catholic social justice doctrine. Two years later, on December 23, 1922, he was ordained a priest by Archbishop Orozco y Jiménez in the Guadalajara Cathedral. Father Toribio performed his first Mass in his hometown, on January 5, 1923, in the church of La Mesita, which had been completed just in time for the occasion.

Immediately after his ordination, Father Toribio received his pastoral assignment to the state of Jalisco, and for the next six years, he served in various places in the region—the usual expectation of a young diocesan priest. During this time, he devoted himself to instructing his parishioners in the catechism, one of his favorite activities. According to James Murphy, author of the only full biography on Toribio Romo available in English as of this writing, it was during Toribio's assignment in Cuquío, Jalisco, that he became involved with the recently created antigovernment Cristero group called La Unión Popular (1925). This grassroots organization was founded in Jalisco by Anacleto González Flores, who also hailed from Los Altos de Jalisco and was a close friend of Toribio's. The two had met when González Flores also attended seminary. Both men would be dead within a few years—González Flores tortured and executed by a firing squad during the Cristero War in 1927, Toribio killed only a year later.[35]

Because of his decision to align with the rebels in Cuquío, Father Toribio was reassigned to the town of Tequila, Jalisco, located almost fifty miles northwest of Guadalajara. The region was a frequent site of violent clashes between the Cristero rebels and government troops. There Toribio lived with his brother Román, also a priest, and their sister Maria Marcos Romo González (known as Quica) in a two-room shack in the Barranca del Agua Caliente, a farming settlement that was a twenty-minute drive from Tequila (Figure 3.2). From this remote location, the two brothers were able to celebrate Mass and conduct other services for Tequila and the surrounding communities in clandestine sites, including an abandoned warehouse, since official Catholic church services were banned in Mexico at that time. As described by the canonization records in the Vatican archives: "At night [Toribio] entered the town of Tequila to help the sick and sometimes he celebrated Holy Mass in the homes of devoted Christian families. Many people from the neighboring towns came to the Canyon of Agua Caliente to get baptized."[36]

Figure 3.2 Outside the shack where Romo was killed, Tequila, Jalisco.
Photo by the author

On February 25, 1928, around 6:00 a.m., an anti-Cristero group comprising local agraristas and government troops broke into the siblings' shack.[37] Toribio was not celebrating Mass that morning because he was too tired from a long night of working on several parish tasks. He was resting in bed when the troops entered his room. Only Toribio and Quica were there; Toribio had sent Román to Tequila the afternoon before to take care of some errands. As described by Román himself, Toribio "gave [him] an enclosed envelope and told him not to open it until he was told to do so" by Toribio.[38] As interpreted by Román, based on the content of the letter he opened days after the killing, Toribio had foreseen the deadly threat and had sent his brother away to save his life. The letter reads "Román, take care of our elderly parents, do everything you can to alleviate their suffering. I also want you to take care of Quica who has been like a mother to us. . . . I would like for you to celebrate two masses for me."[39] It was Román's survival that made possible the emergence of Toribio as a popular saint, for it was Román who wrote the first biography of his brother and was instrumental in preserving an informal archive of relics and documents attached to the history of Toribio's life and martyrdom—many of which are now on display in Santa Ana de Guadalupe, Jalisco.

According to Vatican records, the intruders broke into Toribio's room, and one screamed, "That's the priest; kill him!" Toribio woke up and began to respond, saying, "Yes, I am [a priest] . . . but please don't kill me." He was fatally shot before he even finished speaking. His sister was present during the ordeal, though she was not harmed. She ran to Toribio and cried, "Courage, Father Toribio . . . Merciful Jesus, receive him! Viva Cristo Rey!"—but it was too late.[40]

Toribio's body was put on an improvised stretcher and was taken by several residents of Agua Caliente to Tequila for burial. The transport itself was a spectacle, as Quica and other devotees followed the body, praying the rosary, while those on the other side of the Cristero conflict—the troops and agraristas—were "whistling and singing vulgar songs."[41] Upon arrival in Tequila, the body was dropped off "at the town square . . . for everyone to see."[42] The body was later transported to the local jail, where Quica was detained as well. She spent three days in prison.

Within a day of his death, Toribio's body was released so that the community could prepare it for the viewing and the funeral. People brought objects to be touched by the body and collected Toribio's blood in cotton balls as relics, both here and during the transport of his dead body to Tequila. At noon on the day after his death, a procession brought the body to the cemetery in Tequila and buried him there.[43] His remains stayed there for twenty years, until his family moved them to Santa Ana de Guadalupe in 1948. Eventually, Román became the pastor of Santa Teresita Church in Guadalajara, and he remained in that post for almost fifty years before his death in 1981. Today, their sister Quica is also being considered as a candidate for canonization because of her pious life.[44]

From Los Altos to Rome: The Sainthood of Toribio Romo

Toribio Romo differs in a significant way from the other saints discussed in this book: he is the only one to be officially canonized by the Catholic Church. He was beatified in 1992 and canonized in 2000.[45] I include him here, despite his official status, because his reputation as the Holy Smuggler of undocumented migrants locates him at a unique intersection within the nebulous boundaries of popular religiosity, illegality, and state intervention.

More importantly, this chapter shows how a popular reputation for holiness develops; it requires the active participation of many social players who work—sometimes together, sometimes separately—to emphasize particular facts about the individual, to share experiences of the person's miracles or interventions, and to attach certain meanings to that person's life and legend. To understand Toribio's role as a border saint, we must understand the diverse forces shaping ephemeral discourses of holiness—how popular sainthood is recognized by a community and how economic, cultural, and historical factors shape this process in the context of US-Mexico relations.

Several people and processes were crucial in establishing Toribio Romo's reputation of sanctity before he was officially canonized by the Catholic Church. These players include his brother Román, who spearheaded the efforts to document and popularize Toribio's martyrdom, within the context of a devoted conservative alteño culture ("alteño" refers to people from Los Altos de Jalisco); Monsignor Óscar Sánchez Barba, the person responsible for promoting Toribio's canonization within the Catholic Church; and local pastor Father Gabriel González Pérez, whose campaign promoting and marketing Toribio's image has had a profound impact on the precarious economy of Santa Ana de Guadalupe.

We must also examine another significant factor, which influenced not only his pre-canonization reputation for holiness and his official canonization but his eventual popular adoption after canonization: the migration of the story of one of Toribio Romo's miracles. This story about an encounter with Toribio circulated, became famous, and began to repeat itself on both sides of the US-Mexico border, cementing his cross-border status as the patron saint of immigrants. Over time, these formal and informal factors have attached different meanings to Toribio Romo.

The Brother: Román Romo

Román was not only the brother of Toribio Romo, a metaphorical witness to his martyrdom by virtue of his involvement in the events surrounding it, and the writer of the first biography dedicated to the exaltation of Toribio's holy virtues, but also a key player in initiating and spreading the legend of Toribio Romo, which would establish his reputation for holiness and, eventually, lead to his canonization.[46] As Guadalajaran religious scholar Renée de la Torre explains (writing with Fernando Guzmán Mundo), Román Romo "during his lifetime was in charge of maintaining both the local and family cult to the relics of his brother, who was always considered a holy martyr, and of promoting his beatification before the ecclesial authorities."[47] Román was instrumental in having Archbishop Orozco y Jiménez introduce the case for Toribio Romo's beatification; Orozco y Jiménez, who was archbishop of Guadalajara from 1913 to 1936 and a crucial player during the Cristero War, was the highest-ranking ecclesiastical authority who openly led and protected many of the rebels against the Mexican government during the period.

Román—who was also known as Tata Romo ("Tata" is a colloquialism for "father" or "papa" in the region and is used for all kinds of fatherly figures)— used his control over his brother's mythology, and his own position as local priest, to control the town and its economy.[48] Román insisted on relocating Toribio's body from Tequila, Jalisco, where he died, to their hometown, Santa Ana, to centralize and consolidate his memory and martyrdom in the consciousness of the Jalisco community. It was Román who, before anyone else, envisioned creating a sanctuary to venerate his brother. He did all this from his position as priest in another town, Santa Teresita.

Beginning the 1940s, Román "organized pilgrims to Santa Ana de Guadalupe to visit the remains of his brother, already idealized as a saint."[49] Román was directly involved in preserving and keeping safe the relics related to Toribio's martyrdom, from his bloody clothes to his Bible, rosary, and other objects.[50]

Román continued to be involved in politics in his hometown, Santa Ana, in many ways, even after he left home for Santa Teresita. For example, he created an important picture-framing business in Santa Teresita that hired people from Santa Ana in an effort to (in part) ameliorate the economic devastation wrought by the migration out of Santa Ana during the years following the Cristero War and by droughts and other calamities, which displaced many Santa Ana farmers.[51] So, even from a distance, Román kept tight control over their town through his family ties to the region and his influence in the job market. According to testimonies collected by de la Torre, "In Santa Ana the electric power didn't arrive until 1988, because . . . during his life [Román Romo] did not allow it. . . . [H]e thought that with [it] . . . television would be introduced, and it would deform the conscience and good habits of the town. It was only after the death of Father Román that television would arrive, with no one to stop it."[52] Indeed, telephone lines did not arrive in Santa Ana until 1999.[53]

Such stories clearly reflect something about the personality of Román and about the Catholic Church's effect on these communities. However, they also reveal the character of the inhabitants of Santa Ana and Los Altos de Jalisco more generally. Román, as Toribio's brother, and the Cristero martyrs of Los Altos are located within a particular social and cultural context and cannot be considered in isolation from it. The town is extremely insular, and alteños are very religiously and politically conservative: for many years, the inhabitants of the town refused government public education because they believed that the schoolteachers were "transmitting 'red' [communist] and anti-Catholic ideas," and residents even threw stones at the teachers who tried to open a public school in town.[54] This insularity was only reinforced by the town's resistance to adding television and telephone service; the residents' hostility to outside interference endured for decades.

The Postulator: Monsignor Óscar Sánchez Barba

Accessing documents pertaining to the canonization of Saint Toribio is not an easy task. The Catholic Church shrouds such records in secrecy, in part because so many elements of the process rely on the intangibles of faith, miracles, and popular religiosity. The Vatican office that oversees the process of evaluating candidates for sainthood, called the Congregation for the Causes of Saints, considers all the testimonies, documents, and miracles attributed to each possible saint. The process has no formal timeline; it varies depending on the individual and the circumstances attached to the case. The office's final decision to recommend a candidate for canonization must be approved by the pope.

Monsignor Óscar Sánchez Barba, whose contact information I obtained from the Congregation for the Causes of Saints during one of my visits to the Vatican, was the general postulator for Toribio Romo—that is, he officially presented the case for Toribio Romo's canonization (along with those of all the other martyrs from the Cristero War) to the Catholic Church in the late twentieth century. Sánchez Barba is thus in a unique position to discuss the history of Toribio Romo's canonization process. As a Tapatío (a nickname for people from Guadalajara, the capital of Jalisco), Sánchez Barba understands how Toribio's canonization connects to the very identity of Jalisco and, beyond that, all of Mexico. According to him, the virtues that Toribio manifested in life made him worthy of martyrdom; we can thus view the process of his sanctification having begun in life, as he tended to his Cristero flock, and we cannot divorce his virtues and his sanctification from their context—the persecution of the Catholic faith in Mexico.

The formal process for the cause of canonization was initiated in the 1930s by Archbishop Orozco y Jiménez, at the behest of Román Romo. "Cause" is the Catholic Church term for the petition, procedure, and supporting evidence that begins the process of formal canonization of an individual. Once the cause with its supporting documents was fully prepared, it was sent to Rome. But there it stalled out—as Sánchez Barba puts it, it "slept for over forty years in the hand of the Italians"—because the original postulator in Rome "took the documents, held on to them . . . and never filed the cause."[55] It was not until 1987, a year after Sánchez Barba finished his first year of postgraduate canon law studies in Rome, that he was asked by the Catholic Church in Mexico to assist. Sánchez Barba had come to Rome right after his own ordination as a priest in Guadalajara, and he felt deeply connected to Toribio Romo and all the other Cristero martyrs from the area. As he explains, "I already had a deep sympathy for the martyrs, because I was a seminarian in Totatiche, a town located near Colotlan [Jalisco]. In Colotlan they killed two [during the Cristero War]: Cristóbal Magallanes [Jara] and Agustín Caloca [Cortés]. The leading figure of the list of martyrs [proposed to Rome] was Cristóbal Magallanes. . . . [He had] been the parish priest of Totatiche, the place where I was stationed."[56] Sánchez Barba was moved by the faith and heroic virtuosity of these individuals, and he felt connected to them because they were Jalisciense and Mexican. Thus the canonization of these Cristero rebels was very personal to Sánchez Barba because they were intimately connected to his homeland.

The timing of Sánchez Barba's invitation to take up the cause of Toribio Romo's canonization was not coincidental; it was related to the broader political transformations involving the Mexican government and the Roman Catholic Church taking place at that time. His invitation coincided with the 1988 Mexican presidential transition from Miguel de la Madrid to Carlos Salinas de Gortari. For the first time since the Cristero War, a Mexican president, Salinas de Gortari, invited ecclesiastical authorities to attend the inauguration. The Church's acceptance of this invitation sent a symbolic message of reconciliation and unification to the population. Within a year Mexico reestablished full diplomatic relations with the Vatican, after more than 130 years of rupture. During his administration, Salinas de Gortari also restored many legal rights to religious groups by amending the Mexican

Constitution with the 1992 Ley de Asociaciones Religiosas y Culto Público (Act on Religious Associations and Public Worship).

The first step in continuing the process of canonizing Toribio and the Cristero martyrs required locating the original materials that had been submitted to support the cause. How or why the materials were lost is unclear. They were eventually found stashed away in the back of the sacristy where the previous postulator had served. The original cause included forty-six individuals proposed for consideration as martyrs, but this number shrank to twenty-five, for twenty-one of them were disqualified for killing others or promoting violence in the Cristero War. The crucial element to be considered a martyr, Sánchez Barba explained, is one's willingness to die for their faith: persecutors "take your life because of hatred of faith, and you offer it [willingly]. If you say no [to their threats to kill you because of your faith], then you are not a martyr, even if they kill you [anyway]."[57] As we will see, this became a central point of contention in the discussion of Toribio Romo's canonization. Many of those who directly participated in the Cristero conflict had not met this condition, for they had fought back against, or killed, their persecutors. For each of the twenty-five cases of martyrdom that emerged, Sánchez Barba and others sought to "demonstrate [the candidates'] situation within their historical context, the threats they experienced, their acceptance of the martyrdom, and the fact that they were in effect killed because of their faith."[58]

As mentioned, the question of willingness to be martyred was a point of contention in Saint Toribio's cause for canonization—although it is strange to think that one of the most popular saints in Mexico today almost did not become an official saint. According to Sánchez Barba, the Congregation for the Causes of Saints questioned the circumstances surrounding Toribio's death, because just before he was shot and killed, Toribio reportedly asked his attackers not to kill him. Some in Rome interpreted this as an unwillingness to die for his faith, violating an essential condition for Catholic martyrdom.

According to Sánchez Barba, the postulator team's response was that Toribio, like Jesus of Nazareth the night before he was crucified, had a moment of crisis but nevertheless chose to do God's will. He had the chance to deny being a priest, which might have saved his life, but he chose to be truthful and instead gave his attackers an opportunity to change their minds. Sánchez Barba also emphasized to the Vatican that Toribio had asked many times during his life for the grace of being a martyr. For example, he prayed for martyrdom during a massive religious service in 1925 held by Father

Justino Orona Madrigal (another Cristero priest martyr and saint) in Cuquío. Similarly, when as a young priest Toribio celebrated the First Communion of a group of children, he asked them to pray to God to give him "the opportunity to be a martyr." Sánchez Barba argues that simply having "fear, being afraid, is not a sin" and "does not take away anything." Furthermore, Sánchez Barba emphasized to the Congregation that despite being "very afraid" during the Cristero conflict, Toribio and the others had committed to remaining in the country: "It is one thing to be afraid and not to be here . . . and leave. Many [priests] went to the United States. But these ones stayed here."[59] Sánchez Barba presented this as a sign of the holy character of Toribio Romo and the other martyrs. They knew the dangers they faced by staying in Mexico, yet they chose to remain and risk their lives. Arguably, Romo's death was sealed not on the day of his murder but on the day he opted to stay in Mexico.

The Marketer: Father Gabriel González Pérez

Santo que no es conocido, no es venerado. [A saint who is not known is not revered.]

—El Informador[60]

Román Romo was not the only person who sought to popularize (and commodify) Toribio Romo; Gabriel González Pérez, who has served as the pastor of the church in Santa Ana de Guadalupe in Jalisco since 1997, was also instrumental in spreading Toribio Romo's legend. González Pérez himself was once an undocumented immigrant to the United States, living in California for some months as a teen before returning to Mexico to become a priest.[61] It is fitting, then, that he has played a key role in solidifying Saint Toribio's reputation as the patron saint of immigrants.

During his tenure as the pastor of the Santa Ana church, González Pérez has been directly involved with marketing the saint, working "with business leaders to produce the material objects (stamps, medals, candles, T-shirts, etc.) that spread Toribio Romo's fame."[62] Before Toribio gained his current popularity as a saint for immigrants, the Holy Coyote for those crossing the border, he was associated in Jalisco with children and teens (because of his interest in teaching the catechism) and with soccer (because of the work of González Pérez with several soccer teams in the region).[63] González Pérez sought to promote an influx of tourists into Santa Ana by increasing Toribio's popular sainthood in these areas; he "promoted the visit of soccer players and coaches from popular teams—the Chivas de Guadalajara. These events were publicized in the media so that Santo Toribio would be recognized as the miraculous patron saint of soccer."[64] In addition, he, "convinced the owners of Atletica, a sportswear manufacturer in a neighboring town [San Miguel el Alto, nine miles away, where González Pérez had previously been a pastor], to open an outlet store in Santa Ana."[65] Athletica produces the official team uniforms and other paraphernalia for the Chivas, not only the most popular team in Jalisco but also currently the top soccer team in the Mexican League and one of the founding members of the Mexican First Division.[66] Atletica has also been the official sponsor of both the Mexican Olympic Team and the Mexican national soccer teams. The Santa Ana outlet store brought many sports fans to town and allowed González Pérez to add "sports paraphernalia into the religious assemblage that heightened Santa Ana's profile."[67]

González Pérez understood that pilgrims want to do more than just visit a church that houses the relics of a martyr, and anyway, Los Altos already had several places where they could do that. He understood that people seek a religious experience as part of a larger spiritual journey. Toribio was not so different from the many other local Cristero martyrs, and González Pérez realized that he needed to emphasize the unique spiritual advantage of Santa Ana over the other nearby places with veneration sites to Cristero martyrs. Therefore, González Pérez systematically broke down the life of Toribio and the experience of the Cristero War into a series of distinctive events that people can experience while visiting Santa Ana. Each event or location emphasizes a distinct aspect of Toribio's martyrdom and helps people connect personally with him. The believer can visit his childhood home, a Cristero War calzada (walkway), a museum, and a new megachurch, all of them situated as a network of interconnected sites. This self-contained series of mini-tours converges upon the old main church, La Mesita, which currently holds Saint Toribio's relics (Figure 3.3).

Over time, González Pérez, with his strong "ecclesiastical team of laypeople from San Miguel and Santa Ana," has transformed the small town of Santa Ana into a religious tourist site and a spiritual service provider with multiple amenities centered on Saint Toribio.[68] Both the experience of venerating Saint Toribio and the town of Santa Ana itself have been deeply transformed by the work of González Pérez. These days, the town, which had once almost disappeared due to drought, land seizure, and mass emigration to evade the violence of the Cristero conflicts, now boasts three hundred permanent

Figure 3.3 Churches to Toribio Romo, Santa Ana, Jalisco. *Top:* La Mesita Church. *Bottom:* The new church to Toribio Romo. Both are in Santa Ana, Jalisco, Mexico.
Photos by the author

residents, and between fifteen thousand and eighty thousand pilgrims visit every week.[69] In November 2017, during the month-long celebration of the twenty-fifth anniversary of Toribio's beatification, more than three hundred thousand pilgrims visited Santa Ana—an extraordinary number of visitors in such a short time.[70] To accommodate this huge volume of visitors, the town has changed substantially: there are multiple souvenir stores (both devotional and secular) that sell Saint Toribio busts (made in China), keychains, prayer books, pictures, clothes, hats, travel amulets, lamps, plastic flower arrangements, and more, and there is a state-of-the-art rectory for priests (started in 1998 and finished in 2000) adjacent to the main shrine.

The town also features a half-mile Calzada de los Mártires (Martyrs Walkway) that connects the church of La Mesita, which houses Toribio Romo's relics, to another church dedicated to the Holy Family. The calzada is decorated on both sides by busts of the twenty-five Cristero War martyrs, and speakers play Beethoven's Fifth Symphony as you walk. The journey between the two churches is thus a multisensory experience meant to invite the pilgrim into reflection about the lives and sacrifices of each martyr. However, in practice, the experience is anything but spiritual, quiet or contemplative. The day I was there, it was extremely hot and dusty, and the noise of the many pilgrims walking with their families, as well as the many informal vendors trying to get people's attention along the calzada, made it almost impossible to listen to the music or to read the plaque on each bust with the information about that martyr. Everyone was in a hurry to get to the other church.

When pilgrims finally reach the Holy Family church, they can visit a full-scale replica of the shack in which the Romo family supposedly lived. The two-bedroom structure reinforces visitors' sense of the humble character of the Romo family and the alteño way of life: "the simple, peasant, and religious life, held on the collective imagination of an alteño homeland."[71] The shrine conveys the particular Los Altos asceticism that combines the morality of hard work and sacrifices with pious Catholicism and religiosity.

The town includes other attractions and amenities related to Toribio Romo. A cafeteria/deli and two Church-owned restaurants have been constructed: El Peregrino (The Pilgrim, 2002) and La Casita (The Little House, 2004); the latter is located near the Romo family's replica shack. In 2005 a museum was completed and blessed in memory of Pope Saint John Paul II. According to the locals, this museum shelters the mesquite tree where Toribio taught catechism.[72] There is a large new retreat center for "visiting priests and dignitaries," which includes twenty-four guest rooms, a meeting room, a private chapel, and an indoor pool.[73] Finally, a new megachurch dedicated to Toribio Romo is almost complete. This new sanctuary, able to host two thousand people, is meant to become the new spiritual center; it will replace La Mesita, which can only hold 150 people. Once the building is finished, the relics of Toribio Romo will be transferred there. All of these elements have been built with the money collected and donated by Saint Toribio's followers.

The Migration of a Miracle

Toribio Romo has not always been as overwhelmingly popular as he is today. According to Sánchez Barba, at the beatification of the first group of Cristero martyrs on November 22, 1992, Toribio Romo was not the most popular member of the group—not in Rome nor even in Mexico. Instead, the leading figure on beatification day was Magallanes Jara, another Jalisco priest killed during the conflict, who was already being venerated by his local community "independently of the ecclesiastic decisions" about his formal beatification or canonization.[74] In contrast, as Sánchez Barba describes, "Toribio [Romo] was very much unknown . . . beyond his region, his town, and the various places where he had been." However, within a decade, a story emerged that changed everything. It did not start circulating widely until the early 2000s, when it was picked up by the media, but it was known among local communities before then. Following the spread of that story, the fame of Toribio Romo grew until "it surpassed everyone else [in the group of martyrs]. Now, it can be said that he [Toribio] is probably the most famous Mexican saint."[75]

The Structure of a Miracle: What Happened?
Sometime in the early 1990s, Jesús Buendía Gaytán, a native of the Mexican state of Zacatecas, had an experience that forever changed not only his life but also the popular veneration of Saint Toribio. To travel to California to find employment as a seasonal farmer worker, he hired a pollero (a smuggler) in Mexicali, Baja California, to help him cross the US-Mexico border. However, "as soon as they crossed the border, they were discovered by the Border Patrol, and to escape, [Buendía Gaytán] ran into the desert."[76] After several days under the burning sun of the Sonoran Desert, lost and without water, Buendía Gaytán began to expect the worst. Then "he saw a van approaching. From it descended an individual of youthful appearance,

thin, white skin, and blue eyes, who in perfect Spanish offered him water and food."[77] The generous stranger also gave him money and recommended a place where he could find a job. When Buendía Gaytán asked how he could repay the man's kindness, the man told him not to worry, requesting only, "When you have money and work, come and look for me in Jalostotitlán, Jalisco, ask for Toribio Romo."[78]

Once the harvest season was over, Buendía Gaytán returned to his hometown in Zacatecas and then traveled to Jalostotitlán, where he hoped to find his benefactor and repay his kindness. When he arrived and asked after Toribio Romo, he was redirected to the small settlement of Santa Ana, located just outside town. As he described in an interview: "There I asked about Toribio Romo and they told me I was in the temple. I almost had a heart attack when I saw my friend's photograph on the high altar. It was the priest Toribio Romo, killed during the Cristero War."[79] Now, he explained, every time he embarks on a new trip to the United States, he completely entrusts himself to Saint Toribio.

Similar stories had been circulating among migrants since the 1970s, and the story of Buendía Gaytán was already circulating locally. But in 2002, Marco A. García Gutiérrez, a reporter for the Mexico City–based magazine *Contenido*, interviewed Buendía Gaytán; his story was published on June 1, 2002.[80] Upon the publication of the *Contenido* article, the mythology of Toribio Romo received national and even international attention, bringing forward others with similar accounts.[81] Within two months, a similar story was reported by the *New York Times*. In this new case, an immigrant from Michoacán, identified only as José, described a similar scene of salvation: "He had arrived at the border with no documents and no hope," the article explains. "Then a stranger appeared and offered him safe passage, a good meal and a decent job." Again, the mysterious man asked for no monetary compensation, requesting only "that José visit him sometime in Santa Ana de Guadalupe." As the story goes, it was only much later, when the man was able to return to Mexico and visit Jalisco, that "a dumbfounded José learned that his coyote was a saint."[82]

Though the accounts of migrants' encounters with the saint vary in specific details, recurring themes emerge.[83] As described by the immigrants, Toribio appears as a young Mexican male in his late twenties, with blue eyes and fair skin. In most accounts, he "drove a truck; other times he was walking; and in one instance, he sat next to an emigrant on an airplane."[84] In all the stories, he is a protector of immigrants, in particular those without documentation;

in addition to providing transportation or money, he sometimes reportedly "makes migrants invisible to border agents," and some migrants have reported him visiting the sick, even "appearing to them in the hospital," to comfort them after an accident or as they recover from the border crossing.[85]

The increase in veneration of Toribio Romo and the spread of his legend and fame have coincided with deep social changes in Mexico and in US immigration policies. According to the Pew Research Center, in the years "1965 to 2015, more than 16 million Mexicans migrated to the U.S. in one of the largest mass migrations in modern history."[86] The period of the most "rapid growth began in the 1970s—[and] by 1980 ... Mexico had become the top country of origin for U.S. immigrants."[87] Migration from Mexico to the United States has since declined, and it is no coincidence that Saint Toribio's reputation grew most during the peak decades of migration, at the end of the twentieth century. During this period, new immigration policies were implemented, physical and technological barriers were installed along the southern US border (e.g., Operation Gatekeeper in 1994), and drug cartels increasingly participated in the control and policing of Mexico border's traffic. Taken together, these changes forced undocumented migrants to move into ever more dangerous terrain in their efforts to cross to the United States, making the journey increasingly deadly.

At the same time, migration began to seem more and more appealing as life in Mexico became more difficult from the 1990s onward, thanks to the North American Free Trade Agreement (NAFTA). The neoliberal practices brought by NAFTA dismantled traditional ways of life, privatized ejidos (community lands), and introduced subsidized US goods such as corn, devaluing domestic agricultural production. Suddenly, survival—in Mexico, during the journey to the United States, and in the US once arrived—began to seem to require nothing short of a miracle. As Aguilar Ros explains, people have increasingly turned to Saint Toribio as a mediator who "resolves the contradictions in favor of the undocumented."[88]

Toribio's Racial Typologies: A Tapatío Saint with Blue Eyes

As with Jesús Malverde, Saint Toribio's popularity cannot be disassociated from discourses that are linked to "the axes of differentiation and social exclusion tied to race and social class"[89]—an issue that is particularly relevant in Los Altos de Jalisco, which, as de la Torre notes, is "mostly populated by

[Mexican] whites who brag about their European origin (Spanish or French) and the scarce presence of indigenous people" in the region. These claims of indigenous scarcity highlight both indigenous displacement in the region and residents' racialized boasts regarding their lack of indigenous blood. In this sense, the alteño Cristeros were engaged in not just a religious fight but also a cultural one to preserve and continue their regional racial (and gender) values.

In Los Altos, racial purity is deeply connected to religion and nationalism, and the "alteña Catholic culture, which highlights the pride of their Catholic and Creole conservatism," comes through clearly in countless narratives of Saint Toribio, including in Román's biography of his brother.[90] Analyzing the visual elements of Toribio's appearance that signify European ancestry is key to understanding the migration of racial discourses around this particular vernacular saint. Although in accounts of his apparitions his age and his modus operandi vary, as does the place in which he appears, his racial designation remains constant: again and again, accounts and representations of Toribio emphasize his blue eyes and light complexion. These features are reflected in all of the visual imagery, busts, and figurines sold of Toribio Romo, which always depict him as a white Mexican. This phenotype is used, as Aguilar Ros discusses, to corroborate him as "authentically alteño" and as "one of us." As de la Torre explains, European ancestry, land tenure, and religiosity are all linked together in Los Altos: "It is the land of ranchers (mostly cattle ranchers), who were able to articulate society through strategies rooted in kinship relations and where Catholicism played a decisive role in the maintaining of a local oligarchic system."[91] Toribio Romo's veneration thus also reinforces kinship relationships; Aguilar Ros writes, "Let's remember that alteños reproduce themselves, symbolically and discursively, around a common ethnic origin—that is, whites, criollos, with a fervent Catholicism, all linked to ranching activities."[92] In other words, Toribio's holiness and his membership in the Los Altos clan offer a way to celebrate and cement the racial and cultural bonds of the local community, just as participation in the Cristero war did.

This discursive regeneration of Los Altos is reflected in Guzmán Mundo's interview with Luis Tarcisio González Ramírez, a former mayor of Jalostotitlán, the municipality that includes Santa Ana de Guadalupe. Asked about the relevance of Saint Toribio's canonization, González Ramírez responded: "This is an achievement. It is a triumph for us, for our way of life. Many people from outside call alteños pious, churchy, but time gives the reason. I believe that after years of struggle, not only armed [struggle from the Cristeros], and caring for the true Catholic and family values of each individual, we are finally seeing [our way of life] crowned [in] this historic event [Toribio Romo's canonization]."[93] Here, the canonization of Toribio is constructed as a victory, at least a spiritual one, and as a validation for the subculture of Los Altos, whose members feel judged and misunderstood. Toribio becomes a hero not just of the Cristero War but also of a regional cultural identity placed at risk during subsequent decades because of policies like NAFTA, which wrought deep and fundamental economic changes in the traditional ranching and farming economy in Jalisco. Toribio's canonization—and, more importantly, the marketing of his figure and the subsequent economic success of Santa Ana and the surrounding area—will prove to be the ultimate victory (and revenge) for the region. The representation of Toribio as visually white and blue-eyed not only connects him with alteño culture but also shows how deeply notions about beauty and morality are interconnected in popular religiosity. As we will see shortly, this interconnection becomes even more evident as his veneration spreads to the United States.

Rewriting a Conflicted Past: Toribio Romo's Anti-Immigrant Legacy

Perhaps the most ironic part of Toribio's life is regularly left out of the narratives about him: this popular and well-loved saint of migration in fact opposed immigration to United States. He even wrote a play during his first year as a seminarian, titled *Vámonos p'al Norte* (Let's go north), which examines the dangerous consequences of emigrating to the United States. The one-act comedy centers on two characters: Don Rogaciano, an alteño who returns to his hometown after living in the United States for several years, and Sancho, a street-smart local peasant. Rogaciano initially attracts the attention and admiration of everyone in the small village because of his sophistication and his self-described love for progress and civilization. The tables soon turn, however, when Sancho starts to unveil the truth behind Rogaciano's façade. By the end of the play, Rogaciano represents all that can go wrong for those who emigrate to the United States. He is an irresponsible, materialistic, superficial person of low morals. The play warns Mexicans about what will happen to them and their families if they pursue a similar path. The play asks: "How many people have we seen leaving home crying, who four or five years later have completely abandoned their faith and families, who don't send them so much as a letter, not to speak of economic support?" Those who migrate to the United States, according to the play, betray Mexico not just by leaving but also by going "to strengthen with their work the tyrant who will take advantage of their energies to increasingly humiliate and reduce to ashes our unfortunate Mexico."[94]

In the play, Rogaciano's emigration-induced moral devolution is accompanied by a falling away from traditional Mexican macho masculinity: Toribio suggests that with his new clothes, cologne, mannerisms, and jewelry, Rogaciano has compromised his masculinity and become sexually ambiguous, a "rooster hen that neither crows nor lays eggs." According to the peasant Sancho, men like Rogaciano become afeminado (effeminate). Sancho says: "Take a good look at what becomes of the Mexican who goes north.... He ends up a man without religion, without a country or home ... a coward, an afeminado who is incapable of feeling shame for having abandoned his responsibilities to his family. Despite this, the roads are packed with Mexicans headed toward the United States in search of bitter bread. Everywhere you hear the rallying cry—'Let's go north!'" Through Sancho, Toribio voices the collective fears and resistance of the ecclesiastical authorities around immigration during the first half of the twentieth century in Mexico, as well as his deep homophobia. In the play, manhood and nationalism are fused together; being a man means staying in Mexico and confronting its calamities.

Certainly, for a region such as Los Altos, which is deeply dependent on agricultural workers, the large outflow of peasants to the United States was devastating. For Toribio Romo—the actual person, not the saint—immigration threatened to corrode traditional Mexican moral and religious values and ultimately to destroy Mexican society. The play ends on a harsh note, concluding that in the end Mexico may well be better off without those "traitors" who leave for the United States, "because they leave behind a more peaceful Mexico," made better by their absence.[95] A similar sentiment underpinned Toribio's brother Román's reasons for refusing to let TV and phones come to Santa Ana; both the play and Román's resistance to modern culture manifest the same obsession with hewing to traditional values.

The anti-immigration position expressed in Toribio's play also reflected the official stance of the Catholic Church in Mexico during that time. Orozco y Jiménez, then archbishop of Guadalajara, called in 1920 for a "holy crusade" against emigration in a public apostolic letter titled *Contra la emigración* (Against emigration), which was read during Sunday Mass in all the churches of the archdiocese.[96] The next year, the local Catholic Church convened in Guadalajara for the Curso Social Agrícola Zapopano (Social and Agricultural Discourse of Zapopan), an event that focused on the negative impact of emigration for the farming sector and the local economy.[97] As noted by sociologist David FitzGerald, "Some five hundred clergy, including ten bishops, attended the session on emigration."[98] It was not until the 1960s that the Church's policy on emigration began to change. In the late 1980s, for example, seminarians from the Diocese of San Juan de los Lagos, Jalisco, "circulated the questions on the U.S. naturalization exam so they can teach migrants how to become a U.S. citizen." They also "urg[ed] wives to follow their migrating husbands as soon as possible," attempting to address what the Catholic Church in Mexico saw as "the second major problem caused by emigration": family disintegration.[99]

Importantly, however, Toribio's real-life position on this issue is consistently erased from the popular sainthood narratives about him. Precisely how and why this erasure began is unclear—that is, whether it was a conscious decision by ecclesiastical authorities or whether it was instead a collective preference on the part of devotees. What it shows us, though, is the disconnect between the historical figure and the constructed image of him as a saint—like the disconnect we saw, in Chapter 2, between Juan Castillo Morales the man and Juan Soldado the saint. The gaps and erasures in saints' popular narratives reveal the selective nature of spirituality and commemoration.

Miracle or Mirage: The Blessings of Santa Ana

Perhaps one of the biggest changes attributed to Saint Toribio is the profound economic, cultural, and social transformation of Santa Ana de Guadalupe, Jalisco, wrought by his veneration. The changes began a few years after Toribio's beatification in 1992 and, as noted earlier, coincided more specifically with the arrival of González Pérez in 1997 as the pastor of Santa Ana. The flow of hundreds of thousands of religious visitors to the small town every year has forever changed its civil and religious terrains, the physical and cultural environments, and the psyche of the local community.

Crucially, however, this massive growth in visitors has not translated into an equivalent improvement in the quality of life for the inhabitants of Santa

Ana. An economic and developmental researcher from the University of Guadalajara, Rogelio Martínez-Cárdenas, along with colleagues, points out that (as of 2019) almost one-quarter of all households in the town still lack plumbing and running water, 15 percent do not have a toilet, 9 percent lack refrigerators, and 6 percent do not have access to electricity.[100] Not only is the massive influx of revenue unevenly distributed, but the majority is funneled out of the community. Most of the religious products sold in Santa Ana's stores are produced elsewhere; according to Martínez-Cárdenas in a 2013 article, "only 37% of the items sold are purchased from companies located in the highlands of Jalisco."[101] Most products are brought in by third-party dealers who resell them in town to the small vendors.

The town still has few communal amenities. It has no hotels; most pilgrims travel as part of tours organized by parishes, religious groups, or private companies operating outside Santa Ana. The community has no medical center (one is just now being built) and has only one ambulance, available only on weekends and holidays. Indeed, we might say that the massive influx of tourism is costing the town money; the municipality faces increasing expenditures such as road maintenance, street illumination, trash collection, drinking water accessibility, sewer lines and treatment, and security and fire prevention, among many more services, to accommodate the thousands of new visitors—without any increase in revenues for the municipality. According to Martínez-Cárdenas, each weekend visitors to Santa Ana collectively produce an average of five tons of garbage, or approximately 35.5 pounds per person—an amount far above the national average of 1.69 pounds per person. The town, in short, has become a mono-economy, dangerously dependent on faith-based tourism, which has displaced or eliminated the town's traditional sources of revenue and development, such as ranching and farming.

The negative impact of these transformations has not gone unnoticed. Some local critics have decried what they see as the overcommercialization of devotion to Saint Toribio Romo. When asked about such critiques during an interview by the *New York Times* on August 14, 2002, González Pérez argued, "This is not business, we are not trying to make money on people's faith. We simply want to give the people who visit us the best service we can."[102] He pointed to what he perceives to be the advantages that have flowed from these transformations: "This is about providing a service for our visitors, not about making money or getting rich quickly. When I began my ministry here, in 1997, there wasn't a single place where a visitor to Santa Ana could buy a taco. Now the church has three restaurants where they can buy a plate of carne asada for 25 pesos. That's a very reasonable price.... When we construct new buildings, we could easily hire people from outside, but we prefer to give jobs to the people of Santa Ana."[103] Here, González Pérez's notion of development is focused entirely on the need of pilgrims, not on the needs of the local community. In this way, Santa Ana has turned into a service town, devoted not so much to venerating Saint Toribio as to catering to the needs and wants of his devotees.

Locals often resent the power differential this produces between the pilgrims and the residents. One of the locals expressed his frustration in these terms: "All the blessings are for the peregringos, and very little for those of us who have lived here all our lives."[104] The term "peregringos" brings together two words: "peregrinos," or pilgrims, and "gringos," referring to those coming from El Norte. The term "peregringos" reflects the animosity and hostility against pilgrims (usually Mexican nationals and Latinx Catholics) coming from Canada and the United States. They are part of a complex process of retorno (return), in which Mexicans in diaspora come back to Mexico. In a vicious cycle, as the town serves the pilgrims and becomes more dependent on religious tourism, the traditional ways of life that presumably draw visitors are replaced or forgotten.[105]

The commercial transformation of Santa Ana must be analyzed within the context of the broader growth in religious tourism in Los Altos de Jalisco in the 1990s, and the perpetuation of the Catholic Church's power in the region. Religious tourism is a complex system in which economic and cultural forces work together in the trade of commercial goods, including the goods associated with the ephemeral practices and rituals around faith and religion. According to Martínez-Cárdenas, as of 2016, religious tourism brings an average of eight million pilgrims annually to Jalisco alone. Santa Ana is part of a triangle that connects multiple religious sites, including the Basilica of Our Lady of San Juan of los Lagos and the sanctuary to El Santo Niño de Atocha located in Fresnillo, Zacatecas. Several years ago, the secretaría de turismo, or tourist bureau, of the state of Jalisco created a program known as the Ruta Cristera, or Cristero Route, meant to promote religious tourism in the region by designating four routes (north, south, east, west) that navigate the twenty-four different municipalities of Jalisco and connect all the religious sites.

The tourist bureau even designed a souvenir passport, *El Pasaporte: Mártires Cristeros, Los Altos de Jalisco, Mexico*, in which pilgrims can collect seals as they travel to the different religious sites.[106] The practice of collecting seals from holy places visited goes back to the Middle Ages. This particular passport includes the images of all nine Cristero martyrs from Jalisco, as well a map showing the route corresponding to each saint, including the churches and sites that define each path. The passport also includes a page for the owner to add his or her own picture and information, with a note that reads, "In case the holder of this passport requires information and assistance, it is recommended to go to the tourism representatives or the corresponding church of your municipality." Certainly the document has no legal status, and it redirects the individual to traditional sources of assistance rather than to the Church itself. But it is meant to validate the Church's companionship with the pilgrim, and the politics of retorno.

A Saint of Retorno: The Politics of Religious Remittances and the Peregringos

Just as it is almost impossible to talk about Toribio Romo without referring to the Cristero War or the oppressive policies that govern immigration to the United States, it is also impossible to understand his popularity and his development from a saint of soccer to a saint of immigration in Los Altos without understanding its relation to the process of retorno. In general, scholars use the term "retorno" to refer to the return of diasporic Mexican nationals to their homeland, many of them returning because of forced removal or deportation from the United States; it also refers to the revolving process of leave-and-return that defines immigration, for many Mexican migrants return on their own to Mexico after a period in the United States, and many regularly return again to the United States. Cultural and economic factors, such as xenophobia and economic recessions, affect the fluctuating rates of return to Mexico. As Aguilar Ros describes it, "Los Altos expels migrants, but it also receives them back, creating consequently a migratory culture" in the region.[107] As migrants visit the sanctuary of Saint Toribio, they actively construct the devotional practices and faith surrounding him; by sharing histories and narratives of miracles in crossing to the United States and back, they continually shape him more and more into a saint not of teenagers and soccer but of immigration—the Holy Coyote. Retorno strongly influences religious tourism and can reinforce power differentials between locals and peregringos.

It is not only the migrants who physically return to visit Toribio's sanctuary that take part in this shaping process. In the case of Saint Toribio (and the other saints studied in this book), I am particularly interested in a process I call "spiritual retorno"—the return not just of people but of money: the transfer of donations and remittances sent to Mexico earmarked for religious causes, such as building churches, sponsoring patron saint festivities, or supporting religious activities or charities. Spiritual retorno has had a strong economic and cultural impact in Santa Ana, both on the skyrocketing popularity of Saint Toribio devotion and the physical development of Santa Ana itself.

The total amount of religious financial help sent to Mexico each year from the United States is difficult to calculate. The Catholic Church in the United States, for example, shapes the religious life of all the Americas (North, Central, and South) in formal and informal ways—through sponsoring missionaries, supporting building projects, or even seeking to influence the US government's international aid programs. We also lack data about specific religious remittances sent by Mexican immigrants to their hometowns. We can only explore these religious remittances as part of the larger flow of remittances—billions of dollars sent to Mexico via direct money transfers every year from the United States.[108]

Many remittances are collected, administered, and sent from the United States to Mexico via clubes de oriundos (migrant hometown associations, HTAs) from all over the United States. As scholar Xochitl Bada explains, most HTAs began first as "informal associations, such as soccer clubs, mutual aid societies, or prayer groups," but over time they "have not only become formal organizations but have also scaled up to form federations that represent various communities of origin from that same state."[109] HTAs are created by immigrants who come from a given state or town in their country of origin and now live in the United States. These groups serve as "social support networks, as well as transmitters of culture and values to the U.S.-born generation"; the associations bring together immigrants from particular areas into a critical mass, "increas[ing] migrant leverage with their home state governments" in Mexico and defending members' "rights in the region of settlement" in the United States."[110]

Around the time of the beatification and then canonization of Toribio Romo, as immigration from Mexico was increasing, remittances to Mexico were growing hugely, "from a total of just US$3.7 billion in 1995 to more than US$23 billion in 2006."[111] In 2008—the period when González Pérez was building the new church projects in Santa Ana—almost a thousand HTAs around the United States "contributed more than $30 million to 2,457 projects in 574 municipalities" in Mexico.[112] Jalisco, specifically, is one of the top receivers of remittances from the United States.[113] In the particular case of Santa Ana, migration scholar Shinji Hirai notes: "The recent construction of the new temple to Father Toribio Romo was made possible, in part, by the collaborations of those absent [living] in the United States. The donations were collected through a committee formed by migrants that want to help build the new temple, after receiving a visit of the parish priest of Jalostotitlán [that is, González Pérez], in California in 1996. He tried to promote the devotion to Father Toribio and the construction of his temple among those living in the U.S."[114]

As González Pérez's visit to the United States indicates, the shrine and its related amenities have become part of a larger cultural project of both reconstructing the past and envisioning a better future. Saint Toribio's veneration thus works as a bridge that connects the immigrant experience at both ends—at home and in the host country—and as a signifier of a mobile transnational spirituality. The creation of a committee in the United States to build a church in Mexico, the visit of a priest to California, the pilgrimage of relics through the United States, and the types of miracles attributed to Saint Toribio—all are expressions of the same mobile transnational spirituality.

González Pérez's visits to California in the 1990s took place right after the implementation of NAFTA and just before Toribio Romo's canonization in 2000. They functioned not just as pastoral visits for those living in California who were unable to return to Mexico but also as a way to recognize and tap into the emerging economic power of the diaspora community. It is no coincidence that he chose California, which has over time become a central player in the construction of Saint Toribio as an immigrant saint. In the first decade of the 2000s, for example, a series of relic pilgrimages in California and related marches were organized to support immigration reform in the United States. Those who attended were able to experience not only a personal encounter with Saint Toribio via his relics but also a reconnection with their home country. In this way, Toribio's travels, both literal and imagined, constructed a spiritual Mexican territory that extended beyond Mexico into the United States.

Similarly, the spiritual retorno—the return of money to Mexico—can construct a spiritual United States territory that extends back into home territories in Mexico. Through their many civic, cultural, and religious associations, established immigrants in the United States sponsor and promote numerous development projects back home, often directly deciding—based on their own experiences, sometimes without any consultation with their hometowns—what projects are needed and important. As project sponsors, such immigrants are often able to dictate the design and aesthetic elements of the projects, and cultural understandings of "Americanness" play a vital role in defining how progress should materialize. As Bada explains, HTAs may have a "vision of community development [that] does not necessarily coincide with the priorities and ideas of local governments and international financial institutions."[115] Such conflicts can stem from many ideological, physical, and temporal factors, such as the distance between the immigrant HTA and the community it is trying to serve, the time between immigrants' departure and the moment they are able to help, the many changes the hometown has experienced, and differing notions of progress or development, especially after sponsors have been exposed to life in the United States. This may help to explain how Santa Ana de Guadalupe has seen such growth in religious infrastructural development but so little development in amenities or services for those within the community itself.

More research is needed to fully understand how and to what extent HTAs may transform or influence local decision-making in religious sites like Santa Ana, as well as the roles played by individuals who return to Mexico from the United States. Returnees, who form an essential constituency of Saint Toribio's veneration, have had a significant impact on the transformation of Santa Ana. The "revolving door" of migration is a powerful one: between "2009 and 2016, 1.4 million Mexicans returned and 2.2 million [were] removed from the United States," and between 2010 and 2015, Jalisco was the state with the highest number of returnees, representing 9 percent of the total national number; the adjacent state of Michoacán had the second-highest number, with 7 percent of the national number of returnees.[116] These numbers are important because they contextualize the unique characteristics that define the popularity of Saint Toribio. He is not simply a saint of migration to the United States but also a saint of return. Many of his venerators are those who returned to show their gratitude for favors received: he asks all those he has helped cross the border to *return* to Santa Ana. Saint Toribio is thus a companion to all—those who make it to the United States and succeed, those who have decided on their own to return, and even those who have seen their dreams dashed and have been forced to come home. He is a saint of the entire wide border zone, the big spaces outside/on the edges (and far away) of the line of the border, where the United States and Mexico mix in a kind of gradient.

Santo Inmigrante: Traveling with Toribio Romo in Your Pocket

The many religious objects sold along the streets and within the shops of Santa Ana are more than just mementos of a spiritual visit to a religious shrine. They also have a specific utilitarian function, given Saint Toribio's status as a smuggler saint. For a person migrating north, a rosary from Santa Ana does actual work: it promises to maximize the chances of a safe journey and a successful outcome. Capitalizing on Toribio's specific symbolic and pragmatic value as a coyote is essential to his fame as a migration miracle maker and to the success of his "brand." Consequently, US-Mexico relations are crucial to the meaning of Toribio Romo–related objects.

Many of the objects related to Saint Toribio sold in Santa Ana are talismans, amulets, or material spiritual mantras, meant to be used to help the individual navigate a dangerous immigration journey. One of the most interesting objects sold here is the *Spiritual Passport* (despite the similarity in names, this is different from *El Pasaporte: Mártires Cristeros, Los Altos de Jalisco*, which is the spiritual passport for the Cristero martyrs pilgrimage). The Santa Ana *Spiritual Passport* is a replica of a US passport created by the private American company Pajaro Macua, a Florida-based company that produces and distributes spiritual and esoteric objects. The passport, which is meant to be used by migrants during their journey to the United States, is printed in Spanish. The blue cover, inscribed with the words "Spiritual Passport," reproduces the design of an authentic diplomatic document, bearing the Great Seal of the United States and the words "United States." The company website exhorts buyers, in both Spanish and English, to "visualize your blue American passport and [you] will get one," and it explicitly says, "Este pasaporte espiritual the protejera contra inmigracion" (This spiritual passport will protect you against immigration [Spanish errors are in the original]).[117]

Upon opening the document, one finds not the US secretary of state's request for safe passage for US citizens but a prayer to Saint Toribio. The text—printed on one side in English and on the other side in Spanish—is an updated version of a prayer that can be found in *El devocionario del migrante*, described in the introduction of this book. *El devocionario* is a small book produced by the Diocese of San Juan de los Lagos containing prayers for the various steps of the immigration process. However, this particular prayer has been modified for the *Spiritual Passport* to voice a plea from the family of the person migrating to the United States. The passport thus serves not just those traveling but also those who stay behind. The English version of the prayer reads: "We ask you through the intercession of Santo Toribio Romo to take care and protect our relatives who had to leave the House and go to foreign lands in search of improvement for them and our families, protect them from all evil and make them stand firm in the faith so can return soon to our home and strengthened in the soul and the body."[118] The prayer thus weaves together a request for safe travel with a plea that those who travel north will not lose their faith.

The next page of the *Spiritual Passport* reproduces exactly the signature page found on a US passport, including the preamble of the US Constitution and images of a bald eagle, the American flag, and ears of wheat. The next page presents a modified version of the US passport's data page with information about the passport holder. It reproduces a type P (or personal) US passport, but instead of the passport holder's information, Toribio Romo's information appears:[119]

Surname / Nom / Apellidos	Romo Gonzales
Given Names / Prénoms / Nombres	Santo Toribio
Nationality / Nationalité / Nacionalidad	Mexicano
Date of birth / Date de naissance / Fecha de nacimiento	16 de abril 1900
Place of birth / Lieu de naissance / Lugar de nacimiento	Santa Ana de Guadalupe—México
Date of issue / Date de délivrance / Fecha de expedición	TENER FAITH [Have faith]
Date of expiration / Date d'expiration / Fecha de caducidad	NUNCA-NEVER
Sex / Sexe / Sexo	M
Authority / Autorité / Autoridad	DIOS (God)

This page obviously diverges in several ways from a real US passport, yet the mixture of similar and dissimilar elements gives the presented information its power. These elements combine to give the document an interstitial status—it is a simulacrum that is neither real nor wholly imagined. The passport marshals the spiritual to help the user navigate the real. Neither dimension excludes the other; they must work together.

It is worthwhile to closely read some of the elements of the passport. Note, for example, that the document does not present Saint Toribio as a US citizen or national, even though only US citizens and nationals can carry US passports. In this way, the document plays off both the real and the imaginary; it shows that even when one is in the United States, documented as an American, one is still always Mexican and still holds the border crossing in one's heart. For date of issue, the passport lists only "Have faith." This implies that only faith in Saint Toribio's miraculous intervention counts as the starting point for achieving a positive outcome. Similarly, for the date of expiration, the passport lists "never," implying that the migrant must never give up—on Toribio or on the immigration process itself—or that God's care for the immigrant never stops. The machine-readable strip located on the bottom of this data page—which customarily displays the passport number and the owner's name—in this case shows only the name "Santo Toribio Romo," surrounded by the word "Dios" (God) printed sixty-two times. God is also presented as the authority issuing the document. This detail crucially implies that the migrant's travel—however technically illegal it may be—is endorsed by a higher authority.

The second-to-last page in the *Spiritual Passport* includes a prayer in Spanish that reads like a statement of purpose—a justification of the decision to migrate. It refers to "refugees who are escaping violence" and draws connections to the experience of Jesus himself—someone else who "became a pilgrim, going through the experience of the displaced." At the end, the prayer becomes an exhortation asking that those living in El Norte be protected "from danger and strengthen their faith. So that they seek happiness not only in this world but also, in eternal life."[120]

The *Spiritual Passport*, with its blend of real and imaginary, navigates a Catholic global citizenship that expands beyond national borders. The document manifests a core dilemma for the migration of members of the Catholic Church: how to reconcile the theological values that see all humans as children of one single God, united by their Catholic faith, with the very real boundaries erected by national states and government policies. The passport exemplifies a core paradox for a transnational religious institution whose members must still reckon with secular nationality or citizenship.

On the Other Side: Saint Toribio Romo Moves to the United States

As befits a transnational saint and the Holy Smuggler, Saint Toribio lives simultaneously in both Mexico and the United States. Saints, as spiritual entities, reside in the faith of their followers and devotees, and they can therefore be in many places at once: their "presence" is tied to their followers' mobilization of faith and relocation of devotional practices and of relics. Indeed, the remarkable mobility of many saints' veneration is made possible by the migration of relics—the often transnational sharing of their fragmented bodies and the objects that surrounded their existence.

Indeed, only as a saint has Toribio Romo himself traveled into El Norte. Bone relics of Saint Toribio can now be found in several parishes of the United States. These relics reveal the migration patterns (and settlements) of Mexican immigrants, especially those from the Jalisco region. As the patron of immigrants, Saint Toribio helps map the ways and spaces in which migration and religiosity collide. This section charts the migration of Saint Toribio's relics into the United States, focusing on two Catholic parish sites: Holy Redeemer in Detroit, Michigan, and Sts. Peter and Paul in Tulsa, Oklahoma. In each place, one finds a different presence of Saint Toribio Romo that reveals distinct politics of translocation and community mobilization.

Mexicantown, Detroit: A Saint in Gothic City

> Back in the 1930s and '40s, Holy Redeemer was known as the largest English-language parish in the United States . . . [and now, there] is no doubt that it's a Hispanic parish. . . . An Anglo would come in and look and say, . . . "Y'know I came to the church when I was a kid and it used to be packed." I said, "Well, if you come for the Spanish Masses, it's packed."
> —Most Rev. Donald F. Hanchon, auxiliary bishop of the Archdiocese of Detroit

Mexicantown is a barrio community located in southwest Detroit, Michigan. The area emerged as a Latinx enclave in the early part of the twentieth century when immigrants started to settle along Vernor Street. Known originally as La Badley, the barrio received the name Mexicantown in the 1980s, after the waves of migration from Mexico in previous decades and before the large 1990s immigration resettlement in Detroit. Today a relic of Saint Toribio—a fragment *ex ossibus* (from the bones)—is hosted at Holy Redeemer Roman Catholic Church, one of the central players in this Latinx community. The relic's original arrival in Mexicantown was celebrated with a Mass on November 21, 2010, on the feast of Christ the King. The day was especially fitting given Toribio's status as a martyr of the Cristero War, the slogan of which was "Long live Christ the King."

Most of the paperwork needed to acquire the relic from Mexico was handled by Donald F. Hanchon, then pastor at Holy Redeemer (1999–2005) and now auxiliary bishop of Detroit. Originally from Jackson, Michigan, Hanchon has been involved with Latinx community ministry since the late 1980s. Saint Toribio revealed himself to Hanchon in a simple but almost miraculous way in the very place—Holy Redeemer—where his relic would eventually rest and be venerated by the public. One day, Hanchon went into the church, almost in desperation, asking for help to save the impoverished parish—and God answered his prayers. Hanchon describes the event:

> I was walking through the church and I'd found on the floor . . . a little medallion with the photo of [Saint] Toribio [Romo]. . . . I brought it to the office to Geraldina, the [parish] secretary, who is Dominican. . . . I said, "Geraldina, do you recognize this?" She goes, "Oh, sí, sí, es el Padre Toribio," and I said "¿Quién es él?" . . . Never heard of him before, you know? First time I'd ever seen the image. . . . She said, "He's a saint from Jalisco and there are many people from his area." I said, "Oh, that's very interesting." It's—first mention I'd heard from him. So then I started to . . . ask around and ask people if they knew Father Toribio [Romo] . . . [and they responded] "Oh, sí, ¿como no? [Oh, yes, of course!]"[121]

For believers, the bishop's discovery of the medallion was no random incident, but an act of divine intervention and a sign of Saint Toribio's agency. The saint wanted a shrine in that church. Of course, there are other explanations for the presence of the medallion, but the community is not particularly interested in them. What matters is that the medallion depicted not just any saint but Saint Toribio, who happened to originate from the same region as many in the local community. For almost fifty years, Holy Redeemer has been holding Spanish Masses in Mexicantown, and around 75 percent of its members are from Jalisco.[122] So the interest of Hanchon, as the pastor of that community, in Toribio is not coincidental; it can only be understood within a specific demographic context and transformation. The subsequent creation of a shrine to Saint Toribio within this particular church not only reflects already existing devotional practices within the community but also constructs and reinforces that community's identification with the local church.

Acquiring the Relic of Saint Toribio for Detroit

Eventually Hanchon visited Los Altos de Jalisco in Mexico, where he learned more about Saint Toribio and what he means to immigrants: "I went there several times and I was really moved by the stories I would hear. The people up here who were immigrants . . . would tell me the stories that they had heard or their own experiences of getting helped . . . as they crossed in a difficult moment."[123] Here, Hanchon shows how Toribio Romo connects both sides of the border, linking those located in Mexico, especially in Los Altos de Jalisco, with those from his own parish. With the help of the local bishop in Jalisco and the pastor of Santa Ana, Hanchon secured a bone fragment from the body of Toribio Romo, and by 2010, he was able to bring it to Detroit. The relic was received solemnly by the archbishop of Detroit, Allen Vigneron, on November 3 of that year at the Cathedral of the Most Blessed Sacrament. After visiting several parishes in the area, the relic found its permanent home at Hanchon's own parish, in the Holy Redeemer Church, in a little shrine to the left of the altar, in what used to be a confessional. At Mass on November 21, 2010, the reliquary was blessed and received by the community.[124] Acquiring the relic of Saint Toribio renewed the popularity of Holy Redeemer and helped consolidate the parish as a Latinx enclave in Detroit.

Imagining an Icon: Racial Conflicts over Saint Toribio's Image in Detroit

The bone fragment is not the only object used to venerate Saint Toribio in Detroit. To accompany the fragments, Nancy Lee Smith, a renowned producer of religious icons and a Catholic sister of the Immaculate Heart of Mary, was commissioned to write a religious icon of Saint Toribio. (In Eastern Orthodox iconography, icons are said to be "written," not painted.)

As explained by Hanchon, "A family from the parish . . . wanted to express their gratitude to the parish for all their years as an immigrant family. So they gave a donation" to fund the Toribio Romo icon.[125]

I met Smith at her studio, located within her religious community in Monroe, Michigan. She is a vibrant and energetic artist who has dedicated her career to creating and restoring Christian icons, a form of worship stemming from Eastern Orthodox aesthetic tradition. She told me that the Toribio Romo icon was commissioned by a Latino alumnus of the Holy Redeemer parish who had moved to Novi, Michigan. Smith met with Hanchon, the donor, and various members of the community in the process of writing the icon; following tradition, its creation required several years of research and prayer. When the icon was finally presented to the community during a solemn celebration, Smith recalls, "the place was packed. . . . They carried the icon up over their heads and brought it into the church."[126]

However, the piece was not well received by the community. Two elements in the icon soon became the focus of controversy: a traffic sign held in Saint Toribio's hands and the depiction of the saint as apparently mixed-race, with dark skin (Figure 3.4). The traffic sign controversy was generated because, according to Smith, the congregation (mistakenly) believed that "you can't have [or depict] anything manmade in an icon."[127] Smith's icon has Romo holding a yellow "Caution" traffic sign that also features silhouettes of a family running—a symbol that is, as we will see, especially well suited to represent Toribio Romo, the patron saint of border crossing. The sign in the image is well known to the Latinx immigrant community, because it was widely used during the 1990s along California's I-5, between the San Ysidro port of entry at the US-Mexico border (Tijuana/San Diego) and the San Clemente US Customs and Border Protection checkpoint. The sign was created to warn drivers about undocumented immigrants crossing the freeway, after more than one hundred people were killed along that section of the interstate between 1987 and 1990.

The sign fits the religious icon's cultural context and signifies Saint Toribio's role as the patron saint of immigrants. As Smith puts it, because an icon is not only an image but also a sacred object in itself, she "prayed about what to put in his hands, which is one of the main things in an icon."[128] The inspiration to include an immigration sign that is deeply loaded with political meaning came to Smith after talking with Hanchon. She explains: "Hanchon told me that he [Saint Toribio] shows up at the border in a red pickup truck. So I got in the literature. . . . I read a number of articles and stories about him. . . . It was

200 UNDOCUMENTED SAINTS

Figure 3.4 Icon of Toribio Romo, Detroit. The icon was created by Sr. Nancy Lee Smith. Displayed at Most Holy Redeemer Catholic Church, Mexicantown, Detroit.
© 2012 SSIHM

that whole connection with the immigrants that struck me. And when you do an icon, you read their letters, you read their life, you find out what's said about them, what they said, and you get to know them personally. You pray. You form a relationship."[129] Smith's aesthetic decision turned a religious icon into a powerful political statement about the deadly realities experienced by immigrants as they cross into the United States. As Smith explains: "I put the sign in his hands because he's helping them be illegal immigrants, according to the law, to an unfair law."[130]

These explanations helped reduce the controversy around the traffic sign, but more intractable was the anger over Smith's depiction of Toribio as an Afro-Latino man rather than as a white alteño. As explained earlier in this chapter, the blue eyes and light complexion that usually appear in Saint Toribio's images align him specifically with Los Altos residents' identity as "whites, criollos, with a fervent Catholicism."[131] As previously discussed, Toribio's race works as a signifier of the internalized values of beauty, holiness, and good character that are attached to whiteness in Mexico.

According to Smith, she worked from an image of Romo faxed to her by Hanchon. Describing the final appearance of the icon, she says: "He's kind of dark and foreboding-looking. You know, big bushy hair and he kind of looks . . . like not a grin could ever cross his face, overly serious. So I tried to capture . . . his hairdo, and what he might have looked like without getting real specific. You're not supposed to get real specific in an icon. You have a lot of generic things you follow."[132] Here, she gestures to the visual tropes of icons, many of whose subjects are depicted as darker-skinned and with a larger forehead, representing their wisdom and holiness. Her aesthetic decision was not well received or understood, though; in the eyes of the community, however, she misrepresented the saint, and they have treated the icon accordingly. The community "stuck the icon in a corner and put plants in front of [it]. . . . They didn't understand. . . . I've been praying to him to manifest himself in his own time."[133]

Hanchon attributes the controversy to the fact that "all [Smith] had to work from was a picture from the little holy card" that he had given her as a photo reference for the icon. He adds:

> The icon doesn't really look like Toribio [Romo] and that was a big problem among them. Yeah . . . They said, "No, no se parece nada! No! . . . Se parece a otra persona" [No, it doesn't look anything like him! It looks like another person]. . . . You look at the image, and you see that he has darker skin. . . . That was the main problem . . . the skin color. So I kept it there [in the parish] out of respect for this [donor] family, but we got a larger image of the photograph [of Toribio Romo] and put that over the relic.[134]

The community's response is revealing: it illustrates how religious practices can be deeply influenced by sociopolitical forms of racial speech as they travel and migrate, as the racial discourses around Toribio have crossed over from Mexico into the United States. What is at stake here is not the integrity or authenticity of the icon but the way in which believers self-identify their devotions with a particular racial typology, one that has historically and intentionally erased African or indigenous presence from narratives of holiness.

Tulsa: The Bible Belt and the First National Sanctuary to Saint Toribio Romo

> HB 1804 is the reason we have an image of Saint Toribio Romo in the middle of the United States.
> —Father Tim Davison, Sts. Peter and Paul Church, Tulsa

On February 5, 2007, state representative Randy Terrill introduced bill HB 1804 into Oklahoma's House of Representatives. Officially known as the Oklahoma Taxpayer and Citizen Protection Act 2007, the bill was one of the toughest pieces of legislation to date against undocumented immigrants in the United States. It received overwhelming approval from both Democrats and Republicans in Oklahoma's House of Representatives. On May 8, Governor Brad Henry signed it into law. The act makes it a felony to provide support in the form of housing or transportation to any person suspected to be in the state without authorization. The law also prohibits state agencies from providing health care, education, or public services to undocumented immigrants or their children. It requires local police to enforce the law and to verify the legal status of any individual suspected to be in the country without documentation.

On June 29, 2006, a few months before HB 1804 was introduced, Edward J. Slattery, then the Catholic bishop of Tulsa, met with around sixty white parishioners, all members of Sts. Peter and Paul Catholic Church in the McKinley neighborhood in Tulsa. Slattery met with them to hear their concerns about the rapid demographic transformations in the parish; they complained about what they perceived as "disruption" in the parish under Father Tim Davison, who had arrived as pastor some two years prior and sought to reach out to the growing Hispanic community in the area.[135] The meeting with Slattery was tense and difficult, reflecting deep divisions within the Catholic Church in the United States regarding the issue of immigration.

The conflict had reached a tipping point a few months earlier. The bishop had celebrated a confirmation Mass mostly in Spanish, because most of the attendees were Spanish-speakers. In response, "some people walked out, and the family of at least one confirmand left the parish over the incident."[136] When Slattery tried to explain his pastoral obligation to all people, including those without documentation who were already present in the United States, he asked the attendees, "Should they all—mothers and fathers and children—be sent back?"[137] He was expecting a negative response, but a man in the audience screamed, "Yes, and I'll drive a bus."[138] The bishop, frustrated by what he described as "definite prejudice" against immigrants, told the attendees, "You have something to learn here, and it's the Gospel"—specifically how the Christian holy text expresses the need to show compassion and acceptance toward foreigners.[139] Then he left the meeting.

Despite this kind of xenophobic hostility (which is not uncommon in some parts of the Bible Belt), the Latinx immigrant community has flourished in Oklahoma. According to Oklahoma Watch, a nonprofit reporting group, US Census Bureau data show that "Oklahoma is just a piece of the overall pattern of immigration that is occurring nationwide"; more Latinxs "have been migrating to new destinations in interior states" outside the traditional Mexican immigration destinations of "California, Florida, New York, Texas and Illinois."[140] Such demographic changes, says Oklahoma Watch, point "toward a multicultural future that some Oklahomans consider invigorating, but others find unsettling."[141]

In December 2007, Davison wrote to all the priests of the diocese: "As you are aware many of our Hispanic brothers and sisters are in need of special attention due to HB 1804. They turn to the Church for protection and support and it is for those reasons that a group of Hispanic Catholics at my parish have begun meeting to plan for the establishment of a special place of prayer to the Patron of Immigrants, St. José Toribio Romo Gonzalez."[142] Despite the opposition of many white parishioners, in 2008 Sts. Peter and Paul Catholic Church celebrated the arrival of a newly commissioned six-foot-tall statue of Saint Toribio Romo and the first relic of him to be housed in the United States. The parish eventually spearheaded the construction of the nation's first Saint Toribio Romo shrine.

According to Simón Navarro, a longtime member of the parish and a local activist, the succession of events that led to creating the national shrine to Saint Toribio began unexpectedly. Navarro was responsible for commissioning and transporting the sanctuary's six-foot statue, and he coordinated the negotiations that ended with the eventual arrival of the relic of Saint Toribio in Tulsa. He explained how HB 1804 catalyzed these events:

> Few years ago, there was a very strong law that was going to happen... 1604 [*sic*: HB 1804].... We started, as an organization, to get involved in the protests.... We asked churches and schools to support us, in order to have a place to meet... to give seminars, and to teach people how to protect themselves and protest.... Father Tim [Davison] told me that he wanted

to help [the Latina/o community], but he did not know how. . . . I told him that there was a saint venerated by people in Mexico and they called him the patron of immigrants. Then he said, "Let's work on bringing a statue." I started working with the civil association [Casa de Guanajuato, Navarro's HTA] . . . with the contacts [I had] in Mexico . . . because he [Toribio] is originally from another state, Jalisco, and I am from Guanajuato. They are close to each other . . . like two hours [driving].[143]

Navarro's connection to Casa de Guanajuato is significant. The state of Guanajuato is second only to Jalisco, Toribio's home state, in the number of migrants it sends to the United States.[144] Navarro's account also reveals a new dimension of the crucial role played by HTAs in Toribio's popularity and in transnational religiosity in general. In describing the process of spiritual retorno earlier in the chapter, I focused on the financial support sent home by HTAs and individual immigrants. But in Tulsa we see a different dimension of this process. Here, we see groups of immigrants actively building a spiritual Mexico in exile, within the United States. Saint Toribio spiritually migrates north as migrants seek to reconstruct the familiar, the known, the quotidian within the unknown and the hostile. Saint Toribio reinscribes Mexican spiritual territories within Oklahoma in a way that generates and preserves spaces of security, comfort, and hope for the present and the future.

In addition to moving churches to enter the political fray over immigration, the imminent passage of HB 1804 in Oklahoma also radicalized the HTA Casa de Guanajuato. In this group, the boundaries between religiosity, cultural exchange, and immigration activism became increasingly blurry as Navarro and others built the religious and secular transnational connections necessary to commission and bring a statue and later a relic to the United States from Mexico.

But many see Saint Toribio's journey to Tulsa not only as a story of immigrant activism but also as evidence of his miracles. Due to delays in the construction of the statue, the original schedule changed, and Navarro and others were forced to travel to Mexico themselves and personally bring the object back across the border. Navarro recounts: "Bringing the image of Father Toribio [Romo] to the United States was very difficult. Too much paperwork . . . We had a deadline and the bishop of Tulsa was waiting for us. We could not wait for papers."[145] Consequently, "like many other immigrants have done it before . . . Father Toribio [Romo] crossed the border without [papers]."[146] Four to five people loaded the life-sized statue "in a big box... inside a van." Navarro explains that as they approached the border entry point,

> I asked all of them [those traveling with him] for their [travel] documents. In the haste of everything that was happening, I did not think much about anything. . . . They all gave me their documents . . . and I kept driving. [When we got to the border checkpoint] the guard asked me, "What are you carrying there? What do you bring there?" "A gift for the Church," [I responded]. He asks us to get [out] of the car. . . . Here, it is the first miracle . . . after few minutes, he [the guard] gave us the passports and checked nothing. It was a surprising thing, because they did *not* check *anything*! Afterwards, as I was reviewing the events . . . I began to see that in reality it was something almost miraculous! Because of the people who was there [driving in the van], I am an [American] citizen, but I'm still an immigrant. I'm not gringo! And [there was also] a green card holder [a permanent resident] and a tourist . . . and then there was a person without papers, who was there from Laredo. All the immigrant expressions were represented![147]

The diverse composition of the delegation that brought the statue back to Tulsa was a purposeful decision on Navarro's part, as he explains: "I wanted to showcase the diversity of our immigrant community."[148] For Navarro and the community, in which the story has since become popular lore, the meaning of the incident is clear: "I truly believe Father Toribio helped us. He really wanted to be in Tulsa."[149] This event frames Toribio's journey to the United States as a reenactment of the immigrant experience of crossing the border without documents and then remaining without authorization. For Navarro and those other venerators of Saint Toribio who are involved with his chapel in Tulsa, this event is another example of the many miracles of Toribio. This particular miracle indisputably connects him with the life experience of his many undocumented followers—it miraculously positions him as an undocumented Mexican trapped on one side of the border.

A relic of Toribio Romo, a bone fragment, arrived in Tulsa on April 16, 2008, and the statue arrived on May 19; these events were celebrated together with a series of events that took place between May 21 to May 25. The festivities began with a solemn Mass celebrated by Slattery on the feast day of Saint Toribio Romo, May 21, with a short procession of the statue. A novena was prayed that week, and on Sunday, May 25, a huge community celebration took place. The event included "a pilgrimage from the various communities of Hispanic immigrants [in the Tulsa area] to St. Francis Xavier Church where the pilgrims . . . [began] a walk to Sts. Peter and Paul parish," reaching the church in time for a Spanish Mass, which was followed by an afternoon carnival with "games, live music, [and] food."[150] Soon after the successful arrival of the relic and the statue, plans were underway to construct a chapel that would eventually become the national shrine of Saint Toribio Romo in the United States. As Navarro explains, the decision was announced the same day as the celebration, May 25, 2008: "The bishop was impressed by the huge number of people attending. That's why that same day, [during the celebration] he declared the shrine! We thought [of] asking for it in a few years, but we had not asked yet. . . . [His declaration] encouraged us, even more!"

Even though the two objects, statue and relic, arrived within a few weeks of each other and were unveiled to the Tulsa community during the same event, they have distinct trajectories and forms of spiritual capital within the manda economy of the believers; the community has constructed a unique affective relationship with each object. The bone fragment was donated to Tulsa directly from Santa Ana de Guadalupe, Jalisco, and was given in person to Davison, the Anglo pastor of the church. The relic thus enjoyed a much simpler journey to the United States than the statue did: Davison and the relic passed easily into the United States on April 16, 2008. Legality and race are key components in the differentiation of these sacred objects' migration—both their original border crossing and their afterlives within the community. The relic remains static, protected within the shrine, while the life-sized statue continues to migrate, regularly traveling around Tulsa; it is especially mobile in mid-May, around both the anniversary of its arrival and Toribio Romo's feast day. Today, over four thousand followers gather every year during this time to venerate St. Toribio Romo, moving the statue across town in a grand procession that is both religious and political (Figure 3.5).

The relic, tucked away in its niche, remains more abstract to venerators of St. Toribio; perhaps because of its inaccessibility, they have a less intense emotional connection to it, although (unlike the statue) it is a personal relic of the saint himself. Devotees form a more personal connection with the statue, with its anthropomorphic mobility and real presence. The relic is no less sacred, but it is understood to serve more as a source of spiritual support for the whole community. In a February 21, 2008, letter to the bishop of San Juan de los Lagos, Felipe Salazar Villagrana, Slattery described the significance of the relic: "The presence of his [Toribio's] relic will comfort people as they pray for his intercession during these difficult times in Oklahoma. There

Figure 3.5 Procession of Saint Toribio Romo, May 26, 2019, Tulsa, Oklahoma. Caravan with the statue of Toribio Romo arrives at Sts. Peter and Paul as part of the celebration.
Photo by the author

is a lot of suffering here because of the recent law targeting undocumented immigrants. Many have already left the state with fear. As a consequence of this law, families has been separated."[151] In a previous communication, he had explained, "This is why [it] is an opportune moment to offer this Shrine [to Toribio Romo] as a space for our [migrant] parishioners to obtain spiritual strength, which also will be a support for our pastoral mission."[152]

The shrine that contains the relic directly mimics the aesthetics and architectural spaces of Mexico's churches. Indeed, a central feature of the shrine is a scale reproduction of the original La Mesita church in Santa Ana, the main and original chapel to Saint Toribio (see Figure 3.6). Navarro explains that the reproduction was no small task, but it was well worth the effort and cost: "We collected money selling tamales and donations. . . . It cost us around $450,000. But many materials were brought from Mexico. We wanted to make a small replica of the chapel in Mexico [in Santa Ana]. The only thing that changes, a little here, is that in Mexico they have the Virgin

Figure 3.6 Mirror Altars, Tulsa, Oklahoma. *Top:* Altar (replica) at Sts. Peter and Paul, Tulsa, Oklahoma. *Bottom:* Altar at La Mesita in Santa Ana, Jalisco. The altars are located on the northern and southern sides of the migration journey.
Photos by the author

[of Guadalupe] on the top of the altar, and here we don't. . . . But everything else is the same . . . it's the same thing!"[153] Even the materials to build the chapel "were brought from Mexico," firmly establishing the authenticity of the final product.[154] Anthropologist Aguilar Ros argues that the reproduction in Tulsa serves as a "mirror sanctuary . . . [that] shows that the religious practices of these migrants also transform the American national space."[155]

By recreating La Mesita in Oklahoma, the chapel "allows for this locality [La Mesita] to be rescaled at international levels, and brings this sanctuary [in Tulsa] into the global circuits of Catholicism."[156] The chapel works essentially as a spiritual Mexico-within-Tulsa—a particularly meaningful possibility for Toribio's followers who are unable to return to Mexico because of their legal status. Just as the saint himself helps migrants to cross the border, so too does the shrine's chapel facilitate spiritual passage between distant spaces, gesturing toward the fact that these are spiritual *retornos* in action, bringing the incorporeal self back to Mexico. The replica in the United States works as a portal of sorts, one that keeps migrants connected to their homeland. In the experience of migration, the real and the simulacrum merge, becoming two ends of a continuous line that leads across the border, from Mexico to the United States and back.

A Traveling Coyote Saint

Toribio Romo's 2000 canonization by Saint Pope John Paul II can be understood as the Catholic Church's response to two things: the larger phenomenon of Mexican migration to the United States and the popularization of other border folk saints, such as Juan Soldado and Jesús Malverde. Soldado and Malverde, two "illegal saint[s] of 'illegal' immigrants," represent an unsettling conflict for the Catholic Church, given its large number of Mexican adherents; so many Mexican Catholics venerate these vernacular saints despite their unofficial status, and their very nonrecognition means that the Church is unable to regulate their veneration.[157]

As this chapter shows, Saint Toribio's vernacular canonization as the Holy Coyote, the Holy Smuggler—and his evolution from his early iterations as patron saint of children, teens, and soccer—points to the need to understand not only how the Church seeks to centralize, standardize, and police faith practices but also how vernacular religiosity continues to elude Church control. Saint Toribio plays a key role for many migrants who must negotiate not just the migration policies of the United States but also the religious and cultural boundary patrolling being carried out by the Catholic Church in North America. Saint Toribio helps us understand how the regulation of faith constitutes a central component in US-Mexico relations and conflicts, despite both nations' claims to be secular states.[158] His veneration in the United States, for example, reveals the limitations of state sovereignty in dealing with religiosity and the migration of faith, as transnational migrating communities unsettle state boundaries and recreate new spaces of religious statehoods.

Saint Toribio's veneration (like that of Jesús Malverde) manifests how religiosity intersects with race within the performativity of gender expectations, as his followers construct around him idealizations about whiteness and Mexicanidad—and conservative notions of masculinity. The veneration of St. Toribio pertains to the prospects of making it to El Norte and succeeding there, of course, but it also relates to the question of Mexicanness for those already in the United States, manifesting the expectations (and apprehensions) of what it means to be a good and authentic Mexican outside the homeland. The practices around Saint Toribio recreate a type of Mexico that is glued together by religiosity and national identity but is deeply connected to racial discourses of citizenship.

The largest communities of Saint Toribio's followers outside Mexico have expanded beyond the traditional Southwest Latinx enclaves to find homes in cities like Chicago, Detroit, and Tulsa. Mapping the location and migration of Saint Toribio's relics within the United States leads one through key battlegrounds of immigration debates and charts the tangled intersections of race and religiosity. In 2014, for example, a four-foot-tall wooden statue of the saint, complete with a relic (a bone fragment from the saint's left ankle) enclosed within its heart, arrived in the United States from Jalisco for a tour through three southern California counties.[159] Its first stop in the United States was the Cathedral of Our Lady of the Angels, in downtown Los Angeles, where it was solemnly received on July 20.[160] Over the subsequent days it traveled to the cities of Indio, Rancho Cucamonga, Lake Forest, and Commerce.[161] Thousands of followers gathered to greet the statue as it traveled between parishes. Among the many requests made of the saint were "Please, my mother needs a visa"; "Please, my niece was caught by agents"; and "Please, I can't go on being illegal."[162]

It was no coincidence that the statue's holy tour took place when the national debate over immigration in the United States was intensifying. That summer, an anticipated immigration reform plan, designed to provide a path to citizenship for undocumented immigrants and streamline the immigration and documentation process, was killed in Congress. The bill, which had been under consideration since 2013, had been proposed by a bipartisan group of senators known as the Gang of Eight, but it was killed when it expired due to inaction by the US House of Representatives, led by Speaker John Boehner.[163] In the summer of 2014, an upsurge of media coverage also brought to international attention a new dimension of the immigration crisis: the increased number of unaccompanied children and women from Central America arriving at the US-Mexico border. They came from what is often referred to as the Northern Triangle of Central America, a triple border shared by Guatemala, El Salvador, and Honduras. The refugee children were the source of great concern from many Toribio Romo devotees. For example, Francisca Romero, a fifty-six-year-old Toribio Romo devotee, came to see the statue when it stopped in Commerce, California. She asked the saint to help her family, her friends, and the thousands of Central Americans children arriving at the border that summer; as she put it, "Those children, I want this saint to keep them safe from all harm, and to please help us all."[164] Another believer, Jesse Lopez, and his family came to see the traveling saint at a church in Rancho Cucamonga, explaining: "We're here to ask St. Toribio [Romo] to protect them. These are children in need. They're alone and they're afraid."[165]

During a homily at St. Marcellinus Church in Commerce, California, near East Los Angeles, Father Martin Federico Rizo Soto, the Mexican priest who accompanied the relic on its trip from Jalisco through southern California, spoke directly about the situation at the US-Mexico border that summer:

> Today, all the young immigrants that will travel through so many dangerous paths, this valor that St. Toribio [Romo] had, gives them strength. Although the path is difficult, it is not impossible. If we have his intercession and his protection, we can do anything. Let us then commend to St. Toribio Romo the destiny of our towns. Let us commend this large community of immigrants that live here, with all their problems, their difficulties, their circumstances. May this be the time that we ask for his intercession for our homeland, for the good of our towns so that we may live justice. May this be.[166]

The relic's pilgrimage that summer illustrates how religiosity and political mobilization merge within the veneration of Saint Toribio. The Masses, the travels of the relic, and the explicit context of the pilgrimage combined to provide palliative spiritual assistance to those in distress. But it also created a sense of belonging to a pan-Latinx immigrant community affected by external forces beyond their control. Saint Toribio Romo unifies the community as a heterogenous body-in-suffering—a body trapped between displacement from home and vulnerability in the United States, but held together through faith in the body and living spirit of another.

Postscript: Who Really Killed Toribio Romo?

During the research for this chapter, I encountered again and again essentially the same narrative of the killing of Toribio Romo—namely, that he was murdered by government troops in the context of the Cristero War. The story can be found in everything from academic articles to US and Mexican newspapers to the souvenir handouts printed by the many local shops in Santa Ana de Guadalupe and around Tequila. It appears in the biographies created by the local dioceses and sold in the churches. But while examining the files submitted to the Vatican for Saint Toribio's canonization, I made a stunning (but not entirely surprising) discovery that contradicted all traditional accounts of his death. Within the Vatican records—and notably *only* within the Vatican records—are listed the specific name and identity of the person who shot and killed Toribio Romo: "Lauro Sandoval, who was a member of the agraristas."[167]

Certainly, the Guadalajara diocese had access to all files sent to the Vatican, given that all the documents and testimonies for Toribio Romo's canonization were collected by and within the diocese. My interest, however, lies not in adjudicating the truth of the claim or how it came to appear in the Vatican's records, but rather in considering why the information would unsettle existing narratives and what this tells us about the construction of saintly meaning. If true, erasing this fact from popular memory aligns with the consistent effort, identified by César Eduardo Medina Gallo, to ignore uncomfortable information about the Cristero War. Medina Gallo notes that "since the time of the 'arreglos' that resolved the Cristero conflict, the ecclesiastical hierarchs 'forgot' [certain] events that happened, by prohibiting the consultation of archives or by destroying documents that had some of that information."[168] Here forgetting is not an innocent or fortuitous event but rather a conscious act of creating epistemic ignorance by eliminating or restricting access to information. The question we must ask, however, is why the killer's status as an agrarista would be so problematic.

It is likely that this information has been excluded because of the inconvenient truth it presents. Recognizing an agrarista as the murderer of Toribio would expose unsettled tensions within the peasant community's own history, including unresolved internal land right disputes between and sometimes even within families.

In addition, if the identity of the killer is accurate, it complicates the more straightforward narrative that pits the government against the people. Revealing that an agrarista was Saint Toribio's killer could reveal fractures in the official Catholic account describing the revolts as a clear-cut religious clash between the state, as an evil entity, and the Church, as the victim. Recognizing that the conflict was tainted by land ownership and power disputes unsettles these imposed binaries. On the one hand, the agraristas were informally an enforcement arm of the state, but they remained at the same time full members of the farming community. Moreover, not only were those agraristas Catholics, just like the Cristeros, but they eventually emerged as a landowning class and became crucial benefactors of the Catholic Church. That a local agrarista might have killed Toribio Romo, the man who became the most popular saint in the region, demonstrates how intimately issues of land tenure and rural religiosity were interconnected in the conflict between Cristeros and agraristas: old oligarchs versus new tenants (who would go on to become the new oligarchs because of the government land concessions and their participation in the war). In other words, the Cristero War, particularly in the context of Los Altos de Jalisco, was also a class struggle that saw a rural bourgeoisie and professional lower middle class fighting over the continuity of power as well as land and cultural control. Today, as before, Toribio Romo continues to navigate (and negotiate) the unsettle legacies of those wars, in and out of el Norte.

La Santa Muerte:
The Patrona of the Death-Worlds

4

4

La Santa Muerte

The Patrona of the Death-Worlds

I think she [La Santa Muerte] is the saint of NAFTA.
—Charles Bowden, *Exodus: Coyotes, Pollos, and the Promised Van*

Here [with La Santa Muerte] your job or your sexual preference vanishes to offer you a new identity and a new belonging.
—*La Santa Muerte: Historia, Realidad y Mito de la Niña Blanca*

The Queen of Queens

The undécimo aniversario, or Eleventh Ball, honoring La Santa Muerte (LSM) took place on Saturday, August 19, 2017, in a small ballroom rented for the occasion in Queens, New York.[1] I got to the event just a few minutes before 7:00 p.m., its official starting time. However, this was too early, as everyone else was late. Walking into the room, I felt underdressed and wondered whether I should have worn a tuxedo, because the decor was extravagant. After paying the suggested entry fee of ten dollars, I chose one of the first rows and sat right in the middle. This was my first time attending the ball, and I wanted to have a good view of the stage. The music in the background was a familiar blend of top Latino ballads from the 1990s, including songs by Alejandra Guzman, Eros Ramazotti, and Luis Miguel. The playlist reflected the demographics of the audience—mostly members of Generation X who had immigrated to the United States and now live in and around New York. For immigrants, including myself, the popular music hits we remember from our homelands often serve as powerful timeline markers, more than even the official documentation of our immigration.

The venue's decor—paper flower centerpieces, the DJ in the corner, and the printed programs on the tables—was not that different from what's often seen at a quinceañera party.[2] The theme was simple but elegant, a mix of barrio chic and camp. This family event, open to the public, was organized by Arely Vázquez, a transgender immigrant from Mexico now living with her male partner in Queens, New York; Vázquez is one of the main leaders of the LSM movement in the United States. The night I was there, participants included both Enriqueta Vargas Ortiz from La Santa Muerte Internacional (SMI) in Mexico City and Lucino Morales, the leader of Iglesia Arcangelista México–US, from El Templo Santa Muerte, which has locations in both Los Angeles and Rosarito, Baja California. Overall, the event was a blend of a traditional quinceañera celebration, a charismatic prayer event, and a communal Mexican cultural and political event—although, of course, attendees were not uniformly Mexican (Figure 4.1).

The celebration started with a prayer to LSM that referred to the upcoming solar eclipse and the Trump administration's attacks on the Latinx community. The opening ceremony then moved on to several Christian prayers, including the Our Father and an invocation to God. Thus far, the event looked and felt like many other Christian charismatic renewal events, except that many of the prayers, originally from the Catholic repertoire, were being modified to accommodate LSM. After these introductory prayers came a formal academic lecture about the evolution of LSM, presented by Jorge Adrián Yllescas Illescas, a doctoral student in cultural anthropology from the Universidad Autónoma de Mexico. His presentation was followed by a performance of danza indígena (traditional Mexican indigenous dance) by a local group of teens and children. The rest of the evening program included collective prayers and charismatic interventions by Vargas Ortiz, Morales, and Vázquez interspersed with other cultural performances, including mariachi bands, a Paquita La del Barrio impersonator, and a Latinx lip-syncing show. At center stage, a large statue of LSM was surrounded by several small statues brought by attendees to be blessed for their personal home altars. Many of these statues had been customized to fulfill the needs and requests of the believers. Dressed and decorated with family pictures, dollar bills, ribbons, bows, and amulets, the personal statues revealed the drama of everyday life.

At the emotional level, the event was deeply intimate and personal. Around one hundred fifty people attended, including families with children. During the prayers led by Vargas Ortiz, she walked around the hall, embraced people, and laid hands on participants as a swarm of photographers followed her every move and documented audience members' reactions. It was a spectacle of pious religiosity and cinematographic choreography. The people

218 UNDOCUMENTED SAINTS

Figure 4.1 Promotional poster for Santa Muerte Ball, Queens, New York, 2017, including main performances and religious figures. *Left to right:* Lucino Morales, Ivonne García, Arely Vázquez, Enriqueta Vargas Ortiz.

attending were moved by the atmosphere of personal intimacy created by the spoken-word style of Vargas Ortiz's prayers, which invoked the human tragedies of immigration, racial discrimination, poverty, police profiling, and the overall cultural isolation experienced by many of the attendees. Vargas Ortiz's prayers emphasized the collective nature of everyone's misfortunes. She also pointed out the transnational makeup of the group and the corresponding need to build unity among the different geographic contingencies, emphasizing the interconnectivity between Latinxs in New York and Latinx communities in the American Southwest, such as Texas and California. Like the prayers offered by Vargas Ortiz, this annual event functioned as a pan-Latinx project connecting both sides of the immigration journey, from south to north and from west to east, in the United States.

The next performance of the event was a show by Vázquez and Ivonne García, a trans woman follower of LSM. All the songs selected were top melodramatic hits about love and its pains, and all of them reframed LSM as a lover. One of the songs proclaimed: "The way I love you, better believe it . . . believe it, nobody will love you, nobody, because . . . I love you with the force of the seas . . . with the vehemence of the wind . . . with my soul and with my flesh . . . I love you through turmoil and through calmness . . . I love you so much."[3]

Despite the campy aesthetics, the performers constantly displayed deep solemnity and sadness; on many occasions, the artists were overtaken by their emotions and openly cried during the performance. Their performance of hyperbolic femininity seemed designed to defy many conservative Catholics' belief that they are not "real" women and to testify to the LSM community's acceptance of them. At one point Vargas Ortiz praised Vázquez and introduced Vázquez's husband to the audience because, as Vargas Ortiz said, "behind a great woman there is a great man."[4] As these performances illustrate, the event manifested how deeply integrated the LGBTQ community is into LSM veneration. This integration goes beyond mere tolerance and acceptance of LGBTQ followers; as in the case of Vázquez and García, it presents active points of reference and spiritual leadership within the community. It is noteworthy that Vázquez has been the main leader of the LSM community in New York for over a decade; later in this chapter, I examine the LGBTQ connection to LSM in greater detail.

At this ball, the boundaries between public and private are blurry. The event is public, as anyone who pays the ten-dollar entrance fee can attend. Yet the event is also deeply intimate and private, with people being openly vulnerable and making very personal requests of LSM. While attendees observe an implicit code of privacy, not unlike that I observed in other saints' chapels and shrines, I nevertheless saw many reporters, photographers, newscasters, and film crews walking around, taking pictures, and recording those attending. The media, attracted by the religious spectacle and the exotification of the community, sought to capture both the dramatic spectacle of the performances and the personal nature of the prayers. They were so intent on capturing the personal, emotional angle of LSM worship that they were distracting and disrespectful; they took pictures of people crying, the children attending and running between the performers, and the imagery of LSM, including many tattoos. In many cases this media voyeurism took place with no consideration for people's privacy or dignity, or for the risk that public exposure might pose for vulnerable attendees such as minors or individuals without documentation. Their paparazzi-like antics starkly contrasted with the profoundly personal emotions being expressed.

Yet the organizers feed this desire for drama, for they are well aware of the effect participants' emotions have on the media—and, in turn, on the public awareness of and popularity of LSM veneration. Probably some of the media were actually invited by Vázquez and Vargas Ortiz, as both are media savvy and know how to leverage spectacle to bring attention to their groups. And because the event is technically open to the public, the media can make a fair argument that it is only informing its audience. However, many photographers and videographers were not there for journalistic purposes, and they had not requested permission, announced their intentions, or solicited the community's collective consent.

Ironically, and despite my own efforts to be inconspicuous, I too was pulled into performing, in a way. During her opening prayer, Vargas Ortiz stopped in front of me, laid her hand on my head, and prayed for my research work. She screamed, "¡Tendrás una plaza de trabajo permanente!" (You will get tenure!). She knew my presence and my identity very well: I had been introduced to the community the day before by Arely Vázquez, the organizer, and I had emailed Vargas Ortiz introducing myself and my work to her before arriving at the ball, though this was the first time we had met in person. However, the moment still came as a shock. Rationally, I knew she was working to trigger my own fears and insecurities; emotionally, I could not deny the deep impact the statement had on me. As a minority assistant professor in a field with traditionally low rates of tenure, I was certainly not in a position to refuse any help, including supernatural goodwill. It was validating in other ways, too; I always appreciate having the support and validation of the community I am studying, and Vargas Ortiz is a master at working a room so that everyone feels personally connected to everyone else. As my experience shows, everyone at the ball was essentially part of the show, a participant in the public veneration of LSM.

LSM Goes to Court

The foregoing portrait of LSM veneration is likely unexpected and unfamiliar for many readers. The better-known image of LSM is a sinister one, associated with criminality. I began this chapter by describing the ball because I want to challenge this negative imagery and juxtapose it with an understanding of what LSM really means for those who worship her. Yet I must also acknowledge how LSM has been interpreted on the outside—by those who neither believe in her powers nor belong to the communities who embrace her. This requires telling a very different story, this time from New Mexico.

On June 28, 2011, María Medina-Copete was a passenger in a borrowed car, driving along Interstate 40 in Albuquerque, New Mexico, when Sergeant Arsenio Chávez of the state police stopped the vehicle for "inadequate driving distance."[5] This routine traffic stop soon turned into a complex and serious First Amendment court case, with broader implications for the relationship between the state and religious faith: the case sought to establish whether a person's spiritual affiliations and veneration practices can be used as evidence of criminal activity by the US judicial system. According to Chávez, the officer who performed the traffic stop, he began to suspect the individuals he had pulled over for a traffic violation were involved in illegal drug activities when, in addition to seeming nervous, Medina-Copete began reciting a prayer to LSM. Also known as "Holy Death," LSM—a "popular Mexican folk saint who personifies death"—has gained an increasingly large following since the 2000s in Mexico and the United States.[6]

Chávez searched the car and found two pounds of methamphetamine hidden in a secret compartment. Medina-Copete and the driver, Rafael Goxcon-Chagal, denied any knowledge of the drugs, saying that the car was borrowed from a friend. During their trial, an expert witness, US marshal Robert Almonte of the Western District of Texas, testified that the veneration of LSM was linked to the drug trade, saying that Medina-Copete's prayer to LSM was not only "a very good indicator of possible criminal activity" but also evidence of the defendants' own recognition of the drugs' presence because, he explained, "often criminal drug traffickers and other criminals pray to her [LSM] for protection from law enforcement."[7]

In short, the state prosecutors used Medina-Copete and Goxcon-Chagal's apparent veneration of LSM as evidence against them. The saintly figure, the state argued, "relate[s] solely to the tools of the drug traffickers' trade" and is, in fact, one of the "means for the distribution of illegal drugs."[8] By invoking LSM, prosecutors argued, both defendants revealed not only that they were aware of the drugs inside the car but also that they were purposely transporting them across state lines.

Medina-Copete and Goxcon-Chagal were both convicted of possession of, intent to distribute, and trafficking of drugs. They were sentenced to fifteen years in prison.[9] On July 2, 2014, upon appeal, the Tenth Circuit Court overturned the sentences. The appellate court argued, "The government has persistently failed to explain how the Santa Muerte iconography in this case was a 'means for the distribution of illegal drugs.'"[10] Furthermore, referring to a previous case related to Jesús Malverde (see Chapter 1), the court explicitly stated: "We reject such a broad definition of 'tools of the trade,' which would logically include literally every legal item used or carried by a person who is committing a drug distribution offense. Our precedent requires some showing that a 'tool of the trade' can be used as a 'means for the distribution of illegal drugs.'"[11] (See Figure 4.2.) As Robert Contreras, an Associated Press reporter covering the case, pointed out, "This is the first time . . . that a conviction has been overturned because a folk saint was used in trial" within the United States.[12] The state decided not to retry and instead accepted plea bargains that resulted in prison sentences of ninety months for Goxcon-Chagal and forty-eight months for Medina-Copete.[13] Unfortunately, because Medina-Copete was a Mexican national, deportation proceedings against her had already begun.

Referring to this case, Eugene Volokh—a UCLA law professor and a scholar on religious freedom, First Amendment law, and church-state relations—notes that the government during the trial "persistently failed to explain how the Santa Muerte . . . was a 'means for the distribution of illegal drugs.'" In other words, the prosecution offered "no evidence that Santa Muerte iconography is 'associational,' nor was there any allegation that the 'main purpose' of La Santa Muerte veneration 'was to traffic in' narcotics"—the core of the state's argument against the defendants.[14] That the state was able, even temporarily, to successfully argue this case despite the lack of evidence reveals the tacit hierarchizing of faith within American civil society that renders non-mainstream religious practices and beliefs perpetually suspect.

The case reveals the entangled social norms through which we understand and assess different spiritualities as official versus unofficial, folk versus mainstream, legitimate versus illegitimate, and even criminal/unsanctioned versus licit/sanctioned. In his testimony, Almonte proffered as fact a completely specious and dangerous link between popular religious affiliation and criminality, emphasizing LSM's lack of official sanction from the Catholic Church.[15]

Figure 4.2 Scapular and figurine of La Santa Muerte.
Photo by the author

Of course, as we have seen, many popular saints venerated by Catholics worldwide have not been recognized by the Catholic Church. But the situation with LSM goes further than simple non-recognition; the Catholic Church has been an outspoken critic of LSM, openly condemning her worship.[16] Indeed, Catholic ecclesiastical authorities in both the United States and Mexico, as well as in the Vatican itself, have declared worship of LSM to be in direct contradiction to the Catholic faith.[17] For example, in 2008, the Archdiocese of Mexico City explicitly argued that such veneration opposes the teaching of the Church because "Christ himself overcame death" during his Resurrection and promised "eternal life to those who keep the commandments of the law of God."[18] In 2013, Cardinal Gianfranco Ravasi, president of the Vatican's Pontifical Council for Culture, became the first Vatican official to address the topic, defining LSM devotion as a "degeneration of religion."[19] Such worship, he clarified, "is not religion just because it's dressed up like religion; it's a blasphemy against religion."[20] On February 13, 2016, during his visit to Mexico, Pope Francis himself alluded to LSM, cautioning those who "praise illusions and embrace their macabre symbols to commercialize death in exchange for money."[21] In 2017 several Catholic bishops in the United States joined their Mexican counterparts in declaring LSM veneration as "antithetical" or contrary to the teachings of Jesus Christ and the Catholic Church. John Wester, archbishop of Santa Fe, New Mexico, argued, "She's not a saint. There is nothing good that can come out of praying to her."[22] Two years later he said much the same thing: "It's really wrong."[23]

Yet despite the Church's multiple clear condemnations, the popularity of LSM is increasing. What do her followers, called Santamuertistas, find in her? How can studying her veneration illuminate social connections among faith, popular religiosity, class, and sexuality as these categories shift and change? Certainly, at first glance, the recent emergence of LSM veneration (especially since 2001) can be partially explained as a response to the socioeconomic and cultural effects of the post–Cold War era in Latin America and among communities of color in the United States, as late capitalist policies have intensified poverty among and exploitation of the most vulnerable—policies that include NAFTA and the continuing effects of the so-called war on drugs, especially in Mexico. This first level of analysis provides a useful framework within which to contextualize the emergence and evolution of LSM and similar spiritual movements at the dawn of the new millennium. What this sociopolitical analysis cannot explain, however, is how quickly the movement has grown, or how deeply and rapidly her followers develop emotional attachment to her. (This is especially true of people in disenfranchised sectors of society, like her many LGBTQ followers.) If our basic structural analysis centers solely on the political-economic context, we overlook the complex role of religiosity in communities at the margins—and the role of faith in people's lives.

A deeper analysis reveals that Santamuertistas inhabit a complex, liminal space of religiosity and faith. Most US and Mexican Latinx followers of LSM define themselves as fully practicing Catholics, while others exist within the blurred boundaries of a Catholicism-by-proximity, as cultural Catholics. Some combine worship of LSM with other religious traditions, while still others embrace her as their only deity. The terrains of affiliation are vast, and they always adapt to the individual spiritual context—especially because believing in LSM does not demand a radical rupture or a conversion from the Santamuertistas' central religious beliefs, for veneration of LSM does not exclude other beliefs. The veneration of LSM, then, should be understood as a form of spiritual pragmatism; it is less concerned with the afterlife than with the afflictions of the present.

LSM is, above all, a personification of death, and this speaks to many of her followers. Avoiding a mala muerte, a bad death, is a central concern for those confronted by systematic and consistent violence, and the threat of a bad death is part of their daily reality; conversely, a buena muerte, a good death with minimal pain and suffering, is often seen as a rare miracle. Vargas Ortiz, the leader of SMI, asserts that LSM stands as "an angel of God, one that one day will come for us, when it is our hour," and that "every day there are more devotees to her because she is the fastest miracle maker."[24] Consequently, many followers refer to LSM as La Cumplidora: "the one who gets things done" or "the fixer"—the best miracle granter. This quality is particularly important in Mexico, where many agree that nadie cumple: that is, nobody can keep promises, nobody delivers—particularly not the state or the religious institutions in power. LSM thus represents for her veneradors la segura, security, the safest figure to approach for refuge and resources. For this reason, some even argue that she is better than traditional saints, whose miracle-granting can seem far more capricious.

In this context, the exhortations against LSM offered by Pope Francis and the hierarchy of the Catholic Church seem detached from her followers' lived reality (although many Latinx followers hold a deep affection, care, and cultural affinity toward the Latin American pope). Santamuertistas perceive their devotion to the popular saint as fitting within an extended pantheon of saints and vernacular practice, a pantheon that extends beyond the narrow range of saints that the Vatican recognizes. The array of LSM beliefs and practices is not homogeneous, and there is some overlap with traditional Catholic doctrine and hierarchy. Many Santamuertistas, especially the leaders, believe that through LSM they achieve a spiritual connection with God. As Martin George Quijano, a spiritual leader of the Circulo Espiritual Nacional e Internacional de La Santa Muerte, describes it, "La Santa Muerte takes us by the hand and leads us to God."[25] Other followers view LSM as an intermediary connecting them to Jesus. These Santamuertistas position LSM within the Catholic Church's "spiritual" territories or as an extended version of their Catholic faith. These venerators generally feel deeply connected to the redemptive plan of the same Catholic God, independent of their devotion to LSM.

Others have a somewhat more broadly theistic view. The leaders of the LSM movement, as well as most of its followers, insist that "a devotee of La Santa Muerte never stops believing in God," referring here to the Judeo-Christian understanding of God.[26] Vargas Ortiz, the head of SMI, declares, "I believe that there is only one God with many names. It is the same God for all of us. The same omnipresent God."[27] For Vargas Ortiz, the God above LSM is the same God who guides and unifies all Christianity. As Katia Perdigón Castañeda explains, while many followers' veneration of LSM can be interpreted as a derivation or spin-off from Christianity, it is at the same time "a form of minor theoretical and organized systematization, and [one with] a greater degree of spontaneity."[28] The controversial veneration of LSM should be understood within the context of a sort of vernacular Catholicism and syncretism between Spanish colonial and indigenous death deities. The emergence and expansion of the LSM movement thus highlight the ambiguity of the borders defining Catholicism: irreducible to an institution with a fixed set of cultural practices and beliefs, LSM and the veneration she inspires together constitute a Catholicism by proximity and a populist Catholicism that responds her venerators' current circumstances.

This is why, when asked how Santamuertistas reconcile their beliefs in LSM with their Catholic practices, Vargas Ortiz explains: "As long as you have a strong faith . . . all saints will take you to the same end. La Santa Muerte helps us. . . . We believe in the free will of everyone. We try to keep always a common respect for the religion [faith] of each person."[29] In this expansive vision of Catholicism, LSM is just one of the many saints available. Her followers, for the most part, integrate her with their faith in Jesus Christ and the Virgin Mary, their belief in the events described in the Gospels, and their participation in the many popular pious practices prevailing in Mexico and other parts of Latin America.

According to Quijano, LSM can be included in this vision of Catholicism because her followers consider the practices and beliefs surrounding her to be both "un culto y una devocion"—that is, both a worship and a devotion. He explains: "As a veneration, it is related to our history and our nation's cultural beliefs, and how [death] is known here, not in other places or religions. . . .

Collectively it is both a culto and a devotion."[30] The case of LSM reflects the simultaneous coexistence of belief systems. Both LSM and Christianity are part of the marketplace of practices available to followers, particularly those affected in some way by migration.

Here it is important to note that Quijano—as well as other followers, Mexican scholars, and even the Mexican government—consistently use the term "culto," which can be translated literally as "cult." However, given the extremely negative connotations of this word in the United States, this direct translation would prevent many English-speakers from understanding the real signification of the term in Spanish. I asked Juan Salazar Rojo, an LSM pastor in Puebla and Tlaxcala, Mexico, about this issue and invited him to explain the term after he used it during one of our interviews. He explained, "Culto refers to the spiritual movement around the veneration of La Santa Muerte."[31] In other words, it can be better translated as "worship," because it refers both to the individual spiritual veneration practiced by each follower and to the "spiritual movement" around LSM—her veneration at the collective or community level (see Figure 4.3).

LSM's veneration is arguably a truly Mexican phenomenon because it was born in this individual/collective form within Mexico. Although similar saints associated with death can be found elsewhere in Latin America, and these saints might even share LSM's spiritual and colonial DNA, this chapter shows that LSM is a uniquely Mexican spiritual form. This observation leads to several essential questions: Who is LSM? What are the differences and similarities between her veneration and that of other representations of the dead (such as those associated with El Día de los Muertos, the Day of the Dead)? And how has her veneration become, in just a few years, such a fast-growing spiritual movement, turning LSM into a transborder citizen?

Who Is La Santa Muerte? A Semiotic Differentiation

Andrew Chesnut, author of the first in-depth study on LSM in English, describes LSM as a "Mexican folk saint who personifies death . . . [who is] often depicted as a female Grim Reaper," as a skeleton.[32] She is also known as La Flaca or La Flaquita (Skinny Lady), La Niña Blanca (White Girl), and La Niña Santa (Holy Girl), among many other names.[33] Her name can be translated as "Holy Death," but Chesnut argues that "Saint Death is a more accurate translation" because "it better reveals her identity as a folk saint."[34]

Figure 4.3 Santa Muerte service, Puebla, Mexico. Main altar, 1er. Santuario a Dios y a la Santa Muerte, Puebla, Mexico.
Photo by the author

Quijano explains the name in these terms: "We called her 'Santa' because of our love for her and 'Muerte' because of her nature."[35]

As scholar Desirée A. Martín explains, LSM is "[often] represented as a skeleton, dressed in hooded robes, as a bride, or in other elaborate, hand-made clothing, wigs, and jewelry that change depending on the calendar or the moods of her devotees. She often carries a sickle [note: in fact, it is typically a scythe], a globe of the world, an hourglass, and the scales of justice."[36] Representations of LSM may include a halo or aureole around her head to signify her saintly status. LSM can be dressed in different colors to accentuate a particular devotional element, such as health (amber), prosperity and land wealth (gold), protection from evil (black), love (red), justice (green), job security (blue), and so on. According to Chesnut, the current iconic Mexican image of LSM as a female Grim Reaper symbol of death can be traced back to medieval Catholicism, to the Spanish female skeleton known as La Parca, who was brought to Mexico during the conquest and colonial period.[37] La Parca's image mixed with the pre-Columbian "indigenous goddess (usually Aztec or Mayan) of death" to become the foremother of LSM.[38]

The signifier of the saint incorporates visual references to race and gender. She is racially phenotyped as a fair-skinned saint—not because of the whiteness of her exposed bones but through a series of language and aesthetic tools, not always explicit, that are meant to convey and reinforce her whiteness. For example, one of the most popular names for LSM is La Niña Blanca (White Girl), referring both to her whiteness and also to the spiritual qualities of innocence and purity. Here, whiteness is not used to signal a particular geographic and cultural criollo identity, as it was with Toribio Romo, nor is it exclusively about a racial preference or an association with beauty; here, it is a multi-signifier of the power granted by society to whiteness itself. Certainly, LSM is able to grant miracles and favors because of her spiritual nature. But thanks to her whiteness, she is also able to enact an extra level of social privilege and mobility, which reinforces her superiority over other spiritual entities; it is her whiteness that makes her role as La Cumplidora even more possible.

Although LSM is consistently defined by her followers as the ultimate equalizer—death comes for us all, independent of our race, gender, class, sexuality, origin, and so on—LSM's whiteness emphasizes not similarity but differentiation and disparities, precisely because fair skin remains a holder of real power within society. In a world deeply defined by social disparities and by the uneven distribution of value and resources based on those disparities, LSM's frequent representation as a white saint without flesh reflects both the deep legacy of colonial models of racial superiority and the aspirational desire to wield and benefit from the privilege of whiteness. For LSM's venerators, having a fair-skinned spiritual ally is indeed a powerful tool for survival.

How can we differentiate LSM from other, visually similar figures like the Grim Reaper or the Mexican figures La Catrina or La Calaca, both of whom are colloquial Mexican reflections on death that are popular during El Día de los Muertos?[39] One key aspect that distinguishes LSM from these others can be found in the grassroots nature of her spiritual creation, invocation, and evolution. As Perdigón Castañeda explains, LSM is—unusually—"not a deity created by a religious organization but . . . is rather an object-symbol turned [into a figure of veneration] by a sector of the population"—a set of worshipers which has since "proliferated as a religious group."[40] This grassroots spiritual identity is unique to LSM.[41] As Regnar Alabaek Kristensen explains, followers first created the initial spiritual meaning attached to LSM, and they cemented that meaning as they developed personal attachments to the idea of LSM as a miracle maker.[42]

Yllescas Illescas has studied the veneration of LSM among male prison inmates in Mexico City.[43] Among the inmates, LSM is understood (often retroactively) as an angel who has followed them throughout their lives, protecting them even before they were aware of her existence or began to venerate her. One's "conversion" to LSM is like an act of awakening, when the inmate first recognizes the active intervention of LSM in his life. This intervention can take the form of either action or inaction, either protection or punishment. One inmate interviewed by Yllescas Illescas describes his relationship with LSM as protective: "For me [LSM] is like my guardian angel, my protector—is the one who takes care of me against all evil, against things that may happen to me; she protects me even from my enemies."[44] Another inmate views his apprehension by the police as an act of punishment by LSM after he stole a gold necklace that depicted her.[45] What ties such beliefs together is the inmates' faith in LSM's holy agency—La Cumplidora's ability (and willingness) to work in the world.

Evolution and Structure of the Veneration of LSM

To understand the development of LSM as a peculiarly Mexican vernacular saint, we must see her origins and evolution as growing out of a network or system of interconnected events. As scholar Alberto Hernández Hernández explains in his contemplation of the movement's "temporalities and regions," "It is impossible to identify one single origin [of LSM]."[46] When we trace LSM's transformation over time as her veneration shifts from obscure and ambiguous private practices to a public, spectacular spiritual affair, we glean useful clues about the materialization and consolidation of faith and religion.[47]

To understand LSM's emergence, consolidation, and growth, we must examine the complexities of overlapping forces and events: market consumption, migration and expansion issues, and regulation have all shaped her veneration. Certainly, one key event—the 2001 public opening of an altar by Enriqueta Romero Romero (see Figure 4.4)—is central to the modern history of LSM. However, other factors have also helped create her reputation and her popularity as an illegal saint—by which I mean both her association as a patron of illegal or criminal activities and a purely vernacular saint whose veneration has been named a mortal sin by the Church. These include the migration of her devotion from Mexico to the United States and other countries; the emergence of stable, unifying imagery and aesthetics in her

Figure 4.4 Image of first public altar to La Santa Muerte in Tepito, Mexico, established by Enriqueta Romero Romero in 2001.
Photo by the author

veneration; the backlash against her venerators from the Mexican government and the Catholic Church (both institutions have policed and surveilled groups venerating LSM and have sought to promote other popular but less controversial saints to take her place); and the US and Mexican news and entertainment media's representation of her not as a saint but as a spiritual monster—a socialized and racialized category of decidedly unholy figures. These factors have enabled a particular type of theology to emerge among her followers and have consolidated a ritual repertoire.

LSM: A Mexican Saint of Precariousness?

I locate the popularity of LSM's current spiritual form within the context of the precariousness generated by late capitalism and neoliberalism in Mexico (and across Latin America). For Perdigón Castañeda, LSM is a "deity of the twentieth century, a symbol... [that] represents a group, [and] orders it, both in the level of natural logic, as well as in the social logic, each one with its own axis, but related to each other."[48] This context is particularly shaped by sociopolitical and economic changes: those wrought by transnational trade agreements such as NAFTA, the dismantling of the secular welfare state, the erosion of public trust in the state, massive migration, land dispossessions, the decentralization of labor policies at the turn of the twentieth century, and Santamuertistas' perceptions of the Mexican Catholic Church as neglecting its pastoral (and material) obligations to the poor, as set forth by Jesus and the Bible. Although LSM shares some similarities with earlier Mexican figures of death (and those of other countries), Saint Death, in the modern form of LSM, is foremost a Mexican product of the twentieth century, one that (like Mexicans themselves) is constantly negotiating global and local tensions of signification; she has become a global spiritual citizen who reflects and embodies the meanings and desires of many different constituencies at once. The tensions between the local and the global are made manifest in the figure of LSM, who embodies both a fundamental Mexicanness and the universal nature of death.

One of her followers, Martín Morfín Reyes, agrees that "La Santa Muerte is Mexican," but says that she is not a product of modern Mexico; she argues that "our [Mexican] ancestors already worshiped her, and she appeared first in Mexico," placing LSM's origins in the pre-Columbian period.[49] Here we see the intertwining of a nationalist discourse about LSM with assertions of a pre-Columbian (rather than a twentieth-century) origin. This belief that in her modern manifestation, LSM is a product of both modern Mexico and of its indigenous past is central in the imagination of her among followers, researchers, and detractors alike. Here, I do not debate the accuracy of this belief in her deep historical roots; this section examines her disputed pre-Columbian ancestry because the debate itself has ongoing political implications. As I show, the debate over her origins, like the figure of LSM herself, grows out of multiple sociopolitical, economic, religious, and aesthetic factors in her development—the conditions that have turned her into a transnational global citizen.

This section discusses LSM's evolution at the levels of both the real and the imaginary, divided into five stages: (1) the pre-Columbian period, (2) the encounter with modernity, (3) the development into a proto-saint, (4) the sociopolitical expansion of neoliberalism and the official backlash against LSM veneration that accompanied it, and finally (5) today's innovative efforts to legalize, systemize, and standardize the LSM movement. The first three stages illustrate how the figure of LSM was distilled from the pre-Columbian archetype of death, then developed into a proto-saint, then flowered into the modern persona and spiritual entity that is venerated today. The development of her into a proto-saint and into her current form are, as I show, driven by several factors: the charismatic leaders of the movement that seeks to popularize LSM's veneration, the disjuncture created by migration and the forced dislocation of communities, the changes in economic markets, the resistance to her veneration by the Mexican state and the Catholic Church, and the fight for control and power among spiritual factions. Here I am primarily interested in current leaders' emphasis on the antiquity of LSM and in how this framing influences followers' rituals and spiritual approaches today.

The Arguments for a Pre-Columbian Era
Many Santamuertistas believe, in the words of follower Morfín Reyes, that "during the conquest the Spaniards brought the [Catholic faith of the] Virgin of Guadalupe and Jesus . . . but our ancestors already had a veneration of La Santa Muerte."[50] Many scholars have agreed with this position, believing that LSM is a pseudo-Catholic reappropriation of the Aztec death god Mictlantecuhtli and of his wife, the goddess of the underworld, Mictecacihuatl.[51] Called the Lady of the Dead, Mictecacihuatl rules over the afterlife. She watches over and protects the remains of dead people, and she consequently presides over festivals of the dead, including the modern celebration of El Día de los Muertos.

Other theories argue that LSM is not rooted in the indigenous past but is a product of indigenous people's encounter with European Christianity; these scholars argue that LSM developed in Mexico to personify the centrality of death within the Christian narration of salvation—that is, Christ's Resurrection, which will enable humankind's own resurrection of the body when Christ comes again at the end of time. As Hernández Hernández explains, other scholars take this notion further, seeing LSM not simply as an indigenous manifestation of Christian theological principles but as a syncretic transformation of "Catholic saints such as San Bernardo, San Pascual (or Pascualito), and San Sebastián"; all of these saints are represented in some parts of Latin America with skeleton bodies, manifesting in their saintly forms the ubiquity of death.[52] Consequently, as Perdigón Castañeda asserts, "the history of the present concept of death and its iconography, reflected in the contemporary Santa Muerte, are more related to Judeo-Christian religion (Catholicism in this particular case) than the forgotten and unknown voices of the vanquished, in other words, the pre-Hispanic [or pre-Columbian] people."[53] Under this assertion, our current version of LSM is always partly Christian (ideologically), whether she was a newly generated figure embodying new local understandings of the resurrection created by the encounter with Europe in the Americas, or an evolution of existing official Christian saints.

To reiterate, this chapter is less concerned with either validating or rejecting a pre-Columbian continuity myth about LSM and more interested in exploring the reasons for the modern-day investment in an ancient past and the sociopolitical implications of such beliefs. Certainly, the visual representations of LSM over time connect her with other historical representations of death, but the spiritual connotations of these images should not automatically be fused. Previous representations of death in the Mexican tradition have certainly contributed to the public emergence of (and familiarity with) the modern veneration of LSM, for she emerged not in isolation but within the cultural context of Mexico's relationship with death. However, recognizing these connections does not mean accepting blindly that LSM is simply another iteration of the multiple previous representations of death in Mexico.

Why, then, do movement leaders insist on tracing a genealogy to a pre-Columbian or indigenous past for LSM? The first explanation is simply that establishing the modern veneration of LSM as part of a long-standing religious tradition within Mexico is a crucial strategic and marketing move to achieve official recognition for modern-day veneration of LSM. This recognition is particularly important in light of Santamuertistas' long struggle to have the Mexican government recognize them as a valid religious group, which would allow them to apply for the associated tax exemptions and state protection. This speaks to Mexico's own assumptions of Mexicanidad and its cultural and political bias against non-Christian and non-European practices.[54]

Many followers insist on LSM's indigenous origin for nationalist reasons. The pre-Columbian origin story fits neatly into the post–Mexican Revolution state ideology that emphasizes only a particular type of pre-Columbian past, once that is imagined as homogeneous and stable. In other words, after the Revolution, the Mexican state engaged in a project of "rediscovering" a unifying past that refused contradictions and gives a linear narration to the present, and the notion of LSM as a figure that emerged from this past is one that is more like to be palatable to (and recognized by) the state. This LSM's past is thus a comforting and appealing one to modern Mexicans attempting to negotiate the complexities of national religious sovereignty as people are trying to navigate a global present.

In part, LSM's followers fervently believe in the narrative of LSM's antiquity because it constructs (and reinforces) Mexicanness, anchoring Mexican expatriates and their families to the Mexican homeland. Vargas Ortiz makes this argument clear: "La Santa Muerte is part of the Mexican culture. Our ancestors venerated the deities of death."[55] For Vargas Ortiz, LSM is a way to be Mexican in the United States—that is, to embrace a Mexicanness that is particular to a region, an imagined national identity that has spiritual ramifications. For people forced to leave their homeland behind, whether because of economic reasons or state oppression (as with "sexiles"—the term used by Manolo Guzmán for those who "have had to leave their nations of origin on account of their sexual orientation"), those who cannot return to their homeland can find not only spiritual relief but also national appeasement and solace in LSM as a figure rooted in the ancient Mexican past.[56] LSM, like all the immigrant saints of this book, becomes a traveling enclave of imaginary and spiritual nationhood.

The Encounter with Modernity
As already mentioned, the two familiar Mexican female figures of death, La Calaca and La Catrina, are not to be confused with LSM, although they are all interrelated. However, an early image of La Catrina (or the more generic La Calaca) did influence the development of the figure of LSM, shaping people's understanding (and sometimes misunderstanding) of her and promoting her emergence as a modern, human-like saint—a personification rather than an archetypal, allegorical figure. This transformation was nurtured by the famous Mexican artist José Guadalupe Posada's (1852–1913) representations of La Calaca and La Catrina, which integrated human features and qualities into the concept of death. This created in viewers a more quotidian and familiar relationship with death, one that lasted beyond the single day of El Día de los Muertos—a relationship that enabled the incorporation of LSM as a saint-like figure into the Mexican psyche.

The image of La Catrina created by Posada, as well as the many iterations of the image used by Diego Rivera, manifests a transformation that was happening in Mexico during the late nineteenth century: the encounter with modernity, which was being accelerated by the policies of President Díaz. La Catrina marks the encounter with the deadly practices of industrial exploitation that would eventually lead to the social unrest of the Mexican Revolution. The late nineteenth century in Mexico had no LSM as we understand her today. What we find instead in the images of La Catrina (upon which many of today's representations of LSM are based) is the beginning of the humanization of death, and the dehumanization of humans, produced by the encounter with modernity.

While the Spanish colonial era was characterized by imminent physical, epistemic, and religious genocide, modernity can be defined by "slow violence" and the normalization of death. In the case of the US-Mexico relation in the nineteenth century (and since), the slow violence is that of systemic conditions of greed, exploitation, and resource extraction.[57] As explained in Chapter 1, the pre-Revolution era of Porfirio Díaz was defined by a systematic project of exploitation and the massive endeavor of extracting goods and people from Mexico and transferring them to the so-called First World. Just as Achille Mbembe describes in the case of Africa, in nineteenth-century Mexico we witness the "creation of *death-worlds*, new and unique forms of social existence in which vast populations are subjected to conditions of life conferring upon them the status of *living dead*."[58] Death, like La Catrina, remains, but like LSM, it is transformed into living death—death made human

The Proto-Saint Era: The Great Gestation
LSM appears in her prototypical form beginning after the US Great Depression, which (as discussed in Chapter 2) reverberated through the Mexican political economy and triggered the rise of neoliberalism. The first recorded reference to LSM in this period appears in Frances Toor's 1947 book *Treasury of Mexican Folkways*, where LSM is often associated with love: the book includes a series of prayers to LSM that seek to end the infidelity of husbands or boyfriends, and Toor describes encountering, in her field work, prayers "addressed to Holy Death" asking her to grant the petitioners love. By this period, then, LSM has already become a vernacular saint in her own right, a spiritual entity whom people ask directly for help, miracles, and divine interventions. One such prayer reads:

> Most beloved Muerte, of my heart,
> do not forsake me from your protection
> And don't leave "John Doe" (mention here the man's name)
> in peace for one moment from now on,
> make him restless all the time

molest, mortify and worry him
so, that he is always thinking about me.[59]

Another record of LSM emerges a few years later, in Oscar Lewis's 1961 anthropological book *The Children of Sánchez: Autobiography of a Mexican Family*, an ethnographic monograph on the life of a family in Tepito, Mexico—the same barrio where Romero Romero would open the first public shrine to LSM in 2001, "less than half a block" away from the setting of Lewis's book.[60] *The Children of Sánchez* presents the first recorded reference to LSM as a saint, and it verifies that her popularity began several decades before the shrine was opened in 2001. Like Toor's, Lewis's work also shows LSM's veneration as being associated with the return of strayed lovers or with the repair of broken relationships; his book transcribes a prayer to LSM meant to bring a lover to one's "feet, beaten and tied."[61] This aspect of her devotion remains very much in place today. LSM's red candles, associated with her intervention regarding love affairs, are the most popular and frequently sold-out objects in her repertoire of religious artifacts.

Kristensen argues that in the 1980s and 1990s, LSM evolved from a saint narrowly focused on love affairs into a multitasking saint capable of tackling a huge array of problems and needs. Kristensen links this shift to the large socioeconomic transformations in Mexico in that period (some caused by NAFTA, some caused by the country's financial crisis) and to the social violence created by the incoming Mexican "government's rhetoric on cracking down on crime and criminal corruption" in the late 1980s and 1990s.[62] As Kristensen explains, these sociopolitical changes in Mexico and the accompanying changes in LSM's area of operations co-occurred with another significant transformation, this one of the visual representations of LSM, which moved away from flat images found on prayer cards and toward three-dimensional statues. For Kristensen, this visual transformation was an essential "vehicle for extending the agency and meaning of death."[63] This transformation of LSM into a three-dimensional statue—a further step in her increasing humanization—manifests the deeper transformations occurring in the psyche of the people in relationship to this saint.

The Neoliberal Expansion (and Backlash)
Around the turn of the millennium, the neoliberal economic practices of decentralization and deregulation were introduced into the realm of the

religious, as the Mexican state tried to define, formalize, and regulate its own transactional relationships with institutionalized religiosity. These attempts began with the 1992 enactment of the Ley de Asociaciones Religiosas y Culto Público in Mexico. This law particularly affected the veneration of LSM, for it codified the desire of some Santamuertista leaders to gain visibility and formal governmental recognition.

The culto "worship" of LSM formalized even further in 2001, when LSM veneration went public, triggered by Romero Romero's opening of her public shrine. This new visibility increased social cohesion among her followers, as the public sharing of rituals began to unify what had been a very polymorphous religious group. Laypeople started to form informal religious associations (compadrazcos for males, comadrazcos for females) dedicated to supporting the altars to LSM that began popping up around Mexico City, providing dresses for the statues, flowers, candles, and prayer cards.[64] As Perdigón Castañeda notes, an intricate network of these lay groups surrounding LSM also founded and stewarded chapels, oratories, and neighborhood groups.[65] These relationships and informal collaborations eventually became the seeds for more formal events and structures. In these nurturing and formative spaces, the combination of vernacular Catholic devotional practices with syncretism became normalized.

But the worship forms during this period did not become completely standardized, for they were deeply connected to the charismatic personal stories of founders and leaders of the different spiritual communities dedicated to LSM. Modern venerations of LSM, as a relatively new spiritual phenomenon, vary according to leader, location, and the context of each community; no two communities are alike, even within the same spiritual branch, and new rituals are constantly being created. Consequently, no single ritual or community unifies the veneration of LSM, and the constellation of veneration practices, cultural forms, and religious expressions has created a somewhat volatile mixture. Tensions surrounding control and doctrinal dominance of spiritual practices have emerged among the groups; each "brand's" territorial pattern of growth and distribution has been defined by each founder's or leader's access to social capital—their education, gender, and class mobility—as well as the circumstances surrounding how he or she originally came to the culto of LSM.

Legacy as a Leader's Spiritual Capital: Building a Movement as a Personal Experience

Two key founders and leaders of LSM veneration groups, Enriqueta Romero Romero and Enriqueta Vargas Ortiz (as well as the latter's son, Jonathan Legaría Vargas), have worked in various ways to cement, publicize, and move forward the public veneration of LSM. Each of these leaders defines a particular aspect in the development and transnational migration of LSM's veneration. The following discussions, which summarize many interviews and visits to these leaders' communities and sites, describe the evolution and characteristics of LSM's veneration, as well as the often combative relationship between the LSM spiritual movement, the state of Mexico, and the Catholic Church.

Doña Enriqueta Romero Romero: The Original Godmother

Romero Romero's persona as a spiritual leader is much larger than her physical presence, for she is a petite, sharp, loving, and grandmotherly lady. She is widely recognized as the founder of the modern LSM movement. I met Romero Romero in January 2015 during one of my research trips to Mexico City. We got together at her home—the same place where, on September 7, 2001, she opened the first public altar to LSM, whom she calls La Flaquita Linda (Skinny Pretty Lady).[66] The chapel and home shrine is located at 12 Calle Alfarería, between Calle Panaderos and Calle Mineros, in the barrio of Tepito, Colonia Moreros, Mexico City. The neighborhood of Tepito is located south of the historical downtown of Mexico City, and since Aztec times, this area has been a trading settlement and one of the poorest areas in the city. It is famous for its large outdoor market, or tianguis, that extends across twenty-five blocks, where the visitor can buy almost anything. Today Tepito is considered one of the toughest barrios of Mexico City. In the heart of this neighborhood is the altar to LSM, a large glass niche that faces the street from living room. It is less a shrine inside Romero Romero's home than a projection outside her home, basically a separate room. Chapel rearrangements and the monthly change of dresses for the human-sized statue of LSM are all carried out through a door that separates the niche from the house. This allows visitors to venerate LSM from the street without needing to enter Romero Romero's house.

Meeting Romero Romero required some maneuvers on my part. I was in Mexico already, studying Jesús Malverde (see Chapter 1), and I was struck by the constant presence of LSM around Malverde and alongside another popular saint, Saint Jude. I was familiar with Saint Jude through my previous study of his worship among the transgender community in Phoenix, Arizona. Until this point, I had resisted doing research on LSM due to her overwhelmingly negative representation in the mass media. However, as I was finishing interviews and ethnographic research regarding Malverde, I found myself intrigued by the people following LSM.

I decided to explore Tepito, one of the centers of LSM veneration, and asked my research contacts to help me arrange a meeting with Romero Romero. I encountered much resistance—ironically, not from wary LSM followers but from these research contacts and from local taxi drivers. Nobody wanted me to enter the poor barrio, out of concern for my apparent inexperience with Tepito and my obvious queerness. Several murders had occurred just a few days before my planned visit, so naturally there were safety concerns. Despite these warnings, I found Tepito to be a thriving and energetic, albeit poor, barrio of people trying to survive and do their best with the little that was left to them after a long series of damaging political and economic decisions by the Mexican government. This barrio is no different from many other barrios in Latin America and the United States, many of which are similarly organized by a set of interlocking informal economies. However, in Mexico's consciousness, it is an imagined space of deviancy and crime, not unlike Tijuana in the early twentieth century; in the Mexican imagination, Tepito serves as a borderland frontier in upper- and middle-class discourses, tangibly representing the problems in Mexico while serving as a place where the rich can imagine fulfilling their darker desires.

I first met with Raymundo Romero, Romero Romero's husband, as he was attending the little shop at the shrine. To him I must have seemed like an odd visitor—clearly not from there, overwhelmed and unsettled by Tepito's negative image in the press, and governed by my own prejudices. He was kind and listened with patience to my avalanche of questions. Then he asked me if I was there to meet his wife. I explained who I was and what I was doing. He was able to set up an interview for the next day with la mera mera—a person in charge, Romero Romero herself. The next day I came back, prepared with a list of questions, paper and pencils, a recorder with extra batteries, and water.

Although I myself am a Latino, I fit the stereotype of the typical US-trained researcher who does research in Latin America, and it seemed that Romero Romero wanted to change the typical power dynamics that this relationship entails. After I presented the required introductions and legal formalities, she asked me to "just have a talk" without the recorder or the notepad.[67] Clearly, she was concerned by the risk of negative publicity. She had given interviews many times before and was an expert by this point.

We talked for over two hours. Then, when I was ready to leave, she asked, "Where are you going?" I explained that I was going back to my place to write up the notes from our interview. She looked at me and said, "But m'ijo, we are just beginning. Now that we know each other, we can finally start the interview. Take out your recorder, paper, and pen, and let's start from the first question."[68] We went through all the questions again, plus some more. When we were finished, I told her that I would send her the transcripts as a record of what she said, attempting to reassure her that I was not one of the sensationalist reporters that she feared. But she looked at me and said, "Don't worry, William. If you talk shit about me or La Santa Muerte, she will take care of you. I don't need to do anything. She will take care of you, be sure about it!"[69] Then she smiled. The innuendo was clear. She knew how to play upon my fears in order to protect herself and those she cares about. Tepito, and Romero Romero, proved the savviness of the street.

As Romero Romero explained during our interview, her aunt Leonor had introduced her to the devotion of LSM more than fifty-seven years before our interview—a fact that validated the argument that LSM veneration also existed in the 1950s, though it was not so public or well known then. According to Romero Romero, in 2001 her son gave her the statue of LSM that became the centerpiece of the public altar in her living room. The life-sized statue was an ex-voto (or religious offering) promised to LSM by her son after he was released from jail. That year Romero Romero tore down the exterior living room wall, opening the room to the outside. This bold act marked the beginning of the modern, public LSM veneration movement. According to Romero Romero, at the time she neither expected nor planned the emergence of a transnational spiritual movement, but her decision changed the trajectory of what had until then been a private veneration practice, bringing many more LSM devotees out into the open. As she put it, "I never thought we were thousands and thousands of devotees. Maybe this [our society] was very closed-minded. There was not an altar where people were able to go and pray, and now that there is one, thousands of people come to venerate the most Holy Death."[70] Because of her creation of the shrine, Romero Romero is today considered the founder of the modern movement of LSM worship, and she is probably the most recognized (as well as the most esteemed and least controversial) of its "early" leaders.

It is not coincidental that the first public chapel to LSM—a saint invoked in times of crisis—emerged in one of the most distressed areas of Mexico. I asked Romero Romero about the relationship between LSM and Tepito, the location of that first chapel. She responded, "It would have happened in another colonia [barrio] if God had wanted, but God wanted it here, maybe because he sees us so needy. He sees us, well, so badly taken care of. Maybe this is why it's up here [the chapel], to take care of us all."[71] Her comments illustrate her understanding of the social and economic precariousness faced by the residents of Tepito and the role LSM plays in ameliorating that precariousness—whether materially or spiritually. In the vulnerable community of Tepito, death has become fully normalized, and the neighborhood has thus become a sort of social laboratory for the emergence of LSM.

As Romero Romero explained, when LSM arranged for her altar to be positioned in the middle of Tepito, she was simply carrying out God's will, responding to God's desire to care for the community. This reveals one of the cardinal theological beliefs of the LSM spiritual movement, or at least Romero's branch of the movement—namely, the superlative power of God's will, which works through LSM. As described by Romero Romero, LSM herself is "blind, deaf, and dumb"; she only follows God's orders.[72] For Romero Romero, LSM's spiritual power over humanity comes through God's granted grace. She manifests God's love for those experiencing repression—and his particular love for those in Tepito. As Romero Romero explained, "You know that everything that happens in this world is by God's will, you know that not a leaf moves if is not by the will of God. It happened here [in Tepito] because God wanted. Not because I wanted."[73]

This assertion is particularly important. By framing the creation of the Tepito shrine to LSM as an expression of God's will, Romero creates a space in which those attacking her or the adoration of LSM are forced to confront the possibility that they are resisting God's will. This can help to combat negative responses to LSM and her community of venerators (the same ones I had heard and internalized before I visited Romero Romero). As Romero Romero put it: "People are not well informed. . . . They said, 'Oh, La Santa Muerte is bad. Do not believe in her. She will punish you. Your family is going to die.' This is not true! No one is going to die, if it is not the will of God. . . . It is not her [LSM's] will. It is the will of God" that allows someone to die.[74] Even LSM herself is constrained by God: she can grant favors and perform miracles, but only according to God's commands. Romero Romero says,

"[LSM] helped us . . . as long as we first asked permission from God, our Lord. . . . We ask him to allow our beloved, beautiful, and lovely girl [LSM], so she can take care, and assist us."[75]

As the modern founder of LSM's public veneration, Romero Romero remains a central protagonist of the worship community. She is commonly known as La Madrina (the godmother). Her monthly so-called rosary to LSM, held on the first day of each month, gathers hundreds of followers outside her home for an evening of prayer and popular devotion—one of the most popular and best-known acts of public devotion to LSM in Mexico. This rosary largely reproduces a typical rosary to the Virgin Mary, with the wording changed to replace the references to Mary with references to LSM instead.

Despite Romero Romero's clear prominence as the leader and founder of LSM's modern veneration, her branch of the movement has remained closely confined to Tepito, and the status of her branch of the movement as the public face of LSM veneration has declined somewhat; when her husband, Raymundo, was murdered outside their home on June 7, 2016—a year and a half after I had met him on that first visit—Romero Romero shifted her attention from public acts of veneration to more intimate events. She remained silent about the death of her husband and how it may have affected her own veneration of LSM, but she began to plan for who might replace her.[76]

Going Global: Enriqueta Vargas Ortiz and San Padrino Endoque
"I don't do witchcraft. I don't do dark magic. . . . I only know how to do prayers."[77] This is how Enriqueta Vargas Ortiz described herself during one of our interviews. From 2008 to 2018, Vargas Ortiz was the leader of Mexico City–based La Santa Muerte Internacional (SMI), the largest branch of the LSM movement. SMI should not be confused with La Santa Muerte Universal (SMU), a different organization that emerged from the SMI in the same region several years later. Our last interview took place in October 2018, on the same day she went into the hospital due to complications from cancer. She died on December 20, 2018. Vargas Ortiz was a charismatic, sweet grandmother, deeply dedicated to her community and her family. Like many people I encountered during my research, she was open and direct, but also very much in control of her public persona and aware of the media's constant scrutiny of LSM. Under Vargas Ortiz, her group La Santa Muerte Internacional (SMI) spread across national borders to become the largest

branch of the movement, extending from Mexico into the United States, Central and South America, and Europe.[78]

To understand how Vargas Ortiz rose to prominence in 2008, one must first understand the life and death of her son, Jonathan Legaría Vargas, another LSM devotee who was known as San Padrino (Godfather) Endoque, or Comandante Pantera (Commander Panther). On December 28, 2007, Legaría Vargas inaugurated a shrine to LSM in Tultitlán, a municipality within the greater Mexico City urban area. On Via López Portillo in the barrio of Santa María Coatepec, he erected a seventy-two-foot statue of LSM. Only six months later, in the early hours of July 31, 2008, Legaría Vargas died after being shot more than two hundred times by the police. He was only twenty-six years old.

His death had a lasting effect on the development of LSM's veneration, especially its expansion into the United States. In 2014, he was declared the first saint of LSM—under the name San Padrino Endoque—by his mother and SMI. Prayers, songs, busts, statues, and murals about him, along with LSM, can be found throughout Mexico, although his status as a vernacular saint is strictly limited to SMI.[79]

Legaría Vargas was a complex individual, likely involved in shady business affairs, and the circumstances surrounding his death remain unclear. Explanations vary, linking it to everything from a narco-related crime to road rage, from a power struggle between rival LSM factions to a targeted assassination by the government and the police. Some even chalk it up to an unfortunate mistake. Devastated by the death of her son and frustrated with authorities' slowness in investigating the crime, Vargas Ortiz made a pledge to LSM: "If you give to me the murderers of my son, I will try to lift you as high as I can."[80] According to Vargas Ortiz, within a year, her son's killers were dead. From then on, she became a highly active promoter of LSM. She regularly reported visions and communications with her dead son, who has become a sort of ghostly spiritual co-leader of the group. Under her guidance, her son's original group in Tultitlán, Mexico, with its seventy-five-foot statue of LSM (the largest in the world), has become one of the most influential and recognizable organizations of the development of the global LSM movement, with ties across all the states of Mexico, the United States, and several other continents.[81]

During one of our interviews, Vargas Ortiz described her immersion into the world of LSM—which until then had been her son's world, not her own—as being a sort of spiritual "second" conversion:

It was a completely different world to the one I knew. Suddenly, I saw myself immersed in a totally new world. I was afraid . . . for the culto [worship] to La Santa Muerte . . . imagine, I was Catholic, and full of taboos and fears . . . But when I got there, and I put myself in front [of the organization], I realized that it was full of people trying to comfort me. . . . They adored and loved my son. That gave me a little bit of strength. They tried to offer me a warm hug. . . . They told me, "We love[d] your son, and now we love you." . . . It did me good to know these people [involved in the veneration of La Santa Muerte]. That changed my way of thinking completely![82]

In this explanation, Vargas Ortiz strategically narrated her conversion as being defined by the acts of kindness of LSM's followers during her time of grief. She contextualized her own fears of, and early resistance to, the veneration of LSM in relation to her Catholic upbringing. Importantly, Vargas Ortiz, a powerful and charismatic storyteller, wove a narrative of being introduced to the veneration of LSM with which others could also identify, united around the broader themes of motherly love and grief.

I first met Vargas Ortiz in person in Queens, New York, in the summer of 2017, at the Santa Muerte ball described at the beginning of this chapter, although we had previously communicated by email. We remained in contact and occasionally met during her trips to the United States or during my trips to her main temple in Tultitlán. During our many conversations, she elaborated on how her promise to LSM became reality, on her family's relationship with LSM, and on how her life changed after the death of her son. She explained that her work with SMI enabled her to avoid thinking about his death. She constantly framed her work as fulfilling her promise to LSM and healing her relationship with her son, which before his death had been strained by his involvement with LSM: "I want my son to feel proud of me. Also . . . at a certain point I may have not had a good communication with my son, in part because of his beliefs." She added, "In many ways, I want to be forgiven. . . . In many forms, I am saying to him, 'Here I am, until the moment when we will see each other again. I am going to make you proud of me.'"[83] This narrative of her work as an expiatory motherly sacrifice was a central element in how Vargas Ortiz presented herself to the media.

Motherhood similarly shapes how Vargas Ortiz's followers see her—as La Madrina or the Godmother—and how they see LSM. She recounted that once, when her son was still alive, she tried to leverage her position as his mother to question his devotion to LSM. He responded, "Mamacita, you are my [biological] mother, but she [LSM] is my spiritual mother. Respect, please, what I believe."[84] After forming SMI, Vargas Ortiz made motherhood a recurrent theme in her prayer events and interviews. She constantly reminded devotees of the tripartite connection between their own biological mothers, LSM as a divine mother, and herself as a surrogate spiritual mother.

Intentionally or unintentionally, this approach served as an effective shield against any who might have questioned her leadership of SMI. As a grieving and suffering penitent, a mother who had endured the loss of a child, Vargas Ortiz was largely immune from critique—even within her own family. She told me: "In my family, I am the only one that believes in La Santa Muerte. . . . My daughters do believe in her, a little bit, but they refrain from telling me anything against it, they keep themselves in the margins. . . . Also . . . my family knows the suffering that I went through. They understand!"[85] Having survived the death of her son, Vargas Ortiz connected with others through their tragedies and was rewarded, as she saw it, with an abundance of new children: her followers, the descendants of her son's spiritual work.

In my last interview with her, Vargas Ortiz reflected on the future of SMI. She spoke in particular about her two grandchildren, the son and daughter of Legaría Vargas: "[The kids] believe in La Santa [Muerte]. I think they will be the ones that will lead the community. Not because I have instilled it in them, but rather because they carry it inside them."[86] This hope speaks to the real struggle for continuity that confronts many of the modern branches of LSM veneration. All of the existing organizations are currently run by senior spiritual leaders. Many have also transformed from small, local worship groups into large, complex, and sometimes even international groups. The need to secure continuity is real and pressing. Following the death of Vargas Ortiz in 2018, one of her daughters stepped up to lead SMI; she will have to adapt to the new complexities and global realities of LSM fellowship.

Innovative Legalizations: Santa Muerte Universal Within a Liminal Mexico
As an organic movement, one deeply defined by the personal experiences, needs, and inspirations of its members, the LSM movement is constantly morphing in response to the forces that oppose it. One of these opposition forces has, until recently, been the Mexican state itself; until 2016, none of the various branches had secured the Mexican government's recognition as a religious group. But in 2016, Santa Muerte Universal (SMU)—also referred to as Rosita de Natanahel AC—transformed from a religious group into a nonprofit organization, only eight years after its 2008 founding.[87] This group,

located in Colonia República Mexicana in the municipality of Coacalco, is the first nonprofit organization affiliated with the veneration of LSM to be formally registered with and recognized by the Mexican government.

The history of SMU is intimately linked to the life experiences of Carmen Sandoval and her husband, David Valencia, the founders of the organization. Valencia's devotion to LSM started early in his life. His teen years served as the backdrop for his all-embracing adult conversion to LSM many years after. He described this experience to me in these terms:

> I migrated to the United States as a young adult. I was living in Santa Ana, California, with some of my relatives. . . . On one occasion, as we were painting and replacing the carpet in a house in San Diego, I went to their garage . . . and there in the middle . . . I saw a statue of La Santa Muerte. . . . In that moment . . . I saw my life flash in front of me, like a light . . . everything that led me to that moment. . . . That day when we finished our work, the lady who owned the house called me and without reason gave me the statue. . . . That same day, when I got home, I told everyone I was moving back to Mexico. I bought my ticket and returned with La Santa Muerte. She arrived on December 11, [2004,] with me. . . . She comes from California.[88]

This story manifests the intimate connection between LSM and the US-Mexico border. It features immigration to (and the retorno from) the United States, showing how religion and culture in the two countries cross-pollinate. In the case of SMU, part of the spiritual capital associated with Valencia's LSM statue arises from the fact that he brought it back from the United States. The statue takes part in the familiar process of immigration and retorno—there and back—with LSM there at both the beginning and the end, having roots in both worlds.

The nonprofit arm of SMU was legally recognized by the Mexican government on May 16, 2016. Achieving this designation was no small matter. The nonprofit came after the religious initiative: it was only after eight years (2008–16) of the religious arm's work in social relief services, "collecting clothes and pantry goods that were distributed among needy communities," that the idea of the nonprofit organization developed, with the leaders seeing it as a way for the "government [to] help us to do more, to help others."[89] Currently, because of SMU's legal status, its charitable and religious functions are managed as two distinct entities, although the memberships have significant overlap. "The majority of the people who support [the civil association's] volunteer work . . . are also members of the religious group," Sandoval explains, but "the civil association . . . [is] independent from the religious group, which is about faith and devotion."[90] Maintaining this clear distinction between the civil and religious arms is particularly important for the group's dealings with the purportedly secular Mexican government, which grants funds and approves tax-exempt status for the civil association.

Sandoval told me an illuminating story about how the group gained its legal nonprofit status; the story highlights how crucial the internet has been in the development and spread of the culto of LSM. As Sandoval explained in our interview, the legal process of becoming a nonprofit "was not easy. Actually, in many ways, it was kind of funny . . . because in reality, we did not know how to form a civil [nonprofit] association. We learned everything, all the steps, via the internet."[91] This detail illustrates the centrality of the internet for this veneration. LSM is a migrating saint not just because of her transnational movement between nation-states but also because of her online presence, which has allowed her to fulfill, as a spiritual entity, the promise of being in multiple places at once. The universes of accessibility provided by the internet have become an intrinsic part of LSM's spiritual dominion and identity. Online memes, Photoshopped images, prayer cards, YouTube videos, and the many virtual altars dedicated to LSM have transformed her into a star of the spiritual virtual world.

As the LSM movement has grown, both inside and outside Mexico, new challenges and needs have emerged. Many are directly related to the expansion of LSM's veneration, but others have arisen from issues of continuity, clarification, and consolidation among the early groups as they confront their diversity and the emergence of new leaders. The challenges moving forward cluster around three central issues: (1) lack of a unifying administrative structure within or between the different branches of LSM, which translates into a flexible but uneven approach to group formation and governance across different branches and leaders; (2) the growing use of and dependence on social media and web technology for group formation, organization, and communication—both a boon and a problem, since internet literacy and access are unevenly distributed across generations, regions, and branches; and (3) a wide-open field of core rituals and beliefs with a high level of adaptability and personalization.

The distributed nature of digital LSM veneration produces a kind of atomism in the movement. Other spiritual movements focus heavily on formal processes such as retreats, printed guides, meetings for mentors, and so on, but among followers of LSM there exist no such formal shared practices. Of course, there are informal collective veneration activities—prayer gatherings (e.g., rosaries, Masses, and healing rituals), TV/radio presentations—that work to increase membership and unify communities around LSM. Nevertheless, the profoundly digital context and character of LSM community-building is largely unprecedented. We are witnessing the birth of not just a religious group but a digital spiritual movement, one that combines traditional means of religious interaction with the virtual concept of digital churches without walls.

Online, streaming, or cloud-based spiritual gatherings are a central element of the LSM movement today. They reflect not only the technological and sociocultural times but also the socioeconomic realities of immigration and political resistance experienced by her followers. Because Mexico has denied or delayed all efforts by LSM-affiliated groups to obtain legal recognition as religious entities (recall that only the civil association arm of SMU is legally recognized, as a nonprofit charity rather than a religion), these spiritual groups bear a greater tax burden than do other recognized religious organizations, and it would be more difficult for them to pay for long-term physical spaces of worship. Online gatherings have also emerged as a cornerstone for worship practices because of the experiences of migration and labor-driven mobilization (and the correspondingly vast distances between many members) and because of the stigma associated with LSM veneration. Internet-based devotion allows the groups to create a sense of community, even across national and generational boundaries.

All leaders and main branches hold regular online streaming events, such as weekly Masses and rosaries, where they share news and announcements. As many people have found during the COVID-19 pandemic, web-based worship venues are highly flexible and offer a decentralized, cheap, and always available spiritual experience that can still be very personal. Interestingly, few groups actually have their own websites; at this writing, those that exist are very rudimentary. Instead, they rely almost exclusively on existing social media platforms, such as Facebook, Twitter, and WhatsApp, to distribute, access, and store virtual meetings and video conferences. Thus the popularity of LSM is deeply linked to the formation of social networks via virtual connectivity. Indeed, the online LSM networks are so strong that they are producing an entirely new type of spiritual leader: online ministers whose followers are mostly or even exclusively virtual. LSM is thus one of the first virtual saints of the twenty-first century. One of her biggest miracles is that her venerators can visit her online worship spaces, at any hour of need, day or night, unlike chapels in real space that are sometimes closed or too far away for spur-of-the-moment visits. These virtual chapels are always open, and someone else is always online to worship with you.

Digital social networks are a cornerstone not only of LSM worship but of organization leadership as well. For example, when asked specifically about her closest group of collaborators, Vargas Ortiz explained, "There are leaders, but they are kept in contact via WhatsApp . . . Facebook, and telephone. . . . I visit them during the anniversaries of their temples . . . and the [anniversary of the] death of my son. . . . But we don't have retreats. It is difficult because all of them work and they live very far. . . . They all have jobs."[92] Her comments reflected more than just the composition or geographic distribution of the leaders in her group. They also shed light on a deeper transformation in how religious groups in the new millennium are approaching today's dynamic realities and people's access to technology. This new model requires researchers to change the way we think about how religious organizations develop, factoring in the impact of web-based technologies in constructing and perpetuating religiosity.

In the case of Mexico, this use of online technologies is remarkable, for it is a nation still deeply digitally divided as "a consequence of poverty and inequality," where "less than half of its population" has access to the internet.[93] As of 2017, according to the Organization for Economic Co-operation and Development, Mexico and Colombia have the worst household internet access in Latin America, with only 50.9 percent and 50 percent of households, respectively, able to get online at home.[94] Despite this, Mexico ranks fifth globally in the use of Facebook, surpassing even the United Kingdom—a disparity that calls attention to the importance of mobile technology, especially cellphones, in internet access.[95]

SMU has been particularly adept in using these technologies. Sandoval told me, "We have WhatsApp and [Facebook] Messenger groups. . . . In there we upload the prayers. . . . They ask questions, share their difficulties and problems . . . and anyone [collectively] gives them advice. 'Go and light a green candle . . . or a red candle.' . . . All of that happens via the internet."[96] Vargas Ortiz's group, SMI, also uses technology to integrate new members, introduce new rituals, and make organizational decisions. In short, the virtual world becomes both a real and a metaphorical expression of the physical terrains inhabited by LSM's followers today.

Moreover, Sandoval explained, "the first contact [for new groups] normally happens via WhatsApp . . . this is how everything begins."[97] So the virtual world serves not only as space for encounters and education but also as one of the central terrains for expanding the community's network. Interestingly, expansion focuses not only on individual members but also on already established groups. In other words, Santamuertistas are not only recruiting individual people, they are also working to bring existing small LSM groups under one larger umbrella. For many in the new millennium, the virtual world is the first place they encounter and learn about LSM. Her success in attracting followers online reflects how the virtual world and the spiritual realm intersect. We are witnessing the enactment of a global spiritual e-miracle, as leaders and followers—often separated by great distances in the physical world—invoke LSM's support within the terrains of cyberspace. What proportion of these online followers move into worshiping in person with others is unclear. What is clear is that the anonymity provided by the virtual world is useful to those of LSM's followers who are already socially stigmatized by virtue of their veneration of her.

Not One but Many Santa Muertes: Personalizing Death

Because of the plurality of practices around the veneration of LSM, it is impossible to single out just one form of LSM worship for description. Rather, we must recognize that there are many forms of LSM worship within a polymorphous system. In fact, we might say that there are many Santa Muertes. Each set of devotees believes in a different version of LSM, but all of the versions share the same "job": of humanizing death and helping vulnerable followers deal with the inevitable pains and troubles of life—a form of death-in-life—and with the inevitability of literal physical death. Each group approaches veneration of LSM within a large array of practices defined by that group's unique needs and context. Indeed, sometimes the beliefs of different branches even contradict each other. This phenomenon makes it imperative—and, as the next section will show, nearly inevitable—that a cohesive theology about LSM eventually emerge.

The flexibility and adaptability that characterize LSM's veneration respond to the point, illustrated by Sandoval, that "we all do not have the same needs all the time."[98] Venerating LSM is understood as a dynamic process, in which the altar and the practices around it change over time because her followers' needs change. All saints, including the border saints studied in this book, are responding to their followers' needs. In this case, what LSM's followers have in common is that their needs are very much defined by the precarity created by migration. This highly personalized form of veneration, in which no single branch or entity monitors or regulates the popular practices of LSM worship, stands in sharp contrast with the worship of canonized Catholic saints. This very instability makes it particularly difficult to normalize or identify as central any one form of LSM veneration, even among the most recognized branches within the movement. Sandoval explained: "Everything depends on each person and place. Each person has their own different customs. As you see, we have visited all the republic [of Mexico], and each person and group pray differently. . . . We are open to other ways and customs because we want also to learn. . . . This way we can learn something new all the time. Basically, here we are open to everyone who wants to join our deity, our faith, our belief, our veneration. Everyone has been shaped by their own personal circumstances and experiences."[99] This plurality of styles, forms of prayers, and spiritual approaches might be one of the most appealing characteristics of LSM veneration for many Catholics and ex-Catholics who dislike the rigidity of traditional, institutionalized religious groups.

The leaders of LSM's main groups are aware of the challenges raised by the very flexibility and decentralization that appeals to many members, and some seek to help the movement coalesce around certain shared practices or figures. For Vargas Ortiz, for example, "writing many of the prayers and songs we use" was one of the most important ways to "preserve the name, legacy, and memory" of her son and the movement he helped launch.[100] The leaders of SMI—and the LSM movement as a whole—see the importance of both growing the movement's numbers and creating for the followers of the Holy Death an identity distinct from that of other spiritual groups.

The Theology of LSM: Understanding LSM's Place Among Other (Catholic) Saints

> Para nosotros, primero Dios, luego la virgencita de Guadalupe, San Juditas Tadeo y mi Niña Blanca. [For us, first comes God, then the Virgin of Guadalupe, then Saint Jude Thaddeus and my White Lady (LSM).]
>
> —Enriqueta Romero Romero

Not All Saints Are the Same: Catholic Santamuertistas?

Most followers of LSM locate their belief in her within a large constellation of other religious beliefs, each with its own set of material worship practices. As Perdigón Castañeda explains, believing in LSM does not exclude other beliefs: followers "can believe at the same time in any other Virgin Mary or saint."[101] According to Perdigón Castañeda, Santamuertistas locate God at the top of their spiritual hierarchy, right above Jesus Christ, who is then followed by LSM and the angels at the same level, because they believe that she started off as a universal force instead of a human who ascended to sainthood. On the next level down, LSM followers position the Virgin Mary, and below her other saints (as well as martyrs and other holy people). At the bottom of this structure Santamuertistas locate lay humans.[102] Perdigón Castañeda never questions what kind of God Santamuertistas are referring to. The assumption here is that followers are referring to a Judeo-Christian understanding of God, because many of them have grown up with predominantly Catholic narratives.

Ten years after Perdigón Castañeda's work, my research reveals that a similar structure remains in place—although, as discussed later in this chapter, not all Santamuertistas position the Virgin Mary beneath LSM. For the many followers of LSM who do see her as being above the Virgin in the celestial hierarchy, it is the universal character of death that positions LSM divinely (and naturally) above all other saints. In an interview, Lucino Morales (of El Templo Santa Muerte and Iglesia Arcangelista México–US) explained the superiority of LSM as stemming from the fact that she (unlike all human saints) neither was born nor died: "All the saints have been born of someone, a person. . . . However, Our Most Holy Death is not the daughter of a human. . . . She was not born from a human being. She was created [directly] by God. . . . He created La Santa Muerte, and the Bible speaks about it."[103] Further, all other saints, being human, eventually died and were thus eventually taken under the wing of the Holy Death. In other words, because of the human condition of the other saints—being subject to birth and death—they must naturally be positioned underneath LSM.

Pragmatically, as Morales explains, other saints' relation to LSM is shaped by the latter's unique effectiveness in granting miracles, which is a function of her relative closeness to God. Another believer describes a spiritual and almost utilitarian relationship between God, LSM, and humans as follows: "[LSM] is in unity with God, our Lord. . . . It is because of his command that she one day will come to get us. Because every person ... will eventually die at some time ... and she is the only one who will guide us [to God]."[104] Here, Death as a divine entity works with and for God, guided by the latter's plans for each person and for humanity.

Two themes emerge consistently across the various forms of LSM theology: LSM's position within the heavenly hierarchy and death as a constant element in the human experience. First, as discussed above, LSM holds a superior celestial position within the hierarchy of saints and other spiritual entities. For Morales, LSM is second only to the Holy Trinity (the same in form and essence as in Catholic theology): "God is the Father, the Son, and the Holy Spirit. After God there is my Most Holy Santa Muerte."[105] Another group frames it this way: "God is first, because we need to ask permission from God in order to invoke La Santa Muerte."[106] As these statements show, deep residues of Catholic beliefs inform the veneration of LSM, which frames her as collaborating with (a Christian) God to meet followers' needs.

Objects of LSM worship encode these relations. In the Latinx neighborhood of Detroit, Michigan, known as Mexicantown, one regularly finds traditional six-day glass votive candles—like those found in many grocery stores and botánicas—that are decorated with a black-and-white image of LSM on the front and a Spanish/English prayer on the back. The English version of the prayer reads as follows:

> Lord, before Your Divine Presence God Almighty,
> Father, Son and Holy Spirit, I ask for your
> permission to invoke the Holy Death, my White
> Daughter: I want to humbly ask, that you break and
> destroy all spells and darkness that may present itself
> before my persona, in my home, and on my path.
> Holy Death, please relieve me of all envy, poverty,
> hate, and unemployment. I ask that you please grant
> me _____. Enlighten, with your holy
> presence, my home, my work and those of my loved
> ones. Award us love, prosperity, health, and well-being.
> Blessed and praised by your charity Holy Death.
> Lord, I give you infinite thanks, because I see your
> charity through your tests, which are perfecting my
> spirit. Lord, I give you thanks because in the midst of
> these tests, I will have your Holy Blessing. Amen.[107]

Again, we see that LSM is subordinate to God—in this case, a God who is based on (and refers to) the Catholic model of the Trinity as Three Persons in one God: Father, Son, and Holy Spirit. The prayer also emphasizes and reveals the precarious reality that surrounds those who venerate LSM. Words like "spells," "darkness," and "envy, poverty, hate, and unemployment" refer to the many difficulties experienced by her followers. However, the things that followers are asking for in the prayer's petitions for "love, prosperity, health, and well-being" are not very different from the petitions that are made to other saints.

The second tenet of LSM's theology is its emphasis on death as a constant element of the human condition. This is what provides the foundation of LSM's power. LSM conquers and triumphs over everyone, including other saints in the hierarchy, because all humans succumb to death. Martín argues that it is LSM's egalitarianism in her role as Holy Death that attracts and unifies her followers, bringing them together despite their varied individual needs and histories. Death comes for everyone, rich or poor, downtrodden or privileged, precarious or safe. It is this that explains her popularity: as Martín puts it, "Santa Muerte's devotees . . . embrace her role as an equalizer and unifier of the human race."[108] Romero Romero painted an even more vivid picture when she explained LSM's intimate connection with each human being: "You are born with death [within]. You just need to peel off your skin and you turn into la muerte. You are a skeleton."[109] This inescapable relationship with all humans means that everyone, according to Romero Romero, is a potential follower of LSM, and everyone can potentially share her fundamental message with others; everyone is a candidate to become a disciple. As LSM reminds us of the reality of death, she also reminds us that no matter who you are, when you die (and you will), there will be a reckoning: in Romero Romero's words, "When you die, nobody is going to keep half of your sins. You alone are going to deal with them."[110]

Many Santamuertistas believe in the Resurrection of Christ and the Assumption of Mary, but interweave these beliefs with LSM's story. For example, Morales refers to the Virgin Mary in ways that reinforce his belief in her as the Mother of God. Others, however, diverge sharply from traditional Catholic dogma in their beliefs about the Resurrection—a core Christian value, one that enjoys the status of dogma in the Catholic Church. Believers cite the Resurrection as proving the victory of Christ over death, which confirms for them his omnipotent status as the Son of God, the Second Person of the Trinity, God himself incarnate. As Saint Paul writes of the

Resurrection of Christ, in his first letter to the Corinthians, "O death where is thy victory? / O death where is thy sting?"[111] In this sense, LSM—the Holy Death, death personified—is incongruent with the normative Christian faith, in which Jesus defeats death. As Romero Romero explained to me, some who believe in LSM reconcile this apparent contradiction by arguing that she is only following God's commands. For the followers of LSM, Christ and Mary are no longer human and thus no longer subject to death; Christ's Resurrection and Mary's Assumption into Heaven position them with similar status within the spiritual hierarchy. All other humans, however, are directly subordinate to death. For Santamuertistas, then, human mortality and people's own relationship with death reflect the personal and intimate relationship each person has with LSM, whether (as Romero Romero put it) the individual acknowledges her or not.

These are the theoretical and theological reasons for her followers' belief that LSM is the most powerful saint. Their belief is also influenced by LSM's efficacy as a miracle-granter: as Sandoval explained, she "grants miracles faster than other saints . . . because the other saints are very busy."[112] She added, "In my opinion, she does the most miracles. . . . I believe in it, and many people said that too, that she is the most miraculous of all [saints]."[113] In this case, miracle granting is organized within the logic of accessibility and efficiency. Paradoxically, however, LSM's power to grant miracles is in inverse proportion to her number of followers. For Sandoval, LSM is the most powerful saint precisely because she is not as popular and, consequently, not as busy as the other saints. This presents a transactional dilemma: as she becomes more popular over time, LSM risks becoming busier in attending to her growing numbers of petitioners, and losing her reputation for speed and efficiency in miracle-granting. This conflicts with her followers' desire for her to become more popular.

The relations between the LSM movement and the Catholic Church are contentious and muddy—sometimes even to those following LSM. LSM's followers understand her as being part of a much larger and interconnected matrix of spiritual entities, a matrix that includes some traditional recognized Catholic saints such as the Virgin Mary and others, and others of whom are not. Romero Romero explained this spiritual collaboration between a pantheon of multiple spiritual entities in an interview:

> Nobody is disconnected from anybody. Not of San Juditas [Saint Jude], the Virgin of Guadalupe, Holy Infant of Atocha [Antioch] . . . the Virgin

of Saint John. Nobody is disconnected. Everything is a matter of faith. Everything is good! So, if you connect all those chains . . . when you have a serious problem, they will help you, La Santa Muerte, God our Lord, the Virgin of Guadalupe. They will join forces and move you forward. Because it is not bad. But people are like . . . tricky, [they] remove La Santa Muerte and put God . . . [they] remove little Saint Jude and put to [Jesús] Malverde. No, that cannot be done! You should grab all forces. Because, at the end, when you die, the idea is that you feel comfortable that you joined with the forces . . . to love God, to love death [LSM], to love all the celestial and spiritual court.[114]

LSM is at the center of an economy of spiritual entities in which a constant negotiation of power is taking place. In this matrix, not all entities are the same or part of the same set of dogmas or practices, and different believers structure the hierarchy in different ways. But what is crucial here is how the spiritual movement around LSM remains entangled with and largely dependent on traditional Catholic prayers, rituals, references, and iconographies, despite the Church's lack of formal recognition of LSM.

Establishing Altars: Recognizing Microcosms of Hierarchy

The complex and shifting hierarchies of the interconnected matrix of saints are reflected in home altars to LSM. Vázquez has LSM "on a throne, because she is the most important. And on her right side" she has "the Virgin of Guadalupe."[115] Sandoval explained to me, "La Santa Muerte is not in a fight with any saint. . . . Therefore, it is accepted that each person can have in their altar to La Santa Muerte a little shrine to Saint Jude, or Saint Anthony . . . to whatever they want."[116] Santamuertistas see no contradiction in mixing multiple saints in their altars and related spiritual practices. All saints are perceived as helpers provided to them by God. The boundaries among saints are thus defined not by dogma or organizational borders but by pragmatism and by followers' urgent needs, and their home altars reflect this.

Altars work as tangible manifestations of the needs and struggles of an individual or family. Items in home altars are never selected at random. Vázquez's comments about the relative placement of La Santa Muerte and the Virgin of Guadalupe, for example, reflect her understanding of the coexistence of LSM with other spiritual figures, but they also reveal an important understanding of power and its intersections in the spiritual realm. Specifically, although her altar contains a heterogeneous array of multiple spiritual figures within the same space, not all of these objects or images are treated the same. An implied hierarchy is found among these devotional objects; an explicit disparity of power is manifested through where they are located within the altar. For example, there is a clear power differential expressed in the relative placement of the Virgin of Guadalupe and LSM: it matters who is at the center of the altar and who is on the side.

The centers and peripheries of these compositions together define a narrative, and the altar works as a system in which each piece is carefully positioned to construct a discourse. In an altar the story is told collectively, not individually. Each object has an individual history, yes, but it also has a purpose that connects it with the main narrative. During my visits to people's altars to LSM, followers frequently felt compelled to explain the narrative of their altars to me, telling me the stories of how each piece came to be, where each came from, and how they were all interconnected. In this way, I experienced by proxy the spiritual journey narrated by each altar. The spiritual power and personal connection between followers and their altars to LSM (or to other saints) are amplified by the constant reiteration of the spiritual journey retold and reenacted by the altar.

As people's journeys change over time, so do their altars. People constantly update their altars to reflect their personal experiences and those of their communities. In many cases, as communities dissolve and new ones emerge, statues and sacred objects from one altar may be passed on to other communities. These objects' spiritual capital and relevance shift and intensify as they move from one community or individual to another. Moreover, the genealogy of each object is an important component defining its spiritual (and literal) location on the altar and in the life of the followers. For example, all those interviewed for this book remember (and keep) with special esteem their first statue of LSM. Many started their stories of their personal spiritual journeys or conversions by describing how they obtained their first statue or image of LSM. Often, I heard that interviewees had inherited a first image from a grandmother, a previously important leader or healer, or a close friend in times of distress, and they remember the distressing events as part of their spiritual journeys. These essential elements of personal narrative not only validate the spiritual power of the interviewee's image or statue but also transfer to each person the social and emotional capital the object has accrued through each previous owner's spiritual journey.[117]

In addition to these personal emotional genealogies, followers offer many other spiritual reasons to justify the inclusion of a particular LSM-related object on their altars. In some cases, objects were "adopted" when their previous owners could or would not care for them and venerate them properly. For example, Sandoval explained how SMU was able to "rescue a series of statues that were not well taken care of and honored by their previous owner."[118] In another case, followers explained how statues might first arrive in their community "on consignment," with the object temporarily entering their possession until the owner reclaims it. However, when the original owner is "unable to collect the object," it can become a permanent fixture on the group's altar. In these cases, LSM herself sometimes makes the decision about what objects are to stay at her altars. In one case of a disagreement about ownership, LSM interceded: "Every time [the owner] had tried to pick it up, something happens. . . . That was two years ago! Clearly, she [the statue of LSM] wants to stay here."[119] That particular statue acquired an animistic status, and her "persistence" in remaining with the group was taken as proof that the original owner should not force LSM to relocate.

Vázquez's decision to connect all the saints together—official and unofficial—in her spiritual pantheon reflects her own attachment to and personal history with each of the different spiritual entities. As she explained, her "Catholic saints were already part of [her] life before La Santa Muerte came into [her] life."[120] Vázquez said she has not been able to "get rid of them [the other saints] because they are part of the beliefs and values" that her parents instilled in her very early when she was growing up Catholic in Mexico.[121] Consequently, her home altar has become a repertoire and a historical archive of her entire spiritual journey, from childhood into the present. In her home, LSM, the Virgin of Guadalupe, other traditional Catholic saints, and santería saints all coexist on the altar, because, she said, they are "different things."[122] For Vázquez—as for many followers of LSM, especially those who have grown up Catholic—the veneration of La Flaquita is not about a pure notion of an institutionalized religiosity. Rather, it reflects the interweaving of many elements that have formed followers' individual spiritual life experiences. The altar becomes a spiritual footprint of their struggles and spiritual geneologies.

Assigning Personality to Each Statue of LSM

One of the most intriguing elements about the veneration of LSM is the anthropomorphic or human agency assigned to some of her statues. Many devotees refer to their statues as if they were alive, with personalities. Just as they are often connected in followers' minds with the people who gave the statues to them—a grandmother or grandfather, a friend, shaman, or a curandero—they are also often associated with the followers' conversions or the difficulties they had to overcome at that time. In other cases, the spiritual value comes less from the emotional provenance of the statue than on the process of its construction or on the materials it is made of (for example, some statues incorporate a human skull, hair, or teeth). Many of these objects are seen as having unique power and animistic characteristics. These statues are not only treated differently from others but are held in higher esteem within the hierarchy of other spiritual objects in home altars or public shrines.

Some statues of LSM achieve almost human status among followers. For example, Sandoval described her fear when her husband brought a new statue for their altar: "This one was very realistic, and I got scared that she will take [kill] him."[123] She also recounted how the statue her family had in a former home forced its new owner to return the house to them because she was unhappy with the new tenant. Followers see these statues as having needs and desires and the means to accomplish them, often ascribing to LSM and her physical manifestations human emotions like jealousy, protectiveness, gratitude, and happiness. They believe that it is important to treat her with the utmost respect following the rules and expectations set by a manda economy. As Sandoval explained, "Depending on how you take care of her, she will take care of you."[124] Believers are encouraged to "put flowers, water . . . tequila . . . candy, chocolate" on her altars year-round—not just as ofrendas (offerings) but as ways to keep her "happy."[125] Believers also keep her looking attractive, dressing her in beautiful outfits for the same reason. Sandoval, referring to a large-doll-sized statue SMU obtained from another community that "was not taking good care of her," explained to me how different things are now that she is with them: "Here [with us] she is very happy! We dress her, we cut her hair . . . and she has changed completely! Last year we dressed her as a bride."[126] Every year, as part of the group's annual celebration, the statue of LSM is assigned a madrina de vestido, or a godmother sponsor, who covers the expenses for the new dress that she will wear in the festivities.[127]

Some statues are also given individual names, and even unnamed ones often have their own individual identities and characters and are honored with individual celebrations. Sandoval explained: "This [statue] is called

Macarena.... Each month on the twenty-eighth we have a rosary for her." The group's annual pilgrimage is made for a different statue, called Rosita de Natanahel.[128] Each statue is thus a different personalization of LSM—a different aspect of the human face of the Holy Death—and thus has a history that requires a different set of spiritual practices to fit her needs and personality.[129]

For some followers, the altar tangibly represents the multiplicity of LSM's types and reminds followers of the geographic scope of her veneration: "Most of our Santitas [little Santa Muertes] have been given to us. These here were given to us during a Veracruz meeting. This one here was given to me in a Puebla village.... Most of these ones came from an altar in Anizapan. These ones were given to me in Tepito. This little girl [Santa Muerte statue] was given at San José Iturbide.... This one, and these ones, came from Guanajuato."[130] As this tour of one group's statues illustrates, the altar becomes more than just a display of offerings, mandas, and hopes. It becomes an album that collects the memories and the histories of a community, with each statue "framing" a new picture of the community's evolution, trajectories, and geographic expansion. The altar serves as more than a collection of travel postcards, but rather provides a living testimony to the diversity of the LSM community and the interconnectivity among its network. An altar can become a template, a spiritual topography of a nation inscribed by the veneration of LSM.

A Queer Queen of the Torcidos

One of the most distinctive aspects of LSM's spiritual movement is the abundance of her LGBTQ followers. Their active and open presence has deeply shaped the emergence of the movement in recent decades; they have been an intrinsic part of its constituency, rituals, and practices. As Chesnut observes, "From the most prominent devotional leaders to anonymous believers, the disproportionate number of [LGBTQ] devotees to death can't be ignored."[131] Indeed, "the majority of top Saint Death leaders in the United States, Britain, and the Philippines are LGBT, with gay men predominating." Chesnut attributes this phenomenon to the long history of the "saint's zero-tolerance policy on discrimination": death is the great leveler that comes for everybody, and LSM is equally radically egalitarian.[132] For example, the Iglesia Católica Tradicional México–Estados Unidos (founded by Romo

Guillén)—known also as the Church of Saint Death—became one of the first churches to not only embrace and recognize same-sex marriages in Mexico but also openly officiate at same-sex wedding ceremonies, starting in 2004.[133]

However, the LSM movement goes beyond simple acceptance of LGBTQ members, instead welcoming them into a completely egalitarian community where individual identities fall away in shared contemplation of the inevitable death of all mortal beings: "Here your job or your sexual preference vanishes to offer you a new identity and a new belonging."[134] Similarly, Vargas Ortiz (who for a long time herself "performed marriages [and unions] between LGBTQ couples")[135] explained that the LGBTQ community is seen by the LSM community "as the brothers [and sisters], as the human beings that they are."[136] She added, "We do not care about their sexual orientation; this is why they feel so close to us."[137]

However, this full acceptance of the LGBTQ community has not always been the default within the LSM community; getting to this point has required effort. When Vargas Ortiz first began welcoming LGBTQ followers, she was met with animosity and attacks from many members of her own community. Over time, though, acceptance came from the community of believers—an acceptance that has yet to come from the Mexican government. Vargas Ortiz described how LSM veneration counters the government's resistance to recognizing same-sex marriages outside Mexico City: "We cannot give them the civil registry [rights provided by the government], but we can give them the spiritual rights" that come from union in the eyes of LSM.[138] In this case, the dignity and acceptance that LGBTQ followers experience though spiritual affiliation with LSM afford them a space of spiritual sovereignty, something they felt cannot be openly achieved within the traditional Catholic Church at this time.

One of the leaders of SMU, Valencia, explained to me the group's openness to the LGBTQ community in these terms: "Everyone is welcome here. . . . We are no one to judge others. . . . Here come all types of people . . . [and] everyone is treated equally. We all come here to adore her [LSM] . . . to pray, to honor her, to build her an altar. That's how it is—if you are gay it is not important."[139] Quijano elaborated: "Every person has the right to love, to be respected . . . [and] to search [for] and achieve the happiness with the person that they want. . . . The sexualities in the veneration of La Santa Muerte are physical" (meaning real, part of everyday life) "but they are not criticized" or policed.[140] He added:

The different desires, passions, and tastes in people are absolutely respected . . . and discrimination is put aside. Among us, there is no bullying because someone happens to be gay. . . . We understand that we are all equal, since death does not discriminate. . . . We are united by death. . . . Sexuality has no limits. It is forbidden to forbid. We don't force people to change. People are accepted for who they are. The body, the passions, and the desires are all universal . . . What is love? . . . Love is a feeling accompanied by death.[141]

This sentiment is shared by Arely Vázquez, now one of the main leaders of the LSM movement in the United States, who explained to me that La Flaquita's popularity among the LGBTQ community is deeply connected to her universality. Like death itself, she does not discriminate among people based on sexual orientation, preferences, or the performance of their desires. Vázquez pointed out in our interviews that people come to venerate LSM "because they notice our openness to everybody. Because there is nothing here that prevents you from being yourself."[142] She added, "Here, there are not restrictions. . . . Nobody will judge you, not as in other religions like the Catholic Church." She refers here to the bad reputation associated with LSM, who ministers to criminals and underworld people, the rejected in society—which also includes LGBTQ people. At the same time, Vázquez was very clear and protective in discussing the character of the LGBTQ community involved in the veneration of LSM: "It annoys me that the tabloids say that the veneration of Santa Muerte is full of gay people who are prostitutes. This is simply not true. . . . As in any other community, there are all sorts of people, not just sex workers."[143] This clarification is particularly important, as it corrects the stereotype that LSM venerators are all engaged in illicit or illegal activities—the stereotype that underpinned US law enforcement's attempts to introduce into evidence Medina-Copete's prayers to LSM to "prove" that she knew about the drugs in the car, as discussed in the first section of this chapter.

For Morales, LSM's appeal for LGBTQ individuals navigates both pragmatic and ontological terrains. At the practical level, the LSM community (like LSM herself) does not judge or discriminate against any followers of any stigmatized identity, including LGBTQ people: "La Santa Muerte does not discriminate against anyone. She does not care if you are a thief, a murderer, without this or that. . . . She wants your faith. Your faith and nothing else!"[144] Consequently, "no one in the community discriminates . . . judges

[or] ... criticizes" LGBTQ followers. Vargas Ortiz agreed: "When you don't receive a bad stare in a place, you come back. But if they treat you badly, then you do not return. That's exactly what happens here."[145] Valencia explained SMU's openness in similar terms: "We don't get involved with their [followers'] private conduct, in what they do in their private life . . . as long as they respect the veneration of La Santa Muerte . . . sexuality does not matter."[146] According to Morales of the Iglesia Arcangelista México–US (IAMU), his group's openness to the LGBTQ community (which is modeled on LSM's own) has long been manifested in its actual material practices: he explains that even "before it became legal" to celebrate same-sex unions in the United States, he and his church were "already marrying gay and lesbian couples" in both the United States and Mexico, and this practice continues as a strong component of the IAMU today.[147]

Moving beyond the practical level to the ontological level, we see further explanations of the LSM community's incredible and welcoming openness to LGBTQ followers. Morales argues that this openness comes from the very nature of LSM as a celestial being, which makes it impossible for her to discriminate against anyone on the basis of gender, sexual preference, or gender expression. As Morales argues, divine entities are removed from such petty mundane and material matters. He says, "But what is the sex of the angels and the archangels, anyway? They do not have biological sex."[148] The implication here is that LSM as a spiritual being, the Archangel of Death, does not really have a biological sex or gender (despite the feminine pronouns used to refer to LSM), nor a preference between genders or sexual orientations. In Morales's opinion, angels' absence of biological sex (since they have no biology) implies the irrelevance of this element in regard to people's own relationship to LSM. And as Vázquez notes, LSM's absence of gender at the spiritual level is manifested in the ambiguous aesthetics of images of LSM. As she explained, "The White Child [LSM] can wear earrings and long hair, or she can look more manly, or both. There is no judgment. She does favors for all, without exceptions."[149] This same visual flexibility is expressed in how the statues of LSM are presented, according to Vázquez, who notes that because LSM's followers have great flexibility in choosing outfits for their own images or statues, they can make LSM reflect their own gender flexibilities and unique aesthetic preferences. In other words, followers can project their own desires for gender ambiguity and plasticity onto LSM's celestial form and her material embodiments on altars and in shrines.

Vázquez articulated the beliefs of many LSM followers when she noted that LSM provides a more inclusive space than the Catholic Church. She argued, "The Catholic faith limits you a lot for being gay. La Santa Muerte doesn't have intolerance . . . she tolerates everything from you."[150] This in in stark contrast to the Catholic Church, which does not officially recognize or include organizations or movements that welcome or embrace openly LGBTQ members. The Catholic Church declares that "homosexual acts are intrinsically disordered" and "contrary to the natural law."[151] Consequently, it tolerates only those ministries that condemn same-sex orientation and that seek only to provide pastoral ministry for those "struggling" with a same-sex attraction. Those Catholic organizations and parishes trying to embrace the LGBTQ community stand in danger of excommunication for such activities and teachings.[152] For those who have been disenfranchised and excluded by the Catholic Church, denied the possibility of being full members in the largest and most influential institutionalized religion in the Western Hemisphere, LSM provides a space for valorization and inclusion, one that accepts LGBTQ followers on their own terms.

For many followers, LSM's "queer" devotional attitude undercuts traditional expectations and thus guides them toward their own encounter with death. Those constructed by society as deviants, torcidos (twisted), outsiders, and lost causes (such as the LGBTQ community) can connect to LSM, interpreting her as a figure of insubordination, rebelliousness, and defiance toward the structures of moral and socioeconomic power that govern Mexico and the United States. As discussed above, for some of these followers, LSM might be their only option for building a spiritual space that recognizes their existence and differences on their own terms. Luisa Fernanda Raquel Aguilar, a transsexual (her terminology) originally from the state of Michoacán, Mexico, explains, "I went to Mexico City to totally remake my life as a transsexual, like I wanted. All the girls from my scene, all the girls of the night, and all the transsexuals believed in [LSM]."[153] In Aguilar's case, the devotion to LSM came as a consequence of her path toward becoming the person she truly is and deciding whom she wants to be in community with. Her veneration of LSM grew out of her association with other trans women who have shared some of her life experiences, and from their current experiences as sex workers. This precarious life, defined by everyday social death (and sometimes literal death, for sex workers and trans people are overrepresented as victims of violent crime in both the United States and Mexico) pushes Aguilar and other transgender individuals to approach the saint of death itself, who can offer them some sense of control over the constant shadow looming over their everyday lives.[154] Aguilar explains, "Because a prostitute leaves her house and she doesn't know if she'll come back [alive] or not. They always recited their prayers and they would ask of her [Santa Muerte] to help them to make it back ok. That's why I venerate her, and I adore her."[155]

Aguilar's comments illustrate why LSM has become so popular among LGBTQ Latinx communities: because she reflects their subjugated reality—the slow violence of social death in the eyes of the state and other institutions like the Catholic Church. The LSM community shares with the LGBTQ community a common sense of stigma, of being constantly condemned, rejected, and judged as outsiders and undesirables. When I asked Romero Romero why LSM is so popular among the queer community, she told me,

> Well, because they have so many needs! Perhaps more needs than those that are not like them. They are in desperate need of being loved! That we love them . . . That we give them a fucking hug! That we grab them by the hand! "How are you, my friend? How are you doing? Are you doing well? Good, take care!" [They need that]—not that we attack them. . . . This is why they come to see the little mother [LSM], to tell her, "Mother, save me from bad people, from those people who do not want me. Look, Mom, I do not know why they do not want me. But help me to get accepted by people [such as the followers of LSM]." So they want to be accepted within that [LSM] community.[156]

As Romero Romero explains, members of the LGBTQ community are drawn to LSM precisely because they daily confront difficulties imposed by a homophobic society. For Romero Romero, this homophobia illustrates society's tendency to judge difference and the unknown—a tendency that LSM (and her followers) understand all too well, for she is misjudged by those who misunderstand and thus fear her.

This social prejudice denies the intrinsic diversity already present in the world. This diversity is present in the larger human family and, as Romero Romero notes, in any biological family; any family, large or small, can have a gay or lesbian member, and it is imperative to treat everyone with respect and dignity:

Nobody is exempt.... In our family we [might] have a lot of closeted cases. Yes, they are locked inside the closet! We judge people ... that are [queer]. But how beautiful, that they show who they are. That, like you all say, that they "come out of the closet." Let them be happy. Let them live with dignity. Unfortunately ... society doesn't let them. It attacks them. Let them live! ... Give them a hand. Take care of them. Love them. They are human beings! ... Me, personally, I love them a shitload....

[LGBTQ people] don't want to be mistreated. They want to have a good quality of life, a good life. We are all human beings. We are all alive and we all are going to die. Why not let us live in peace? Why are we discriminated against? Why do they attack us? The same applies to girls who are lesbians. Let them live. They are not harming anyone. You should let people live, to be happy. You know, many times people die and they are not happy. Why? Because we gossip about everyone around us.... But you know what, when we turn around, we [may] have a gay son. We [may] have a lesbian daughter.... We have everything [in our families].... Watch your home and care for your children! ... Don't waste your time looking after your neighbor's business![157]

Here, Romero Romero follows her beliefs to their ultimate conclusion: LSM represents the fact that at the end of people's lives, all differences are eliminated, and death will come for us all, no matter how we have lived our lives. It is this benevolent nonjudging approach, combined with the stigma and ostracization shared by the venerators of LSM (whether because of their identities or because her worship is itself stigmatized), that has made LSM particularly attractive to the LGBTQ community.

Conclusion

> We pray for our enemies, because theirs will be the kingdom of misery and despair. May La Santa Muerte make us invisible in the eyes of our enemies.
> —Enriqueta Vargas Ortiz

Despite the mainstream Catholic Church's explicit denunciation of LSM veneration as a bizarre and morally wrong spiritual phenomenon, this unorthodox religious movement is growing exponentially in both Mexico and the

United States. This growth stems in part from the unique characteristics that define the times during which LSM's popularity took off—decades in which death, vulnerability, and precarity have become increasingly normalized for more and more people. The movement's expansion has also been facilitated by its remarkable heterogeneity: with no central organizing structure, rules, or even forms of worship, a multiplicity of practices and beliefs has blossomed instead, tailored to each community of worshipers or even each individual's needs and desires.

Within this diversity, though, members do subscribe to a fundamental set of shared ideas about the identity and nature of LSM. For the most part, the movement has almost exclusively drawn on Judeo-Catholic and some Mesoamerican beliefs, without necessarily altering followers' spiritual self-definition as Catholic or their belief in the Catholic pantheon of saints, allowing them to continue their Catholic piety and practices in everyday life. Indeed, most followers who affiliate with LSM have already decided whether to remain in or formally leave the Catholic Church before they come to her. Many Santamuertistas have broken from their original faith because they feel abandoned by the hierarchy of the Catholic Church or other church.

LSM's communities function, then, as an extended system of support, one that works both spiritually and emotionally. For those who have immigrated to the United States, LSM communities allow followers to create a sense of pan-Latinidad and to remember their homelands; for LGBTQ individuals and other marginalized populations, LSM communities allow them to find acceptance while also meeting their spiritual needs. Precisely because of the stigma and resistance LSM followers face, her veneration has different boundaries between public and private than that of other vernacular saints, who have not been explicitly repudiated by the Church. Many spiritual ceremonies are performed during closed-door events in the privacy of people's houses, around their personal altars. People often worship privately, connecting at the personal level with their specific LSM images and narratives, and their personal altars serve as microcosms of that follower's life experiences, needs, and expectations. At the same time, the multiple different statues in more public shrines work as reminders of different events and communities, forming a complex network of memories—networks that are reinforced by services that take place online, using technology to connect worshipers in different locations.

Around LSM, in short, we are witnessing the emergence of a modern spiritual movement, one that is extraordinarily decentralized, transnational, often virtual, and simultaneously deeply personal and communal. As a spiritual movement of the new millennium, the worship of LSM is profoundly shaped by web-based technologies—not just for community organization, but also for the development of leaders and the distribution of prayers and rituals. Since the unveiling of the first public altar to LSM in 2001, new public styles and spiritual associations have emerged. These currently coexist with the previous groups and styles, although if and when the movement becomes more institutionalized and standardized, these different groups, beliefs, and practices will likely come into conflict. This chapter has sought to give a more personal face to LSM's followers and unveil the complex factors involved in the worship of LSM, which for the most part has been demonized and rejected. Understanding the characteristics and context of this spiritual movement as it emerges into the mainstream can help us understand how migrating communities navigate the complex experience of managing and transferring faith.

Conclusion

On Earth as It Is in Heaven

> I think it is one of the tragedies of our nation, one of the shameful tragedies, that . . . Sunday morning is one of the most segregated hours, if not the most segregated hours, in Christian America.
> —Martin Luther King Jr.[1]

> You're going into a segregated church; you must be worshiping a segregated God.
> —Rev. Ashton Jones[2]

Holy Demons of Segregation: Separate and Unequal

Saint Mary's Basilica, the center of worship for the Catholic Diocese of Phoenix, was completed in 1914, just two years after Arizona achieved statehood and became part of the United States. In many ways, the church is a tangible symbol of this political transition, and of the deep demographic transformations and ongoing racial tensions that define the Catholic religious terrains of the American Southwest. The land on which Saint Mary's Basilica stands was donated by the local Latino community, which was actively involved not only in collecting funds but also in actually constructing the church. In the following years, Saint Mary's—the only parish in the city at the time—became an epicenter of racial tensions and a site in and through which the connections between religion, race, and migration in the United States were negotiated.

Following the 1848 signing of the Treaty of Guadalupe Hidalgo, which ended the Mexican-American War, Arizona, like the rest of the conquered territories, experienced a profound shift in demography and power as the Mexican ruling class gave way to new Anglo settlers. In the decades following the treaty, processes of mobilization and forced displacement gradually transformed Phoenix—first established as a settlement in 1867—into a predominantly Anglo city. By 1889, Phoenix had become the territorial capital of what would eventually be the state of Arizona. This transformation was accompanied by the displacement of Latina/os living in the city of Phoenix (many of whom moved to Tucson, which emerged as a Mexican and Mexican American enclave); their numbers declined sharply "from 52 percent [of the city's population] in 1870 to 14 percent in 1890."[3]

The Catholic Church responded to these demographic and power shifts in Arizona. In 1896, the Franciscan Order of Friars Minor was assigned to operate Saint Mary's Basilica, which at the time was a simple adobe structure described by the friars as resembling "a barn rather than a place of worship."[4] In 1902 the friars began the two-phase construction of the new church, with the majority of funds for the project raised from and by Latina/o parishioners. The project included demolition of the old structure and promised to deliver "one of early Phoenix's most outstanding buildings."[5] In 1914, a "handsome upper church was erected and decorated with fine altars, statuary and exquisite stained glass." In 1915, within months after the completion of Saint Mary's, Father Novatus Benzing, its pastor, made a highly controversial announcement: Spanish-speaking parishioners would continue to have their services in the basement, and the new upper church would be reserved for English-speaking parishioners.[6] Deeply offended, many Latina/os left Saint Mary's. According to Barrios, at that time, "about half the population was Mexican [or] Mexican Americans and almost all of them were Catholic."[7] They formed the Mexican Catholic Society and took their concerns to Bishop Henry Granjon in Tucson.[8] The local ecclesiastic authorities argued that the best solution to the "Latino problem" in Phoenix was the creation of a second, separate parish specifically for that community. To that end, Granjon donated $500 to construct a separate church. The Latina/o congregation, now segregated from the Saint Mary's flock, was assigned to Father Antimo G. Nebreda, a Claretian priest. In 1922, Bishop Granjon replaced Saint Mary's pastor, Benzing, with Father Ferdinand Ortiz, a Mexican American, and the first ordained Catholic priest born in Arizona.[9] His appointment was not welcomed by the English-speaking parishioners.

By 1924 the Catholic Latino community in Phoenix was able to purchase a piece of land for their own church. Meanwhile, the parishioners of Saint Mary's continued to refuse to accept Ortiz as their pastor—a fight that had been going on since his appointment two years earlier.[10] The same year, in

1924, Bishop Daniel James Gercke replaced Granjon as the new regional bishop, and Gercke finally acceded to the parishioners' demands, bringing Benzing back and ousting Ortiz. This cemented the huge racial distance that separated the two churches, physically only half a mile apart. In 1928, after much "intense fund-raising" by Nebreda, there was finally enough money to build the structure.[11] It was named Inmaculado Corazón de María (Immaculate Heart of Mary) and was constructed less than half a mile from Saint Mary's, the previous church. The new church was dedicated in the same year, and in attendance were the new regional authority, Bishop Gercke, and two Mexican bishops: Bishop Juan María Navarrete y Guerrero of Sonora and Bishop Agustín Aguirre y Ramos of Sinaloa. The presence of both American and Mexican Church authorities emphasized both the deeply Latino character and mission of the new parish and its transnational nature. Over time, the new church, Inmaculado Corazón de María, became the spiritual and activist center of the Latino Catholic community in Phoenix.

Such rifts between churches were far from isolated, reflecting as they did the deep racial divides that defined the early twentieth-century religious experience of Latinxs in the Southwest and that continue to haunt contemporary Latina/o/x Catholic communities in the region.[12] As racial demographics continue to change, the anti-Latino/a racism within the church is having consequences for mostly-white churches. Now, Latino/as make up 40 percent of American Catholics, an increase from 25 percent in the 1980s, and Latino/a churches have booming attendance and engagement.[13] White churches who have resisted the growth in Latino/a membership have begun to wither. For example, today, Saint Mary's only holds two masses on Sundays; the congregation of Inmaculado Corazón is so large that it must hold six—only one of which is conducted in English, reflecting the ongoing demographic changes in Phoenix. Inmaculado Corazón has become one of the most active and important churches for the Latina/o Catholic community in Phoenix. Yet the tacit Church hierarchy established at the beginning of Arizona's statehood remains very much in place today. Bishop Thomas J. Olmsted serves as the head of the Diocese of Phoenix, while Bishop Eduardo Alanis Nevares, a Mexican American from Texas and the son of Mexican immigrants—who in 2010 became the first and only Latino bishop in the Diocese of Phoenix—functions only as an auxiliary bishop, despite the city's very large Hispanic/Latinx population: as of 2018, Hispanic/Latinxs represented around 42.6 percent of the population of Phoenix, and 58 percent of them identify as Catholic.[14]

Feeding on Vulnerability: Race, Power, and Sexual Abuse

Of course, the battleground created at the intersection of religion and race expands beyond spaces of worship to define many aspects of the lives of Latinxs in Phoenix, just as it does within the US Catholic Church more broadly. Despite official statements offered by the local Church hierarchy, and despite the efforts of many local priests and lay and religious organizations alike, Latinxs continue to perceive themselves as being segregated, pushed outside the larger structures and processes of decision-making within the Catholic Church in the United States. They express a shared sense that there are two separate Catholic Churches in the United States, constituted along racial, class, migration, and cultural divides. There are multiple reasons for this: for example, the Church reduces questions about diversity in faith and culture to oversimplified discussions about language, focusing on liturgical translation. But there is much more than just language at stake for Latinxs and their involvement with the Catholic Church in the United States (and indeed in the nation's Evangelical Christian churches as well): US churches need to reckon in a real, material way with what it would mean to have real cultural diversity and integration within church congregations and their larger systems of power.

Explicit and implicit factors within the US Catholic Church have consistently perpetuated the mistreatment of Latinx Catholics in ways that have made many of them feel unwelcome and less valuable than their mainstream Catholic counterparts. The Church's lack of care for its Latinx congregants is exemplified by how it has handled priest sexual abuse cases. A 2003 *Arizona Republic* report about sexual abuse in the Diocese of Phoenix uncovered a pattern showing not only that Catholic Church leaders were "reassigning priests rather than disciplining them"—a now well-known policy—but also that "some of the worst repeat offenders were transferred into predominantly Hispanic parishes."[15] Overall, the priests identified during the state investigation into sexual misconduct "worked in 10 of the 12 parishes with the highest numbers of Hispanic faithful"—83 percent of the Latinx-designated parishes in Phoenix.[16] And as the nation has learned, in so many cases, these predatory priests "went on to abuse other children" in their new Latinx parishes.[17]

The actual number of victims and the extent of the abuse of Latinx parishioners may never be known, especially given the intersections of poverty, language access, cultural values, legal status, secrecy, fear, and the stigma of sexual abuse. Race, gender, class, and social capital are strongly connected to whether or not victims report abuse. Add to this the fact that most Latinx immigrants come to the United States from Latin America, where Catholic priests are often particularly powerful figures in their hometowns, and it is not hard to understand that there are extra barriers that prevent the Latinx community from reporting sexual abuse cases to ecclesiastical and civil authorities.

This set of pressures that discourage people from reporting abuse is intensified by the fact that many immigrants already fear and mistrust both law enforcement and the judicial system—sometimes because they do not have legal status, but often because many of them fled their home countries because of police brutality, abuse, and totalitarian systems. During the period covered by the *Arizona Republic* report, Joe Arpaio, the notorious and controversial sheriff of Maricopa County (which includes Phoenix), ruled the county with an iron fist and intimidation tactics. Arpaio has been accused of abuse of power, unlawful enforcement of immigration laws, and racial profiling of Latinxs, as well as failure to investigate sex crimes, particularly in cases where "many of the victims ... were children of illegal [undocumented] immigrants."[18] In addition, the overall climate in Arizona in the first decade of the century was deeply anti-immigrant; in 2010 the controversial SB1070 legislation, at that time the strictest anti-immigrant legislation in the United States, was signed into law by then Arizona governor Jan Brewer.

This example illustrates what I have sought to demonstrate throughout this book: ecclesiastical and secular powers are often tightly connected. In Arizona, the intersecting policies of church and state have created conditions of extreme vulnerability for Latinxs in Phoenix. The intersections of the secular and the spiritual have important implications for scholarship in religious studies. Because these two sets of powers work together to create these conditions, they must be analyzed together for us to understand their real workings in the lives of devotees.

The Border as Stigmata: Litanies for a Crumbling World

Gloria Anzaldúa defines the US-Mexico border as "*una herida abierta* [an open wound] where the Third World grates against the first and bleeds. And before a scab forms, it hemorrhages again."[19] In this sense, the border can be read as modern stigmata: a constellation of constantly bleeding wounds that materialize the legacies of colonial violence and greed. The border is the site of an ongoing social, epistemic, and religious crucifixion. This is not only the ongoing metaphysical crucifixion of Jesus Christ, which is enacted again and again as he lifts the burden of sin from his followers and protects them from the travails of the world as they cross the border, but also a metaphorical crucifixion of the migrants themselves as they seek various kinds of salvation in their crossing. The vernacular saints explored here can be understood as the external manifestations of the wounds borne by the social body of these communities, continuously produced by the border's mobile lacerations.

As described in this book, the saints created and venerated by these migrant communities fulfill many functions, both spiritual and material, for their venerators, who are subjects in constant economic and social distress. Each of the saints explored here occupies a space where religiosity, culture, and politics merge. Far from static relics, these saints are living objects, constantly adapting and transforming in an ever-changing world.

In this conclusion, I identify fourteen elements that can systematize and distill the complexity of these vernacular venerations in the context of migration. I am not attempting to establish the criteria or properties of sainthood or holiness; rather, here I highlight characteristics and aesthetics of saintly devotions, especially within the realm of the vernacular and the migratory experience of settling in El Norte. Many of these observations are also true of officially recognized saints; to some degree, canonized saints and their veneration exist also within social constructs of piety, holiness, and the marketplace of the believers' needs. But these elements are most visible within the veneration of popular saints, who more closely correspond to and address their worshipers' most immediate needs and circumstances.

Vernacular Saints Are Loud

They are a depository of localized knowledge and therefore come to exist within specific cultural, historical, and political contexts.

This essential element not only unifies the vernacular saints studied here with official saints and forms of popular piety but also frames vernacular religiosity within larger discourses about community agency and resiliency. Because they are inscribed within specific times and cultural contexts, saints "speak" loudly about how communities relate to their past, deal with the present, and actively hope toward their future.

Saints—all saints, both vernacular and official—are neither innocent nor naive; they are sophisticated cultural and historic products. The people who create and sustain these saints are also not naïve but are instead responding appropriately to their circumstances with their spiritual practices and expressions. The narratives about saints' lives, miracles, and adventures are written and passed on within a social context. They are inscribed with a unique language used by particular communities to describe its realities. They tell the human history of a community or region and often narrate how people adapt to change. They are part of a network of epistemic practices used by vulnerable and marginalized communities to deal with the contradictions and complications of the real world. In Latin America, as in many other places, a collective communal history is inscribed within the stories of miracles and adventures that people tell about their saints and pass on through generations.

In many ways, saints are what Rossana Reguillo defines as "critical social knowledge . . . transmissible through an oral register that attains its force precisely because [they are] deploy[ed]. . . . in the form of myths."[20] This social knowledge travels undetected in part because, as "subjugated knowledges," the stories have historically been dismissed as inadequate and naive.[21] But as cultural entities, vernacular border saints hold specific cultural information for the everyday survival of their believers, and they belong to a larger network of border productions beyond the spiritual.[22] The narratives about Jesús Malverde, for example, depict the changes wrought by modernity in Sinaloa, but also the anxieties over land expropriation and the transnational exploitation of farmers. The intertwined stories of Olga Camacho and Juan Soldado speak to sexual violence along the border. The myths around Saint Toribio Romo manifest the dramas of migration and settlement in the United States, as well as the tensions surrounding racial diversity within traditional religious institutions. Vernacular saints are not silent entities. They speak loudly from their altares.

Vernacular Saints Emerge at Historical Moments of Rupture or Crisis

They always respond to specific acts of social violence or "sinful" change.

Vernacular saints, by their nature, always manifest a community response to particular acts of violence or change (e.g., the evil effects of industrialization, increasingly stringent immigration policies, changes in the roles of women, sexual abuse) inflicted on the social body. Certainly, on a basic level, saints are used to exemplify heroic virtues and inspire works of charity and compassion, but they do something more: they are social reminders of violence that has been experienced collectively.

The "heroic" nature of a vernacular saint emerges precisely in the absence of others' love and care. That saint exists, culturally, as evidence of a social wound that has not been healed and resolved. The wound might result from lack of religious freedom, as in the cases of martyrs; more often, however, a saint's wounds reflect conditions of poverty, disempowerment, patriarchy, sexual violence, racism, greed, the anxieties of gender performance, the imposition of gender norms, and so on. Saints witness to and reflect the messiness of social interactions. They remind us of the effects of human violence and of the possibility of acting differently.

Saintly devotions adapt constantly to the conditions of their time and place. The history of the US-Mexico border region can be traced through the sequence of spiritual and uncanny beings who have inhabited these lands. Because each saint speaks to a specific historical context, saintly devotions map the sociopolitical changes of a region as they have affected particular communities. Saints tell us about people's fears and anxieties, and about the huge sociopolitical transformations with which people must reckon. They tell us not only how oppression is experienced but also how it is recorded in the social body. This is very clear with Saint Toribio Romo, who is a saint of migrants precisely because migration is at the center of today's drama, especially for Latinxs. The same applies to La Santa Muerte; a figure of death comes to be seen as a saint during a period in which social death has become normalized.

The Stories Told About Saints' Adventures and Their Miracles Are Real

People tell what is real for them.

People do not lie when recounting stories of saints' adventures or the favors they have granted. Their accounts may not be strictly accurate or empirically verifiable, but as Jacques Lacan has explained, the real is not synonymous with reality. Furthermore, as Alessandro Portelli says of all oral traditions, the "errors" in accounts tell us about the anxieties, desires, and fears of the narrators and their communities. People tell saints' stories that matter and are meaningful for them, stories that explain their world. At the same time, echoing Mircea Eliade, one can say that narratives about these saints (or their miracles) are a type of "true history" because, beyond the accuracy of the events, they "always deal with [the] realities" created by greed, exploitation, racism, sexism, homophobia.[23] Border tales, myths, and legends about the saints do not contradict historical beliefs but run parallel to them as part of a complex cosmology and spirituality where many realities coexist. These fantastic tales are more than real. They are hyper-real.[24] Border tales allow the narrator to transform themselves from a "social actor into an 'author'" by recentering the periphery, shaping stories around their own experiences of precarity.[25] The stories people tell about the adventures of Jesús Malverde, for example, may not be historically accurate, but they provide the means for a community to grapple with the disruptions of neoliberalism and late capitalism. The history such stories record reimagines the past in order to deal with a very real present.

Saints Were Dead Once, and They Can Die Again

They survive through the stories and narratives about them.

Saints need people. They live on in the miracles, memorabilia, spiritual practices, rituals, prayers, amulets, spells, and spaces created to remember and venerate them. Certainly, vernacular saints tell us about the struggles experienced by their communities. However, to understand these saints and spiritual entities, one must analyze the cultural products created around (and for) them, such as corridos, tattoos, murals, mandas, chapels, poems, cartoons, TV shows, jokes, and so on. The emotions attached to such artifacts and practices as they get embedded in people's social networks (as gifts, inheritances, offerings, mandas) reflect the complexity of these entities as they shift, and they gain or change meaning over time in people's lives.

If a saint (or the idea of a saint) cannot fulfill promises, accomplish spiritual favors and miracles, and meet the social expectations of devotees, that saint will be replaced, go out of fashion, or simply fade from social memory. Like the artifacts that surround them, saints themselves are consumable goods that compete and are traded within the vast marketplace of religious and spiritual figures and miracle makers available for worship. The devotion of saints, therefore, is a highly fragile cultural product. La Santa Muerte, for example, is growing in popularity even now because she is framed as La Cumplidora (or sometimes as La Poderosa, which similarly conveys her efficacy in granting favors in miracles)—the most powerful and most reliable of the many saints available to her followers. Her current popularity is directly related to her reputation for fulfilling supplicants' needs quickly. The more she performs miracles, in the eyes of her followers, the more she lives on and expands in popularity. In the marketplace of saints, popularity means survival.

Saints Have Social Bodies

Their shapes, qualities and human representations are social marketing constructs.

The shapes taken by these vernacular saints—their aesthetics, the objects surrounding them, and their ways of operating in the world—are not random. Because saints are essentially a concept, an ideal, a need turned into social flesh, their bodies are social products that expand beyond any real historical individual. Their bodies belong no longer to themselves, but rather to the communities that believe in them.

Juan Soldado, for example, is venerated as a saint for immigrants in the territory around the US-Mexico border, which sees a constant flow of cheap, transnational labor flowing from the South to the North. To serve the needs of border crossers, Juan Soldado has been transformed: the image of the historical Juan Castillo Morales as an adult capable of raping and murdering a child has been deleted from people's consciousness and memory, replaced by the image of Juan Soldado as a young, exploited soldier who manifests innocence. Similarly, La Santa Muerte's omnipresent powers are represented by the globe she holds, but also by the absence of flesh—an absence that turns her into everyone all at once. Reimagining Jesús Malverde as the actor and singer Pedro Infante is deeply tied to the construction of Mexicanness and masculinity in post-Revolution Mexico. The study of saints implies the study of their imaginary bodies as they are created, maintained, and transformed by their worshippers.

Saints Can Have Contradictory Meanings

As social beings, saints can serve as sources of both liberation and oppression (including violence), even at the same time.

Contradictory meanings can exist simultaneously in the same social body, as different communities attach different meanings and values to a saint. Geography, class, gender, race, sexuality, age, citizenship status, entitlement, and so on—all shape the many meanings attributed to a saint. A saint's original meaning is always altruistic, in support of the social good. Over time, however, that meaning can decay, become corrupted, or get lost within the marketplace of spiritual entities fighting for their own survival. In this sense, vernacular saints can enact social fantasies of liberation and emancipation that are based on the demand for justice—but they can just as easily be yoked to fantasies of revenge.

The wider the differences in power and position among a saint's followers, the more contradictory the meanings that can be attached to that saint. Juan Soldado is seen by some as a source of community resilience against state military power, but for others he represents patriarchal oppression and violence against women. Similarly, Jesús Malverde serves as a local saint for peasants and farmers grappling with the effects of modernity in Sinaloa, while also gaining infamy as the saint of narco-trafficking activities. Because the process of attributing meaning to saints is socially and individually constructed, multiple versions of a saint can exist simultaneously.

Saints Live in Their Own Territories

Because of their epistemic bodies, saints cannot be controlled, contained, or owned.

Despite the assertions by Church and political authorities, saints cannot be owned, for they belong to multiple constituencies. No one can claim exclusive authority over a saint's meaning or the spiritual favors attributed to the saint, as he or she grants miracles freely to followers. Furthermore, saints come in many different forms that are not always easy to identify or quantify. In other words, because of their shifting and unstable nature, saints cannot be contained by institutional or national domains. Saintly devotions move and exist within their own spiritual sovereignties, beyond the constraints of state and ecclesiastical limits. Saints do miracles as they please; they are free agents.

Thus vernacular saints (and the devotions around them) present complications for religious and secular entities (such as formal Church hierarchies or nation-states) that rely on the premise of homogeneity and epistemic uniformity. Saints move between and across borders, and their spiritual domains are continually remapped as they travel with their devotees to new territories, often slipping under the radar and evading authorities. They migrate, adapt, and reconstitute themselves all the time, as part of their process of survival. Because saints' meanings can shift and can become sources of resistance and non-normative ideology, states and religious entities constantly try to control, conform, or contain saintly devotions. But they consistently fail. Despite the efforts of the Mexican government and the Catholic Church to prevent the spread of the devotion of La Santa Muerte, for example, her popularity has expanded into the United States and continues to grow. Not even those who lead her devotion can claim ownership over her. Saintly devotions—like the forms they take and the places they go—are capricious and in many ways unpredictable.

Saints Are Everywhere, but They Prefer Vulnerable and Distressed Areas

Saints emerge in spaces of distress.

Saints are both everywhere and nowhere, but they can usually be found in spaces where violence has been inflicted and normalized. The stories surrounding saints hold together a world that appears to be falling apart. This is true of the border saints discussed in this book: in a sense, the border is a war zone, and its inhabitants are under siege. They are constantly exposed to violence and the effects of extreme and long-lasting vulnerability. Thus the spiritual and the uncanny are marshaled to make sense of the extreme reality of oppression. Life on the border is fragile and is constantly under attack.

Following Achille Mbembe's concepts of the contemporary construction of extreme forms of subjugation, we can argue that the border is a "topography of cruelty," where subjects are put into a "third zone between subjecthood and objecthood," positioned as racialized bodies for labor—as counterparts to inhabitants of maquiladora or plantation zones.[26] It is no coincidence, for example, that La Santa Muerte was first unveiled publicly in Tepito, Mexico, one of the most distressed areas in Mexico City. As many of her followers explained in interviews, she appeared there because it was the place where she was most needed.

Saints Are Deeply Political

They exist between human and divine spaces.

Saints are foremost intercessors, political negotiators, between two worlds—one that exists and one that is possible. They intercede for favors and miracles in order to fix a world that has been corrupted by human greed and exploitation. Saints are, in essence, politicians, continually negotiating the messy governance of everyday life. They bring back the hope that things could be better—that health could be restored, that a job could be granted, the justice could be achieved, and so on. Saints exist to fix this world and, when that is not possible, to allow us to imagine an alternative. For capitalism, saints are consumable goods that respond to the market's need for everyday solutions to large structural problems.

Saints Can Be State-Building Agents

Saints' devotions are not excluded from the workings of nationalism and ethnocentric ideologies, but the migration of saintly devotions also manifests the vulnerability of state sovereignty.

Although neither states nor religious institutions can completely control the devotional practices, ethos, or beliefs around a vernacular saint, this does not mean that saintly devotions cannot become allies of state authority and control. Saints can become state-building agents—for example, by creating spiritual intrastates or translocating state territories outside their border domains, through the migration of cultural, religious, and political practices. When this happens, a piece of one state can live and thrive within another state. In this way, the spiritual practices around saints and other religious entities—such as those associated with particular devotions to the Virgin Mary (e.g., Virgin of Guadalupe, Our Lady of El Cobre, etc.)—can work as spaces for cultural, political, and state revival. They exist outside their nations of origin.

For expatriates and migrants, religious performance can also work as a tool to recreate elements of their nations of origin within the new spaces to which they have migrated. For migrants, saintly devotions are spaces where cultural nationalism can be performed in defiance of xenophobic policies, under the protective shield of religious observance. This state performativity through religiosity is an integral part of the migration process, often enacted through the aesthetics of events, performances, food, music, language, parades, clothing, and so on. Saints' social bodies exist within their publicly visible domains, where they serve as gatekeepers of culture and national identity.

Saints Perform the Politics of Sexuality, Race, and Gender

> As social entities, saints manifest society's unresolved racial, sexual, and gender power disparities.

Saintly devotions can never exist outside the terrains of gender, sexuality, and race, for at their center are the racialized, gendered, and sexualized bodies of the devotees, who shape the saints' images to reflect their own beliefs, anxieties, and desires. The social bodies of saints, official and vernacular, have been used, in many occasions, to impose racial, class, or gender stereotypes in society—and to remind people of the consequences of not following social norms. Many saints' narratives not only reflect but also reinforce the social hierarchies of communities. In this way, saints manifest the contradictions and limitations created by gender and racial stereotypes: society wants to believe that they represent altruistic values, but they are trapped within the same matrix of social forces that created racial and gender violence. This is evident in the hypermasculinity assigned to Jesús Malverde as a narco-saint, and in followers' efforts to maintain Saint Toribio Romo's whiteness.

At the same time, saintly devotions can also provide spaces wherein different sexualities and performances of gender can coexist and flourish. Many female saints, for example, as in the case of Santa Olguita, were strong women who are depicted as challenging the gendered hierarchies of power and sexual abuse; others, like La Santa Muerte, work to protect non-normative sexual and gender identities.

Saints Can Be Deeply Catholic, Even When Officially Disavowed by the Catholic Church

Saintly devotions manifest the diverse and complicated terrains of religious affiliation, not religious doctrine.

Saints are, by definition, Catholic. But this does not always mean that they are part of the official Catholic Church. They can and do often live beyond spaces recognized by the formal institution. Even official Catholic saints are not completely under the Church's control; when devotions to an official saint get out of line, the Catholic Church can intervene and try to correct course, but this is not always successful. Vernacular saints—even those deeply rooted in traditional Catholic hierarchies and belief systems—are even farther outside the Church's official control. And some popular saints, such as La Santa Muerte, are completely independent of Church control, having been deemed non-Catholic (or even anti-Catholic—unreconcilable with Catholicism) from their beginning.

Regardless of their official status, however, popular saintly devotions can still be profoundly Catholic in terms of aesthetics and frames of reference. Saints' devotions reflect the vast diversity of people's own relationships and layers of affiliation with the Catholic Church. As such, the unofficial, potentially even disavowed forms of worship around vernacular saints expand the definition of what it really means to be a member of the Catholic Church—or, indeed, a member of any religious institution. Devotees may identify themselves as Catholics, cultural Catholics, exiles, or other types of dissidents. They can occupy multiple and contradictory positions in relation to religious communities: they can locate themselves within or outside these communities, or they can have a foot in each camp, inhabiting the border zone between them.

Studying Vernacular Saints Requires a Unique Methodology

Given the often unstable, ambiguous nature of vernacular saints as religious-cultural objects, apprehending and analyzing them requires special research tools (and an incisive eye).

Precisely because saints are produced and sustained by very particular forms of knowledge, their study requires a flexible, adaptable, multidisciplinary methodology capable of revealing what traditionally has been invisible, segregated, and forced into clandestine expressions. This is why it is imperative to develop what Emma Pérez defines as a "decolonial queer gaze"—a critical investigative eye that can read between the lines and apply a non-white, non-colonial, non-heteronormative lens. A decolonial queer gaze permits scholars to critically interrogate medical texts, newspapers, court records, wills, novels, and corridos, attending to the structures of power in which such records are produced and legitimized.[27]

This decolonial and cross-disciplinary approach is particularly crucial because official archives about oppressed communities are so limited. In this sense, saints, who as repositories of community history and conditions are themselves social archives, are a methodology in and of themselves. As objects of analysis, saints themselves constitute a method that can be used to study the human experience. They embody a set of questions, problems, and solutions as they embody and enact social agency in context.

Saints Are a Call for Action

Saints are not passive bystanders.

Saints can be understood as social plans of action. They are, as Reguillo proposes, a "bridge of intersection between representation and action."[28] They allow us to understand that supernatural forces may be required to destroy or contain an almost indestructible, always changing, and omnipresent system of harm. The brutality and extent of the violence enacted on border communities are so out of proportion that devotees feel the harms can only be rectified by otherworldly beings—by miracles. Because saintly devotions exist to palliate the effects of social violence, they can thus serve as road maps that identify the spaces of vulnerability; the saints embody these social, political, and economic wounds that need to be healed.

The Drama That Keeps Unfolding: Pastoral Implications

> Sometimes, a devotion arises simply because it touches hearts and minds at a time of particular need.
> —Woodeene Koenig-Bricker, "Our Lady: Undoer of Knots"

One of the threads running through this book is its recognition of the ontological and pragmatic distinction between official and unofficial Catholicism. As I have shown, we cannot talk about Catholicism as if it were stable and universal; we must talk instead about a multiplicity of Catholic affiliations and a plurality of typologies of Catholicism. In other words, for many people, their sense of belonging to their Catholic faith exists beyond the institution's formal terrains of acknowledgment, in such ways that the venerations of vernacular or folk saints, including those opposed by the institution, can coexist with sanctioned venerations without posing a conflict for believers. The real conflict seems mostly to take place at the hierarchical level within the formal church institution, as it tries to define and control believers' spiritual landscapes. As shown throughout this book, people's affiliation and engagement levels are driven by many different factors beyond faith alone. Some may be exclusively or intersectively cultural or emotive, driven by necessity, familiarity, or social pressure.

Although this book was never intended as an appeal to the Catholic Church, I hope that its description of the multidimensional impact of migration in faith practices and of the indisputable diversity of Catholic affiliations at play between migrant and local communities calls for a more caring and flexible pastoral approach toward those who want to continue being part of the Church as an institution. Religion and faith overlap and are intertwined.

Similarly, I hope this book will show the Catholic Church the importance of other types of openness to and flexibility with all members of their flock. Integrating and accepting migrants as members of religious groups requires the Church and its members to confront the existing fears of cultural differences, expectations around religious assimilation, socioeconomic class differences, and normalization of privilege and power. This book reminds us that immigrants should be encountered where they are, spiritually and culturally, always with love and care, and never with judgment or the assumption of forced assimilation.

Religious experiences are always anchored within cultural and historical contexts. For many immigrants, their faith is no abstraction. It is tangible, grounded in the grassroots realities of their everyday experiences of survival, resistance, oppression, forced displacement, sexism, racism, lack of assistance, and invisibility. But faith goes even beyond these experiences. As I see it, faith is defined foremost by hope: the desire to have a better life and the fulfillment of the promise of a more just society "on earth as it is in heaven." In this sense, we are all migrants, refugees, and exiles, as we all long for a new society that is not here yet: one that recognizes difference as a value and as a treasure. It is the responsibility of Church leaders—the managerial class—to evaluate their pastoral practices and assess their commitment to embracing all humanity with all its complexities and ambiguities. As the Gospels have it, just before he died Jesus experienced the absurdity of feeling abandoned by God his Father—an experience that allowed him to encounter and love humanity. This love and care (which, as Christ showed us, demands sacrifice) is also the mandate of his Church. Why, then, does the Church not follow his example, by losing God (as in the doctrine, the tradition, the norm) to encounter and love God in the struggles of humanity (as in those who have been abandoned, rejected, disqualified)?

For many of the devotees discussed in this book, it does not matter whether the official Catholic Church recognizes or validates their practices of veneration. They have found a place for their convictions and devotions within the liminal spaces that exist and move between the official and the unofficial, the sacred and the profane. Indeed, those categories feel almost obsolete, insufficient to accommodate the vast array of religious experiences, particularly those of people located in the margins. As this book has shown, religious affiliations in liminal zones—the border itself, the line between official and unofficial, legal and illegal—are shifting and always-unsettled terrains defined by the politics of religion and migration. Perhaps the most important thing we can see in these border saints (and the religious and physical migrations that they respond to) is the eternal human desire to believe in love, despite the barriers and dangers we encounter in life; faith and hope tell us there is always the possibility of a better future on the other side.

Notes

Introduction

1. Although over time this research became a Catholic studies project, I did not intend it to be so—even though the objects of study are vernacular folk saints, and even though most of the people interviewed or involved (as well as me) have some type of affiliation or contact with the Catholic Church. If anything, I tried to use my position and personal history only as research tools available to me, in terms of knowledge and familiarity. Following Robert Orsi's lead, "I wanted to make a contribution to the project of understanding what *Catholicm* is" (Orsi 1985, xxi) and how Catholic cartographies expand, shift, and migrate.
2. From now on, I will use the term "Church" to refer to the Catholic Church.
3. Araújo 1996. Araújo, Vera. Dottrina sociale della chiesa, Class notes Mariapolis Renata Loppiano, Campogiallo, Incisa Valdarno FI, Italy, Fall 1996.
4. Flores and González 2019. I use the term "Latina/o/x" here to recognize gender diversity; however, other terms, such as "Latin@" and "Latinx," have been proposed as gender-neutral options that can be used to avoid the gender-binary bias implied by the terms "Latina" (female) and "Latino" (male). "Latinx" aims to open possibilities for other gender and sexual expressions. The plural form is "Latinxs." This term will be used in cases where the differentiations and emphasis of gender or sexual diversity are needed for an understanding of the material. However, since this book project expands over a hundred years, as a conscious move I try to also use the terms "Latino," "Latina/o," and "Latinx" as temporal markers of social change, and as identifiers of gender disparity and oppression over time. I recognize that the use of the term "Latinx" may simplify people's identities or assume layers of awareness that are not yet collective. In other words, I use these terms to recognize both the transformation experienced by society over time and the continuing prevalence of oppression, for each term in the progression illustrates the evolution of social consciousness, acceptance, and visibility of diversity. For more on this, see Love and Blay 2017.
5. As exemplified by the United Farm Workers' (UFW) peregrinations, long fasts, and use of imagery of the Virgin of Guadalupe in protests and actions organized by Cesar Chavez in the late 1960s. See García 2010.
6. Calvillo 2020, 4.
7. Pedraza 2007, 260.
8. Title translations are my own.
9. Hagan 2008, 5.
10. Fadeke 2017, 18.
11. Diocesís de San Juan 2007, 7.

12. Vásquez and Friedmann 2003, 5.
13. Calvillo 2020, 32.
14. Masci and Smith 2018; Kanter 2020, 6.
15. Crary 2020.
16. Crary 2020.
17. Ospino, quoted in Acosta 2017.
18. Do and Gaunt 2019, 8.
19. Martinez 2018, 6; Diaz 2017; Cooperman et al. 2014.
20. "Changing Faiths: Latinos"
21. Castañeda-Liles 2018, 4–5.
22. Castañeda-Liles 2018, 168, 215.
23. Hagan 2008, 5.
24. In this case, "Caudillo" refers to a male leader who serves also as a spiritual patron, an expression of and referential model of patriarchal hierarchy and superiority.
25. Since 1990 several American newspapers have reported on multiple cases of undocumented immigrants who survived Arizona's Sonoran Desert after receiving help from Saint Toribio Romo. Mexican newspapers also reported similar accounts. Some of them are

    Thompson 2002; Borden 2002, 2003; Williams 2005; Spagat 2005; Corchado 2006; "Oracion" 2006, 8; Avila 2008, 29; "Martyred Priest" 2008, A16; "Santo Toribio Romo" 2008, 7; "Migrantes reportan" 2012.
26. This conflict was a reaction to the secular and anticlerical policies implemented by the Mexican government against the Catholic Church. Toribio was beatified by John Paul II in 1992 and canonized in 2000.
27. The 1994 Tequila Crisis, also known as the Mexican Peso Crisis, was a currency devaluation crisis experienced by Mexico that propelled a series of economic downturns in Latin America, especially in the Southern Cone (Argentine, Chile, Uruguay, Paraguay, and Brazil).
28. Vargas, Mirabal, and La Fountain-Stokes 2017, 192.
29. Graziano 2016, xii.
30. Anzaldúa 1999, 102, 91.
31. Saldívar 2006, 59; Foucault 1997, 7; Mignolo 2000, 13.
32. Anzaldúa 1999, 19, 195.
33. Madrid 2008.
34. De Certeau 1988.
35. Hernández 2002, 11.
36. Barthes 2001, 109.
37. Masferrer 2013, 25.
38. Masferrer 2013, 24, 25.
39. Vásquez and Marquardt 2003, 7.
40. Masferrer 2013, 27.
41. Orsi 1985, xiii, xvii.
42. Masferrer 2013, 27.
43. Masferrer 2013, 37.

44. Orsi 1985, xvii.
45. Vásquez and Marquardt 2003, 3.
46. Anzaldúa 1999, 25.
47. Saldívar 1997.
48. Pérez 1999.
49. Pratt 1991, 34.
50. Castañeda-Liles 2018, 64.
51. Vásquez and Marquardt 2003, 63.
52. Vásquez and Marquardt 2003, 45.
53. Price 2004, 122. See also Eliade 1987 [1959], 11.
54. Price 2004, 123.
55. Anzaldúa 1999,103; Delgadillo 2011, 4.
56. Medina 2014, 170.
57. Medina 2014, 170. This mestizaje is not syncretism; as Marzal has pointed out, syncretism as a construct overlooks its roots in colonizing thought. In its narrative of the prevalence of certain dominant religious systems, it tends to resist recognizing the inherited power disparity between European and pre-Columbian systems of belief. I therefore move away from syncretism and toward notions of religious eclecticism, enculturation, and secularization to explain the reality of the religious landscape of Latin America (Marzal 2002, 196–206)—and, here, of the border.
58. Elenes 2014, 44. See also Anzaldúa 2000, 38, 178.
59. Cantú 2014, 215–216.
60. Kanter 2020, 2.
61. Kanter 2020, 4.
62. Tuzin 1984, 580.
63. Vásquez and Marquardt 2003, 53; Levitt 2001.
64. Marzal 2002, 499.
65. Woodward 1996, 12.
66. Woodward 1996, 52.
67. Woodward 1996, 21–49, 69.
68. Woodward 1996, 65.
69. Woodward 1996, 55.
70. Popes can overrule or waive the five-year waiting period, as happened in the case of Mother Teresa of Calcutta, whose canonization process was initiated sooner.
71. Monsignor Óscar Sánchez Barba, interview with the author, Guadajara, Mexico, November 9, 2018.
72. The three theological virtues in Catholicism are faith, hope, and charity, while the four cardinal virtues are prudence, justice, fortitude, and temperance.
73. As Woodward (1996) explains, in the cases of martyrs—those who have been killed because of their faith—the process is a little different. In the Catholic tradition, "even the sins the saint had committed were erased by martyrdom, since nothing more could be asked of a faithful Christian. Martyrdom, in short, was the perfect sacrifice and implied the achievement of spiritual perfection" (61). In this case heroic death may fast-track the process of canonization.

74. Woodward 1996, 18.
75. Woodward 1996, 68.
76. Woodward 1996, 16, 6.
77. Woodward 1996, 5.
78. López 1999, 57.
79. Mbembe 2003, 40.
80. Woodward 1996, 62.
81. Woodward 1996, 17.
82. Marzal 2002, 375.
83. Graziano 2016, 59.
84. Marzal 2002, 375.
85. Woodward 1996, 7, 18.
86. It is important also to recognize that even though a one-on-one relationship always exists between the petitioner and the saint expected to grant the miracle, this relationship is not prerequisite to the individual's receiving the miracle or favor. Someone can petition for a miracle for another person, as a proxy; a petitioner might request a miracle for someone else who is ill, in prison, or in danger (Graziano 2016, 60), and the grantee does not need to be Christian, to believe in the saint, or even to be aware that a petition has been made on his or her behalf (Graziano 2016, 90).
87. Technically, in Catholic teaching, saints do not grant miracles on their own; rather, they intercede with God on people's behalf. The Catholic Church teaches that since saints are close to God in Heaven, prayers to them carry special weight. Not all Catholics understand these distinctions, and this Catholic tenet has also been a point of contention with several Protestant denominations that see the practice of praying to saints as idolatrous.
88. Derrida 1997.
89. Other cultures have terms to define similar religious vows, such as *panata* in the Philippines.
90. Krause and Batista 2012, 812.
91. Graziano 2016, 60.
92. Graziano 2016, 60, 70.
93. Graziano 2016, 60.
94. Graziano 2016, 71.
95. Graziano 2016, 61–62.
96. Graziano 2016, 80.
97. Graziano 2016, 80–81.

Chapter 1

1. *El señor de los cielos*, season 2, episode 31, "Denuncia," aired July 8, 2014, on Telemundo, https://www.telemundo.com/super-series/2014/07/08/el-senor-de-los-cielos-segunda-temporada-capitulo-31-parte-1-de-5.

2. Zorrilla 2021.
3. Murphy 2008; Volokh 2014; Grillo 2008; Bonello 2015.
4. Chesnut 2014.
5. Saul 2018.
6. Birth certificate, Archivo Histórico General del Estado de Sinaloa, 1888, Act No. 108, record 522/2014A-F/898. Provided by Gilberto López Alanís by letter on April 11, 2016.
7. Cadín 2009; Sada 2001, 96. Griffith (2003) argues that the name "Malverde" can be also read as the "Bad Green One," given the name's association with the trafficking of marijuana and the laundering of money in US dollars—both activities associated with the color green (Griffith 2003, 66). Alternatively, Price (2004) says that Malverde may have been born as "Jesús Juárez Mazo around 1870 in a small town near Culiacán." Mejía (1999), like Price, argues that Malverde's original name was Jesús Juárez Mazo and that it was only in the 1920s that people began to refer to him using the surname Malverde. Sada, the well-known Mexican writer, has also introduced Meza and Garcia as other possible last names given to the saint during the early years of the emergence of the legend (Sada 2001, 95).
8. Sada 2001, 90.
9. Sada 2001, 97.
10. Quinones 2001, 227.
11. Griffith 2003, 66–68.
12. Flores and González 2006, 32.
13. All my requests to discuss the issue with the local church authorities during my trips to Culiacán received no response.
14. Grillo 2011, 188.
15. Amaral 2001.
16. See Miller 2012; Einstein 2008.
17. Price 2005, 189.
18. Gómez and Park 2014, 204.
19. Ibid., 202.
20. See Robinson 2009, 5–31.
21. Walsh 1984, 16.
22. Sada 2007, 96.
23. Griffith 2003, 67; Sada 2007, 96.
24. Sada 2007, 96.
25. Ibid., 89. Perhaps not coincidentally, in 1909 the Catholic Church still observed the Feast of the Discovery of the Holy Cross on May 3 (Griffith 2003, 67). Despite the fact that this feast no longer appears on the current liturgical calendar for the United States in the revised *Roman Missal*, it is still celebrated in Mexico and in many parts of Latin America today.
26. Flores and González 2006, 32; Mendoza 2001, 22–25.
27. Price 2005, 176.
28. Ibid.
29. Sada 2007, 89.

30. For an extended and comprehensive analysis of the sexual construction of bandits, especially the distinctions between Mexican and US bandits, see Alonzo 2009, 85–108.
31. Mendoza 2001, 24.
32. Griffith 2003, 67.
33. Griffith 2003, 67; Price 2005, 176.
34. Griffith 2003, 67.
35. Griffith 2003, 67.
36. Aguilar Aguilar 1997, 118; Romero Gil 2001, 330.
37. Martínez Barreda in Verdugo Quintero 1997, 163.
38. The Yoremen, also known as the Mayo, are large American Indian communities originally from the Mexican states of Sonora and Sinaloa, along the valleys between the rivers Mayo and Fuerte. These communities have suffered consistent persecution, exploitation, and forced relocation over the years. Due to these communities' constant rebellions, strikes, and uprisings, mining corporations and the Mexican federal government resisted their employment and instead promoted the migration of Chinese labor.
39. In the play, Malverde learns how to survive in the wild, navigate the Sinaloan mountains, and use natural herbs as part of a journey of spiritual purification. To protect the Mayo Indians, Malverde leaves their community and becomes the saint of drug trafficking. Playwright Óscar Liera's real name was Jesús Cabanillas Flores. He was born in Culiacán.
40. Esquivel 2009, 44.
41. This expanded into the United States. See Castañeda-Liles 2018, 31–54; Elizondo 1997.
42. Knight 1986, 71.
43. Ortega Noriega 1999, 290.
44. Esquivel 2009, 151.
45. Liera 2008, 362.
46. Sada 2007, 91.
47. Price 2005, 181.
48. Sada 2007; Mendoza 2001, 25.
49. The address of the chapel is 863 Independencia, Culiacán Rosales, Sinaloa 80000, Culiacán, Mexico. This chapel is within walking distance of the old main train station in Culiacán.
50. Price 2005, 180, 192.
51. López Sánchez 1996, 37.
52. Pérez López et al. 1997, 287–88.
53. López Sánchez 1996, 37.
54. Ibid., 38.
55. Sada 2007, 93.
56. López Sánchez 1996, 37; Sada 2007, 93.
57. Mendoza 1964, 14.
58. Quinones 2001, 228; Sada 2007, 99.

59. According to Grillo, in 1980 the government of Culiacán donated a parcel of land for the relocation and construction of a new shrine in response to the multiple protests and negotiations. Grillo 2011, 189.
60. Cody 1986.
61. Interview with Jesús Manuel González Sánchez, Culiacán, Sinaloa, January 20, 2015.
62. "El mito de Malverde" 2016.
63. Quinones, "Jesús Malverde," 231.
64. Interview with Jesús Manuel González Sánchez, Culiacán, Sinaloa, January 20, 2015.
65. López Sánchez, a native of Sinaloa (Culiacán), is a cofounder of the Taller de Teatro de la Universidad Autónoma de Sinaloa (TATUAS), with Liera. In 1988 he relocated to Mexico City, where he is an actor and writer. He was directly involved in the publication of Liera's book *Teatro complete*.
66. Sada 2007, 99.
67. Interview with Jesús Manuel González Sánchez, Culiacán, Sinaloa, January 20, 2015.
68. De la Mora 2006, 69.
69. Ibid., 71.
70. Ibid., 77.
71. Ibid.
72. Ibid., 85, 79.
73. Both emerged in the same period, but in different places. Tapatío refers to a person from Guadalajara, Jalisco.
74. Esquivel 2009, 100.
75. De la Mora 2006, 86.
76. Ibid.
77. Dyer 1997, 67–68.
78. Interview with Jesús Manuel González Sánchez, Culiacán, Sinaloa, January 20, 2015.
79. The branding of saints (and other religious sites) is not new. The marketing of holy relics (and reliquaries) thrived in the Middle Ages.
80. Jameson 1991.
81. Ibid., 17.
82. For a comprehensive understanding of marketing changes in the 1980s and 1990s, see Marwick 2013; Duffy 2017; Banet-Weiser 2012; Aronczyk and Powers 2010; Chinn 2001; Aronczyk 2013; Klein 1999; Serazio 2013.
83. Chesnut 2014.
84. Price 2005, 153–57.
85. Chesnut 2014.
86. Price 2005, 153–57.
87. From a more moralist point of view, Armando Partida Tayzan argues that Malverde's transformation into a "miraculous accomplice" and protector of narco-traffickers has "invalidated" his "original meaning" as a benevolent saint and turned him into an "evil hero" whose main role is to endorse criminal activities, which emphasizes only his "role of bandit." For him Malverde's transformation is a reflection of the "decomposition and deterioration of the national social and public fabric, triggered by impunity and the absence of law" (Partida Tayzan 2011, 47–48).

88. Creechan and Herrán Garcia 2005, 27, 21.
89. Ibid., 26.
90. Quoted in Murphy, 2019.
91. Donald Trump made remarks to this effect as he announced his campaign for US president in Manhattan on June 16, 2015, setting the tone for an unpredictable and polarizing campaign.
92. More information about the exhibition can be found at https://www.fowler.ucla.edu/exhibitions/sinful-saints-and-saintly-sinners-margins-americas/.
93. Interview with María Romero, Mexico City, February 3, 2015.
94. Ibid.
95. Ibid.
96. "Reaparece" 2015.
97. Sada 2007, 97.
98. Rubio 2016a.
99. During the first seven years, the performance was held sporadically. Over time, the idea was to turn this particular day into a feast day for the Novia de Culiacán (Rubio 2016a).
100. Interview with María Romero, Mexico City, February 3, 2015.
101. "Novias y feminismo en Sinaloa" 2018.
102. Home page, Sabuesos Guerreras A.C., http://sabuesosguerreras.wixsite.com/website, accessed July 23, 2019.
103. Rodríguez 2016.
104. Rubio 2016b.
105. Alvarado 2017.
106. Sanchez 2018.
107. Zorrilla 2021.
108. "Narcos no quesieron" 2021.
109. "No lo querían" 2021.
110. Rodriguez 2021.
111. Hernández 2021.
112. Hotson 2021; "No lo querían porque era gay" 2021.
113. This case came on the heels of a related scandal about the optics of masculinity around the Mexican Revolution. A year before, Mexican artist Fabian Chairez had showed a painting of Emiliano Zapata, a leading figure in the Mexican Revolution, "nude and in an effeminate pose." The controversy "led about 100 farmers to block the entrance" of the gallery where the piece was displayed, and several "relatives of . . . Zapata threatened to sue a Mexico City gallery, saying 'depicting him as gay' denigrates his legacy." In both cases, queerness was misinterpreted as a threat to the masculinity of an icon of the Mexican Revolution and the imaginaries of a heteronormative state.

Chapter 2

1. "Troops Slay" 1938; "La Multitud Prende Fuego" 1938; "Machine Guns" 1938.
2. Specifically, the home was located at 615 Second Avenue, between F and G Street. Rivera and Saldaña Rico 2000.
3. "Mueren mas inocentes" 1938.
4. Balderrama and Rodriguez 2006, 150.
5. Ramírez 2018, 322.
6. "Mueren mas inocentes" 1938, 1.
7. Olga's mother had originally assumed that Lili had accompanied Olga to the store, which was the property of Mariano and Roberta Mendívil. For more information retracing Olga's steps, see Alcántara 2005, 4, 11; Rivera and Saldaña Rico 2000; "Mueren mas inocentes" 1938, 1.
8. Rivera and Saldaña Rico 2000; Alcántara 2005, 4.
9. "Mueren mas inocentes" 1938, 1; "Troops Slay" 1938, 2; "Incendian el Palacio" 1938, 1.
10. "A Juan Castillo Morales" 1938, 1.
11. "La Ley Fuga" 1938, 1.
12. Portelli 1991, 2.
13. Ibid., 14.
14. Anzaldúa 1999, 3.
15. This is the same Arpaio who was pardoned by US president Donald Trump in 2017 after being convicted of police misconduct, abuse of power, unlawful enforcement of immigration laws, and racial profiling against Latinxs in Arizona. Horwitz 2011.
16. Hernández 2018.
17. These observations took place between fall 2012 and winter 2015 when I visited Tijuana. As a result, my descriptions apply to the cemeteries as they appeared at that time and may not accurately reflect their appearance since then, given the dynamic nature of the sites and the shifting practices of those who visit them.
18. See Eggener 2010; Aries and Weaver 2008; Dethlefsen 1981, 137–58; Bille, Hastrup, and Flohr Soerensen 2010.
19. Carvajal 2006, 139.
20. Valenzuela Arce 2000, 102. See also Vanderwood 2004, 41; Alcántara 2005, 5.
21. Alcántara 2005, 5.
22. Carvajal 2006, 34.
23. "Mueren mas inocentes" 1938, 1.
24. Tijuana Civil Registry, Libro de defunciones, 1, c. 36, s. 30, 1938.
25. He ordered the creation of a temporary garrison in order to coordinate the investigation. The garrison, under the control of Contreras, was quartered in a nearby rented house between the fort and the Camacho Martínez home. Vanderwood 2004, 7–8; "La Multitud Prende Fuego," l.
26. The results of the autopsy were presented to the press, confirming the cause of death, and revealing that Olga had also been raped. It is unlikely that the Camacho Martínez family was consulted before this information was given to the press. Carvajal 2006, 46.
27. "Troops Slay" 1938, 2; Carvajal 2006, 43.

28. In one version of the events, Concha (a diminutive form of the name Concepción) turned over the evidence voluntarily. In another version, the police found the bloody clothes after they searched Castillo Morales's residence. Concha also declared that a week before, she had caught the soldier trying to rape her niece. Those defending Castillo Morales's innocence argued that Concha was paid by the police or the military to frame him, based on the fact that Concha never spoke with the media and disappeared afterward, with no records of her whereabouts. Alcántara 2005, 4; "La Confesion" 1938, 1, 8. Also see Carvajal 2006, 63; Alcántara 2005, 5; Piñera Ramírez and Ortiz Figueroa 1989, 375.
29. Alcántara 2005, 5; "La Confesion" 1938, 1, 8.
30. Vanderwood 2004, 20.
31. Carvajal 2006, 69.
32. As reported in the same *Los Angeles Times* article, the names of the victims were Roman Maldonado (eight years old), Salvador Vasquez (fourteen years old), and Vidal Torres (fifty-six years old). "Troops Slay" 1938, 2. The names were also confirmed by *La Opinion*: "La Confesion" 1938, 8.
33. Rodolfo Sánchez Taboada to the Department of Interior, Mexico, February 28, 1938, Historical Archives, Baja California, file 4014, exp. 852/100/2819.
34. Rivera and Saldaña Rico 2000; Alcántara 2005, 4.
35. Rivera and Saldaña Rico 2000; Alcántara 2005, 4.
36. "La Multitud Prende Fuego," 1; Carvajal 2006, 80.
37. Rivera and Saldaña Rico 2000.
38. "Troops Slay" 1938, 1, 2; Alcántara 2005, 4.
39. "Troops Slay" 1938, 1.
40. Rodolfo Sánchez Taboada to the Department of Interior, February 28, 1938.
41. CROM is sometimes also referred to as the Confederación Regional de Obreros Mexicanos (CROM). "Severas medidas" 1938, 1.
42. Quote from "Troops Slay" 1938, 1; see also "Los Soldados Dan Muerte" 1938, 8.
43. Silva Hernández 1991, 20; also see *San Diego Evening Tribune*, February 16, 1938. The *Evening Tribune* merged with the *San Diego Union* in 1992, after which the publication was called the *San Diego Union-Tribune*. See also Rivera and Saldaña Rico 2000.
44. "Troops Slay" 1938, 1; "Mueren mas inocentes pidiendo justicia," 1. In another version of the events, Contreras spoke to the community in a radio address; see "Los Soldados Dan Muerte" 1938, 1.
45. Carvajal 2006, 88.
46. Ibid.
47. Vanderwood 2004, 42–43.
48. Rivera and Saldaña Rico 2000.
49. "Los Soldados Dan Muerte" 1938, 1; "Severas medidas" 1938, 1. In the many different accounts of events offered by Martínez de Camacho, Olga's mother, one finds repeated support for the popular belief that more than one person was involved in the crime. For example, two different sets of footprints were found, including one set on the military's side of the location where the body was found. Indeed, Olga's mother went so far as to suggest that Contreras himself might have been involved. This allegation

is significant, as the general was also the one responsible for the military trial after the civil court refused to hear the case. He had access to the evidence and oversaw the execution; and the day after the body was found, it was he who ordered that the location be burned. No charges were ever brought against Contreras. Rivera and Saldaña Rico 2000.
50. "Morales Muerto a balazos" 1938, 1.
51. Ibid.; Vanderwood 2004, 45; Rivera and Saldaña Rico 2000.
52. Ibid.
53. Ibid.
54. Carvajal 2006, 17.
55. Jimenez Beltran 2004.
56. Lázaro Cárdenas, "Declaracion de Expropiacion de 'Agua Calientes' en Tijuana," executive order, December 18, 1937, *Diario Oficial del Gobierno Constitucional de los Estados Unidos Mexicanos*, vol. 105, no. 43, December 29, 1937, Archivo General de la Nación, Mexico City.
57. CTM is sometimes also referred to as the Confederación de Trabajadores Mexicanos. Carvajal 2006, 10–12.
58. Lee 1996.
59. Vanderwood 2004, 78. This massive migration has defined most of the city's current shape. Mexico census data substantiate the magnitude of this rapid growth: Tijuana went from 1,228 inhabitants in 1921 to 11,271 in 1930—a 900 percent increase in only nine years. Between 1930 and 1940 its population doubled again to 21,977 people, amounting to almost eighteenfold growth in just two decades. See Herzog 1990, 107.
60. These grants were part of a larger project of land reform and expropriation of foreign companies that characterized the post-Revolution period in Mexico under President Cardenas.
61. Dwyer 2008, 12.
62. Ibid., 48.
63. Vanderwood 2004, 155.
64. Carrillo Viveros 1991, 128; Alcántara 2005, 5.
65. Vanderwood 2004, 16; Rivera and Saldaña Rico 2000.
66. Garduño 2004, 47.
67. In fact Sánchez Taboada, the governor for the Northern District of the state of Baja California, had been appointed to his position only a year previously, in part to secure the transition of the land expropriations in the region. The Camacho Martínez family was personally involved in a citywide dispute after the closure of several casinos affected them directly. Like Tijuana in general, they depended on the casinos as their main source of income. Juan Castillo Morales, on the other hand, had experienced major losses of his own: the death of his father, mother, and younger brother (due to different causes) in the two months prior to the events.
68. "Severas medidas" 1938, 1.
69. Carvajal 2006, 55.
70. Trujillo Muñoz 2001, 33.
71. Carvajal 2006, 35.

72. Ibid., 65.
73. Rodolfo Sánchez Taboada to the Secretary of State, Mexicali, February 15, 1938, Archivo General de la Nación, Dirección General de Gobierno, IIHUABC, exp. 10.105, f. 2.
74. William Smale telegram to Cordell Hull, February 16, 1938, US National Archives, Record Group 59, Records of the Department of State Relating to the Internal Affairs of Mexico, 1930–1944, Consular Reports, Lower (Baja) California, no. 281.
75. "Severas medidas" 1938, 1.
76. William Smale telegram to Cordell Hull, *Consular Report #284*, February 18, 1938.
77. Carvajal 2006, 82, 86.
78. Ibid., 85; Vanderwood 2004, 32.
79. "Hungry Tijuanans,'" 59.
80. Castañeda in de la Torre and Pesquera 1993, 29.
81. As reported by Vanderwood, in August 1952, fourteen years after the crimes, local Tijuana editor and reporter Antonio Morales Tamborrel, writing for *El Imparcial*, summarized the popular opinion that Castillo Morales was "an innocent man [who] had died demanding justice." Morales Tamborrel 1952; Vanderwood 2004, 62.
82. Vanderwood 2004, 69.
83. Rivera and Saldaña Rico 2000.
84. Lugo Perales in Alcántara 2005, 5.
85. Interview with Marco Antonio, Tijuana, January 17, 2013.
86. "Abajo Frontera" 1938.
87. The image was published on February 17, 1938, in the *San Diego Evening Tribune*, February 16, 1938.
88. Griffith 1993, 114.
89. López Gaspar 1997; Latorre 2008, 131–50.
90. López Gaspar 1999.
91. She has recently exhibited *Juan Soldado* at the UCLA Fowler Museum's 2014 exhibition *Sinful Saints and Saintly Sinners*, where she showed also her series *Queer Santas* (*Sinful Saints* 2014).
92. Interview with Alma López Gaspar de Alba, Los Angeles, April 5, 2014.
93. While the piece has some parallels with the Juan Soldado narrative (as scholar Guisela Latorre points out, in the *Santa Niña de Mochis* piece, López "fashioned a completely new saint. . . . [and] implies that 'saintly' attributes can be found in anyone." Latorre 2008.
94. Ibid.
95. Interview with Alma López Gaspar de Alba, Los Angeles, April 5, 2014.
96. Valenzuela Arce 2000.
97. Garduño Pulido 1991, 7–10.
98. Valenzuela Arce 2000, 104.
99. Piñera Ramírez and Ortiz Figueroa 1989, 137; Watson 2001; López 1999, 57; Griffith 2003.
100. Monarres in Valenzuela Arce 2000, 106.

101. Operation Gatekeeper was a series of on-the-ground practices, judicial measurements, policies, and ideological changes started in 1994 by the Clinton administration, meant to control undocumented immigration into the United States through the Mexican border around the San Diego–Tijuana region. Operation Gatekeeper can be understood as part of the transformations generated in the context of the implementation of the North American Free Trade Agreement (NAFTA). For more information, see Nevins 2002. For more information about ICE's biometric project, see the website of the Office of Biometric Identity Management, US Department of Homeland Security, https://www.dhs.gov/obim.
102. Given the intensely personal nature of some of the petitions, and to preserve the petitioners' identities, all names of the petitioners in documents that I photographed or otherwise recorded have been changed, and any similarity to real persons is pure coincidence. In addition, the faces of individuals in all images have been blurred. All English translations from such letters are my own unless stated otherwise. Some original spelling has been preserved to maintain the context of the message. I have sought to preserve the characteristics of the language used by the petitioners because these details reveal their levels of literacy in Spanish and their socioeconomic class as it relates to education access or even the presence of an indigenous first language.
103. On the Secure Communities Program, see US Immigration and Customs Enforcement, "Delegation of Immigration Authority Section 287(g) Immigration and Nationality Act," https://www.ice.gov/287g, accessed July 30, 2018.
104. Valenzuela Arce 2000, 105.
105. Ibid.
106. Ibid.
107. "Gender Wage Gap" 2019.
108. Since I last visited the site, the housing crisis in Mexico has not improved; indeed, according to a 2017 article from the *Los Angeles Times*, it has been getting worse. Marosi 2017.
109. The name of this restaurant has been changed.
110. Garduño Pulido 1991, 7–10.
111. Castañeda-Liles 2018, 140; for a detailed analysis on the importance of virginity in Mexican Catholicism, see 135–45.
112. Vanderwood 2004, 290.
113. Carvajal 2006, 20; Vanderwood 2004, 290.
114. Gaspar de Alba and Guzmán 2010, 11.
115. Domínguez-Ruvalcaba and Corona 2012, 4.
116. The term "Black Legend" refers to an anti-Spanish bias expressed by many European historians who negatively represent Spain and its American colonies. For more, see Gibson 1971; Maltby 1996, 346–48.
117. Vanderwood 2004, 16.
118. Perales in Alcántara 2005, 5.
119. Castañeda 1993, 29.
120. Ibid., 16.

121. Most notable, given its similarity with Olga's case, was the disappearance in the San Diego area of Virginia Brooks, a ten-year-old girl who was kidnapped on her way to school on February 11, 1931. Almost a month after her disappearance, her mutilated body was found at a military site near San Diego, known as Camp Kearny Mesa ("Mutilated Body" 1931, 10). The case garnered immense attention and notoriety in the region, with over four thousand people attending Virginia's funeral. "Thousands See Brooks Rites" 1931, 3.
122. Elvia Arriola in Gaspar de Alba and Guzmán 2010, 55.
123. Gaspar de Alba and Guzmán 2010, 10.
124. Federici 2004, 14.
125. Yépez 2002, 30.
126. Ibid.
127. Ibid., 31.
128. Yépez 2002, 31.
129. An preliminary/exploratory version of this project took place in 2000 and 2001, as he said "by talking with people." Yépez 2002, 30.
130. Yépez 2002, 31.
131. For detailed discussions of several of the controversies surrounding Yépez, see Sarano 2018; Rosko 2018; Staff 2014; Abaroa 2016; Meza Jara 2016. At the time of this publication Yepez's letter "Carta a un Crítico de derecha literaria" is no longer available. However, it can be found at: https://www.scribd.com/document/335960928/CARTA-A-UN-CRI-TICO-DE-DERECHA-LITERARIA.
132. Ibid.
133. Rebolledo 2002, 31.
134. Yépez 2002, 30.
135. Ibid.
136. Vanderwood 2004, 290.
137. Yépez 2006, 39–40.
138. Vanderwood 2004, 291.

Chapter 3

1. Interview with Marcos Lopez, Chicago, November 7, 2016.
2. Society of Saint Toribio Romo, Chicago, bylaws.
3. Interview with Concepción Rodríguez, Chicago, November 7, 2016.
4. Ibid.
5. Aguilar in Ortiz 2016.
6. Murphy 2007, 44.
7. FitzGerald 2008, 70.
8. Fussell 2014, 479–98; Flores 2018, 1649–90; Flores and Schachter 2018, 839–68.
9. Romo 2010; Tejeda 2010; Chavez-Martinez 2016.
10. Aguilar Ros 2016, 104.

11. Massey, Rugh, and Pren 2010, 133.
12. This pattern has by no means diminished. Ibid., 135; Durand, Massey, and Zenteno 2001, 109; Suro 2005.
13. Young 2015b, 157.
14. Young 2017.
15. Young 2017.
16. Young 2015b, 158.
17. This event in 1925 was not the first time that someone tried to create a Mexican national Catholic Church. For a detailed historical analysis of circumstances leading to this schismatic event, see Meyer 2005, 156.
18. Potter 2006.
19. CROM is sometimes also referred to as the Confederación Regional de Obrera de México, or the Confederación Regional de Obreros Mexicanos. Meyer 2005, 148.
20. By 1936 the close relationship between CROM and the Mexican government deteriorated to the point where the government not only prohibited federal workers from joining CROM but also promoted the creation of another organization, the Confederación de Trabajadores de México, also referred to as the Confederación de Trabajadores Mexicanos (CTM, or Confederation of Mexican Workers).
21. Young 2015a.
22. The first violent revolt of the Cristero War took place in Guadalajara, capital of Jalisco, on August 3, 1926, when more than four hundred Cristeros entrenched inside the Santuario de Nuestra Señora de Guadalupe engaged in a gunfight again Mexican federal troops. The ordeal left eighteen dead and forty wounded, and it ended only when the Cristeros ran out of ammunition. This event was followed by a succession of violent militia attacks from different factions of the Cristeros against government forces.
23. Archbishop Orozco y Jiménez refused to use violence.
24. Meyer 1976, 108.
25. Ibid., 109.
26. Meyer 2013, 85.
27. Meyer 1976, 106.
28. Archives of the Society of Jesus, Mexican Province, April 9, 1929, cited in Meyer 1976, 107.
29. Ibid., 106.
30. Young 2015a.
31. Romo G. F. 2000, 24. The edition of Toribio Romo's biography cited here by the author is a reprint created at the request of Javier Navarro Rodríguez, bishop of the Diocese of San Juan de los Lagos, Jalisco, in commemoration of Toribio Romo's canonization in 2000. I purchased this during a research visit to Santa Ana, Jalisco, in November 2018. The book states that the English translation was "validated and authorized by Msgr. Jorge Elías Chávez, second vicar general of the Diocese of Juan de los Lagos" in Jalisco, Mexico, but there is no record of who did the translation.
32. Recently a new, larger church has been built to hold the thousands of pilgrims visiting the town.
33. De la Torre and Guzmán Mundo 2010, 111.

34. Romo G. F. 2000, 13.
35. "José Anacleto González" 2005.
36. Vatican Papers I, 2.
37. Some reports state that he died on February 24, 1928. However, the Vatican records show that he died early in the morning, around 6:00 a.m., on February 25. Vatican Papers I, 3.
38. Romo G. F. 2000, 48.
39. Ibid., 53.
40. Murphy 2007, 44.
41. Vatican Papers I, 3.
42. Ibid., 52.
43. Ibid., 4.
44. Interview with Óscar Sánchez Barba, Guadalajara, Mexico, November 9, 2018.
45. The differences between beatification and canonization may not be familiar to many people. In beatification the Vatican authorizes the limited veneration of individuals, mostly in the vicinities where they used to live or work, whereas canonization is a global status. See the introduction to this book for an extended explanation of the process, limitations, and characteristics. See also Simón 2018, 143–64.
46. De la Torre and Guzmán Mundo 2010, 124.
47. Ibid., 116.
48. Aguilar Ros 2016, 107.
49. Aguilar Ros 2016, 97.
50. De la Torre and Guzmán Mundo 2010, 116.
51. Interview with Renée de la Torre, Guadalajara, Mexico, November 10, 2018; de la Torre and Guzmán Mundo 2010, 116.
52. De la Torre and Guzmán Mundo 2010, 117.
53. Martínez-Cárdenas, Machaen López, and Madrigal Loza 2019, 30428.
54. Ibid., 117.
55. Interview with Óscar Sánchez Barba, Guadalajara, Mexico, November 9, 2018.
56. Ibid.
57. Ibid.
58. Ibid.
59. Ibid.
60. "Santo que no es conocido" 2012.
61. Hirai 2009, 252.
62. Levitt and de la Torre 2018, 344.
63. De la Torre and Levitt 2017, 144.
64. Ibid.
65. Levitt and de la Torre 2018, 344.
66. Officially known as the Club Deportivo Guadalajara.
67. Levitt and de la Torre 2018, 345.
68. Aguilar Ros 2016, 108.
69. "Santo que no es conocido" 2012. Data are from Rogelio Martínez-Cárdenas's keynote presentation, "El turismo religioso, de la fé al product turístico," at the XXXIII

Congreso de Religión, Sociedad y Política: Dinámicas geográficas del patrimonio, el turismo y lo religioso, Ciudad Guzman, Mexico, November 9, 2018, which I attended.
70. "Esperan más de 300 mil" 2019.
71. Aguilar Ros 2016, 105.
72. Ibid., 106.
73. Romo 2010. In 2003 a winery was built within the premises of the museum to John Paul II. That same year Father González Pérez also opened a house for consecrated religious that are staying in Santa Ana to attend to the visitors. Martínez-Cárdenas, Machaen López, and Madrigal Loza 2019, 30428–29.
74. Medina Gallo 2015, 205.
75. Interview with Óscar Sánchez Barba, Guadalajara, Mexico, November 9, 2018.
76. García Gutiérrez 2002.
77. Ibid.
78. Ibid.
79. Buendía Gaytán in García Gutiérrez 2002.
80. García Gutiérrez 2002.
81. Corchado 2006.
82. Thompson 2002.
83. Sanchez 2005, 15–16.
84. Young 2015b, 156.
85. Agren 2012.
86. Krogstad 2016.
87. Passel, Cohn, and Gonzalez-Barrera 2012, 19.
88. Aguilar Ros 2016, 99.
89. Palomar Verea 2005, 24.
90. De la Torre and Guzmán Mundo 2010, 113.
91. De la Torre 1992, 60.
92. Aguilar Ros 2016, 111.
93. De la Torre and Guzmán Mundo 2010, 118.
94. Romo 1920, 2–9. Also cited in Alarcón and Cárdenas 2013, 241–58; FitzGerald 2008, 71–73.
95. Romo 1920, 2–9.
96. Orozco1920; FitzGerald 2008, 193.
97. Curso Social Agrícola Zapopano: desarrollado en Guadalajara, con ocasión de la pontificia coronación de la imagen de Nstra. Sra de Zapopan, en enero de 1921. Archive of the Archdiocese of Guadalajara, Guadalajara, Mexico.
98. FitzGerald 2008, 193.
99. Ibid., 87, 77.
100. Martínez-Cárdenas, Machaen López, and Madrigal Loza 2019, 30429.
101. Martínez-Cárdenas 2013, 15.
102. Thompson 2002.
103. Romo to González Pérez, in Romo 2010.
104. Romo 2010.
105. Medina Gallo 2015, 206.

106. *Pasaporte* n.d. Other references to the *Pasaporte* can be found in Martínez Cárdenas and Mínguez García 2014, 1580; de la Torre and Levitt 2018, 146.
107. Aguilar Ros 2016, 101.
108. BBVA 2018.
109. Bada 2016, 345.
110. Fox and Bada 2008, 443.
111. Ibid., 438.
112. Burgess 2012, 122.
113. Fox and Bada 2008, 438.
114. Hirai 2009, 252.
115. Bada 2016, 344.
116. BBVA 2018, 70, 79.
117. "Spiritual Passport" n.d., 1. However, it looks like the company Pajaro Macua, Salud Dinero y Amor LLC has stopped producing the *Spiritual Passport*, as the webpage for the product has disappeared.
118. Ibid., 2. Translation from their Spanish prayer version.
119. Ibid., 4.
120. Ibid., 4.
121. Interview with Donald F. Hanchon, Detroit, March 31, 2017.
122. Delaney 2010.
123. Interview with Donald F. Hanchon, Detroit, March 31, 2017.
124. Delaney 2010.
125. Interview with Donald F. Hanchon, Detroit, March 31, 2017.
126. Interview with Nancy Lee Smith, Monroe, Michigan, 2017. Her art studio, Saint Joseph Studio, is located at 610 W Elm Ave., Monroe, MI 48162.
127. Interview with Nancy Lee Smith, Monroe, Michigan, 2017.
128. Ibid.
129. Ibid.
130. Ibid.
131. Aguilar Ros 2016, 111.
132. Interview with Nancy Lee Smith, Monroe, Michigan, 2017.
133. Ibid.
134. Interview with Donald F. Hanchon, Detroit, March 31, 2017.
135. Duck 2006.
136. Ibid.
137. Ibid.
138. Ibid.
139. Ibid.
140. Borgerding 2012.
141. Ibid.
142. Father Tim Davison, letter to Catholic priests in the diocese of Tulsa, December 2007, Sts. Peter and Paul Parish Archive, Tulsa, Oklahoma.
143. Interview with Simón Navarro, Tulsa, Oklahoma, 2018, Sts. Peter and Paul Parish, Tulsa, Oklahoma.

144. Medina Gallo 2015, 211.
145. Miret 2013.
146. Ibid.
147. Interview with Simón Navarro, Tulsa, Oklahoma, 2018.
148. Miret 2013.
149. Ibid.
150. Father Tim Davison, letter to Edward J. Slattery, bishop of Tulsa, April 16, 2008, Sts. Peter and Paul Parish Archive, Tulsa, Oklahoma.
151. Edward J. Slattery, bishop of Tulsa, letter to Felipe Salazar Villagrana, bishop of San Juan de los Lagos, February 21, 2008, Sts. Peter and Paul Parish Archive, Tulsa, Oklahoma.
152. Edward J. Slattery, bishop of Tulsa, letter to Felipe Salazar Villagrana, bishop of San Juan de los Lagos, December 19, 2007, Sts. Peter and Paul Parish Archive, Tulsa, Oklahoma.
153. Interview with Simón Navarro, Tulsa, Oklahoma, 2018.
154. Ibid.
155. Aguilar Ros 2016, 102.
156. Ibid.
157. López 1999, 57.
158. Some American fraternal's groups, including the Knights of Columbus (Young 2015a), the Freemasons, and the Ku Klux Klan, became involved in the Mexican Cristero War.
159. Sanders 2014.
160. "Inmigrantes 'le deben'" 2014.
161. Ibid.
162. Bermudez 2014.
163. The legislation was proposed in 2013 by a bipartisan group of senators that included Robert Menendez (D-NJ), Jeff Flake (R-AZ), Lindsey Graham (R-SC), Marco Rubio (R-FL), and John McCain (R-AZ). Although the bill passed the Senate in June 2013, the bill was never considered in the House of Representatives and eventually expired.
164. Bermudez 2014.
165. Olson 2014.
166. Sanders 2014.
167. Vatican Papers I, 3; Vatican Papers II, 338.
168. Medina Gallo 2015, 202.

Chapter 4

1. In this chapter and throughout the book, I use her full Spanish name, La Santa Muerte, abbreviated to LSM, for two reasons. First, I want to preserve her Mexican identity and Latina locality within the hierarchies that define our society today. Second, because the politics of language define the terrain of race-based

interactions in the United States, I use her Spanish name to preserve her position as racialized object-subject. Finally, I also retain the Spanish article "La" as part of her name to recognize her implied gender-constructed feminine identity. As discussed later in this chapter, many of her followers have interpreted LSM as a gender-nonconforming saint; but I choose to emphasize her gender here as a strategic move, in order to differentiate her from similar yet male counterparts found in other places in the Americas, such as El Rey Pascual, in Guatemala, and San La Muerte, in Paraguay. Though these figures are also associated with the veneration of death, these are not the same spiritual entities. It remains unclear why LSM is clearly a female-infused entity while these other two are clearly male. A genealogical analysis of the construction of gender across these different figures is needed. All these semantic distinctions and complexities are essential to avoid cross-cultural and gender generalizations and misunderstandings about LSM and other icons associated with death.

2. As a manifestation of the plurality and cross-pollination between migrant groups that characterize religious experiences in the United States, the ballroom is not only located within a South Asian neighborhood but is decorated with Hindu religious imagery, which formed the backdrop for the event.

3. Rafael, vocalist, "Como yo te amo," by Manuel Álvarez-Beigbeder Pérez, recorded 1980, track 6 on *Y . . . sigo mi camino*, Hispavox, S.S. [vinyl LP].

4. Enriqueta Vargas Ortiz, remarks at the La Santa Muerte Ball, Queens, New York, August 19, 2017.

5. *United States v. Maria Vianey Medina-Copete and Rafael Goxcon-Chagal*, 757 F. 3d 1092 at 3 (10th Cir. 2014); Walker 2015.

6. Chesnut 2012, 6.

7. *United States v. Maria Vianey Medina-Copete and Rafael Goxcon-Chagal*.

8. This is similar to how the DEA users Malverde imagery in testimony against drug dealers. *United States v. Maria Vianey Medina-Copete and Rafael Goxcon-Chagal*.

9. Ibid., 12.

10. Ibid., 17.

11. *United States v. Bobadilla-Campos*, 839 F. Supp. 2d 1230, at 1234 (D.N.M. 2012).

12. Contreras 2014.

13. One of the many complications noted by defense attorneys for Medina-Copete and Goxcon-Chagal was the impossibility of accessing or even verifying any involvement by the National Security Agency (NSA)—a key player in such cases. The NSA has been directly involved in the monitoring, collection, and sharing of information with the US Department of Justice and the DEA over the past decades. But because its involvement is classified, no information provided by the NSA can be accessed or disputed. Walker 2015.

14. Because of the state's insistence on using a very "broad definition" of what constitutes "tools of the trade" for drug traffickers, they dangerously devalued the premise that sustains that domain in the first place. See Volokh 2014.

15. Today Almonte—along with other ex-DEA, police, and border patrol agents—runs a national consulting firm that provides training services to local, national,

and international enforcement agencies. Almonte's firm is not interested only in warning about LSM; its current list of seminars includes "Hispanic Gangs in the USA," "Narcocorridos," "Mexican Culture and Traditions," "Hotel and Motel Investigations," and "Stash House Investigation." See Almonte n.d.
16. Chesnut 2017.
17. "La Iglesia no avala culto" 2007.
18. "Archdiocese of Mexico" 2019.
19. Ravasi in "Vatican Declares" 2013.
20. Ravasi in Guillermoprieto 2013.
21. Kingsbury and Chesnut 2019.
22. Contreras 2017.
23. Contreras 2019.
24. Telephone interview with Enriqueta Vargas Ortiz, October 22, 2018.
25. Interview with Martin George Quijano, Mexico City, September 29, 2018; Quijano 2010, 50.
26. Interview with Martin George Quijano, Mexico City, September 29, 2018.
27. Telephone interview with Enriqueta Vargas Ortiz, October 22, 2018.
28. Perdigón Castañeda 2008, 64.
29. Telephone interview with Enriqueta Vargas Ortiz, October 22, 2018.
30. Interview with Martin George Quijano, Mexico City, September 29, 2018.
31. Interview with Juan Salazar Rojo, Tlaxcala, Mexico, September 17, 2019. The service took place at 1er. Santuario a Dios y a la Santa Muerte (First Sanctuary to God and La Santa Muerte), 12 Pte, Calle 9 Nte, San Pablo de los Frailes, 72090 Puebla, Puebla, Mexico.
32. Chesnut 2012, 3.
33. As Martín (2014) enumerates, other names include "'La Niña Blanca (White Girl) or 'La Flaca' (Skinny Girl), and many of her followers refer to her with loving, familial endearments such as 'Mi Reina' (My Queen), 'Mi Niña Bonita' (My Beautiful Girl), 'Madrina' (Godmother) or 'Holy Mother.'" Martín 2014, 183.
34. Chesnut 2012, 7.
35. Interview with Martin George Quijano, Mexico City, September 29, 2018. Though others are more conservative in their estimates, Chesnut deems it likely her followers have reached between ten and twelve million devotees, with many uncounted given the stigma and secrecy that still define her veneration. Chesnut 2012, 6. See also Chesnut quoted in Paulas 2014; Bragg 2014.
36. Martín 2014, 183.
37. In Roman mythology, the Parcae (sing. Parca) were three female deities—Nona, Decima, and Morta—known as the Fates, or deities of destiny. They were responsible for defining the length and fate of each god's and each person's life. Morta's task was to cut the thread of life of the individual.
38. Chesnut 2012, 27. In New Mexico, a female representation of death known as Doña Sebastina has been an intrinsic and constant element of the Penitente Brotherhood since the Mexican colonial era in the region. The image merges the concepts of La Parca, the Grim Reaper, and Saint Sebastian.

39. The most popular image of La Calaca is La Catrina, and it was produced by the artist Posada in the 1890s.
40. Perdigón Castañeda 2008, 56.
41. In its most general form, La Calaca is a skeleton, mostly of human form. LSM differs from the popular Mexican figure La Catrina, a personification of Death, in several ways. Perhaps the most important that "La Catrina has not sacred power," whereas LSM is perceived as a saint "because she does saint-like things (e.g., protecting ... and granting ... favours)." Kristensen 2016, 411.
42. Ibid., 413.
43. Yllescas Illescas 2018.
44. Ibid., 168.
45. Ibid., 84.
46. Hernández Hernández 2016, 22.
47. He defines three stages in the evolution of this saint based on the visibility of veneration practices: "the clandestine, the boom expansion, and ... consolidation." Yllescas Illescas 2016, 73.
48. Perdigón Castañeda 2008, 58.
49. Interview with Martín Morfín Reyes, Coacalco, México state, Mexico, November 18, 2018. In discussing the evolution and structure of LSM and her veneration, I do not seek to explain the many similar manifestations of LSM across other cultures and nations—from Argentina to the Philippines, from Europe to Asia and Africa—because other scholars are doing more extensive and comprehensive work in that area. R. Andrew Chesnut's recent work is recommended reading, as he has traveled around the world tracing La Santa Muerte–related venerations and other representations of Death.
50. Interview with Martín Morfín Reyes, Coacalco, México state, Mexico, November 18, 2018.
51. Chesnut 2012, 27.
52. Hernández Hernández 2016, 22.
53. Perdigón Castañeda 2008, 21.
54. But there is an irony here: alongside this bias toward pre-European Mexico runs another bias counteracting it, for modern Mexican values assign more weight to European-inspired practices, including religion, over indigenous productions (as when fine arts are privileged over artesanías, or local crafts). Given the tension between these two sets of values and beliefs, this strategy—rooting LSM's identity and a past in antiquity—may in fact sabotage the group's attempts to gain state-sanctioned economic support.
55. Telephone interview with Enriqueta Vargas Ortiz, October 22, 2018.
56. Guzmán 1997, 227. See also Roque Ramirez 2005, 164.
57. See Nixon 2013.
58. Mbembe 2003, 40.
59. The original prayer appears in Toor 1947, 144.
60. Kristensen 2016, 406.
61. Lewis 2011, 290.

62. Kristensen 2015, 553.
63. Kristensen 2016, 412.
64. Perdigón Castañeda 2008, 61; interview with Martin George Quijano, Mexico City, September 29, 2018.
65. Perdigón Castañeda 2008, 61.
66. Other sources claim that the altar to LSM was erected on All Saints' Day, November 1, 2001. See Chesnut 2012, 11.
67. Interview with Enriqueta Romero Romero, Mexico City, January 19, 2015.
68. Ibid.
69. Ibid.
70. Ibid.
71. Ibid.
72. Ibid.
73. Ibid.
74. Ibid.
75. Ibid.
76. Following the opening of Romero Romero's altar in Tepito, another, more controversial figure, David Romo Guillén, emerged almost immediately and then faded just as quickly—but not without first transforming the way Mexicans (and the world in general) perceive the veneration of LSM. For a detailed description of the events that culminated with Romo Guillén's imprisonment, see Chesnut 2012, 42–43. See also Romo Guillén quoted in "Iglesia advierte" 2009; Bromley and Edelman 2012; "La Guerra Santa" 2009; Tuckman 2009.
77. Telephone interview with Enriqueta Vargas Ortiz, October 22, 2018.
78. Locations can be checked at the website of SMI: https://www.internationalsantamuerte.com/find-locations/.
79. Metcalfe and Chesnut 2015.
80. Enriqueta Vargas Ortiz, remarks at the La Santa Muerte Ball, Queens, NY, August 19, 2017.
81. Kingsbury 2021.
82. Telephone interview with Enriqueta Vargas Ortiz, October 22, 2018.
83. Ibid.
84. Ibid.
85. Ibid. Vargas Ortiz claimed to live exclusively on donations and contributions. According to Chesnut, her husband was an affluent attorney. The exact amount of money received as donations, however, remains unknown as most contributions are still in the form of cash.
86. Ibid.
87. Interview with David Valencia, Coacalco, Mexico, November 18, 2018.
88. Ibid.
89. Interview with Carmen Sandoval, Coacalco, Mexico. November 18, 2018.
90. Ibid.
91. Ibid.
92. Telephone interview with Enriqueta Vargas Ortiz, October 22, 2018.

93. Mecinas Montiel 2016.
94. OECD 2019.
95. Clement 2019.
96. Interview with Carmen Sandoval, Mexico, November 18, 2018.
97. Ibid.
98. Ibid.
99. Ibid.
100. Telephone interview with Enriqueta Vargas Ortiz, October 22, 2018.
101. Perdigón Castañeda 2008, 57.
102. Ibid., 60.
103. Telephone interview with Lucino Morales, October 30, 2017.
104. Interview with Carmen Sandoval, Mexico, November 18, 2018.
105. Telephone interview with Lucino Morales, October 30, 2017.
106. Interview with Carmen Sandoval, Mexico, November 18, 2018.
107. This is the text appearing on a candle I purchased in Detroit. The candle was produced by Eternalux, Commerce, California.
108. Martín 2014, 184.
109. Interview with Enriqueta Romero Romero, Mexico City, January 19, 2015.
110. Ibid.
111. 1 Corinthians 15:55 (Revised Standard Version, Catholic Edition).
112. Interview with Carmen Sandoval, Mexico, November 18, 2018.
113. Ibid.
114. Interview with Enriqueta Romero Romero, Mexico City, January 19, 2015.
115. Interview with Arely Vázquez, Queens, NY, August 19, 2017.
116. Interview with Carmen Sandoval, Mexico, November 18, 2018.
117. As in the case of Jesús Malverde, the social or class status of the original donor also plays a central part in the social power assigned to the object inherited.
118. Interview with Carmen Sandoval, Coacalco, Mexico. November 18, 2018.
119. Ibid.
120. Interview with Arely Vázquez, Queens, NY, August 19, 2017.
121. Ibid.
122. Ibid.
123. Interview with Carmen Sandoval, Coacalco, Mexico. November 18, 2018.
124. Ibid.
125. Ibid.
126. Ibid.
127. Ibid.
128. Ibid.
129. Ibid.
130. Ibid.
131. Ibid., 126.
132. Ibid., 127.

133. The Iglesia Católica Tradicional México–Estados Unidos should not be confused with the Iglesia Arcangelista México–US; they are different entities. "Detienen a David Romo" 2011.
134. "Los Rosarios" 2010, 66.
135. Ibid.
136. Telephone interview with Enriqueta Vargas Ortiz, October 22, 2018.
137. Ibid.
138. Ibid.
139. Ibid.
140. Interview with Martin George Quijano, Mexico City, September 29, 2018.
141. Ibid.
142. Interview with Arely Vázquez, Queens, NY, August 19, 2017.
143. Ibid.
144. Telephone interview with Lucino Morales, October 30, 2017.
145. Telephone interview with Enriqueta Vargas Ortiz, October 22, 2018.
146. Interview with David Valencia, Coacalco, México state, Mexico, November 18, 2018.
147. Ibid.
148. Telephone interview with Lucino Morales, October 30, 2017.
149. Interview with Arely Vázquez, Queens, NY, August 19, 2017.
150. Ibid.
151. *Persona humana* 1975; Catechism of the Catholic Church, n. 2357.
152. See the case of Father Robert Nugent and Sister Jeannine Gramick in Rosin 2019.
153. From Aguilar's interview in *You Can Ask Her for Anything*, video, produced by 590films and Adrian Fernandez Baumann, at 2:29, accessed February 11, 2019, http://faithinthefiveboroughs.org/video/you-can-ask-her-for-anything/.
154. According to the annual report for Transgender Day Remembrance (TDoR), 2021 was the deadliest year for transgender people around the world, and the trend is not improving. About 25% of the victims "were killed in their own homes," and "the majority of the murders happened in Central and South America (70%)." Wareham 2021.

    Moreover, the intersections of misogyny, transphobia, xenophobia, health care access, and hate towards sex workers have created the condition for premature death for transgender people. As shown by a study released in 2021 and conducted in the Netherlands between 1972 and 2018, "Transgender people have double the odds of dying early compared to folks whose identity matches the sex they were assigned at birth (cisgender)." Preidt 2021; "Murders of Transgender People" 2020.
155. From Aguilar's interview in *You Can Ask Her for Anything*, video, produced by 590films and Adrian Fernandez Baumann, at 2:29, accessed February 11, 2019, http://faithinthefiveboroughs.org/video/you-can-ask-her-for-anything/.
156. Interview with Enriqueta Romero Romero, Mexico City, January 19, 2015.
157. Ibid.

Conclusion

1. King 2005, 435.
2. Brown 1965, 46.
3. Avella and Hanley 2009, 19.
4. Ibid.
5. Weland 2014.
6. Avella and Hanley 2009, 19.
7. Bridget Dowd, 2020.
8. Barrios 2008, 60.
9. According to historian Thomas E. Sheridan in his book *Los Tucsonenses: The Mexican Community in Tucson, 1854–1941*, Tucson "did not ordain its first Mexican American priest until 1946," several decades after Phoenix. Sheridan 1986, 156.
10. Barrios 2008, 60.
11. Avella and Hanley 2009, 20.
12. At the same time, in 1926, "a similar kind of segregation took place" in Flagstaff, Arizona, when Father Edward Albouy, who would later become Monsignor Albouy, decided to separate Anglo and Latino parishioners rather to have them worship together in the same church. For the Latinos, he pushed for the construction of Our Lady of Guadalupe church, which was finished in 1926, while Nativity Church, now known as Nativity of the Blessed Virgin Mary, was constructed and designated as the parish for the Anglo community in the city. As explained by Diocese of Phoenix documents, "In a variety of ways[,] it was made known, Hispanics were not welcome as members" of Nativity Church, and the lines of separation got normalized over time. Avella and Hanley 2009, 20.
13. Crary 2020; Funk and Martínez 2014.
14. Crary 2020; US Census Bureau, QuickFacts Phoenix City Arizona, https://www.census.gov/quickfacts/fact/table/phoenixcityarizona/RHI725218#RHI725218.
15. Reaves and Ettenborough 2003, 7.
16. Ibid.
17. Ibid.
18. Billeaud 2019. It was during Arpaio's tenure that Pope Benedict installed (on November 25, 2003) the deeply conservative Bishop Thomas J. Olmsted as the head of the Diocese of Phoenix.
19. Anzaldúa 1999, 25.
20. Reguillo 2004, 40.
21. Foucault 1997, 7.
22. Paredes 1982, I.
23. Eliade 1998, 2.
24. Baudrillard 1983, 23–26.
25. Reguillo 2004, 42.
26. Mbembe 2003, 11–40.
27. Pérez 2007, 128.
28. Reguillo 2004, 40.

Bibliography

"A Juan Castillo Morales se le aplicó la Ley Fuga." 1938. *La Época, Periódico Independiente* (Tijuana), February 18, 1938.

"Abajo Frontera." 1938. *San Ysidro Border Press*, November 11, 1938.

Abaroa, Eduardo. 2016. "Ante la crisis instituciona." *La Tempestad*, September 2, 2016. https://www.latempestad.mx/ante-la-crisis-institucional.

Acosta, Andrea. 2017. "Growing U.S. Hispanic Population Is a Blessing for the Church, Says Theologian." *America: The Jesuit Review*, February 7, 2017. https://www.americam agazine.org/faith/2017/02/07/growing-us-hispanic-population-blessing-church-says-theologian.

Agren, David. 2012. "Cristero Martyr Now Popular Patron of Mexican Migrants Headed to US." *Catholic Sun*, May 31, 2012. https://www.catholicsun.org/2012/05/31/cristero-martyr-now-popular-patron-of-mexican-migrants-headed-to-us/.

Aguilar Aguilar, Gustavo, Azalia Lopez González, Rigoberto Arturo Román Alarcón, and Arturo Carrillo Rojas. 1997. "Siglo XIX." In *Historia de Sinaloa*, edited by Jorge Verdugo Quintero et al., 9–149. Culiacán, SI: Gobierno del Estado de Sinaloa, SEPyC, COBAES, DIFUCUR.

Aguilar Ros, Alejandra. 2016. "El santuario de Santo Toribio Romo en los altos jaliscienses: La periferia en el Centro." *Nueva Antropología* 29 (84): 91–116.

Alarcón, Rafael, and Macrina Cárdenas Montaño. 2013. "Los santos patronos de los migrantes Mexicanos a Estados Unidos." *Revista Interdisciplinar da Mobilidade Humana* 41: 241–58.

Alcántara, Hamlet. 2005. "Olguita, la víctima de Juan Soldado." *Frontera*, January 16, 2005, 4–5.

Almonte, Robert. n.d. "Seminar Overview." *Almonte Consulting and Training*. Accessed February 10, 2019. https://robertalmonte.com/program-topics/.

Alonzo, Juan José. 2009. *Badmen, Bandits, and Folk Heroes: The Ambivalence of Mexican American Identity in Literature and Film*. Tucson: University of Arizona Press.

Alvarado, Sergio. 2017. "La Novia de Culiacán recorrerá el centro este Viernes." *Debate*, December 21, 2017. https://www.debate.com.mx/cultura/La-Novia-de-Culiacan-recorrera-el-centro-este--viernes-20171221-0067.html.

Amaral, Martín. 2001. "Vuelo libre: La manda de María Romero." *El Noreste* (Culiacán, SI), December 30, 2001, sec. Cultura, 8C.

Anzaldúa, Gloria. 1999. *Borderlands/La Frontera: The New Mestiza Consciousness*. San Francisco: Aunt Lute.

Anzaldúa, Gloria. 2000. *Interviews/Entrevistas*. Edited by AnaLouise Keating. New York: Routledge.

Araújo, Vera. "Dottrina sociale della chiesa." *Mariapolis Renata Loppiano*, Campogiallo, Incisa Valdarno FI, Italy, Fall 1996.

"Archdiocese of Mexico City Issues Clarification About St. Jude and the 'St. Death.'" 2008. Catholic News Agency, November 3, 2008. https://www.catholicnewsagency.com/

news/archdiocese_of_mexico_city_issues_clarification_about_st._jude_and_the_ st._death.
Aries, Philippe, and Helen Weaver. 2008. *The Hour of Our Death: The Classic History of Western Attitudes Toward Death over the Last Thousand Years.* New York: Vintage Books.
Aronczyk, Melissa. 2013. *Branding the Nation: The Global Business of National Identity.* New York: Oxford University Press.
Aronczyk, Melissa, and Devon Powers. 2010. *Blowing Up the Brand: Critical Perspectives on Promotional Culture.* New York: Peter Lang.
Arriola, Elvia. 2010. "Accountability for Murder in the Maquiladoras: Linking Corporate Indifference to Gender Violence at the US-Mexico Border." In *Making a Killing: Femicide, Free Trade, and La Frontera,* edited by Alicia Gaspar de Alba and Georgina Guzmán, 25–62. Austin: University of Texas Press.
Avella, Steven M., and John Hanley. 2009. "Division in Phoenix: Anglos Versus Mexicans." In *The Diocese of Phoenix: Celebrating 40 Years 1969-2009: Encountering the Living Christ.* Strasbourg, France: Editions du Signe.
Avila, Oscar. 2008. "A Protector for Journey Full of Danger." *Chicago Tribune,* November 9, 2008, sec. 1, 29.
Bada, Xóchitl. 2016. "Collective Remittances and Development in Rural Mexico." *Population, Space and Place* 22: 343–55.
Balderrama, Francisco E., and Raymond Rodriguez. 2006. *Decade of Betrayal: Mexican Repatriation in the 1930s.* Albuquerque: University of New Mexico Press.
Banet-Weiser, Sarah. 2012. *Authentic™: The Politics of Ambivalence in a Brand Culture.* New York: New York University Press.
Barrios, Frank M. 2008. *Mexicans in Phoenix.* Charleston, SC: Arcadia.
Barthes, Roland. 2001. *Mythologies.* Translated by Annette Lavers. New York: Hill and Wang.
Barton, Paul. 2005. "Ya Basta! Latino/a Protestant Activism in the Chicano/a and Farm Workers Movements." In *Latino Religions and Civic Activism in the United States,* edited by Gastón Espinosa, Virgilio P. Elizondo and Jesse Miranda, 127–44. New York: Oxford University Press.
Baudrillard, Jean. 1983. *Simulations.* Translated by Paul Foss, Paul Patton, and Philip Beitchman. New York: Semiotext(e).
BBVA. 2018. *Mexico: Yearbook of Migration and Remittances 2018.* Mexico City: BBVA.
Bermudez, Esmeralda. 2014. "Faithful Flock to See Statue of Santo Toribio, the Immigrants' Saint." *Los Angeles Times,* July 12, 2014. https://www.latimes.com/local/la-me-immigrants-saint-20140713-story.html.
Bilinkoff, Jodi. 2003. "Introduction." In *Colonial Saints: Discovering the Holy in the Americas,* edited by Allan Greer and Jodi Bilinkoff, xiii–xxii. New York: Routledge.
Bille, Mikkel, Frida Hastrup, and Tim Flohr Soerensen. 2010. *An Anthropology of Absence: Materializations of Transcendence and Loss.* New York: Springer.
Billeaud, Jacques. 2011. "Critics: 'Tough' Sheriff Botched Sex-Crime Cases." Associated Press, December 4, 2011. http://archive.boston.com/news/nation/articles/2011/12/04/critics_tough_sheriff_botched_sex_crime_cases/?page=full.
Bonello, Deborah. 2015. "In His Hometown, Fugitive Mexican Lord 'El Chapo' Is Hero to Many." *Los Angeles Times,* August 10, 2015. https://www.latimes.com/world/mexico-americas/la-fg-mexico-culiacan-guzman-20150810-story.html.
Borden, Tessie. 2002. "Migrants' Saints Give Security, Hope While Stories Multiply, Shrines Keep Growing." *Arizona Republic,* December 11, 2002, A1, A21.

Borden, Tessie. 2003. "Saint, Shrines Offer Serenity to Faithful Migrants Crossing Mexican Border." *The Leaft-Chronicle* (Clarksville, TN), January 18, 2003, sec. Living, 1D.

Borgerding, Katherine. 2012. "Hispanic Population Surges Statewide." *Oklahoma Watch*, November 29, 2012. https://oklahomawatch.org/2012/11/29/hispanic-population-surges-statewide/.

Bragg, Steven. 2014. "Growing Devotion to Santa Muerte in U.S. and Abroad." *NBC News Latino*, December 29, 2014. http://www.nbcnews.com/news/latino/growing-devotion-santa-muerte-u-s-abroad-n275856.

Bromley, David G., and Stephanie Edelman. 2012. "Mexican-U.S. Catholic Apostolic Traditional Church Timeline," *World Religions and Spirituality*, March 27, 2012. https://wrldrels.org/2016/10/08/mexican-u-s-catholic/.

Brown, Charles. 1965. "The Epic of Ashton Jones: Dixie-Born White Minister Leads One-Man Crusade for Interracial Brotherhood." *Ebony*, October 1965.

Burgess, Katrina. 2012. "Collective Remittances and Migrant-State Collaboration in Mexico and El Salvador." *Latin American Politics and Society* 54 (4): 119–46.

Busto, Rudy V. 2005. *King Tiger: The Religious Vision of Reíes López Tijerina*. Albuquerque: University of New Mexico Press.

Cadín Enviado, Iván. 2009. "Un siglo con Malverde." *El Universal*, May 3, 2009. http://www.eluniversal.com.mx/nacion/167777.html.

Calvillo, Jonathan E. 2020. *The Saints of Santa Ana: Faith and Ethnicity in a Mexican Majority City*. New York: Oxford University Press.

Cantú, Norma E. 2014. "Living La Vida Santa." In *Fleshing the Spirit: Spirituality and Activism in Chicana, Latina, and Indigenous Women's Lives*, edited by Elisa Facio and Irene Lara, 202–17. Tucson: University of Arizona Press.

Carrillo Viveros, Jorge. 1999. "Comercios sindicalizados y grupos de visitantes en Tijuana." In *Grupos de visitantes y actividades turísticas en Tijuana*, edited by Nora L. Bringas and Jorge Carrillo V., 123–39. Tijuana, BC: El Colegio de la Frontera Norte.

Carvajal, Mario A. 2006. *Juan Soldado: La verdad y el mito*. Tijuana, BC: Carvajal Editores.

Castañeda, Antonia. 1993. "Sexual Violence in the Politics and Policies of Conquest: Amerindian Women and the Spanish of Alta California." In *Building with Our Hands: New Directions in Chicana Studies*, edited by Adela de la Torre and Beatriz M. Pesquera, 15–33. Berkeley: University of California Press.

Castañeda-Liles, María Del Socorro. 2018. *Our Lady of Everyday Life: La Virgen de Guadalupe and the Catholic Imagination of Mexican Women in America*. New York: Oxford University Press.

Castor, N. Fadeke. 2017. *Spiritual Citizenship: Transnational Pathways from Black Power to Ifá in Trinidad*. Durham, NC: Duke University Press.

"Changing Faiths: Latinos and the Transformation of America Religion." *Hispanic/Latino Identity*, April 25, 2007. https://www.pewresearch.org/hispanic/2007/04/25/changing-faiths-latinos-and-the-transformation-of-american-religion/

Chavez-Martinez, Gloria. 2016. "Bishop Barnes Blesses New Santo Toribio Immigration Center." *Inland Catholic Byte* (Diocese of San Bernardino), June 1, 2016. https://www.icbyte.org/index.php/news/diocesan-news/1498-bishop-barnes-blesses-new-santo-toribio-immigration-center.

Chesnut, R. Andrew. 2012. *Devoted to Death: Santa Muerte, the Skeleton Saint*. 2nd ed. New York: Oxford University Press.

Chesnut, R. Andrew. 2014. "El Chapo Guzman's Patron Saints." *Huffington Post*, last updated April 27, 2014. https://www.huffingtonpost.com/r-andrew-chesnut/jesus-malverde-el-chapo_b_4852830.html.

Chesnut, R. Andrew [rachesnut]. 2017. "Top Vatican Official Rebukes Santa Muerte—Again." *Skeleton Saint*, September 8, 2017. https://skeletonsaint.com/2017/09/08/top-vatican-official-rebukes-santa-muerte-again.

Chinn, Elizabeth. 2001. *Purchasing Power: Black Kids and American Consumer Culture*. Minneapolis: University of Minnesota Press.

Clement, J. 2019. "Countries with the Most Facebook Users 2019." *Statista*. https://www.statista.com/statistics/268136/top-15-countries-based-on-number-of-facebook-users/.

Cody, Edward. 1985. "Some Mexican See Smuggler as Hero." *Washington Post*, June 11, 1986. https://www.washingtonpost.com/archive/politics/1986/06/11/some-mexicans-see-smuggler-as-hero/e05ffbd4-34ec-481e-895a-8b58d773a894/?noredirect=on.

Contreras, Russell. 2014. "Drug Convictions Overturned Thanks to Death Saint." *Santa Fe New Mexican*, July 2, 2014. https://www.santafenewmexican.com/news/local_news/drug-convictions-overturned-thanks-to-death-saint/article_2677e7ed-973d-595f-bdb3-d85d96a91744.html.

Contreras, Russell. 2017. "US Bishops Join Mexico Colleagues, Denounce 'Santa Muerte.'" *U.S. News and World Report*, February 20, 2017. https://www.usnews.com/news/new-mexico/articles/2017-02-20/us-bishops-join-mexico-colleagues-denounce-santa-muerte.

Contreras, Russell. 2019. "Santa Fe Archbishop Again Denounces 'Santa Muerte.'" *Santa Fe New Mexican/Associated Press*, March 25, 2019. https://www.santafenewmexican.com/news/local_news/santa-fe-archbishop-again-denounces-santa-muerte/article_8af68455-62a1-507c-aa93-5667f5d936ce.html.

Corchado, Alfredo. 2006. "The Migrant's Saint: Toribio Romo Is a Favorite of Mexicans Crossing the Border." *Banderas News*, July 2006. http://www.banderasnews.com/0607/nr-migrantssaint.htm.

Crary, David. 2020. "US Hispanic Catholic Are Future, but Priest Numbers Dismal." Associated Press, March 14, 2020. https://apnews.com/article/0cd91a02ad1bfe947d77c3e1a2c313a8.

Creechan, James H., and Jorge de la Herrán Garcia. 2005. "Without God or Law: Narcoculture and Belief in Jesús Malverde." *Religious Studies and Theology* 24 (2): 5–57.

Cunningham, Lawrence S. 1987. *Catholic Experience: Space, Time, Silence, Prayer, Catholicity, Community and Expectations*. New York: Crossroad.

de Certeau, Michael. 1988. *The Writing of History*. Translated by Tom Conley. New York: Columbia University Press.

de la Mora, Sergio. 2006. *Cinemachismo: Masculinities and Sexuality in Mexican Film*. Austin: University of Texas Press.

de la Torre, Renée. 1992. "Toribio a Los Altares." *Siglo 21*, March 6, 1992.

de la Torre, Renée, and Peggy Levitt. 2017. "Religión y reescalamiento: cómo santo Toribio colocó a Santa Ana en el mapa transnacional religioso?" *Desacatos* 55: 128–51.

de la Torre, Renée, and Fernando Guzmán Mundo. 2010. "Santo Toribio: De mártir de Los Altos a santo de los emigrantes." In *Santuarios, Peregrinaciones y Religiosidad Popular*, edited by María J. Rodríguez-Shadow and Ricardo Ávila, 107–27. Estudios

del Hombre, Antropología, no. 25. Guadalajara, JA: Centro Universitario de Ciencias Sociales y Humanidades–Universidad de Guadalajara.
Delaney, Robert. 2010. "Mexican Martyr's Relic to Have Permanent Home in Detroit." *Michigan Catholic*, November 18, 2010. http://www.themichigancatholic.org/2010/11/mexican-martyr-relic-to-have-home-in-detroit/.
Delaney, Robert. 2010. "Relic of Mexican Saint Received at Blessed Sacrament Cathedral." *Detroit Catholic*, November 3, 2010. https://detroitcatholic.com/news/robert-delaney/relic-of-mexican-saint-received-at-blessed-sacrament-cathedral.
Delgadillo, Teresa. 2011. *Spiritual Mestizaje: Religion, Gender, Race, and Nation in Contemporary Chicana Narrative*. Durham, NC: Duke University Press.
Derrida, Jacques. 1997. *Of Grammatology*. Translated by Gayatri Chakravorty Spivak. Baltimore: Johns Hopkins University Press.
Dethlefsen, Edwin. 1981. "The Cemetery and Culture Change: Archaeological Focus and Ethnographic Perspective." In *Modern Material Culture: The Archaeology of Us*, edited by Richard Gould and Michael Schiffer, 137–58. New York: Academic Press.
"Detienen a David Romo, líder del culto a 'La Santa Muerte.'" 2011. *Proceso*, January 4, 2011. http://www.proceso.com.mx/260225/detienen-a-david-romo-lider-del-culto-a-la-santa-muerte.
Diaz, Elizabeth. 2017. "The Rise of Evangélicos." *America: The Jesuit Review*, April 7, 2017. https://www.americamagazine.org/faith/2017/02/07/growing-us-hispanic-population-blessing-church-says-theologian.
Diócesis de San Juan de los Lagos. (2007) *El devocionario del migrante*. Jalisco, Mexico.
Do, Thu T., and Thomas P. Gaunt. 2019. "Women and Men Professing Perpetual Vows in Religious Life: The Profession Class of 2019." *United States Conference of Catholic Bishops and Center for Applied Research in the Apostolate*, Georgetown University, Washington, DC. http://www.usccb.org/_cs_upload/beliefs-and-teachings/vocations/consecrated-life/profession-class/298808_1.pdf.
Domínguez-Ruvalcaba, Héctor, and Ignacio Corona. 2012. "Gender Violence: An Introduction." In *Gender Violence at the U.S.–Mexico Border: Media Representation and Public Response*, edited by Héctor Domínguez-Ruvalcaba and Ignacio Corona, 1–13. Tucson: University of Arizona Press.
Dowd, Bridget. 2020. "Untold Arizona: Amid Discrimination, Hispanics Found Community at Immaculate Heart of Mary Parish." *91.5 KJZZ*, February 7, 2020. https://kjzz.org/content/1427371/untold-arizona-amid-discrimination-hispanics-found-community-immaculate-heart-mary.
Duck, Marilyn. 2006. "Bishop Meets with Parishioners Angry over Perceived Slight." *National Catholic Reporter*, July 26, 2006. http://www.nationalcatholicreporter.org/update/nt072606.htm.
Duffy, Brooke. 2017. *(Not) Getting Paid to Do What You Love: Gender, Social Media, and Aspirational Work*. New Haven, CT: Yale University Press.
Durand, Jorge, Douglas S. Massey, and René M. Zenteno. 2001. "Mexican Immigration to the United States: Continuities and Changes." *Latin American Research Review* 36 (1): 107–27.
Durkheim, Emile. 1995. *The Elementary Forms of Religious Life*. New York: Free Press.
Dwyer, John Joseph. 2008. *The Agrarian Dispute: The Expropriation of American-Owned Rural Land in Post-Revolutionary Mexico*. Durham, NC: Duke University Press.
Dyer, Richard. 1997. *White*. New York: Routledge.

"E. A. Dieckmann Services Today." 2018. *San Diego Police Museum Online.* http://www.sdpolicemuseum.com/Edward-Dieckmann.html.

Eggener, Keith. 2010. *Cemeteries.* New York: W. W. Norton.

Einstein, Mara. 2008. *Brands of Faith: Marketing Religion in a Commercial Age.* New York: Routledge.

"El mito de Malverde, el Bandido generoso, antes y después de Eligio González." 2016. *RíoDoce*, July 3, 2016. https://riodoce.mx/2016/07/03/el-mito-de-malverde-el-bandido-generoso-antes-y-despues-de-eligio-gonzalez/.

Elenes, C. Alejandra. 2014. "Spiritual Roots of Chicana Feminist Borderlands Pedagogies." In *Fleshing the Spirit: Spirituality and Activism in Chicana, Latina, and Indigenous Women's Lives*, edited by Elisa Facio and Irene Lara, 43–58. Tucson: University of Arizona Press.

Eliade, Mircea. 1987 [1959]. *The Sacred and the Profane.* New York: Harcourt Brace Jovanovich.

Eliade, Mircea. 1998. *Myth and Reality.* Long Grove, IL: Waveland Press.

Elizondo, Virgilio. 1997. *Guadalupe: Mother of the New Creation.* Maryknoll, NY: Orbis Books.

"Esperan más de 300 mil peregrinos en Jalisco en santuario de Toribio Romo." 2017. *Televisa News*, November 12, 2017. https://noticieros.televisa.com/ultimas-noticias/esperan-mas-300-mil-peregrinos-santuario-toribio-romo/.

Espinosa, Gastón, and Mario T. García. 2008. *Mexican American Religious: Spirituality, Activism, and Culture.* Durham, NC: Duke University Press.

Esquivel, Manuel. 2009. *Jesús Malverde: El santo popular de Sinaloa.* Mexico City: Editorial Jus.

Federici, Silvia. 2004. *Caliban and the Witch: Women, the Body, and Primitive Accumulation* Brooklyn, NY: Autonomedia.

FitzGerald, David. 2008. *Nation of Emigrants: How Mexico Manages Its Migration.* Berkeley: University of California Press.

Flores, Enrique, and Raúl Eduardo González. 2006. "Jesús Malverde: Plegarias y corridos." *Revista de literaturas populares* 6 (1): 32-60.

Flores, René. 2018. "Can Elites Shape Public Attitudes Toward Immigrants? Evidence from the 2016 U.S. Presidential Election." *Social Forces* 96: 1649–90.

Flores, René, and Ariela Schachter. 2018. "Who Are the 'Illegals'? The Social Construction of Illegality in the U.S." *American Sociological Review* 83 (5): 839–68.

Foucault, Michel. 1997. *Society Must Be Defended: Lectures at the Collège de France 1975–1976.* Translated by David Macey. New York: Picador.

Fox, Jonathan, and Xochitl Bada. 2008. "Migrant Organization and Hometown Impacts in Rural Mexico." *Journal of Agrarian Change* 8 (3): 435–61.

Funk, Cary, and Jessica Martínez. 2014. "Fewer Hispanics Are Catholic, So How Can More Catholics Be Hispanic?" *FactTank*, Pew Research Center, May 7, 2014. https://www.pewresearch.org/fact-tank/2014/05/07/fewer-hispanics-are-catholic-so-how-can-more-catholics-be-hispanic/.

Fussell, Elizabeth. 2014. "Warmth of the Welcome: Attitudes Toward Immigrants and Immigration Policy." *Annual Review of Sociology* 40: 479–98.

Gallagher, Delia. 2020. "Pope Francis Prays for a Coronavirus Miracle at 'Plague' Crucifix Church." CNN, March 16, 2020. https://www.cnn.com/2020/03/16/europe/pope-francis-prayer-coronavirus-plague-crucifix-intl/index.html.

García, Mario T. 2007. *The Gospel of César Chávez: My Faith in Action.* Lanham, MD: Sheed & Ward.
García, Mario T. 2010. *Católicos: Resistance and Affirmation in Chicano Catholic History.* Austin: University of Texas Press.
García Gutiérrez, Marco A. 2002. "Toribio Romo González, protector de los mojados: Es un espejismo del desierto que hace milagros de carne y hueso." *Contenido*, June 1, 2002. http://www.zermeno.com/Toribio_Romo.html.
Garduño, Everardo. 2004. *La disputa por la tierra—la disputa por la voz: Historia oral del movimiento agrario en el valle de Mexicali.* Mexicali, BC: Universidad Autónoma de Baja California.
Garduño Pulido, Blanca. 1991. "Diego Rivera y Frida Kahlo en el rescate de los retablos mexicanas." In *Milagros en la frontera: Los mojados de la Virgen de San Juan dan gracias por su favor*, edited by Blanca Garduño Pulido, Carolina Sada, and María Eugenia López Saldaña, 7–10. Mexico City: Consejo Nacional para la Cultura y las Artes y el Instituto Nacional de Bellas Artes.
Gaspar de Alba, Alicia, and Georgina Guzmán. 2010. "Introduction: *Feminincido*: The 'Black Legend' of the Border." In *Making a Killing: Femicide, Free Trade, and La Frontera*, edited by Alicia Gaspar de Alba and Georgina Guzmán, 1–21. Austin: University of Texas Press.
"Gender Wage Gap." 2019. Organization for Economic Co-operation and Development. https://data.oecd.org/earnwage/gender-wage-gap.htm.
Gibson, Charles. 1971. *The Black Legend: Anti-Spanish Attitudes in the Old World and the New.* New York: Alfred A. Knopf.
Gil Olmos, José. 2010. *La Santa Muerte: La virgen de los olvidados.* México, DF: Debolsillo.
Gómez Michel, Gerardo, and Jungwon Park. 2014. "The Cult of Jesús Malverde: Crime and Sanctity as Elements of a Heterogeneous Modernity." *Latin American Perspective* 41 (2): 202–14.
Goodich, Michael. 1975. "Politics of Canonization." *Church History* 44 (3): 294–307.
Graziano, Frank. 2007. *Cultures of Devotion: Folk Saints of Spanish America.* 2nd ed. New York: Oxford University Press.
Graziano, Frank. 2016. *Miraculous Images and Votive Offering in Mexico.* New York: Oxford University Press.
Griffith, James S. 1993. *Beliefs and Holy Places: A Spiritual Geography of the Pimería Alta.* Tempe: University of Arizona Press.
Griffith, James S. 2003. *Folk Saints of the Borderlands: Victims, Bandits and Healers.* Tucson, AZ: Rio Nuevo.
Grillo, Ioan. 2008. "Mexico's Drug War Goes 'Behind Enemy Lines.'" *Time*, May 29, 2008. http://content.time.com/time/world/article/0,8599,1810489,00.html.
Grillo, Ioan. 2011. *El Narco: Inside Mexico's Criminal Insurgency.* New York: Bloomsbury.
Guillermoprieto, Alma. 2013. "Vatican in a Bind About Santa Muerte." *National Geographic*, May 14, 2013. http://news.nationalgeographic.com/news/2013/13/130 512-vatican-santa-muerte-mexico-cult-catholic-church-cultures-world/.
Guzmán, Manolo. 1997. "Pa' la escuelita con mucho cuidaò y por la orillita: A Journey Through the Contested Terrains of the Nation and Sexual Orientation." In *Puerto Rican Jam: Rethinking Colonialism and Nationalism*, edited by Frances Negrón-Muntaner and Ramón Grosfoguel, 209–28. Minneapolis: University of Minnesota Press.
Hagan, Jacqueline Maria. 2008. *Migration Miracle: Faith, Hope, and Meaning on the Undocumented Journey.* Cambridge, MA: Harvard University Press.

Hernández, Jonathan. 2021. "Fernando Colunga dejó Malverde tras ser amenazado por narcos por ser 'gay.'" *La Noticia*, March 3, 2021. https://lanoticia.com/primerafila/fernando-colunga-dejo-malverde-tras-ser-amenazado-por-narcos-por-ser-gay/

Hernández, Marie-Theresa. 2002. *Delirio—The Fantastic, the Demonic, and the Réel: The Buried History of Nuevo León*. Austin: University of Texas Press.

Hernández, Roberto D. 2018. *Coloniality of the US/Mexico Border: Power, Violence, and the Decolonial Imperative*. Tucson: University of Arizona Press.

Hernández Hernández, Alberto. 2016. "Introducción: La Santa Muerte." In *La Santa Muerte: Espacios, cultos y devociones*, edited by Alberto Hernández Hernández, 13–29. Tijuana, BC: El Colegio de la Frontera Norte and El Colegio de San Luis Potosí.

Herzog, Lawrence A. 1990. *Where North Meets South: Cities, Space, and Politics on the U.S.-Mexico Border*. Austin: University of Texas Press.

Hirai, Shinji. 2009. *Economía política de la nostalgia: Un estudio sobre la transformación del paisaje urbano en la migración transnacional entre México y Estados Unidos*. Mexico City: Universidad Autónoma Metropolitana, Ixtapalapa/Casa de Juan Pablos.

Hondagneu-Sotelo, Pierrette, Genelle Gaudinez, Hector Lara, and Billie C. Ortiz. 2004. "There's a Spirit That Transcends the Border: Faith, Ritual, and Postnational Protest at the U.S.-Mexico Border." *Sociological Perspectives* 47 (2): 133–59.

Horwitz, Sari. 2011. "Operation Fast and Furious: A Gunrunning Sting Gone Wrong." *Washington Post*, July 26, 2011. http://www.washingtonpost.com/investigations/us-anti-gunrunning-effort-turns-fatally-wrong/2011/07/14/gIQAH5d6YI_story_1.html.

Hotson, Will. 2021. "Fernando Colunga Left Malverde After Being Threatened by Drug Traffickers for Being 'Gay.'" *Light Home News*, March 4, 2021. https://www.lighthome.in/entertainment/hollywood/fernando-colunga-left-malverde-after-being-threatened-by-drug-traffickers-for-being-gay/.

"Hungry Tijuanans' Revolt Ignited by Murder Spark." 1938. *San Diego Sun*, February 15, 1938.

"Iglesia advierte sobre 'guerra santa' convocada por el culto a 'santa muerte.'" 2009. *ACI Prensa*, April 7, 2009. https://www.aciprensa.com/noticias/iglesia-advierte-sobre-guerra-santa-convocada-por-el-culto-a-santa-muerte.

"Incendian el Palacio Municipal de Tijuana." 1938. *La Opinión* (Los Angeles), February 18, 1938, 1.

"Inmigrantes 'le deben todo' a su santo patrón." 2014. *Servicios Informativos y Publicitarios del Sureste*, July 14, 2014. https://sipse.com/mundo/eu-inmigrantes-veneran-imagen-de-santo-toribio-romo-en-california-101674.html.

"Is This Charles Olson?" 2013. *Abandon All Despaire Ye Who Enter Here* (blog), City Lights, September 12, 2013. http://www.blogcitylights.com/2013/09/12/is-this-charles-olson.

Jameson, Fredric. 1991. *Postmodernism, or, the Cultural Logic of Late Capitalism*. Durham, NC: Duke University Press.

Jimenez Beltran, David. 2004. *The Agua Caliente Story: Remembering Mexico's Legendary Racetrack*. Lexington, KY: Blood-Horse Publications/Eclipse Press.

"José Anacleto González Flores and Eight Companions." 2005. *Vatican News Service*, November 20, 2005. http://www.vatican.va/news_services/liturgy/saints/ns_lit_doc_20051120_anacleto-gonzalez_en.html.

Kanter, Deborah E. 2020. *Chicago Católico: Making Catholic Parishes Mexican*. Champaign, IL: University of Illinois Press.

King, Martin Luther, Jr. 2005. "Interview on 'Meet the Press: 17 April 1960.'" *The Papers of Martin Luther King, Jr.*, vol. V, *Threshold of a New Decade, January 1959–December 1960*, edited by Clayborne Carson, Tenisha Armstrong, Susan Carson, Adrienne Clay, and Kieran Taylor, 428–35. Berkeley: University of California Press.

Kingsbury, Kate. 2021. "Disrespecting Death: The Trials and Tribulations of Santa Muerte Internacional and the Martyrdom of Comandante Pantera." *Small Wars Journal*, September 26, 2021. https://smallwarsjournal.com/jrnl/art/death-disrespected-trials-and-tribulations-santa-muerte-internacional-and-martyrdom.

Kingsbury, Kate, and Andrew Chesnut. 2019. "The Church's Life-and-Death Struggle with Santa Muerte." *Catholic Herald*, April 11, 2019. https://catholicherald.co.uk/magazine/the-churchs-life-and-death-struggle-with-santa-muerte/.

Klein, Naomi. 1999. *No Logo: Taking Aim at the Brand Bullies*. Toronto, ON: Random House of Canada.

Knight, Alan. 1986. *The Mexican Revolution I: Porfirians, Liberals and Peasants*. Lincoln: University of Nebraska Press.

Krause, Neal, and Elena Batista. 2012. "Religion and Health Among Older Mexican Americans: Exploring the Influence of Making Mandas." *Journal of Religion and Health* 51 (3): 812–24.

Kristensen, Regnar Alabaek. 2015. "La Santa Muerte in Mexico City: The Cult and Its Ambiguities." *Journal of Latin American Studies* 47 (3): 543–66.

Kristensen, Regnar Alabaek. 2016. "How Did Death Become a Saint in Mexico?" *Ethnos: Journal of Anthropology* 81 (3): 402–24.

Krogstad, Jens Manuel. 2016. "5 Factors About Mexico and Immigration to the U.S." *FactTank*, Pew Research Center, February 11, 2016. http://www.pewresearch.org/fact-tank/2016/02/11/mexico-and-immigration-to-us/.

"La Confesion del Asesino!" 1938. *La Opinion* (Los Angeles), February 16, 1938, 1, 8.

"La Iglesia no avala culto a la 'Santa Muerte,' advierte sacerdote mexicano." 2007. *ACI Prensa*, August 15, 2007. https://www.aciprensa.com/noticias/la-iglesia-no-avala-culto-a-la-santa-muerte-advierte-sacerdote-mexicano.

"La Ley Fuga en Tijuana al Asesino de la Niña Camacho." 1938. *La Opinión* (Los Angeles), February 18, 1938, 1.

"La Multitud Prende Fuego al Palacio Municipal de Tijuana." 1938. *La Opinion* (Los Angeles), February 16, 1938, 1.

Lara Salas, Juan Fernando. 2020. "Virgen de Los Ángeles cierra este domingo vuelo para inspirar esperanza y fortaleza frente al Covid-19." *La Nación*, March 21, 2020. https://www.nacion.com/el-pais/servicios/virgen-de-los-angeles-sobrevuela-pais-para/ngbnhgwcljeivo6e3refjmzob4/story/.

Latorre, Guisela. 2008. "Icons of Love and Devotion: Alma López's Art." *Feminist Studies* 34, nos. 1/2: 131–50.

Lee, Loren. 1996. "The San Diego Tijuana Regional Border." Unpublished paper. http://www2.palomar.edu/users/llee/II4BRDER.doc.

Levitt, Peggy. 2001. "Between God, Ethnicity, and Country: An Approach to the Study of Transnational Religion." Presentation at Transnational Migration: Comparative Perspectives workshop, Princeton University, Princeton, NJ, June 29–July 1.

Levitt, Peggy, and Renée de la Torre Castellanos. 2018. "Remapping and Rescaling the Religious World from Below: The Case of Santo Toribio and Santa Ana de Guadalupe in Mexico." *Current Sociology* 66 (3): 337–55.

Lewis, Oscar. 2011. *The Children of Sánchez: Autobiography of a Mexican Family*. 1961; repr., New York: Vintage Books.
Li Ng, Juan José. 2019. "Migration Watch, End of Year 2019." *BBVA Research*, December 18, 2019, 3. https://www.bbvaresearch.com/en/tag/remittances/.
Liera, Óscar. 2008. *El jinete de la divina providencia*, in *Teatro Escondido*. Mexico City: Fondo de Cultura Económica.
López, Alma. 1999. "Juan Soldado." In *Urban Latino Cultures: La Vida Latina en L.A.*, edited by Gustavo Leclerc et al., 56–57. Thousand Oaks, CA: Sage Publications.
López Sánchez, Sérgio. 1996. "Malverde: Un bandido generoso." *Fronteras: Revista de diálogo cultural entre las fronteras de México* 1 (2): 32–40.
"Los Rosarios: Crónica de la fe." 2010. In *La Santa Muerte: Historia, Realidad y Mito de la Niña Blanca*. Mexico City: Editorial Porrúa.
"Los Soldados Dan Muerte a Tres en Formidable Motín." 1938. *La Opinion* (Los Angeles), February 16, 1938.
Love Ramirez, Tanisha, and Zeba Blay. 2017. "Why People Are Using the Term 'Latinx': Do You Identify as 'Latinx'?" *Huffington Post*, last updated October 17, 2017. https://www.huffingtonpost.com/entry/why-people-are-using-the-term-latinx_us_57753328e4b0cc0fa136a159.
"Machine Guns Command Tijuana; 10 Shot in Riot; Building Fired." 1938. *San Diego Union*, February 16, 1938, 1.
Madrid, Alejandro L. 2008. *Nor-Tec Rifa! Electronic Dance Music from Tijuana to the World*. New York: Oxford University Press.
Maltby, William B. 1996. "The Black Legend." In *Encyclopedia of Latin American History and Culture*, vol. 1, edited by Barbara Tenenbaum and Georgette M. Dom, 346–48. New York: Charles Scribner's Sons.
Marosi, Richard. 2017. "A Failed Vision." *Los Angeles Times*, November 26, 2017. http://www.latimes.com/projects/la-me-mexico-housing.
Martín, Desirée A. 2014. *Borderlands Saints: Secular Sanctity in Chicano/a and Mexican Culture*. New Brunswick, NJ: Rutgers University Press.
Martinez, Juan Francisco. 2018. *The Story of Latino Protestants in the United States*. Grand Rapids, MI: William B. Eerdmans.
Martínez Barreda, Alonso, Jorge Verdugo Quintero, Guillermo Ibarra Escobar, and Matías Hiram Lazcano Armienta. 1997. "Revolución, contrarrevolución y reforma." In *Historia de Sinaloa*, edited by Jorge Verdugo Quintero et al., 157–225. Culiacán, SI: Gobierno del Estado de Sinaloa, SEPyC, COBAES, DIFUCUR.
Martínez-Cárdenas, Rogelio. 2013. "Regional Development Through Religious Tourism: San Juan de los Lagos and Jalostotitlán in Los Altos de Jalisco, Mexico." *Études caribéennes* (online), August 15, 2013. https://journals.openedition.org/etudescaribeennes/5352.
Martínez-Cárdenas, Rogelio, Luz Elena Machaen López, and Carolina Elizabeth Madrigal Loza. 2019. "Analysis of Sustainability in a Pilgrimage Site: The Case of Santa Ana de Guadalupe, Mexico." *Indian Journal of Scientific Research* 10 (1): 30426–31.
Martínez Cárdenas, Rogelio, and María del Carmen Mínguez García. 2014. "La Ruta Cristera: Valoración de un producto turístico religioso." In *Proceedings of the VIII Congreso International de Geografía de América Latina*, 1569–84. Madrid: Universidad Complutense de Madrid.
"Martyred Priest Seen as Migrants' Guardian." 2008. *Arizona Daily Star*, November 16, 2008, A16.

Marwick, Alice. 2013. *Status Update: Celebrity, Publicity, and Branding in the Social Media Age*. New Haven, CT: Yale University Press.
Marzal, Manuel M. 2002. *Tierra encantada: Tratado de antropología religosa de América Latina*. Lima: Pontificia Universidad Católica del Perú.
Masci, David, and Gregory A. Smith. 2018. "7 Facts About American Catholics." *Fact Tank*: Pew Research Center, October 10, 2018. https://www.pewresearch.org/fact-tank/2018/10/10/7-facts-about-american-catholics/.
Masferrer Kan, Elio. 2013. *Religión, política y metodologías: Aportes al studio de los sistemas religiosios*. Buenos Aires: Libros de la Araucaria.
Massey, Douglas S., Jacob S. Rugh, and Karen A. Pren. 2010. "The Geography of Undocumented Mexican Migration." *Mexican Studies/Estudios Mexicanos* 26 (1): 129–52.
Mbembe, Achille. 2003. "Necropolis." Translated by Libby Meintjes. *Public Culture* 15 (1): 11–40.
Mecinas Montiel, Juan Manuel. 2016. "The Digital Divide in Mexico: A Mirror of Poverty." *Mexican Law Review* 9 (1): 93–102.
Medina, Lara. 2004. *Las Hermanas: Chicana/Latina Religious-Political Activism in the U.S. Catholic Church*. Philadelphia: Temple University Press.
Medina, Lara. 2014. "Nepantla Spirituality: My Path to the Source(s) of Healing." In *Fleshing the Spirit: Spirituality and Activism in Chicana, Latina, and Indigenous Women's Lives*, edited by Elisa Facio and Irene Lara, 167–86. Tucson: University of Arizona Press.
Medina Gallo, César Eduardo. 2015. "Magnetismo espiritual: Toribio Romo sus reliquias y la expansion territorial del culto." *Espaço e Cultura* 37: 195–217. https://www.e-publ icacoes.uerj.br/index.php/espacoecultura/article/view/21944/15898.
Mejía Madrid, Fabrizio. 1999. "Tiempo fuera: El lamento de Malverde." *La Jornada Semanal*, September 26, 1999. http://www.jornada.com.mx/1999/09/26/sem-mejia.html.
Mendoza, Élder. 2010. "Ground Zero in Sinaloa." *New York Times*, October 16, 2010. https://www.nytimes.com/2010/10/17/opinion/17Mendoza.html.
Mendoza, Leo Eduardo. 2002. "Jesús Malverde: El santo bandido." *Generación: Santos Profanos* 14 (46): 22–25.
Mendoza, Vicente T. 1964. *Lírica narrativa de México: El corrido*. Estudios de Folklore 2. Mexico City: Universidad Autónoma de Mexico, Instituto de Investigaciones Estéticas.
Metcalfe, David, and Andrew Chesnut. 2015. "San Padrino Endoque: First Saint of Santa Muerte." www.skeletonsaint.com.
Meyer, Jean A. 1976. *The Cristero Rebellion: The Mexican People Between Church and State, 1926–1929*. Translated by Richard Southern. New York: Cambridge University Press.
Meyer, Jean A. 2005. *La Cristiada*, vol. I, *El conflicto entre la Iglesia y el estado 1926–1929*. Coyoacán, DF: Siglo Veintiuno Editores.
Meyer, Jean A. 2013. *La Cristiada*, vol. II, *Los Cristeros*. Coyoacán, DF: Siglo Veintiuno Editores.
Mignolo, Walter. 2000. *Local Histories/Global Designs: Coloniality, Subaltern Knowledges, and Border Thinking*. Princeton, NJ: Princeton University Press.
"Migrantes reportan supuestas apariciones de San Toribio en Sonora." 2012. *Excelsior* (Mexico), May 12, 2012. http://www.excelsior.com.mx/2012/05/12/nacional/833534.

Mikkel Bille, Frida Hastrup, and Tim Flohr Soerensen. 2010. *An Anthropology of Absence: Materializations of Transcendence and Loss*. New York: Springer.

Miller, Vincent J. 2012. *Consuming Religion: Christian Faith and Practice in a Consumer Culture*. New York: Bloomsbury Academic.

Millhiser, Ian. 2020. "Texas Pastors Demand a 'Religious Liberty' Exemption to Coronavirus Stay-at-Home Order." *Vox*, April 1, 2020. https://www.vox.com/2020/4/1/21201104/texas-pastors-religious-liberty-coronavirus-stay-at-home-hotze.

Miret, Juan. 2013. "Only Shrine in U.S. Dedicated to Patron Saint of Immigrants Lies in the Heart of Anti-Immigrant Territory." *Latina Lista*, June 3, 2013. http://latinalista.com/culture-2/only-shrine-in-u-s-dedicated-to-patron-saint-of-immigrants-lies-in-the-heart-of-anti-immigrant-territory.

Meza Jara, Leonardo. 2016. "Otra vez la confrontación entre las posturas divergentes de la crítica literaria en México: Yépez versus Domínguez Michael." *Holo-gramático* (blog), June 20, 2016. http://holo-gramatico.blogspot.com/2016/06/otra-vez-la-confrontacion-entre-las.html.

"Morales Muerto a balazos." 1938. *La Opinion* (Los Angeles), February 16, 1938.

Morales Tamborrel, Antonio. 1952. "Había Muerto un inocente clamando Justicia." *El Imparcial*, August 1952. Special edition, n.p.

"Mueren mas inocentes pidiendo justicia." 1938. *El Chiquito* (Tijuana, BC), February 14, 1938.

"Murders of Transgender People in 2020 Surpasses Total for Last Year in Just Seven Months." 2020. The National Center for Transgender Equality (NCTE). August 7, 2020. https://transequality.org/blog/murders-of-transgender-people-in-2020-surpasses-total-for-last-year-in-just-seven-months.

Murphy, James. 2007. *The Martyrdom of Saint Toribio Romo: Patron of Immigrants*. Liguori, MO: Liguori Publications.

Murphy, James. 2019. *Saints and Sinners in the Cristero War: Stories of Martyrdom from Mexico*. San Francisco: Ignatius Press.

Murphy, Kate. 2008. "Mexican Robin Hood Figure Gains a Kind of Notoriety in U.S." *New York Times*, February 8, 2008. https://www.nytimes.com/2008/02/08/us/08narcosaint.html.

"Narcos no quesieron a Columba como Malverde por creerlo gay." 2021. *Municipios Puebla*, March 2, 2021. https://municipiospuebla.mx/nota/2021-03-02/virales/narcos-no-quisieron-colunga-como-malverde-por-creerlo-gay.

Nevins, Joseph. 2002. *Operation Gatekeeper: The Rise of the Illegal Alien and the Making of the U.S.-Mexico Boundary*. New York: Routledge.

Nixon, Rob. 2013. *Slow Violence and the Environmentalism of the Poor*. Cambridge, MA: Harvard University Press.

"No Della Chiesa a Contiguità Religione-Clan." 2017. *Il Giorniale di Calabria*, September 7, 2017. http://www.giornaledicalabria.it/?p=76767.

"'No lo querían porque era gay,' La supuesta AMENAZA a Fernando Colunga que lo hizo dejar 'Malverde.'" 2021. *Gluc*, March 3, 2021. https://gluc.mx/entretenimiento/2021/3/3/no-lo-querian-porque-era-gay-la-supuesta-amenaza-fernando-colunga-que-lo-hizo-dejar-malverde-33002.html.

Noe-Bustamente, Luis, Mark Hugo Lopez, and Jens Manuel Krogstad. 2020. "U.S. Hispanic Population Surpassed 60 Million in 2019, but Growth Has Slowed." Pew Research Center, July 7, 2020. https://www.pewresearch.org/fact-tank/2020/07/07/u-s-hispanic-population-surpassed-60-million-in-2019-but-growth-has-slowed/.

"Novias y feminismo en Sinaloa." 2018. *Teléfono Rojo*, December 23, 2018. https://telefonorojo.mx/novias-y-feminismo-en-sinaloa/.
OECD. 2019. "Internet Access." Organization for Economic Co-operation and Development. https://data.oecd.org/ict/internet-access.htm.
O'Loughlin, Michael. 2019. "Plague: Untold Stories of AIDS and the Catholic Church." *America: The Jesuit Review*, December 1, 2019. https://www.americamagazine.org/plague.
Olson, David. 2014. "Rancho Cucamonga: Relic of Immigrant-Protector Saint Brings Out Faithful." *Press-Enterprise* (Riverside, CA), July 16, 2014. https://www.pe.com/2014/07/16/rancho-cucamonga-relic-of-immigrant-protector-saint-brings-out-faithful.
"Oracion de Santo Toribio Romo, patron de los Immigrantes." 2006. *The Catholic Advance* (Wichita, KS), February 24, 2006, 8.
Orozco, José Francisco. 1920. "Contra la emigración." *La Época*, September 12, 1920.
Orsi, Robert Anthony. 1985. *The Madonna of 115th Street: Faith and Community in Italian Harlen, 1880–1950*. New Haven, CT: Yale University Press.
Ortega Noriega, Sergio. 1999. *Breve historia de Sinaloa*. Mexico City: Fideicomiso Historia de la Américas.
Ortiz, Alex. 2016. "A Vote of Faith: Converting Latinos to Registered Voters." *Medill Reports Chicago*, October 11, 2016. http://news.medill.northwestern.edu/chicago/a-vote-of-faith-converting-latinos-to-registered-voters/.
Palomar Verea, Cristina. 2005. *El orden discursivo de género en los Altos de Jalisco*. Guadalajara, JA: CUCSH-UdeG.
Paredes, Américo. 1982. "Folklore, Lo Mexicano, and Proverbs." *Aztlán* 13: 1–11.
Partida Tayzan, Armando. 2011. "Malverde: De santo familiar a protector de narcotraficantes." *Latin American Theater Review* 44 (2): 39–53.
Pasaporte:Mártires Cristeros. n.d. Secretaría de Turismo del Estado de Jalisco. Los Altos de Jalisco, Mexico.
Passel, Jeffrey, D'Vera Cohn, and Ana Gonzalez-Barrera. 2012. "Net Migration from Mexico Falls to Zero—and Perhaps Less." Pew Research Center/Pew Hispanic Center.
Paulas, Rick. 2014. "Our Lady of the Holy Death Is the World's Fastest Growing Religious Movement." *Vice*, November 13, 2014. http://www.vice.com/read/our-lady-of-the-holy-death-is-the-worlds-fastest-growing-religious-movement-456.
Pedraza, Silvia. 2007. *Political Disaffection in Cuba's Revolution and Exodus*. New York: Cambridge University Press.
Perdigón Castañeda, Katia. 2008. *La Santa Muerte, protectora de los hombres*. Mexico City: Instituto Nacional de Antropología e Historia.
Pérez, Emma E. 1999. *The Decolonial Imaginary: Writing Chicanas into History*. Bloomington: Indiana University Press.
Pérez, Emma E. 2007. "Queering the Borderlands: The Challenges of Excavating the Invisible and Unheard." In *Gender on the Borderlands: The Frontiers Reader*, edited by Antonia Castañeda, Susan H. Armitage, Patricia Hart, and Karen Weathermon, 122–31. Lincoln: University of Nebraska Press.
Pérez López, Francisco Jesús, Jorge Verdugo Quintero, Francisco Padilla Beltrán, and Ronaldo González Valdés. 1997. "Época Moderna." In *Historia de Sinaloa*, vol. 2, edited by Jorge Verdugo Quintero, 244–56. Culiacán, SI: Gobierno del Estado de Sinaloa, Colegio de Bachillers del Estado de Sinaloa.
"*Persona humana*: Declaration on Certain Questions Concerning Sexual Ethics." 1975. Sacred Congregation for the Doctrine of the Faith, Vatican City, December 29, 1975.

http://www.vatican.va/roman_curia/congregations/cfaith/documents/rc_con_cfaith_doc_19751229_persona-humana_en.html.

Piñera Ramírez, David, and Jesús Ortiz Figueroa. 1989. *Historia de Tijuana: Edición Conmemorative del Centenario de su Fundación, 1889–1989*. Ensenada, BC: UABC.

Portelli, Allessandro. 1991. *The Death of Luigi Transtulli and Other Stories: Form and Meaning in Oral History*. Albany: State University of New York Press.

Potter, Gary. 2006. "Valor and Betrayal—The Historical Background and Story of the Cristeros." *Catholicism.org*, January 30, 2006. https://catholicism.org/valor-betrayal-cristeros.html.

Pratt, Mary Louise. 1991. "Arts of the Contact Zone." *Profession* (1991): 33–40.

Preidt, Robert. 2021. "Transgender People Face Twice the Odds for Early Death: Study." *U.S.News and World Report*, September 3, 2021. https://www.usnews.com/news/health-news/articles/2021-09-03/transgender-people-face-twice-the-odds-for-early-death-study.

Price, Patricia L. 2004. *Dry Place: Landscapes of Belonging and Exclusion*. Minneapolis: University of Minnesota Press.

Price, Patricia L. 2005. "Of Bandits and Saints: Jesús Malverde and the Struggle for Place in Sinaloa, Mexico." *Cultural Geographies* 12 (2): 175–97.

Quijano, Martin George. 2010. "Oficiante del Culto de La Santa Muerte." In *La Santa Muerte: Historia, Realidad y Mito de la Niña Blanca*. Mexico City: Editorial Porrúa.

Quinones, Sam. 2001. *True Tales from Another Mexico: The Lynch Mob, the Popsicle Kings, Chalino, and the Bronx*. Albuquerque: University of New Mexico Press.

Ramírez, Marla A. 2018. "The Making of Mexican Illegality: Immigration Exclusions Based on Race, Class Status, and Gender." *New Political Science* 40 (2): 317–35.

"Reaparece 'la novia de Culiacán.'" 2015. *RíoDoce*, December 27, 2015. https://riodoce.mx/2015/12/27/reaparece-la-novia-de-culiacan/.

Reaves, Joseph A., and Kelly Ettenborough. 2003. "An 'Arizona Republic' Analysis Examines the Histories of Sexual Abuse and Harassment in the Phoenix: Diocese Priests with Troubled Pasts." *Arizona Republic*, May 4, 2003.

Rebolledo, Efrén. 2002. "Santa Olguita." *Generación: Santos Profanos* 14 (46): 31.

Reguillo, Rossana. 2004. "The Oracle in the City: Beliefs, Practices, and Symbolic Geographies." *Social Text* 22 (4): 35–46.

Rivera, José Gabriel, and José Saldaña Rico. 2000. "Religiosidad popular en Tijuana: El culto de Juan Soldado." *Calafia: Revista de la Universidad Autónoma de Baja California* 10 (5): 14–24. http://iih.tij.uabc.mx/iihDigital/Calafia/Contenido/Vol-X/Numer05/Religiosidadpopularenlafrontera.htm.

Robinson, Amy. 2009. "Mexican Banditry and Discourses of Class: The Case of Chucho el Roto." *Latin American Research Review* 44 (1): 5–31.

Rodríguez, Brenda. 2016. "Lupita, la Novia de Culiacán, saludó al Santo Padre." *Proyecto 3*, February 16, 2016. https://proyecto3.mx/2016/02/lupita-la-novia-de-culiacan-saludo-al-santo-padre/.

Rodriguez, Jeanette. 1994. *Our Lady of Guadalupe: Faith and Empowerment Among Mexican-American Women*. Austin: University of Texas Press.

Rodriguez, M. 2021 "Narcos habrían amenazado a Fernando Colunga para abandonar el papel de Malverde por rumores de que es gay." *El Salvador*, March 3, 2021. https://www.elsalvador.com/entretenimiento/espectaculos/fernando-colunga-amenazas-narcos-malverde/812646/2021/

Romero Gil, Juan Manuel. 2001. *La minería en el noroeste de Mexico: Utopía y realidad 1850–1910*. Mexico City: Plaza y Valdés.
Romo, David. 2010. "My Tío, the Saint." *Texas Monthly*, November 2010. https://www.texasmonthly.com/articles/my-tio-the-saint/.
Romo, Toribio. 1920. *¡Vamos p'al norte!* Archive of the Archdiocese of Guadalajara.
Romo G. F., Román. 2000. *Saint Toribio Romo: The Extraordinary Life of an Ordinary Man*. Jalisco: Diocese of San Juan de los Lagos.
Roque Ramirez, Horacio N. 2005. "Claiming Queer Cultural Citizenship: Gay Latino (Im)Migrant Acts in San Francisco." In *Queer Migrations: Sexuality, U.S. Citizenship, and Border Crossings*, edited by Eithne Luibhéid and Lionel Cantu Jr., 161–88. Minneapolis: University of Minnesota Press.
Rosin, Hanna. 1999. "Vatican Intervenes Against Gay Ministry." *Washington Post*, July 14, 1999. http://www.washingtonpost.com/wp-srv/national/daily/july99/ministry14.htm?noredirect=on.
Rosko, Zora. 2018. "Heriberto Yépez Is a Forceful Antipoet, a Technician of the Boundaries, a Split-Form Border Zone Nagualist." *Zora Rosko Vacuum Player* (blog), January 5, 2018. https://zorosko.blogspot.com/2018/01/heriberto-yepez-is-forceful-antipoet.html.
Rubio, Alexis. 2016a. "'Hay que hacer del mito de la novia de Culiacán un acto artístico': María Romero." *Espejo*, December 20, 2016. https://revistaespejo.com/2016/12/20/hay-que-hacer-del-mito-de-la-novia-de-culiacan-un-acto-artistico-maria-romero/.
Rubio, Alexis. 2016b. "El mundo entero . . . un nuevo recorrido para 'La Novia de Culiacán.'" *Espejo*, December 21, 2016. http://revistaespejo.com/2016/12/el-mundo-entero-un-nuevo-recorrido-para-la-novia-de-culiacan/.
Sada, Daniel. 2001. "Cada piedra es un deseo." *Guaraguao* (Asociacion Centro de Estudios y Cooperacion para American Latina) 5 (13): 90–100.
Saldívar, José David. 1997. *Border Matters: Remapping American Cultural Studies*. Berkeley: University of California Press.
Saldívar, Ramón. 2006. *The Borderlands of Culture: Américo Paredes and the Transnational Imaginary*. Durham, NC: Duke University Press.
Sanchez, Mateo. 2005. "The Meanings of Mexican Immigrant Devotion to Santo Toribio Romo, Patron Saint of Immigrants." Master's thesis, Claremont University.
Sanchez, Nelly. 2018. "Ilustra y anima María Romero a la Novia de Culiacán." *Noreste*, May 5, 2018. https://www.noroeste.com.mx/publicaciones/view/ilustra-y-anima-mara-romero-a-la-novia-de-culiacn-1128916.
Sanders, Sam. 2014. "Relics of the Patron Saint of Immigrants Take a Pilgrimage." *All Things Considered*, NPR, July 14, 2014. https://www.npr.org/sections/codeswitch/2014/07/14/330663328/relics-of-the-patron-saint-of-immigrants-take-a-pilgrimage.
"Santo que no es conocido, no es venerado." 2012. *El Informador*, July 15, 2012. https://www.informador.mx/Suplementos/Santo-que-no-es-conocido-no-es-venerado-20120715-0174.html.
"Santo Toribio Romo, Patron de los Migrantes." 2008. *The Catholic Advance* (Wichita, KS), November 21, 2008, 7.
Sarano, Sergio. 2018. "A Counter Interview with Heriberto Yépez." *Asymptote*, January 4, 2018. https://www.asymptotejournal.com/blog/2018/01/04/a-counterinterview-with-heriberto-yepez.

Saul, Emily. 2018. "El Chapo's Lawyers Are Literally Praying for an Acquittal." *New York Post*, November 20, 2018. https://nypost.com/2018/11/20/el-chapos-lawyers-are-litera lly-praying-for-an-acquittal/.

Scott, James C. 1990. *Domination and the Arts of Resistance: Hidden Transcripts*. New Haven, CT: Yale University Press.

Serazio, Michael. 2013. *Your Ad Here: The Cool Sell of Guerrilla Marketing*. New York: New York University Press.

"Severas medidas tomadas." 1938. *La Opinion* (Los Angeles), February 17, 1938, 1.

Sheridan, Thomas S. 1986. *Los Tucsoneneses: The Mexican Community in Tucson, 1854–1941*. Tucson: University of Arizona Press.

Simón, Alfredo. 2018. "Teologia della beatificazione e della canonizzazione." In *Le Cause dei Santi*, edited by Vincenzo Criscuolo, Carmelo Pellegrino, and Robert J. Sarno, 143–64. Rome: Libreria Editrice Vaticana.

Silva Hernández, Aída. 1991. "La historia de Juan Soldado, ese del panteón." *Zeta*, July 5–11, 1991, 1889–989.

Spagat, Elliot. 2005. "Border Patrol Follows Migrants to Mountain Area Near San Diego." *The Daily Spectrum* (Saint George, UT), November 20, 2005, A11.

"Spiritual Passport: United States of America." n.d. Nido del Pajaro Macua, Salud Dinero y Amor LLC. Accessed October 12, 2018. https://www.pajaromacua.com/spiritual-passport/ and www.exitoyamor.com.

Staff, Harriet. 2014. "The Writing Project That Was Heriberto Yépez." Poetry Foundation, September 19, 2014. https://www.poetryfoundation.org/harriet/2014/09/the-writing-project-that-was-heriberto-yepez.

Suro, Roberto. 2005. "V. States of Origin in Mexico." Hispanic Trends, Pew Research Center, March 14, 2005. http://www.pewhispanic.org/2005/03/14/v-states-of-origin-in-mexico/.

Tejeda, Gregory. 2010. "St. Mary's Gains Religious Relic for Immigration Center: Mexican Priests Bring the Relic of St. Toribio." *Northwest Indiana Times*, August 4, 2010. https://www.nwitimes.com/news/foreign-language/st-mary-s-gains-religious-relic-for-immi gration-center/article_ee1b0094-bdd8-5a66-84bc-0cf152b7e072.html.

The Associated Press. 2019. "In Mexico, Controversy over Effeminate Emiliano Zapata Painting." *NBC News*, December 11, 2019. https://www.nbcnews.com/feature/nbc-out/mexico-controversy-over-effeminate-emiliano-zapata-painting-n1099756.

Thompson, Ginger. 2002. "A Saint Who Guides Migrants to a Promised Land." *New York Times*, August 14, 2002. https://www.nytimes.com/2002/08/14/world/santa-ana-de-guadalupe-journal-a-saint-who-guides-migrants-to-a-promised-land.html.

Toor, Frances. 1947. *Treasury of Mexican Folkways*. New York: Crown Publishers.

"Troops Slay Three in Tijuana Riot; Guns Guard Girl Killer from Lynch Mob. Enraged Crowd Sets Jail and City Hall Afire." 1938. *Los Angeles Times*, February 16, 1938.

Trujillo Muñoz, Gabriel. 2002. "Juan Soldado: En olor a santidad." *Generación: Santos Profanos* 14 (46): 32–33.

Tuckman, Jo. "Mexican 'Saint Death' Cult Members Protest at Destruction of Shrines." *The Guardian*, April 10, 2009. https://www.theguardian.com/world/2009/apr/10/santa-muerte-cult-mexico.

Tuzin, Donald. 1984. "Miraculous Voices: The Auditory Experience of Numinous Objects." *Current Anthropology* 25 (5): 579–96.

Valenzuela Arce, José Manuel. 2000. "Por los milagros recibidos: Religiosidad popular a través del culto a Juan Soldado." In *Entre la magia y la historia: Tradiciones, mitos y leyendas de la frontera*, edited by José Manuel Valenzuela Arce, 93–106. Tijuana, BC: Programa Cultural de las Fronteras, El Colegio de la Frontera Norte.

Vanderwood, Paul J. 2004. *Juan Soldado: Rapist, Murderer, Martyr, Saint*. Durham: Duke University Press.

Vargas, Deborah R., Nancy Raquel Mirabal, and Lawrence La Fountain-Stokes. 2017. *Keywords for Latina/o Studies*. New York: New York University Press.

Vásquez, Manuel A., and Marie Friedmann Marquardt. 2003. *Globalizing the Sacred: Religion Across the Americas*. New Brunswick, NJ: Rutgers University Press.

"Vatican Declares Mexican Death Saint Blasphemous." 2013. *BBC News*, May 9, 2013. http://www.bbc.com/news/world-latin-america-22462181.

Volokh, Eugene. 2014. "Narco-Saints and Expert Evidence." *Washington Post*, July 8, 2014. https://www.washingtonpost.com/news/volokh-conspiracy/wp/2014/07/08/narco-saints-and-expert-evidence/.

Vonk, Levi. 2016. "Big in Mexico: The Migrants' Saint." *The Atlantic*, June 2016.

Walker, Clarence. 2015. "Praying to a Saint Is Evidence You're a Criminal? That's the Insanity of the Drug War for You." *Alternet*, July 22, 2015. https://www.alternet.org/drugs/santa-muerte-goes-court-curious-case-narco-saint-prayer.

Walker, Clarence. 2015. "Santa Muerte Goes to Court: The Curious Case of the Narco Saint's Prayer." *Stop the Drug War*, July 21, 2015. http://stopthedrugwar.org/chronicle/2015/jul/21/santa_muerte_goes_court_curious.

Walsh Sanderson, Susan R. 1984. *Land Reform in Mexico: 1910–1980*. Orlando, FL: Academic Press.

Wareham, Jamie. 2021. "375 Transgender People Murdered In 2021—'Deadliest Year' Since Records Began." *Forbes*, November 11, 2021. https://www.forbes.com/sites/jamiewareham/2021/11/11/375-transgender-people-murdered-in-2021-deadliest-year-since-records-began/?sh=292f895e321c.

Watson, Julie. 2001. "Residents Along U.S.–Mexican Border Find Strength in Local Folk Saints." *Miami Herald*, December 16, 2001.

Weland, Gary. 2014. "Rifleys—Father and Son." *AZ Capitol Times*, February 17, 2014. https://azcapitoltimes.com/news/2014/02/17/rifleys-father-and-son/.

Williams, Juliet. 2005. "Heart of Sacramento Diocese Set to Reopen." *The Signal*, November 18, 2005, A4.

Woodruff, Judy, and Ray Suarez. 2011. "Catholic Church Looks to Lead Conversation on Combating HIV/AIDS." *PBS NewsHour*, May 27, 2011. https://www.pbs.org/newshour/show/vatican-looks-to-lead-conversation-on-combating-hiv-aids#transcript.

Woodward, Kenneth L. 1996. *Making Saints: How the Catholic Church Determines Who Becomes a Saint, Who Doesn't, and Why*. New York: Touchstone.

Yépez, Heriberto. 2002. "Mito, culto y arte urbano (Soldado, pedófilo y asesino convirtíose en santo)." *Generación: Santos Profanos* 14 (46): 28–31.

Yépez, Heriberto. 2006. *Tijuanologías*. Mexicali, BC: Universidad Autónoma de Baja California.

Yllescas Illescas, Jorge A. 2016. "La Santa Muerte, ¿Un culto en consolidación?" In *La Santa Muerte: Espacios, cultos y devociones*, edited by Alberto Hernández Hernández, 65–84. Tijuana, BC: El Colegio de la Frontera Norte and El Colegio de San Luis Potosí.

Yllescas Illescas, Jorge A. 2018. *Ver, oir y callar: Creer en la Santa Muerte durante el encierro*. Mexico City: Universidad Nacional Autónoma de México.

Young, Julia G. 2015a. "Smuggling for Christ the King." *OUPblog*, Oxford University Press, July 23, 2015. https://blog.oup.com/2015/07/mexican-catholics-cristero-war/.

Young, Julia G. 2015b. *Mexican Exodus: Emigrants, Exiles, and Refugees of the Cristero Wars*. New York: Oxford University Press.

Young, Julia G. 2017. "Mexican Migration History in the Era of Border Walls." *Perspectives on History*, May 15, 2017. https://www.historians.org/publications-and-directories/perspectives-on-history/may-2017/mexican-migration-history-in-the-era-of-border-walls.

Zorrilla, Mónica Marie. 2021. "Behind the Scenes on 'Malverde: El Santo Patrón,' Telemundo's Most Ambitious Project to Date," *Variety*, July 7–22, 2021. https://variety.com/2021/tv/news/malverde-el-santo-patron-telemundos-1235025419/.

Index

For the benefit of digital users, indexed terms that span two pages (e.g., 52–53) may, on occasion, appear on only one of those pages.

Figures are indicated by *f* following the page number

2008 economic recession, 131

activism, 26, 78, 147, 203, 271–72
  immigration, 204
  and religion, 2
  spiritual, 20, 22
Acutis, Carlos, 30
Adventists, 22–23
Africa, 19–20, 201, 236, 310n.50
Afro-Latinos, 200–1
agency, 153, 197–98, 230, 237, 259–60, 275–76, 285
  gendered, 52–53
Agnes of Bohemia, 159
agraristas, 110–12, 114–15, 154, 164–66, 169–70, 212–13
Agua Caliente Casino, 109, 111, 113–14
Aguascalientes, Mexico, 164
  See also Bajío, Mexico
Aguilar, Luisa Fernanda Raquel, 265–66
Aguilar, Rita, 159
Aguilar Ros, Alejandra, 160–61, 182, 183, 189, 207–9
Aguirre y Ramos, Agustín, 271–72
Alba Roja, 111
Albouy, Edward, 314n.12
Almonte, Robert, 221, 222, 308–9n.15
altars, 8, 18–19, 26, 271, 276
  for Jesús Malverde, 44f, 74–76
  for Juan Soldado, 126–27
  for La Santa Muerte, 217, 228f, 230–31, 231f, 238, 239, 241, 242, 248, 251–52, 257–61, 262, 264, 268–69, 311n.77
  for Toribio Romo, 2–3, 181, 198, 207–9, 208f
  virtual, 248

alteño culture, 171, 173, 179, 182–85, 200–1
Amaral, Martín, 39
Amaya, Rafael, 32–33
American studies, 14
A.M.P., 128–29
Anglos, 19–20, 196, 206, 270–71, 314n.12
Anthony, Saint, 134, 257
anthropology, 160–61, 207–9, 217, 237
anthropomorphism, 206–7, 259–60
Antonio, Marco, 119–20
Anzaldúa, Gloria, 13, 17–18, 19–20, 92, 274–75
Araújo, Vera, 1–2
Archdiocese of Chicago, 158
Archdiocese of Detroit, 196
Archdiocese of Mexico City, 223–24
Archivo histórico general del estado de Sinaloa, 34–35
Argentina, 11–12, 22–23, 290n.27, 310n.50
Arizona, USA, 12, 64, 274, 290n.25, 297nn.14–15
  Flagstaff, 314n.13
  Maricopa County, 2, 92–93, 274
  Phoenix, 2–3, 239–40, 270–74, 314n.11, 314n.13, 314n.20
  Pima County, 92–93
  Tucson, 270–71, 314n.11
Arizona Republic, 160, 273, 274
Arizona Senate, 2
Arpaio, Joe, 2, 92–93, 274, 297n.14, 314n.18, 314n.20
Arreola sisters (Melisa and Mónica), 149–52
Arriola, Elvia, 145

334 INDEX

Associated Press, 222
Athletica, 176–77
Aztecs, 19–20, 125, 228, 233, 239

Bachomo, Felipe, 35
Bada, Xochitl, 190, 191–92
Baja California, Mexico, 64, 113, 122, 142–43, 154
   El Rosario, 110–11, 114–15
   Ensenada, 110–11, 113–15
   Mexicali, 87, 110–11, 113–15, 180–81
   Rosarito, 132, 216–17
   Tecate, 110–11
   See also Tijuana, Baja California, Mexico
Bajío, Mexico, 164
Balarezo, Ángel Eduardo, 33–34
bandits, 46, 52–54, 59, 61, 67, 73–74, 81–83
   generous bandit figure, 9–10, 35–36, 47–48, 50, 70–72
Barenque Jarquín, Marco, 79
Barthes, Roland, 15–16
Basilica of Our Lady of San Juan of Los Lagos, 188
Batista, Elena, 28–29
beatification, 25–26, 27
   versus canonization, 304n.47
   of Carlos Acutis, 30
   definition, 25
   of Juan Soldado, 91–92
   of Toribio Romo, 170–72, 177–79, 180, 186, 190–91, 303n.26
Beethoven
   Fifth Symphony, 179
Benedict, Pope, 314n.20
Benzing, Novatus, 271–72
Bernal, Heraclio, 35
Bernardo, San, 233–34
Bible, 172, 231–32, 253
Bible Belt, 203
Bilinkoff, Jodi, 12
Black Legend, 142, 301n.111
Boston College
   School of Theology and Ministry, 5–6
Bowden, Charles, 216
Bracero Program (1942–64), 145
branding, 69–70, 193, 238, 300n.77

Brewer, Jan, 2, 274
Brooks, Virginia, 301n.118
Buendía Gaytán, Jesús, 180–81
burial/grave sites, 125
   of Jesús Malverde, 55–58, 59, 62, 98
   of Juan Castillo Morales, 93–96, 94*f*, 95*f*, 97–104, 99*f*, 118–21, 128
   of Olga Camacho, 10, 93–98, 94*f*, 95*f*, 103–4, 147–48
   of Toribio Romo, 170
   See also cemeteries

Calderón, Alfonso G., 57, 59
California, USA, 115, 117, 143–44, 145–46, 176, 180–81, 190–91, 203, 217–19
   Commerce, 210–11
   East Los Angeles, 211
   Indio, 210
   Lake Forest, 210
   Los Angeles, 33, 74–76, 107–8, 125, 129–30, 210, 216–17
   Rancho Cucamonga, 210–11
   San Clemente, 199
   San Diego (city), 86, 105, 106–7, 114, 121, 129–30, 140–41, 143, 199, 247, 300n.98, 301n.118
   San Diego County, 144
   Santa Ana, 247
   San Ysidro, 199
Calles, Plutarco Elías, 162–65, 166
Caloca Cortés, Agustín, 174
Calvillo, Jonathan E., 2
Camacho, Lili, 88, 297n.6
Camacho, Olga, 86, 87*f*, 276, 297n.6, 298n.37
   erasure of, 86, 91, 98, 101, 116–17, 122–25, 127, 136, 138–40, 141–44, 146, 148–49, 153, 155
   grave, 10, 92, 93–98, 94*f*, 95*f*, 148
   racialization of, 67
   rape and murder of, 10, 86–92, 101, 103–9, 110–13, 114–15, 116–18, 120, 121, 123–24, 127, 137–46, 151, 153–55, 164, 297n.24
   veneration of, 9, 10, 144, 146, 147–53
   See also Olguita, Santa
Camacho León, Aurelio, 88, 109, 111, 112, 113

Camp Kearny Mesa, 301n.118
Canada, 3–4, 188
Cañedo, Francisco, 49–52, 53–55, 59, 67
canonization, 6–7, 27, 28, 137, 168, 170, 180, 251–52, 275, 291n.73
  versus beatification, 304n.45
  of Jesús Malverde, 37
  of Juan Soldado, 10, 86, 90, 116, 124, 139–40
  of Junípero Serra, 143–44
  of Maria Goretti, 137
  of Mother Teresa, 291n.70
  process, 23–26
  of Toribio Romo, 2–3, 9, 11, 26, 160–62, 164, 166–67, 168, 170–71, 173–75, 183–84, 190–91, 209–10, 212–13, 290n.26, 303n.29
Cantú, Norma E., 20
capitalism, 48–49, 50, 152–53
  gendered, 52–53, 125, 139, 145–46, 154–55
  and Jesús Malverde, 45, 54–55, 69, 70–72, 81–83
  and La Santa Muerte, 224, 231–32
  late, 69, 224, 231–32, 277–78
  narco-, 9–10, 35–36, 70–72, 81–83
  and religion, 5, 7–8, 282
  See also maquiladoras; neoliberalism
Cárdenas, Lázaro, 87–88, 108, 109, 110–11, 112, 115, 118
Carillo Fuentes, Amado, 32–33
Carvajal, Mario A., 109, 112, 113
Casa de Guanajuato, 203–4
casinos, 109, 111–15, 151–52, 153, 154, 299n.67
Castañeda, Antonia, 143–44
Castañeda-Liles, María del Socorro, 7, 137
Castillo Morales, Juan, 87*f*
  execution, 10, 88–90, 96–97, 100, 101–3, 102*f*, 104, 108–81
  grave, 92, 93–96, 94*f*, 95*f*, 97–104, 99*f*, 118–21, 128
  rape and murder of Olga Camacho, 86, 88–90, 91–92, 97, 101, 103–5, 106–8, 109, 110, 112–13, 116–17, 122–23, 127, 136–55, 279–80, 297n.24, 297n.26

  veneration of, 90–92, 96, 97, 99–101, 116–36, 138, 139–40, 144, 162–63, 186
  See also Soldado, Juan (Juan the Soldier)
Castor, N. Fadeke, 4
Cathedral of Our Lady of the Angels, 210
caudillos, 9–10, 52–53, 54, 81–83, 290n.24
Cecilia, Saint, 25
cemeteries, 60, 93–104, 107–8, 118–21, 128, 140–41, 170
  Panteón Municipal no. 1, 93, 94*f*, 95–96, 97–104, 99*f*, 102*f*, 107–8
  Panteón Municipal no. 2, 93, 94*f*, 95–97, 95*f*
  See also burial/grave sites; Panteón Municipal no. 1; Panteón Municipal no. 2
cempaúchil, 98
Central America, 86, 243–44, 313n.156
  Northern Triangle, 210–11
Chaplin, Charlie, 109
Charbel, San, 44*f*
Chávez, Arsenio, 221
Chavez, Cesar, 289n.5
Chávez, Jorge Elías, 304n.34
Chesnut, R. Andrew, 71, 227–28, 261–62, 309n.35, 310n.49, 311n.85
Chicago Tribune, 160
Chicana/o studies, 12–13, 14
Chihuahua, Mexico
  Ciudad Juárez, 10, 138, 139, 145–46, 152
Chinese immigrants, 53–54, 294n.39
Chisme en vivo, 80–81
Chivas, 176–77
Christianity, 15–16, 120, 168, 199, 202–3, 273, 292n.86
  burial practices, 49–50, 63–64
  and colonialism, 7–8, 12–13, 233–34
  demographics of, 5–6
  Evangelical, 5–6, 273
  and immigration, 13, 136
  and La Santa Muerte, 217, 226–27, 233–34, 253, 254, 255–56
  martyrdom in, 291n.73
  and national identity, 8, 18, 234
  racialized, 68–69, 270
  role of saints in, 23, 27

Circulo Espiritual Nacional e Internacional de La Santa Muerte, 225–26
citizenship, 5, 12, 93, 159, 188, 195, 210, 280
  cultural, 93
  naturalization, 185–86
  and passports, 193–95
  path to, 210–11
  racialized, 210
  religious, 18, 195
Claretians, 271
clubes de oriundos (HTAs), 190–93, 203–4
Coacalco, Mexico State, Mexico, 246–47
Coatlicue, 125
Cold War, 144–45, 224
Colima, Mexico, 164
Collins, Patricia Hill, 14
Colombia, 32–33, 250
colonialism, 12–13, 17–18, 54–55, 125, 139, 145–46, 149–50, 154, 227, 228, 229, 274–75, 310n.39
  and Christianity, 7–8, 12–13, 233–34
  Spanish, 117, 143–44, 226, 233, 236, 301n.111
  See also decoloniality
colonias, 13, 110, 242
  Castillo, 108
  República Mexicana, 246–47
  Ruiz Cortines, 46, 57–59, 60–61
Colorado River Land Company (CRLC), 110–11, 112, 115
Colunga, Fernando, 80–81
community ministry, 197
compadrazcos/comadrazcos, 238
Concha, 106, 141, 297n.26
Confederación de Trabajadores de México (CTM), 109, 111–12, 113, 114–15, 154, 162–63, 299n.56, 303n.20
Confederación Regional Obrera de México (CROM), 107, 109, 111–12, 113–15, 154, 162–63, 164, 298n.39, 303nn.19–20, 303n.20
contact zones, 18
Contenido, 181
Contreas, Robert, 222
Contreras, Manuel J., 105–7, 106n.25, 108, 117–18, 139, 140–41, 298n.37, 298n.42

Corona, Ignacio, 138–39
corridos, 278, 285
  and Jesús Malverde, 35–36, 56, 61–62, 63, 65, 69, 73–74
Costa Ricans, 22–23
COVID-19 pandemic, 80, 249–50
Coyolxauhqui, 125
Creechan, James H., 72
Creoles, 182–83
criollos, 68, 183, 200–1, 229
crisis, 69, 151–52, 175–76, 210–11, 237, 242, 276–77
  housing, 131, 132–33, 301n.105
  See also Tequila Crisis/Mexican Peso Crisis (1994)
Cristero War, 10, 163, 164, 165, 166, 179, 303n.22, 307n.156
  and CROM, 111, 162–63, 164
  and *El Pasaporte*, 188–89, 193
  and ICAM, 162–63, 164, 165–66
  los arreglos (1929), 166, 212–13
  martyrs of, 167n.32
  and Toribio Romo, 11, 160–61, 162, 164, 167, 168–70, 171–72, 173–76, 177–79, 180, 181, 182–84, 189, 196–97, 212–13
cultos, 174–75, 226–27, 237–38, 245, 248
cultural Catholics, 224–25, 284
cultural religiosity, 96
culture jamming, 149
curanderos, 259–60
Curso Social Agrícola Zapopano, 185–86

Dallas Morning News, 160
danza indígena, 217
Davison, Tim, 202, 203–4, 206
death-worlds, 236
decoloniality, 12–13, 285
de la Herrán Garcia, Jorge, 72
de la Madrid, Miguel, 174–75
de la Mora, Sergio, 65–66, 68
de la Torre, Renée, 171–72, 182–83
Delgadillo, Teresa, 19–20
Democratic Party, 202
Departamento Autónomo de Prensa y Publicidad de la Secretaría de Gobernación, 113
deportation, 2, 3–4, 87–88, 129, 159, 163, 222

INDEX   337

Derrida, Jacques, 28–29
Díaz, Porfirio, 7–8, 9–10, 47, 48–49, 50–51, 53, 235–36
Díaz, Raúl, 131
Dieckmann, Ed, 106
digital spiritual movements, 248–51, 268–69
Diocese of Guadalajara, 212–13
Diocese of Phoenix, 5–6, 270, 272, 273, 314n.13, 314n.18, 314n.20
Diocese of San Juan de los Lagos, 3–4, 185–86, 193–94, 303n.29
displacement, 5, 7–8, 18, 22–23, 270–71, 287
  and Jesús Malverde, 39–40, 59, 60–61, 79–80
  and Juan Soldado, 112, 121–22
  and Toribio Romo, 172, 182–83, 187, 195, 211–12
domestic violence, 77–78
Domínguez-Ruvalcaba, Hector, 138, 139
Doña Sebastina, 310n.39
drug cartels, 38–39, 92–93, 182
  and Jesús Malverde, 32–34, 39, 62, 71–73, 80–81
Dyer, Richard, 68

Eastern Orthodox Church, 198–99
ejidos, 58, 182
El Chapo. *See* Guzman Loera, Joaquín (El Chapo)
El devocionario del migrante, 3–5, 193–94
El Día de los Muertos, 120, 227, 229, 233, 235
Elenes, C. Alejandra, 20
Eliade, Mircea, 19, 277–78
El Informador, 176
El Noreste, 39
El Norte, 3–4, 134, 188, 195, 196, 210, 213, 275
El Pasaporte: Mártires Criseros, Los Altos de Jalisco, Mexico, 188–89, 193
El Peregrino, 179–80
El Rey Pascual, 307–8n.1
El Salvador, 210–11
El Santo Niño de Atocha, 44f, 188, 256–57
El Santo Pollero. *See* Toribio Romo, Saint
El señor de los cielos, 32–33
El Sindicato de Empleados de Cantinas, Hoteles y Restaurantes, 111

El Templo Santa Muerte, 216–17, 253
Enlightenment, 163
epistemic religious closet, 12–13
escapularios, 69, 75f, 98, 223f
Esquivel, Manuel, 53–54, 67
Estrella TV, 80–81
ethnography, 128, 237, 239–40
Eucharist, 158
Excelsior, 160
execution
  of Anacleto González Flores, 168
  of Jesús Malverde, 50, 55, 63–64
  of Juan Castillo Morales, 10, 88–90, 96–97, 100, 101–3, 102f, 104, 108–81
exile, 2–3, 5, 21, 96, 204, 284, 287
  sexiles, 235
expatriates, 110, 235, 283
ex-votos, 127, 241

Facebook, 249–50
Fast and Furious program, 92–93
Federici, Silvia, 145–46
Féliz, Adrián, 107–8
femicide, 10, 97, 144–46, 152, 153–54
feminism, 7, 10, 13–14, 74, 90, 91, 124, 125, 149
Fernández, Pedro, 80
Ferrocarril Occidental de México, 48–49
FitzGerald, David, 185–86
Flake, Jeff, 307n.161
Florida, USA, 32–33, 193, 203
Foucault, Michel, 13
Francis, Pope, 78–79, 136, 223–24, 225–26
Franciscan Order of Friars Minor, 271
Franciscans, 137, 143–44, 271
Freemasons, 307n.156
Frontera, 143

Gang of Eight, 210–11
García, Ivonne, 218f, 219
Garcia, Rico, 73
García Gutiérrez, Marco A., 181
Garduño Pulido, Blanca, 127
Gaspar de Alba, Alicia, 138
gay men
  and Emiliano Zapata, 296n.113
  and Jesús Malverde, 36, 76, 80–83
  and La Santa Muerte, 261–64, 265, 266, 267
  See also LGBTQ communities

gender studies, 14
Generation X, 216
genocide, 236
Gercke, Daniel James, 271–72
Gillo, Ioan, 39
Giordani, Igino, 1
Golden Age of Mexican Cinema, 9–10, 65, 68
Gómez Michel, Gerardo, 47
González, Juana, 167
González Flores, Anacleto, 168
González León, Don Eligio, 37–38, 45–46, 62–64, 65, 66–67, 66f, 68–69, 70, 74–76
González Mata, Roberto, 60–61, 62, 70
González Pérez, Gabriel, 171, 176–79, 186, 187–88, 190–91, 305n.73
González Ramírez, Luis Tarcisio, 183–84
González Romo, José, 165
González Sánchez, Jesús Manuel, 37–38, 45–46, 62, 63, 65, 68–69
Goretti, Assunta, 137
Goretti, Saint Maria, 136, 137, 139, 149–50
Goxcon-Chagal, Rafael, 221, 222, 308n.13
Graham, Lindsey, 307n.161
Granjon, Henry, 271–72
graves. *See* burial/grave sites
Graziano, Frank, 13, 27–28, 29
Great Britain, 261–62
  See also United Kingdom
Great Depression, 7–8, 10, 87–88, 91, 110, 115, 153, 236
Griffith, James S., 35, 122, 293n.8
Grim Reaper, 11–12, 227–28, 229, 310n.39
gringos, 71–72, 188, 205
  See also peregringos
Grupo Horma, 79
G.T., Ricardo and Susana, 133–34
Guanajuato, Mexico, 164, 203–4
  San José Iturbide, 261
Guatemala, 210–11, 307–8n.1
Gulf War (first), 130–31
Guzman, Alejandra, 216
Guzmán, Georgina, 138
Guzmán, Manolo, 235
Guzman Loera, Joaquín (El Chapo), 33–34
Guzmán Mundo, Fernando, 171–72, 183–84

haciendas (including "hacendados' as subcategory), 48, 58
  hacendados, 35, 48
Hagan, Jacqueline Maria, 4, 7
Hanchon, Donald F., 196–200, 201
Hardy, Oliver, 109
Hayworth, Rita, 109
Henry, Brad, 202
Hernández, Marie-Theresa, 15–16
Hernández, Roberto D., 92–93
Hernández Hernández, Alberto, 230, 233–34
heteronormativity, 134–35, 285
hierophany, 19
Hipódromo de Agua Caliente, 109
Hirai, Shinji, 190–91
historiography, 14, 93–94, 104–5
Holy Coyote. *See* Toribio Romo, Saint
Holy Death. *See* La Santa Muerte (LSM)
Holy Family Catholic Church, 2
Holy Redeemer Roman Catholic Church, 196–98, 199, 200f
Holy 23, 163, See,
Holy Smuggler. *See* Toribio Romo, Saint
homophobia, 51, 80–83, 185, 266, 277–78
Honduras, 210–11
housing crisis, 131, 132–33, 301n.105
Huelga de los Sentados, 109, 112
Hull, Cordell, 113
hypermasculinity, 50–52, 54, 61–62, 74, 81–83, 143, 283

I-5, 199
I-40, 221
Iglesia Arcangelista México–US, 216–17, 253, 263–64, 313n.133
Iglesia Católica Apostólica Mexicana (ICAM), 162–63, 164, 165–66
Iglesia Católica Tradicional México–Estados Unidos, 261–62, 313n.133
Iglesias Transplantadas, 22–23
Illinois, USA, 11, 203
  Chicago, 18–19, 20–21, 33, 158, 159f, 210
  La Villita (Chicago), 158
Immaculate Heart of Mary, 198–99, 271–72

immigration reform, 11, 158, 162, 191, 210–11
Industrial Revolution, 145–46
Infante, Pedro, 9–10, 65–67, 66f, 68, 69–70, 279–80
injustice, 10, 36, 86, 90, 118, 120, 150, 151, 153–54
institutionalization, 6–7, 47–48, 104, 140–41, 143–44, 151–52, 237–38, 251–52, 259, 268–69
International Monetary Fund, 4–5
invocation, 3, 21, 217, 229
Italy
　Florence, 1
　Nettuno, 136
　Padua, 134
　Rome, 136, 163, 174, 175, 180
　Tuscany, 1–2
　See also Vatican

Jalisco, Mexico, 160, 161, 180, 196, 197–98, 203–4, 210, 211
　Ahuijulo, 165
　Barranca del Agua Caliente, 168, 170
　Colotlan, 174
　Cuquío, 168, 175–76
　Guadalajara, 24, 164, 165, 167–68, 170, 171–72, 173–74, 176–77, 185–87, 212–13, 303n.22
　Jalostotitlán, 167, 180–81, 183–84, 190–91
　Los Altos de Jalisco, 160–61, 164, 167, 168, 171, 173, 177, 179, 182–84, 185, 188–89, 193, 198, 200–1, 213
　San Juan de los Lagos, 3–4, 167–68, 185–86, 193–94, 206–7, 303n.29
　San Miguel el Alto, 176–79
　Santa Ana de Abajo/Santa Ana de Guadalupe, 167
　Santa Ana de Guadalupe, 160, 167, 169–70, 171, 172, 173, 176–79, 178f, 181, 183–84, 185, 186–88, 190–93, 198, 207–9, 208f, 212
　Santa Teresita, 172
　Tequila, 166, 168–70, 169f, 172, 212
　See also Bajío, Mexico
Jameson, Fredric, 69
J.C.M., Germán, 131

Jesus Christ, 23, 175–76, 195, 223–24, 274–75, 287
　and Jesús Malverde, 35, 42, 44, 68–69, 131
　and Juan Soldado, 101–3
　and La Santa Muerte, 223–24, 225–26, 231–32, 233–34, 253, 255–56
　Resurrection, 223–24, 233–34, 255–56
　Sacred Heart, 97–98
　and Toribio Romo, 158, 164, 196–97
Jesús Malverde Chapel, 9–10, 33–34, 37–46, 40f, 44f, 55–58, 59–60, 93–94, 96, 99–100
John, Saint, 256–57
John Paul II, Pope, 24, 25–26, 160, 179–80, 209, 290n.26
Jones, Ashton, 270
Juarez, Benito, 163
Juárez Cartel, 32–33
Jude, Saint, 42, 239–40, 252, 256–57
Judeo-Christian religions, 226, 233–34, 253, 268
justice, 211, 280, 282, 291n.72, 300n.78
　labor, 112–13
　and La Santa Muerte, 228
　for Olga Camacho, 90, 106–7, 113, 147, 149, 153–54
　social, 20, 167–68
　See also injustice

Kanter, Deborah E., 20–21
King, Martin Luther, Jr., 270
Knights of Columbus, 307n.156
Knights of the Order of Guadalupe, 162
Koenig-Bricker, Woodeene, 286
Krause, Neal, 28–29
Kristensen, Regnar Alabaek, 229, 237
Ku Klux Klan, 307n.156

La Calaca, 229, 235, 310n.40, 310n.42
Lacan, Jacques, 277–78
La Casita, 179–80
La Catrina, 229, 235–36, 310n.40, 310n.42
La Cumplidora. See La Santa Muerte (LSM)
La Flaca. See La Santa Muerte (LSM)
La Frontera, 93
la linea, 92–93

La Lomita, 77–78
La Lupita, 76–79
La Madrina. *See* Romero Romero, Enriqueta (La Madrina)
La Mesita, 167–68, 177, 178f, 179–80, 207–9, 208f
La Migra, 92–93, 129–30
  See also US Immigration and Customs Enforcement (ICE)
La Niña Blanca. *See* La Santa Muerte (LSM)
La Niña Santa. *See* La Santa Muerte (LSM)
La Opinion, 107–8
La Orden de los Caballeros Custodios de la Tumba de Malverde, 60–61, 62, 70
La Parca, 228, 310n.39
La Poderosa. *See* La Santa Muerte (LSM)
La Santa Muerte (LSM), 9, 21, 42, 223f, 228f, 267, 279–80, 281–82, 310n.50
  altars for, 217, 228f, 230–31, 231f, 238, 239, 241, 242, 248, 251–52, 257–61, 262, 264, 268–69, 311n.77
  and capitalism, 11–12, 216, 224, 231–33, 236, 237–38, 259
  and Catholic Church, 217, 222–27, 230–32, 233–34, 252–57, 267–68, 281, 284
  culto of, 238, 245, 248
  and death, 227–28, 229, 232–34, 235–36, 237, 251, 277, 310n.42
  and digital spiritual movements, 220–22, 248–51, 268–69
  and drugs, 220–22, 263
  as Holy Death, 221, 227–28, 236, 241, 252, 253, 254, 255–56, 260–61
  and Indigeneity, 228, 232–35, 310n.56
  as La Cumplidora, 225, 227–28, 229, 230, 278–79
  as La Flaca, 227–28, 309n.34
  as La Niña Blanca, 227–28, 309n.35
  as La Poderosa, 278–79
  and love, 236–37
  name, 307–8n.1
  and queerness, 11–12, 219, 224, 261–67, 268, 284
  racialization of, 67, 229
  Santa Muerte Ball, 216–21, 218f, 245
  shrines to, 237, 238, 239, 240, 241, 242–43, 244, 257, 259–60, 264, 268

veneration leaders, 239–52
  See also Santamuertistas
La Santa Muerte Internacional (SMI), 216–17, 225, 226, 243–44, 245–46, 250, 252
La Santa Muerte Universal (SMU), 243–44, 246–48, 249, 250–51, 259, 260, 262, 263–64
La Soledad, 162–63
Las Vegas, Nevada, USA, 115
Latina/o studies, 12–13
Latorre, Guisela, 300n.90
La Unión Popular, 168
Laurel, Stan, 109
Lee, Loren, 110
Legaría Vargas, Jonathan (San Padrino Endoque), 239, 244, 246
Leo XIII, Pope
  Rerun Novarum, 167–68
lesbians, 263–64, 266, 267
  See also LGBTQ communities
Lewis, Oscar, 237
Ley Calles, 163–64
Ley de Asociaciones Religiosas y Culto Público (1992), 174–75, 237–38
ley de fuga, 101–3, 108
Leyva Flores, Guadalupe, 76–77, 79
  See also La Lupita
LGBTQ communities, 124–25, 240, 285
  and La Santa Muerte, 11–12, 219, 224, 261–67, 268
  See also gay men; lesbians; queerness; transgender people
Liera, Óscar, 53–54, 56, 77–78, 294n.40, 295n.66
López, Baldemar, 49
Lopez, Jesse, 210–11
López Alanís, Gilberto, 34–35
López Gaspar de Alba, Alma, 26
  Juan Soldado, 124–27, 124f, 148
  Santa Niña de Mochis, 125, 148, 300n.90
López Sánchez, Sergio, 58–59, 63–64, 295n.66
Los Angeles Times, 107–8, 129, 298n.30, 301n.105
loudness, 275–76
Lugo Perales, Alejandra F., 118–19, 143

machismo, 116, 138
  See also misogyny; patriarchy
Madero, Francisco, 55
Magallanes, Cristóbal Jara, 174, 180
Maldonado, Roman, 298n.32
Malverde, Guadalupe, 34–35
Malverde, Jesús, 9, 34*f*, 90, 182–83, 312n.117
  altars for, 44*f*, 74–76
  branding of, 64–71
  canonization of, 37
  and capitalism, 9–10, 45, 54–55, 69, 70–72, 81–83, 277–78
  and Catholic Church, 37–38, 39–40, 44–45, 46, 57–58, 59, 60–64, 70, 209
  chapels for, 9–10, 33–34, 37–46, 40*f*, 44*f*, 55–58, 59–67, 68–69, 70, 72, 76, 93–94, 96, 99–100, 118–19
  corridos about, 35–36, 56, 61–62, 63, 65, 69, 73–74
  and displacement, 39–40, 59, 60–61, 79–80
  and drugs, 9–10, 11–12, 32–34, 39, 62, 71–73, 72n.87, 80–81, 82, 222, 283, 294n.40, 308n.8
  execution of, 50, 55, 63–64
  grave, 55–58, 59, 62, 98
  and heteronormativity, 36, 76, 80–83
  as historical figure, 34–36, 293n.8
  and La Santa Muerte, 239–40, 256–57
  in María Romero's performances, 74–80
  and masculinity, 9–10, 50–53, 54–55, 61–62, 65–66, 67, 69–70, 74, 81–83, 279–80, 283, 296n.113
  and migration, 209
  and nationalism, 52, 71–72, 73–74
  and Pedro Infante, 9–10, 65–67, 66*f*, 279–80
  as popular bandit, 47–50, 73–74
  racialization of, 67–69, 210
  rocks as holy relics, 44–45, 49–50, 57, 59, 100
  role in Sinaloa, 9–10, 32–35, 36–39, 40*f*, 44*f*, 46–50, 52, 53–59, 61–64, 66–67, 70–72, 73–74, 76–79, 82–83, 93, 276, 280, 293n.8, 294n.40
  sanctification of, 47–48
Malverde: El santo patrón, 32–33

mandas, 32, 45, 76–77, 79–80, 119–20, 130, 135–36, 261, 278
  manda economics, 28–30, 98, 100–1, 118–19, 206, 260
maquiladoras, 138–39, 144–46, 149–50, 152–53, 281–82
Marquardt, Marie Friedmann, 5, 15–16, 17, 19
Martín, Desirée A., 228, 255, 309n.34
Martínez, Anne M., 12–13
Martínez, Luis G., 108
Martínez-Cárdenas, Rogelio, 186–87, 188
Martínez de Camacho, Feliza, 88, 96–97, 141, 298n.37
Marzal, Manuel, 22, 27–28, 291n.57
masculinity, 7–8, 185, 210
  hyper-, 50–52, 54, 61–62, 74, 81–83, 143, 283
  and Jesús Malverde, 9–10, 50–53, 54–55, 61–62, 65–66, 67, 69–70, 74, 81–83, 279–80, 283, 296n.113
  and violence against women, 139–41, 143
Masferrer Kan, Elio, 15–16
Maya People, 228
Mayo/Yoreme People, 53–54, 294nn.39–40
Mbembe, Achille, 236, 281–82
McCain, John, 307n.161
M.C.T., 132–33
Medina, Lara, 19–20
Medina-Copete, María, 221, 222, 263, 308n.13
Medina Gallo, César Eduardo, 212–13
Medina Ríos, Jesús, 108
Mendívil, Mariano, 88, 297n.6
Mendoza, Vicente T., 61–62
Menendez, Robert, 307n.161
Mesoamerica, 268
mestizaje
  mestiza consciousness, 13
  spiritual, 19–20, 291n.57
methodology of book, 14–17
  See also ethnography
#MeToo, 152
Mexican-American War, 87–88, 124–25, 270–71
  See also Treaty of Guadalupe Hidalgo (1848)

Mexican Catholic Church, 166, 231–32
Mexican Catholic Society, 271
Mexican Constitution, 115, 163, 166, 174–75
  See also Ley de Asociaciones Religiosas y Culto Público (1992)
Mexican Constitution (1917), 115, 163, 166, 174–75
Mexican Farm Labor Agreement (1942), 145
Mexicanidad, 20–21, 54, 65–66, 210, 234
Mexican League, 176–77
Mexican Olympic Team, 176–77
Mexican Revolution, 7–8, 10, 87, 91, 109, 153, 162–63, 234–36, 296n.113
  and Cristero War, 165–66
  and Jesús Malverde, 9–10, 33, 36, 47–48, 51, 52, 54–56, 58–59, 61–62, 64, 67, 70, 82, 279–80
Mexico City, Mexico, 39, 72, 74, 79, 164, 181, 216–17, 238, 243–44, 262, 265–66, 295n.66
  Archdiocese, 223–24
  La Merced, 162
  Santa María Coatepec, 244
  Tepito, 231*f*, 237, 239, 240, 241, 242–43, 261, 281–82, 311n.77
  Tultitlán, 244, 245
  Zócalo, 78–79
Meyer, Jean, 165
Michigan, USA, 11, 38
  Ann Arbor, 22–23
  Detroit, 33, 162, 196, 210
  Jackson, 197
  Mexicantown (Detroit), 18–19, 196–99, 200*f*, 254
  Monroe, 199
  Novi, 199
Michoacán, Mexico, 164, 181, 192–93, 265–66
Mictecacihuatl, 233
Mictlantecuhtli, 233
Mignolo, Walter, 13
Miguel, Luis, 216
misogyny, 10, 103–4, 116–22, 127, 134–35, 138, 139, 154–55, 313n.156
  See also machismo; patriarchy; sexual violence

Monarres, Arturo, 128–29
Monge, Manuel Luis, 162
Morales, Lucino, 216–17, 218*f*, 253–54, 255–56, 263–64
Morales Tamborrel, Antonio, 300n.81
Morfín, Jesús, 165
Morfín Reyes, Martín, 232, 233
Morrow, Dwight Whitney, 166
Moya, Estéban, 133
Murphy, James T., 165–66, 168

Nahuatl (language), 19–20
narco-capitalism, 9–10, 35–36, 70–72, 81–83
narco-saints, 33–34, 36, 46, 51, 59, 61, 70–74, 72n.87, 76, 79, 82, 283
narco-telenovelas, 32–33
National Center for Institutional Diversity, 38
nationalism, 5, 18, 112, 182–83, 282, 283
  gendered, 185
  and Jesús Malverde, 52, 71–72, 73–74
  and La Santa Muerte, 232, 234–35
  populist, 136
  racialized, 183
  See also agraristas
National Revolutionary Party, 110–11
National Security Agency (NSA), 308n.13
Nativity Church (Nativity of the Blessed Virgin Mary), 314n.13
Navarrete y Guerrero, Juan María, 271–72
Navarro, Simón, 203–6, 207–9
Navarro Rodríguez, Javier, 303n.29
Nayarit, Mexico, 64, 164
Nebreda, Antimo G., 271–72
neoliberalism, 7–8, 11, 17, 22–23, 69, 152–53, 162
  and Jesús Malverde, 69, 277–78
  and La Santa Muerte, 231–33, 236, 237–38, 259
  and violence against women, 10, 144–46, 152, 182
  See also maquiladoras; North American Free Trade Agreement (NAFTA)
Nepantla, 19–20, 22, 26
Nevares, Eduardo Alanis, 272
Neve, Felipe de, 143–44
New Mexico, USA, 220–21, 310n.39

Albuquerque, 221
Chimayo, 44f
Santa Fe, 223–24
New York City, 33, 217–19
    Brooklyn, 33–34
    Queens, 21, 216–17, 218f, 245
New York Post, 33–34
New York State, 203
New York Times, 160, 181, 187–88
nichos, 41
#NiUnaMás, 10, 152
nonprofits, 159, 203, 246–48, 249
norteños, 33, 43–44, 69–70
North American Free Trade Agreement (NAFTA), 182
    and La Santa Muerte, 11–12, 216, 224, 231–32, 237–38
    and Operation Gatekeeper, 300n.98
    and Toribio Romo, 183–84, 191

Oklahoma, 11, 202
    McKinley (Tulsa), 18–19, 202–9
    Tulsa, 21, 162, 196, 202, 207f, 208f, 210
Oklahoma House of Representatives, 202
Oklahoma Taxpayer and Citizen Protection Act (HB 1804), 202, 203–4
Oklahoma Watch, 203
Olguita, Santa, 86, 91–92, 104, 153
    as feminist saint, 90, 91, 149–50, 284
    prayer cards, 147f, 149–51
    veneration of, 93, 144, 146, 147–53
Olmstead, Thomas J., 272, 314n.20
online spiritual movements, 248–51, 268–69
Operation Gatekeeper, 129, 182, 300n.98
Orendain, Juan Luis, 32–33
Organization for Economic Co-operation and Development, 250
Orona Madrigal, Justino, 175–76
Orozco y Jiménez, José Francisco, 164, 165, 167–68, 171–72, 174
    Contra la emigración, 185–86
Orsi, Robert, 16, 289n.1
Ortiz, Ferdinand, 271–72
Osornio Camareña, Severano, 105–6
Ospino, Hosffman, 5–6
Our Lady of El Cobre, 282–83

Our Lady of Guadalupe (church), 314n.13
Our Lady of Guadalupe (figure), 54, 77–78, 148

P., Carlos, 133–34
Padrino Endoque, San. *See* Legaría Vargas, Jonathan (San Padrino Endoque)
Pajaro Macua, Salud Dinero y Amor LLC, 193, 193n.117
pan-Latinx communities, 211–12, 217–19
Panteón de la Puerta Blanca. *See* Panteón Municipal no. 1
Panteón Municipal no. 1, 93, 94f, 95–96, 97–104, 99f, 102f, 107–8
Panteón Municipal no. 2, 93, 94f, 95f, 95–97
Pantera, Comadante. *See* Legaría Vargas, Jonathan (San Padrino Endoque)
Paquita La del Barrio, 217
Paraguay, 290n.27, 307–8n.1
Parcae (Fates), 309n.38
Paredes, Américo, 13
Park, Jungwon, 47
partner recession, 134
Pascual (Pascualito), San, 233–34
patriarchy, 162, 277, 280
    and Jesús Malverde, 48, 50, 52–53, 54–55, 61–62, 81
    and Olga Camacho, 91, 96–97, 116–17, 121–22, 124, 125–26, 127, 137, 138, 139, 140–42, 146, 148, 149–50, 151, 154, 155
    See also machismo; misoginy
Patrick, Saint, 25
Paul, Saint, 255–56
Pearce, Russell K., 2
Pedraza, Silvia, 2–3
Penitente Brotherhood, 310n.39
Perdigón Castañeda, Katia, 226, 229, 231–32, 233–34, 238, 253
peregringos, 188, 189
Pérez, Emma, 17–18, 285
Pérez Budar, José Juaquin, 162
performativity, 210, 283
Pew Research Center, 5–6, 182
Philippines, 261–62, 292n.89, 310n.50
Pius XII, Pope, 137

polleros/smugglers, 53–54, 70–71, 73, 147–48, 160, 180–81
  El Santo Pollero, 11, 160, 162, 170–71, 193, 196, 209–10
Portelli, Alessandro, 90–91, 277–78
Portes Gil, Emilio, 165
Posada, José Guadalupe, 235–36, 309n.31
P.P., 131
pre-Columbian era, 228, 232–35, 291n.57
Price, Patricia A., 19, 47, 57–58, 59, 71, 293n.8
processions, 170, 205–6, 207f
Prohibition era, 87–88, 91, 110, 153
Protestantism, 5–6, 22–23, 292n.87
Puebla, Mexico, 227, 228f, 261

queerness, 11–13, 50–51, 80–83, 124–25, 219, 224, 240, 261–67, 268, 296n.113
  decolonial queer gaze, 285
  See also gay men; lesbians; LGBTQ communities
Querétano, Mexico, 164
Quijano, Martin George, 225–28, 262
Quinones, Sam, 35

racial segregation, 6, 270–73, 314n.13
racism, 3–4, 12, 73, 136, 154, 272, 277–78, 287
  by Arpaio, 273–74, 297n.14
  See also Oklahoma Taxpayer and Citizen Protection Act (HB 1804)
Ramazotti, Eros, 216
Ramírez, Adriana, 135–36
Ramírez, Marla, 87–88
Ravasi, Gianfranco, 223–24
Rebolledo, Efrén, 86
referential epistemic standpoint, 14
Reguillo, Rossana, 276, 285–86
religious intrastates, 20–23, 282–83
religious systems, 15–17, 291n.57
remittances, 4, 21, 190–91
Republican Party, 202
resurrection, 17–18
  of Jesus Christ, 223–24, 233–34, 255–56
  of Jesús Malverde, 64
  of Juan Soldado, 117, 118
  of Olga Camacho, 10, 146, 149–50, 152–53

retorno, 188–89, 247
  spiritual, 21, 189–93, 204, 209
Risita de Natanhel. See La Santa Muerte Universal (SMU)
Rivera, Diego, 235–36
Rivera, Gabriel, 118–19
Rizo Soto, Martin Federico, 211
Robin Hood, 35, 47–48, 71–72
Rodríguez, Concepción, 158
Rodriguez, Pedro, 167
Rojas, José Antonio (pseudonym), 129–30
Romero, Francisca, 210–11
Romero, María, 39, 43, 74, 76, 79–80
  El sagrado corazón del beato Mesús Malverde, 74
  La busqueda del tesoro de la divina gracia, 77–78
  La manda de María, 76
  La novia de Cualiacán, 75f, 76–79
  La novia de Cualiacán, ni loca, ni novia: Misionera, 79
  Quitapesares, 74–76, 75f
Romero, María (Meimi) de, 105–6, 141
Romero, Raymundo, 240, 243
Romero Romero, Enriqueta (La Madrina), 230–31, 231f, 237, 238–43, 252, 255–57, 266–67, 311n.77
Romo, Román "Tata," 169–70
Romo González, María Marcos (Quica), 168–70
Romo Guillén, David, 261–62, 311n.77
Romo Pérez, Patricio, 167
rosary, 4, 35, 43, 45, 98, 158, 167, 170, 172, 193, 243, 248–50, 260–61
Rosita de Natanhel AC. See La Santa Muerte Universal (SMU)
Rubio, Marco, 307n.161
Ruta Cristera, 188

Saavedra, Rafa, 149
sabidurías populares, 13
Sabuesos Guerreras A.C., 78
Sacred Heart of Christ, 97–98
Sada, Daniel, 35, 63–64, 293n.8
Saint Agnes of Bohemia (parish), 158, 159
Saint Mary's Basilica, 270, 271–72
Saint Peter's Basilica, 137
Salazar Rojo, Juan, 227

Salazar Villagrana, Felipe, 206–7
Saldaña Rico, José, 118–19
Saldívar, José David, 17–18
Salinas de Gortari, Carlos, 174–75
Sánchez, Lázaro, 32–33
Sánchez, Oscár, 167n.32
Sánchez Barba, Óscar, 24, 171, 173–76, 180
Sánchez Taboada, Rodolfo, 107, 108, 113, 299n.66
sanctification, 40–41, 70
 of Jesús Malverde, 47–48
 of Juan Soldado, 10, 98, 103–4, 110, 118–19, 144, 148–49
 of Maria Goretti, 149
 of Olga Camacho, 137, 149, 152
 of Toribio Romo, 173–74
Sanderson, Susan R. Walsh, 48
San Diego Evening Tribune, 120, 298n.42
San Diego State University, 92–93
San Diego Sun, 116
Sandoval, Carmen, 247–48, 250–52, 256, 257, 259, 260–61
Sandoval, Lauro, 212
San La Muerte, 307–8n.1
San Luis Potosi, Mexico, 164
Santa Muerte Ball, 216–21, 218f, 245
Santamuertistas, 224–26, 232, 233, 234, 238, 251, 253–57, 268
 See also La Santa Muerte (LSM)
Santana, Marcos, 80
Santa Teresita Church, 170
santería, 259
Santuario de Nuestra Señora de Guadalupe, 303n.22
San Ysidro Border Press, 120
Sebastián, San, 233
Secretariat of Clergy, Consecrated Life, and Vocations of the United States Conference of Catholic Bishops, 5–6
Seminario Conciliar de Guadalajara, 167–68
September 11, 2001, 11, 129, 160–61
Serenelli, Alessandro, 137
Serra, Junípero, 143–44
sexual violence, 10, 77–78, 277, 284
 by Alessandro Serenelli of Maria Goretti, 93–94, 137–45, 149–50
 Arpaio enabling, 273–74
 and capitalism, 10, 138–39, 144–46, 152, 182
 by clergy, 12, 273–74
 by Juan Castillo Morales of Olga Camacho, 86, 88–90, 91–92, 97, 101, 103–6, 110, 112–13, 116–17, 122–23, 127, 136–55, 279–80, 297n.24, 297n.26
sex work, 263, 265–66, 313n.156
Sheridan, Thomas E., 314n.11
shrines, 14, 23, 206–7, 219–20
 to Jesús Malverde, 43, 44f, 60–61, 295n.60
 to La Santa Muerte, 237, 238, 239, 240, 241, 242–43, 244, 257, 259–60, 264, 268
 to Toribio Romo, 177–79, 191, 193, 197–98, 203, 205–9
simulacrum, 21, 194–95, 209
Sinaloa, Mexico, 271–72, 294n.39
 Colonia Ruiz Cortines, 46, 57–59, 60–61
 Culiacán, 32–34, 35, 37–40, 40f, 42–43, 44f, 46, 49–50, 55, 56, 57, 60, 66–67, 72, 74, 76–78, 79, 82, 293n.8, 293n.14, 294n.50, 295n.60, 295n.66
 and Jesús Malverde, 9–10, 32–35, 36–39, 40f, 44f, 46–50, 52, 53–59, 61–64, 66–67, 70–72, 73–74, 76–79, 82, 93, 276, 280, 293n.8, 294n.40
 Los Mochis, 125
Sinaloa Cartel, 33–34, 38–39
Sinful Saints and Saintly Sinners (exhibition), 74–76
Slattery, Edward J., 202–3, 205–7
slavery, 68, 145–46
slow violence, 236, 266
Smale, William, 113–14
Smith, Nancy Lee, 198–201, 200f
social bodies, 4–5, 13, 35–36, 46, 127, 146, 158, 164, 277, 279–80, 283
Sociedad de Historia de Tijuana, 143
Society of Saint Toribio Romo (SSTR), 158–59
Soldado, Juan (Juan the Soldier), 86, 104, 151–52, 162–63, 186
 altars for, 126–27
 beatification of, 91–92

Soldado, Juan (Juan the Soldier) (*cont.*)
   and border identity, 93
   canonization of, 10, 86, 90, 116, 124, 139–40
   chapels for, 97–103, 99*f*, 102*f*, 119–20, 127–28
   and displacement, 112, 121–22
   followers' violence, 95–97, 103–4, 148
   grave of, 94*f*, 95*f*, 96, 120
   López Gaspar de Alba painting, 124–27, 124*f*, 148
   and love and family, 134–36
   patron saint of migrants, 10, 107, 124–25, 126–27, 128–30, 209, 279–80
   racialization of, 67
   rocks as holy relics, 49–50, 100–3, 118–20
   sanctification of, 10, 98, 103–4, 110, 118–19, 144, 148–49
   and sexual violence, 90–92, 97, 103–4, 116–18, 120–27, 136, 138–40, 144, 146–49, 153, 154–55, 276, 279–80
   and social vulnerability, 130–34
   veneration of, 9
   See also Castillo Morales, Juan
Sonora, Mexico, 64, 271–72, 294n.39
Sonoran Desert, 160, 180–81, 290n.25
South America, 22, 243–44, 313n.156
Spain, 68, 118–19, 162, 182–83, 228
   Spanish colonialism, 117, 143–44, 226, 233, 236, 301n.111
spiritual activism, 20, 22
Spiritual Passport, 193–95, 306n.117
spiritual pragmatism, 224–25
spiritual retorno, 21, 189–93, 204, 209
St. Francis Xavier Church, 205–6
St. Marcellinus Church, 211
Sts. Peter and Paul Catholic Church, 196, 202, 203–9, 207*f*, 208*f*
subaltern modernities, 13
subjugated knowledges, 13, 266, 276
Sud Pacífico de México, 48–49
Support Our Law Enforcement and Safe Neighborhoods Act (SB 1070), 2, 274
syncretism, 226, 238, 291n.57
syndicate movement, 113, 114, 115, 162–63
   See also Confederación Regional Obrera de México (CROM)

Tapatíos, 173–74, 295n.74
Tecate, 110–11
Telemundo, 22–23, 32–33, 36, 81
Tenth Circuit Court of Appeals, 221
Tequila Crisis/Mexican Peso Crisis (1994), 290n.27
Teresa, Mother, 24, 291n.70
terra nullius, 54
Terrill, Randy, 202
Texas, USA, 203, 217–19, 221, 272
Third Agricultural Revolution, 57–58
Third World, 17–18, 274–75
Tijuana, Baja California, Mexico, 33–34, 86, 199, 240, 299n.59, 299n.67
   Colonia Castillo, 108
   and Olga Camacho/Juan Soldado, 10, 86–155, 162–63, 164
   and Operation Gatekeeper, 301n.101
   Zona Centro, 87
#TimesUp, 152
Tlaxcala, Mexico, 168
tlīlli tlapalli, 13
Toor, Frances, 236, 237
Toribio Romo, Saint, 21, 24, 111, 166–68, 178*f*, 276
   altars for, 2–3, 181, 198, 207–9, 208*f*
   anti-immigrant legacy of, 184–86
   beatification of, 170–72, 177–79, 180, 186, 190–91, 303n.26
   brother of, 166–67, 168–70, 171–73, 183, 185
   canonization of, 2–3, 9, 11, 26, 160–62, 164, 166–67, 168, 170–71, 173–76, 183–84, 190–91, 209–10, 212–13, 290n.26, 303n.29
   and Cristero War, 11, 160–61, 162, 164, 167, 168–70, 171–72, 173–76, 177–79, 180, 181, 182–84, 189, 196–97, 212–13
   and displacement, 172, 182–83, 187, 195, 211–12
   as El Santo Pollero/Holy Coyote, 11, 160, 162, 170–71, 176–77, 189, 193, 196, 209–10
   grave, 170
   as Holy Smuggler, 160, 162, 170–71, 196, 209–10
   icons of, 200*f*

marketing of, 176–80
patron saint of migrants, 2–3, 9, 11, 158–61, 180–82, 189–93, 209–12, 277, 290n.25
processions for, 207f
racialization of, 67, 182–84, 210, 229, 283
relics of, 11, 162, 169–70, 171–72, 177, 179–80, 191, 196–97, 198, 201, 203, 204, 205–9, 210, 211–12
religious objects of, 193–95
role in Santa Ana de Guadalupe, 186–89
role in the US, 196–209, 210–12
shrines for, 177–79, 191, 193, 197–98, 203, 205–9
Vámanos al Norte, 184–85
Toribo Romo Immigration Center, 158
Torres, Vidal, 298n.30
tourism, 110, 115, 133, 134, 142, 176–79, 187–89, 205
transgender people, 216–17, 239–40, 265–66, 313n.156
See also LGBTQ communities
transplanted churches, 22–23
Treaty of Guadalupe Hidalgo (1848), 124–25, 270–71
Treviño, Ricardo, 162–63
Trujillo Muñoz, Gabriel, 113
Trump, Donald, 217, 296n.92, 297n.14
Twitter, 249–50
Tyrrhenian Sea, 136

United Kingdom, 250
See also Great Britain
Universidad Autónoma de Mexico, 217
Universidad Autónoma de Sinaloa, 58, 77–78
University of California, Los Angeles (UCLA), 222
Fowler Museum, 74–76
University of Michigan, 38
Univision, 22–23
US Border Patrol, 180–81, 308–9n.15
US Census Bureau, 203
US Congress
House of Representatives, 210–11, 307n.161
Senate, 210–11, 307n.161

US Constitution, 194
First Amendment, 221, 222
US Customs and Border Protection, 199
US Department of Justice, 308n.13
US Drug Enforcement Administration (DEA), 11–12, 33, 221, 308n.8, 308n.13, 308–9n.15
US Immigration and Customs Enforcement (ICE), 33, 92–93, 129–30
Secure Communities Program, 129–30
See also La Migra
US presidential elections
2012, 92
2016, 159
2020, 158

Valdés, Alfredo and Carmen, 131
Valencia, David, 247, 262, 263–64
Valenzuela Arce, José Manuel, 127, 128–29, 130, 131
Vanderwood, Paul J., 118, 137, 142, 151–52, 300n.78
Vargas Ortiz, Enriqueta, 216–17
Vásquez, Manuel A., 5, 15–16, 17, 19
Vasquez, Salvador, 298n.30
Vatican, 14, 160, 168, 170, 173–76, 212–13, 223–24, 225–26, 304n.36, 304n.47
beatification/canonization by, 304n.45
Congregation for the Causes of Saints, 24, 25, 173–74, 175–76
Dicastery for Promoting Integral Human Development, 136
Pontifical Council for Culture, 223–24
Vázquez, Arely, 216–17, 218f, 219–20, 257–58, 259, 263, 264–65
Veracruz, Mexico, 261
vernacular Catholicism, 226, 238
Vigneron, Allen, 198
Viñals Carsi, Luis, 105–6
virginity, 52–53, 77–78, 137–38, 148, 149
Virgin Mary, 29, 42, 44–45, 76, 226, 243, 253
Assumption of, 255–56
See also Our Lady of El Cobre; Virgin of Guadalupe
Virgin of Guadalupe, 2–3, 19, 44–45, 101–3, 102f, 125, 164, 167, 207–9, 233, 252, 256–58, 259, 282–83, 289n.5

Volokh, Eugene, 222
vox populi, 25–26

war on drugs, 9–10, 38–39, 62, 152–53, 224
Washington Post, 33, 62
Wester, John, 223–24
WhatsApp, 249–50
Wilde, Oscar, 23
Woodward, Kenneth L., 23, 25–26, 27, 28, 291n.73
World Council of Churches, 136
World War II, 144–45

xenophobia, 18, 53, 82–83, 136, 152–53, 159, 160–61, 189, 202–3, 273–74, 283, 297n.14, 313n.156
  See also Oklahoma Taxpayer and Citizen Protection Act (HB 1804); Support Our Law Enforcement and Safe Neighborhoods Act (SB 1070)
Xenophobia, Racism, and Populist Nationalism in the Context of Global Migration conference, 136

Yépez, Heriberto, 144, 147–50, 151–52
Yllescas Illescas, Jorge Adrián, 217, 230
Young, Julia G., 161
YouTube, 248

Zacatecas, Mexico, 164, 180–81
  Fresnillo, 188
  Plateros, 44*f*
Zambada, Jesus, 33–34
Zazueta, Heriberto, 50
Zócalo, 78–79

www.ingramcontent.com/pod-product-compliance
Lightning Source LLC
Chambersburg PA
CBHW072159290825
31867CB00026B/1163